THE EMBODIMENT OF BHAKTI

To Frank
With thanks
and best wishes

Karen

THE EMBODIMENT OF BHAKTI

Karen Pechilis Prentiss

New York Oxford
Oxford University Press
1999

Oxford University Press

Oxford New York
Athens Auckland Bangkok Bogotá Buenos Aires Calcutta
Cape Town Chennai Dar es Salaam Delhi Florence Hong Kong Istanbul
Karachi Kuala Lumpur Madrid Melbourne Mexico City Mumbai
Nairobi Paris São Paulo Singapore Taipei Tokyo Toronto Warsaw

and associated companies in
Berlin Ibadan

Published by Oxford University Press, Inc.
198 Madison Avenue, New York, New York 10016

Oxford is a registered trademark of Oxford University Press

Library of Congress Cataloging-in-Publication Data
Prentiss, Karen Pechilis.
The embodiment of bhakti / Karen Pechilis Prentiss.
p. cm.
Includes bibliographical references and index.
ISBN 0-19-512813-3
1. Bhakti—History. 2. Hindu literature—History and criticism.
3. Bhakti in literature. 4. Religious poetry, Tamil—Translations
into English.
BL1214.32.B53P75 1999
294.5'4—dc21 98-45874

1 3 5 7 9 8 6 4 2

Printed in the United States of America
on acid-free paper

Acknowledgments

It was 1987, and I was in south India on the American Institute of Indian Studies' Tamil Language Program, which is based in Madurai. The charismatic and learned Dr. K. Paramasivam, a guru to generations of American students of the Tamil language, directed the program and worked tirelessly to introduce us to a wide variety of Tamil writings and aspects of Tamil culture. Encouraged by his outgoing approach, I independently undertook weekend tours of temples in Tamilnadu, which became one of my favorite activities that year. I went to places I had studied in art history or had heard described as important pilgrimage sites by local friends. I accomplished these tours with minimal planning; I simply chose a destination and then showed up at the Madurai bus station after class on Friday, hoping a bus would be going my way. In this manner, I crisscrossed Tamil country several times that year. I will always be grateful to those Tamil people who spontaneously offered me friendly assistance on those trips, even in remote towns.

At some point during those travels, I became aware of the pattern in temples to Śiva of displaying a group of figurines in a line on one side of the sanctum. To me, they looked like models of patience. I learned that they are the nāyaṉmār, or saints, who represent bhakti to Śiva. As I continued to ask about them, I came to realize that they were understood to represent passion as well as patience, themes richly developed in stories about them. My interest was piqued.

Prior to 1987, there were very few authoritative translations of Tamil bhakti poetry in modern English. In the late 1980s, a number of such books were published, including Norman J. Cutler's *Songs of Experience: The Poetics of Tamil Devotion* (1987). It was my good fortune that Professor Cutler was teaching Tamil at the University of Chicago, and that I had studied with him prior to my trip. I am grateful to him for encouraging my interest in the nāyaṉmār upon my return by patiently guiding me in the translation of hymns and stories of the saints in a series of independent study classes. His teaching and scholarship have illuminated Tamil bhakti poetry for me and many others.

I returned to south India in 1992 on a Fulbright dissertation research grant. For that academic year I was affiliated with the Kuppuswami Sastri Research Institute; I am grateful to S. S. Janaki, N. R. Bhatt, and the staff at the KSRI for their erudite conversation and guidance. During that trip, I worked mainly on understanding the worldview of the Tamil school of Śaiva Siddhānta philosophy. I was guided in this endeavor by Professor Emeritus Vai. Irattiṉacapāpati of the University of Madras and eminent interpreter of the Tamil Śaiva Siddhānta's canon of fourteen texts. With his help, I translated one of the canonical texts, the *Tiruvaruṭpayaṉ*, and discussed in detail the foundational philosophical ideas within it. Members of this Tamil school of philosophy are very active in Madras (Chennai) today, and I benefited from attending their conferences and engaging in discussion with them. One erudite scholar in the group, Dr. Vaidilingam, shared his historical perspective with me in several discussions.

On that trip, I was able to obtain a copy of the *Tēvāra Aruḷmuṟaittiraṭṭu*, an anthology of Śiva-bhakti hymns by a historical Tamil Śaiva Siddhānta philosopher. It was a gem of a find, as was my introduction to Dr. A. A. Manavalan through the advice of Professor Cutler. At that time, Dr. Manavalan was chair of the Tamil Language and Literature Department at the University of Madras. He generously guided me in translating the anthology. A brilliant scholar of Tamil literature and comparative literature, Dr. Manavalan has been an inspiring senior colleague to me for these years.

On my return, I soon completed my dissertation, which was a very early stage in the process leading toward this book. Professor Cutler was a reader for the dissertation, and I thank him for his conscientious and careful review of my work. His comments have guided me over the past several years as I have developed this project. Professor Frank E. Reynolds was my advisor, and I thank him for his many insightful comments, especially those on the nature of religious change.

My deepest intellectual debt is to Professor Jonathan Z. Smith, who was a reader for the dissertation and a mentor for everything else. He saw through me and saw me through (to borrow a phrase from J. Anthony Lukas).

Since it is the custom in Indian tradition never to tell only one story when you can tell two (or more), this project grew even more fascinating over time as I learned more of the texts by and about the nāyaṉmār. Through my encounters with these works, I sought to understand the story of the development of Tamil Śiva-bhakti tradition in the medieval period. Library support for this endeavor was crucial, and I express gratitude to the directors and staff at the University of Chicago Regenstein Library, especially the South Asia Collection and the Adayar Library in Madras. A faculty research travel grant from Drew University enabled me to perform additional research at the School of Oriental and African Studies in London.

My colleagues in the religious studies department at Drew University have created a supportive environment that encouraged me in my research.

I was fortunate to have the opportunity to present portions of this project at the Conference on Religion in South India and at Columbia University's Seminar on Asian Thought and Religion.

I would like to thank the two anonymous scholarly reviewers for Oxford University Press, and Cynthia Read and Cynthia Garver at the Press. I also thank Margaret H. Case for her editorial suggestions as I prepared the final version of the manuscript; a faculty research grant from Drew University supported this preparation work.

Very special thanks are due to friends whose comments on my work consistently helped me to see things in new ways: Paul Younger, Joanne and Dick Waghorne, Richard Davis, Lalgudi Swaminathan and his family, Ganesh Satchitananda and his friend Ganapati, Dr. P. V. Rao, Selva Raj, Rodney and Chrystal Easdon and their sons, and Kathryn Sargent Ciffolillo.

This book is dedicated to those who have helped me the most, my family.

Contents

Note on Transliteration

Tamil terms are transliterated as per the *Tamil Lexicon*. In order that the text not be overcrowded with italics, I have chosen not to italicize Tamil and Sanskrit words unless I am discussing them as terms.

Much of Tamil religious terminology is derived from Sanskrit; I have used both the Sanskrit terms and Tamil transliterations of them.

There is considerable variation in the treatment of proper names. In general, I have used transliterated terms with diacritics. When recognition is an issue, I have dropped the diacritical marks and used the form most often used in scholarly works. In a few cases, I have used sources that do not provide the diacritics, and I have been unable to locate a corroborating source to put in the diacritics with accuracy; therefore, I have followed the source's spelling.

THE EMBODIMENT OF BHAKTI

Introduction

On the face of it, to students of Indian culture, bhakti needs no introduction. Celebrated as an Indian version of Protestant Christianity by nineteenth-century missionaries and scholars, immortalized in the *Bhagavad Gītā*, promoted as "India's Bible" by orientalists and now reclaimed as such by Hindu immigrants in Western countries, and praised by poet-saints in all the major languages of India, bhakti became firmly established in the canon of scholarship on Indian religions.

There had been a consensus on what bhakti means, which contributed to its inclusion in the canon of scholarship. Revealing orientalist scholars' approval of this religious path, by the turn of this century *bhakti* had come to be defined as "devotion to a personal deity" in English-language scholarship, a definition still influential today.[1] For orientalist scholars such as H. H. Wilson, M. Monier-Williams, and G. A. Grierson, bhakti was a monotheistic reform movement, the first real instance of monotheism in India. By this assertion, they challenged the views of F. Max Müller, regarded as a founder of the discipline called *Religionswissenschaft*, or the history of religions; he and his followers deemed the Sanskrit Vedas as India's true and original religion. In Max Müller's view, the scholars of bhakti were studying the compromise of history; in their own view, they were identifying the jewel in the crown of India's living religious traditions.

They rivaled Max Müller's identification of the Vedas as India's true religion by linking the religion of the *Bhagavad Gītā* to Christianity, through both phenomenological themes and historical events. Several themes encouraged the identification of bhakti with Christianity: Bhakti was a monotheistic tradition, centered around the god Viṣṇu; the nature of Viṣṇu was as a "God of love"; bhakti was a reform movement through its emphasis on feeling and its criticism of caste; and the medieval "reformers," especially the sixteenth-century bhakta (practitioner of bhakti) Caitanya, whom they likened to Luther, played the same role as Protestant reformers in Europe.

The historical study of the origins of bhakti was intended to support these thematic parallels by grounding them in a situation of contact with Christianity, but ultimately this vector in the study of bhakti proved to be a dismal failure. Following the episteme of the search for origins that guided much of scholarship on religion from the sixteenth to the nineteenth century, scholars searched for the origins of bhakti.[2] Albrecht Weber, a preeminent German scholar of Sanskrit, hypothesized that bhakti originated from contact between Christians and Hindus in the remote historical past. His proof text was the Śvetadvīpa legend in the twelfth book of the *Mahābhārata*, which he understood to refer to the pilgrimage of a group of Kṛṣṇa worshipers to the "white island" where Christians practiced their religion. Weber was relatively cautious in his approach—he distinguished "borrowing," his term of choice, from "direct influence," though in part to distance his thesis from the contemporary "passionate and licentious descriptions of Krishṇa's loves among the shepherdesses." He even suggested the possibility of mutual influence between the traditions.[3] None of his cautiousness was shared by his colleague, M. F. Lorinser, who sought to prove Weber's hypothesis by direct comparison of passages in the *Bhagavad Gītā* with passages from the New Testament.[4] Orientalist scholars responded to Weber's assertion that Christian ideas had influenced the identity and worship of Kṛṣṇa by tending to agree with him in part, perhaps with a sensitivity that reflected his eminence in the field of Indology. In contrast, they tended to disagree radically with Lorinser, who had tried to prove the more forceful case of direct influence.[5]

One of their most important critics was R. G. Bhandarkar, a professor of Sanskrit at Elphinstone College and former governor of Bombay. His aim was to trace indigenous developments of Vaiṣṇava religiosity, for which he drew on his considerable experience with manuscripts and epigraphical materials and ultimately emerged with a euhemeristic argument. Through an analysis of Patañjali's *Mahābhāṣya*, he claimed that Kṛṣṇa was originally a kṣatriya (warrior caste) named Vāsudeva who had been elevated to divine status.[6] Expanding on the theme of a non-Brahman founder of bhakti—thus bringing it into comparison with Buddhism—in a subsequent work, Bhandarkar endowed bhakti with the revival of devotion that had once, but no longer, inspired Brahmanic sacrifice: "Cold and dead formalities took the place of warm and living devotion and the very verses and hymns which contained the fervent prayers of the old Ṛṣis, were repeated mechanically in the course of the formal worship, without even an attempt to apprehend the sense."[7] This image of the history of bhakti would influence subsequent scholarship up to the present day.[8]

The historical study of bhakti thus flopped at first and then became formulaic. This lack of success was due, in part, to the tendency to mire historical studies in the search for origins, but it was also due to the orientalists' failure to view different texts' discussions of bhakti as distinctive representations of bhakti. It is true that they focused on texts that explicitly promote bhakti, chief among them the *Gītā*, although including other Sanskrit texts such as the *Śāṇḍilya Bhakti Sūtra*, but in their quest to find "devotion to a personal deity," they tended to collapse the rhetorical voice of the texts in favor of a univocal definition of bhakti. Rather than serving to challenge this definition of bhakti, religious phenomena that did not fit into the paradigm were cast in the role of foil. This was the case, for example, with south Indian formulations of bhakti, especially those that focused on Śiva. To the orientalist eye, Śiva was, in contrast to Viṣṇu, the god of fear; the "fact" that Śiva was more prominent in south India did not bode well for the region, and it tended to be ignored at best in orientalist scholarship.

My study seeks to reclaim the historical study of bhakti through a consideration of the distinctive representations of bhakti that different proponents within one regional tradition, Tamil Śiva-bhakti, made during the medieval period. Tamil Śiva-bhakti tradition was actively developed during this period: My analysis of the tradition begins with the seventh century, when bhakti hymns to Śiva were composed, and concludes with the fourteenth century, when the hymns and other Śiva-bhakti texts were established as a written canon.

In focusing on a regional tradition of bhakti, I join many contemporary scholars in the study of bhakti in regional-language poetry. Many excellent translations of bhakti poems in a variety of regional languages, including Kannada, Hindi, Bengali, Marathi, and Tamil, have recently been published, bringing these traditions to a wider audience. These translations have established conventions for rendering the poems into English, and they have located the poems in the literary history of regional cultures.

These translations make possible a broad comparative study of bhakti, which would be less accessible if the poems were left in the many regional languages of their composition. In particular, the translated poems allow us to gain a comparative understanding of the perspectives of the bhakti authors. It is clear from most translations that tradition designated the poems as expressions of bhakti; less clear in some cases is whether the authors of the poems themselves considered their work to represent bhakti. The *Gītā* is the first text we know of that uses the term *bhakti* as a technical term to designate a religious path. In its earliest usage, the term encompassed meanings of affection and attachment, but the *Gītā* transformed the word into a technical religious term, specifying a religious path that encouraged active participation in worship without the sense of material and familial attachment that had characterized earlier uses of the word. Through comparison with traditional religious paths, the *Gītā* distinguished bhakti and endowed it with autonomy as its own religious path; in the *Gītā*, bhakti denotes a method of religious experience that leads to liberation. As many scholars have noted, the *Gītā* can be understood as a response to widespread Indian religious perspectives that view the body negatively. For the *Gītā*, the field of human worship is coextensive with the field of ordinary human activity, if one's mind is focused upon God. Unlike classical law books, which sought to legislate correct human action, and unlike formalized prayers and ritual manuals, which located worship in a specific time and place, bhakti is represented in the *Gītā* as a religious perspective that can inform all actions, at any time and in any place. This technical meaning of *bhakti* became authoritative, and the *Gītā* was considered one of the three foundational texts (prasthānatrayā) for Hindu religious commentary by the great philosophers Śankara and Rāmānuja, as well as in later Sanskrit philosophical tradition.[9]

It is this technical meaning of *bhakti* as a religious path that informs the representation of bhakti in regional-language texts. In a rare case, such as the representation of bhakti in a thirteenth-century text from Maharashtra, there is an attempt to link bhakti in a regional language specifically to the bhakti of the Sanskrit *Gītā*.[10] Other authors, such as the Tamil poets, use a transliteration of the Sanskrit bhakti (Tam. *patti*) in their poetry. Sometimes it is not clear from the translation whether bhakti poets actually use the term *bhakti* in their poetry; this would be important comparative information for translators to provide.

Beyond the presence of the term *bhakti* in the poetry of regional-language authors, common themes can be identified through comparison. One of the most important commonalities is that authors explicitly refer to themselves in their poetry, either through the first-person voice or through the mention of their names (the authors refer to themselves in the third person). The agency of the poet is thus highlighted. The importance of human agency in the poetry has implications for our understanding and definition of bhakti. In general, as the study of bhakti has reached out to regional traditions, there has been much less scholarly reflection on the definition of bhakti, especially as compared to the orientalists' view.[11] The importance of a definition lies in its nature as a stipulated domain for scholarly discourse; it facilitates bringing diverse materials into a shared discussion. From a comparison of voices within bhakti, it becomes clear that active human agency is a premise of this religious perspective. As John Carman has pointed out, the term *bhakti* is used specifically to describe the human response to God and never to characterize God's response to human beings.[12] In actively encouraging participation (which is a root meaning of *bhakti*), the poets represent bhakti as a theology of embodiment. Their thesis is that engagement with (or participation in) God should inform all of one's activities in worldly life. The poets encourage a diversity of activities, not limiting bhakti to established modes of worship—indeed, some poets harshly criticize such modes—but, instead, making it the foundation of human life and activity in the world. As a theology of embodiment, bhakti is embedded in the details of human life.

Although the *Gītā* and the poems in regional languages share this thesis, there is a major difference in their perspectives. The *Gītā* is a teaching text in the question-and-answer format, in which the protagonist (Arjuna) learns—at times, painfully slowly—about bhakti. In contrast, the regional-language bhakti poems presuppose that the author has bhakti; the poems are generated from the experience of bhakti. The bhakti authors detail their response to God and their response to their contexts in their poems. There is an important dynamic at work in the poems, as the authors join together transcendent and local themes. The poems are personal, yet the authors encourage others to participate in their worldview; similarly, God is transcendent, yet he is locally concerned.

This dynamic tends to be obscured by contemporary authors' inclination to classify regional-language bhakti poets into two categories: *nirguṇa*, in which the poet imagines a formless God without attributes, and *saguṇa*, in which the poet imagines God with attributes. This distinction resonates with the orientalist premise that understanding the imagined form of God (a "personal deity"; saguṇa in modern scholarship) is a key to understanding bhakti. The classification also resonates with the orientalists' concern with protest and reform; nirguṇa bhakti is viewed as a criticism of inherited tradition, whereas saguṇa bhakti is viewed as an accommodation to it; in this discourse, bhakti is characterized as a movement.[13]

However, the genesis of the nirguṇa and saguṇa classificatory schema can be traced to a very different historical context than that of the poems' composition. According to John Stratton Hawley, the schema was developed and used by late medieval anthologizers of bhakti hymns in Hindi.[14] The time period between authors and redactors cannot be collapsed in a historical study, for these groups of people exist in different historical contexts and possess distinctive concerns. In many of the translations of the bhakti poems, scholars introduce the poets by way of their hagiographies. Their approach is justifiable in that contemporary people understand the poems through these biographies, but it is also ahistorical.

Significantly, it is a shared theme in regional-language bhakti traditions that the attention of later anthologizers and interpreters focused on representing bhakti poets as saints. Later interpreters thus worked creatively within bhakti's thesis on embodiment. This theme is so pervasive that it is not an overstatement to suggest that saints became the primary embodiment of bhakti. The result was extensive biographical literatures written in regional languages. This aspect of bhakti tradition distinguishes it from other religious perspectives in India, including the *Gītā*. The *Gītā* provided one example of a bhakta; his plight was expressed in a manner that had implications for others by Kṛṣṇa's admonition that he "do his dharma." This explicit link between caste and the practice of bhakti is not a focus of most regional-language bhakti poems, although there is infrequent illustration of a bhakta who is worshiping appropriate to her or his status.[15] In contrast, the biographies detailed the specific embodiment of each bhakta, including caste, family, hometown, and actions. Generally speaking, it was an issue of concern to biographers who wrote in regional languages to represent the diversity of those on the path of bhakti; through their texts, they asserted that in spite of their differences all bhaktas are on the same religious path.

The poems and the biographies are distinctive yet related representations of bhakti. What unites them is their attempt to represent bhakti to Śiva in their works, often involving a conscious intertextual approach. What separates them is time and cultural milieu. In medieval Tamilnadu, south India, from the seventh to the fourteenth centuries A.D., there were far-reaching transformations in diverse fields of culture, including poetry, art, kingship, ritual space, and philosophy. A thread of continuity through this great time period is Śiva-bhakti, a path of participation in the worship of Lord Śiva. Actively developed in this period, it was an important contributing factor to the wider cultural developments, particularly in the arts and the construction of a distinctly Tamil mode of religiosity. These historical transformations in Tamil culture highlight the participation of diverse agents in building tradition. Tradition itself comprises many different agents acting in many different spheres; hymnists on pilgrimage, kings and priests in temples, and philosophers in educational centers had all played a role in developing Śiva-bhakti, but their agendas had been different, resulting in distinctive interpretations—and thus representations—of bhakti. How then to acknowledge bhakti as a technical religious term with a consistent and coherent meaning, yet incorporate the fact of a variety of interpretive traditions that played on both the authority and the fluidity of the term as it could relate to specific contexts?

The interpreters of bhakti I discuss in this book have in common the praxis of representation. Representation is a praxis, insofar as it is a method by which agents participate in a public discourse and invest their subjectivities in the public arguments they make. The cultural historian Rajeswari Sunder Rajan views the idea of representation as just such an intersection between private and public, reality and culture, and the real and the imagined: "The concept of 'representation', it seems, is useful precisely because and to the extent that it can serve a mediating function between the two positions, neither foundationalist (privileging 'reality') nor superstructural (privileging 'culture'), not denying the category of the real, or essentializing it as some pre-given metaphysical ground for representation."[16] This viewpoint has guided my attempt to find a way of discussing the Tamil agents and, to some extent, the orientalists, who tend to privilege "reality" in their perspectives on bhakti as ultimate truth, in comparison with modern scholars, who tend to privilege "culture" in their descriptions and analysis. The issue is understanding how the proponents and interpreters of Tamil Śiva-bhakti represented their visions of the real in their own historical contexts. Representation acknowledges the human effort of interpretation; it is the creative space in which cultural agents act. A representation can be analyzed to "seek to arrive at an understanding of the issues at stake" in any given cultural construction.[17] The main issue at stake in the development of Tamil Śiva-bhakti was to define bhakti as a religious path that related to the conditions of embodiment as they were understood by different agents in different historical periods. The meaning of bhakti as participation was not an issue at stake, for it was presupposed by all authors; at stake was the way to understand its significance for their era.

Tamil Śiva-bhakti was established as part of Tamil culture through many centuries, from the time of the bhakti hymns' composition in the early medieval period (seventh through ninth centuries) through their active interpretation in later medieval times (to the fourteenth century), and it is accepted today as a major contribution to a distinctive Tamil cultural heritage. Tamils today appreciate the bhakti hymns as a classical element of Tamil history, along with the Caṅkam poems, the *Tirukkuṟaḷ*, Vaiṣṇava bhakti poetry, the *Rāmāyaṇa* of Kampaṉ, and the poetry of Māṇikkavācakar, among a wealth of writings in Tamil.

Since the early years of this century, appreciation of Tamil heritage has been promoted by the Tamil nationalism movement. This movement had many strands; for example, the Tamil literary and cultural heritage was a focus of the Tamil Renaissance, whereas caste and religious practice were the focus of the Non-Brahman movement. The Tamil Renaissance sought to restore classic Tamil texts. The Caṅkam poems had fallen into disuse and were known only by name when U. Vē. Cāminātaiyar made a determined search for old manuscripts in the late 1800s, which resulted in a published volume of eight major anthologies in 1905. Tamil religious texts, such as the canon of Śiva-bhakti texts (*Tirumuṟai*) and the canon of Śaiva Siddhānta philosophical texts (*Mēykaṇṭa Cāttiraṅkaḷ*), became a focus of the Non-Brahman movement in its attempt to prove that there was a historical, distinctive Tamil religion that eschewed brahman leadership. The Tamil Śiva-bhakti hymns I discuss in this book were promoted by the Tamil Icai (Music) Movement of the 1930s and 1940s.[18]

In the field of Tamil cultural studies, including those that deal with religion, it is certainly possible to come across modern works of scholarship that more or less explicitly participate in the polarized discussion of Tamil versus Sanskrit, in an effort to distinguish a preexisting Tamil heritage from Aryan influence. These works invert the Indological language of a generation ago to understand the process of cultural interaction as the Tamilization of Sanskrit rather than the Sanskritization of Tamil.[19] The question of the origin and original nature of Tamil cultural formulations may be an important locus of study, but it is not the approach I take here. In this study, I identify and analyze the values that selected agents invested in bhakti over time.

Tradition understands Tamil Śiva-bhakti to have begun with hymns composed by the three famous hymnists, Campantar (Tiruñāṉacampantar), Appar (Tirunāvukkaracar), and Cuntarar (Nampi Ārūrar), referred to as "the three" (mūvar). There is no apparent reason to doubt the historicity of these poets and that they lived during the seventh to ninth centuries A.D., although a minority of scholars would date them either earlier or later. Their hymns participate in a shared discourse of praise to Śiva, with similar language and poetic techniques, yet there are also differences among the three in terms of content and tone, which are alluded to in various popular characterizations, including "Campantar and Appar sang of the Lord, while Cuntarar sang of himself," and "Campantar is the child of the Lord, Appar His servant, and Cuntarar His friend."

Through the hymns' prominent themes of pilgrimage and praise, I analyze the selections the hymnists made from both Sanskrit and Tamil sources, while I emphasize their perspective that bhakti was greater than the sum of these parts. In particular, I focus on their localization of bhakti in the Tamil lands and in Tamil culture, through which they equated being a good bhakta with being a good Tamil. The hymnists' emphasis on place was a key feature by which they distinguished bhakti from other Hindu practices. The autobiographical nature of their poetry both expressed their experience of Śiva and encouraged their audience to eschew a complacent worldview in favor of a critical look at themselves and others and a rejection of all that impeded the opening of their hearts for love of God and the opening of their minds to contemplate God. Through their pilgrimages, they established a community of bhaktas distinct from other communities within Hinduism. In response to non-Hindus, their rhetoric emphasized a moral distinction between themselves and these groups, especially Buddhists and Jains, who are explicitly attacked in the Tamil bhakti hymns. I discuss the case of Jainism in particular to challenge the scholarly view that Tamil Śiva-bhakti represented a "revival" of Hinduism.

In defining bhakti as a religious path, the mūvar represented bhakti as a theology of embodiment. They embodied bhakti in their own experiences, their visions of Śiva, their pilgrimages to Tamil towns, and the community of bhaktas. Representations of Tamil Śiva-bhakti were, from the beginning, concerned with issues of embodiment, not only in the imagining of God but also in the embodiment of humanity and the questions it raised. Issues of embodiment constituted a rhetoric that informed the composition and development of Tamil Śiva-bhakti in the works of Tamil authors. Later interpreters understood the hymns of the early bhakti poets to be authentic and original Tamil expressions of bhakti and thus sources of inspiration for various understandings of the path of participation in the worship of God. Yet, each group also brought its own perspective to bhakti; their perspectives understood bhakti to be an autonomous religious path yet related it to developments in their time, including imperial temple worship and philosophical writing in Tamil.

In the tenth through twelfth centuries, the development of imperial stone temples, both symbols and actualizations of the potent material and spiritual powers of kings, reached a summit with the Chola dynasty. How the hymns, which were unabashedly regional in comparison with the increasingly systematized modes of priestly worship in these temples, came to be an established part of worship informs my analysis in this section. It was in this context of imperial temples that a principal stream of Tamil Śiva-bhakti's development became stories of the bhaktas themselves, which were depicted in paintings and sculptures and written in verse. These stories explored details of caste, family, employment, actions of worship, and salvation. Detailed knowledge of these practitioners of Śiva-bhakti thus became knowledge of bhakti; bhakti became embodied as saints (nāyaṉmār). Telling stories of the nāyaṉmār culminated in the twelfth-century *Periya Purāṇam* (Great Traditional Story), a multivolumed text attributed to Cēkkiḻār. In contradistinction to earlier biographies, Cēkkiḻār firmly contextualizes the nāyaṉmār in imperial temple culture by reasserting the access to Śiva, certainty of salvation, and diversity of bhaktas on the same religious path that characterize Tamil Śiva-bhakti but that had become negotiated in the imperial temple culture.

In the fourteenth century, Tamil Śaiva Siddhānta philosophers found in the bhakti hymns a speculative angle that illustrated their principles. Toward this end, a Tamil Śaiva Siddhānta philosopher, Umāpati Civācāryār, systematized Śiva-bhakti. One of the texts attributed to him describes the making of the Tamil Śiva-bhakti canon, the *Tirumuṟai* as we know it today, by persons who lived before him. The text is understood by contemporary scholars to accurately portray events that took place prior to Umāpati's time, yet I demonstrate that the text actually points to his own identity as the composer of the canon, based on his interest in creating a Tamil heritage for his own philosophical writings in Tamil. His interest in Tamil Śiva-bhakti pervades the Tamil works attributable to him, including the first known anthology of the Tamil Śiva-bhakti hymns, a selection that he suggests embodies Śaiva Siddhānta philosophy. The themes of representation, identity, and heritage are thus brought to the fore as the tradition of Tamil Śiva-bhakti becomes established in the late medieval period.

Although some might view these historical developments as accretions on the original formulations of bhakti by the three poets, they are, in fact, all original understandings of bhakti. Later interpreters of Tamil Śiva-bhakti drew upon bhakti's thesis on embodiment while they contextualized the mūvar's hymns and stories of the nāyaṉmār in their distinctive worldviews. The Tamil agents from the periods of the composition of the hymns, those who brought the hymns into imperial temple culture, and those who composed philosophical interpretations of the hymns were all actively engaged in the worship of Śiva. They were composers on pilgrimage, singing the praises of Śiva; followers of the saintly hymnists, who hoped for liberation by actively engaging in worship; and religious leaders experiencing mystical access to Śiva. All of these images of the agents involved convey a sense of bhakti as participation. For all of the Tamil Śiva-bhakti agents, bhakti is a theology of embodiment that encourages active participation in the worship of Śiva and that values human experience. Bhakti became embodied, then, in the words, actions, and images of agents who gave it distinctive representation, based on their engagement with their own historical contexts and rhetoric.

There are many images of bhakti because representations of bhakti are created through the interpretive and practical activities of many different agents in disparate ages. The cultural agents I discuss in this book, including scholars, bhakti poets, medieval kings and priests, and a late medieval philosopher, are all responsible for creating distinctive images of bhakti. Although authors are individuals, the discourses in which they participate are collective. They each seek to ground their representations in the issues that shape their lives, so that the meanings they give bhakti respond to their own situation, even while their formulations contribute to the body of material and symbolic realities accepted as a shared ideal. Through this dialectic, bhakti became a cultural reference point in Tamil heritage. The meeting point between the individual and the collective, the real and the imagined, the material and the symbolic, is precisely that agents invest their own subjectivity in the construction of culture. In so doing, they created distinctive, yet purposefully overlapping, images of bhakti.

PART I

Images of Bhakti

Scholars writing on bhakti in the late nineteenth and early twentieth centuries were agreed that bhakti in India was preeminently a monotheistic reform movement. For these scholars, the inextricable connection between monotheism and reform had both theological and social significance in terms of the development of Indian culture. Equally important were the ways in which these scholars could identify with the ideals of monotheism and reform. The orientalist images of bhakti were formulated in a context of discovery: a time of organized cultural contact, in which many agencies, including administrative, scholarly, and missionary—sometimes embodied in a single person—sought knowledge of India. Through the Indo-European language connection, early orientalists believed that they were, in a sense, seeing their own ancestry in the antique texts and "antiquated" customs of Indian peoples. In this respect, certain scholars could identify with the monotheism of bhakti. Seen as a reform movement, bhakti presented a parallel to the orientalist agenda of intervention in the service of empire.

Bhakti also represented an example, or even a case study, of what orientalist authors considered to be universal processes in the development of religion. In the orientalist episteme, monotheism represented the culmination of religious development; in terms of world religion, monotheism was thus the ultimate reform. In terms of the history of Christianity, however, it was the penultimate reform, later to be refined through sectarian reform—that is, Protestantism. The orientalist scholars of bhakti worked within this frame of historicity, though their location of bhakti in history tended to differ. H. H. Wilson viewed bhakti as a modern, sectarian innovation, an image that implicitly resonated with the Protestant idea of reform. A. Weber and M. F. Lorinser represented the monotheism of bhakti as an ancient idea in India, based upon the proof text of the *Bhagavad Gītā*; however, they maintained that monotheism could not have been Indian in origin but was, instead, borrowed from Christianity. R. G. Bhandarkar, taking up the issue that monotheism as a culminating religious idea need not have been modern in India any more than it was in Christian history, sought to prove that monotheism was an indigenous Hindu development that preceded

Christianity. For Bhandarkar, bhakti was a kṣatriya reform of brahman religion; this image became influential in bhakti scholarship. M. Monier-Williams, who was probably the most widely read among these orientalist scholars, made explicit the connection between Protestant reform and bhakti prefigured by H. H. Wilson and contextualized it in a discussion of orthodoxy and heterodoxy.

These diverse but complementary perspectives were what George A. Grierson had to draw upon for his comprehensive and authoritative article on Bhakti-Mārga for the 1910 *Encyclopædia of Religion and Ethics*. As with any encyclopedia article, it was supposed to represent the current state of knowledge about a given topic. What is remarkable is the impression it gives of virtual unbroken continuity with the ideas of scholars who had written a generation before.

Grierson defined the term *bhakti* as having the primary meaning of "adoration," while the related term *Bhāgavata* (which the author always capitalizes) means "the Adorable One" (in the sense of "One who is adored").[1] In discussing how Indian monotheism originated and became centered around this figure—the embodiment of bhakti—Grierson grudgingly identified a first stage in nature worship, representing his nod to a discourse that was marginal in academic scholarship on bhakti but dominant in scholarship on the Vedas. Grierson suggested that early bhakti may or may not have been related to worship of the sun. The idea was that the sun is unitary; some of the earlier orientalists had, in fact, likened Viṣṇu's avatāras (forms in which God descends to earth) to rays of the sun.

Though many had attempted to find the origins of monotheism in the Vedas, scholarly consensus deemed this ultimately not possible. Knowing that Bhandarkar had argued for a kṣatriya development of bhakti monotheism, Grierson identified a second stage in the development of bhakti accordingly. He imagined competing communities in which divergent ideas of God were localized: Specifically, the brahmans were advocates of pantheism, and the kṣatriyas were advocates of monotheism. Grierson even attempted to plot them geographically: The center of the map was located to the north of modern-day Delhi, representing the Midland, inhabited by brahmans who knew the Vedas. The periphery of this center was an Outland inhabited by kṣatriyas: "and here, during the thousand years that precede our era, while the Brāhmans of the Midland were developing their pantheistic 'Brahmanism,' the leading spirits of the Kṣatriyas thought out their monotheism."[2]

In this situation, the "Bhāgavata religion" was founded by the kṣatriya "Krisna Vāsudeva" (the latter term a patronym), which Grierson understood to be Kṛṣṇa as a real person, inhabiting the Outland. This religion went through various stages of contact with other systems that from Grierson's description can be interpreted as an alternation of threats to monotheism and fodder for the development of monotheism. First, the Outland negotiated the new philosophies of Sānkhya and Yoga; then these were appropriated by the Midland brahmans and transformed into Brahmanism. Then the Outland had contact with the polytheism of the "lower orders"—these are presumably the "aborigines" noted in several of the orientalist discourses on Hinduism—as a result of which they created a pantheon of gods, the personal deities of bhakti. Finally, the Outland inhabitants had to cope with a major challenge to "their monotheism" from the Midland, the Vedānta of Śankara (which, according to the orientalists, was pantheistic).

This latter event precipitated a reform movement initiated by Rāmānuja and Mādhva that changed forever the Bhāgavata religion and represented the third stage of development, according to Grierson: "With the appearance of these two great reformers commences the third stage in the development of the Bhāgavata religion—the modern *Bhakti-mārga*."[3] This modern Bhakti-mārga is a religion: It has doctrines, such as monotheism, grace, creation, salvation, works, immortality of the soul, and "four churches of the reformation," that is, Rāmānuja, Mādhva, Viṣṇusvāmin, and Nimbāditya. It also has ritual features such as the mantra, sectarian marks, and the authority of the guru (which Monier-Williams believed analogous to baptism, initiation, and communion).

The map of bhakti in this article was not gratuitious. It was a spatial depiction of the orientalists' sense of the orthodox (center) and the unorthodox (periphery), with bhakti consistently located on the unorthodox side in opposition to Śankara. The origin and tenacity of the Bhāgavata religion depended upon nonbrahman kṣatriyas, following Bhandakar's analysis, who were not traditionally invested with religious power. Grierson's map "explained" the genesis of monotheism, and the development of the Bhāgavata religion, in terms of polarities. But whence came the reformers who created the modern bhakti-mārga? By the time Grierson wrote this article, scholars had linked bhakti to the Vedānta of Rāmānuja and others, and even he acknowledged this. His answer was to suggest a gap between the early Bhāgavata religion and the modern bhakti-mārga, the latter a reform that "almost seems as if a new doctrine, coming from some unknown land, had suddenly been revealed, and had swept with irresistible force in one mighty wave across the peninsula."[4] The image of a wave is in keeping with his, and earlier orientalists', idea of a reform movement and with their persistent image of bhakti as an overwhelming emotional response to God.

In a contemporaneous article, Grierson sought to explain the source of the wave that propelled bhakti from the periphery to, as it were, the mainstream. He revived the thesis of bhakti's Christian origin but with a difference: He postulated that Christianity had influenced medieval bhakti, rather than providing a source for bhakti in ancient times, as the German orientalists had held. For example, he noted that Rāmānuja was "born at Perumbūr and studied at Kāñcīpura (Conjeeveram), each of which is within a few miles of the Nestorian Christian shrine of St. Thomas at Mylapore."[5] Medieval bhakti had thus begun in the south, under Christian influence. From there, it went north: "Late in the 14th century, or early in the 15th, a teacher of Rāmānuja's school, named Rāmānanda, drank afresh at the well of Christian influence, and, quarrelling with his co-religionists on a question of discipline, founded a new sect, which he carried with him northwards to the Gangetic plain. From his time Sanskrit was no longer the official language of the *bhakti*-cult."[6]

There are many facets to Grierson's depictions of bhakti, including his historical argument that Christianity was the origin of bhakti, his continued use of Christian ideas to understand bhakti, his emphasis on bhakti as an emotional and practical religious cult, and his understanding that bhakti in a regional language is a transmission of the original Sanskrit bhakti (for him, the official textbook of bhakti is Śāṇḍilya's *Bhakti Sūtra*).[7] All of them served to reify an ideal of the radical outsider as reformer, characterized in various ways, including kṣatriya, the Outland, Christianity, and a language other than Sanskrit.

The concern with locating bhakti accurately in the development of religion in India and with understanding the nature of bhakti as a religious perspective continues in contemporary scholarship, which has, however, dropped the language of radical otherness, monotheism, and reform of orthodoxy. Instead, scholars today represent bhakti as a religious perspective that developed from reflections on the Vedic context; rather than innovation, it is understood to be a reworking of tradition within a distinctive religious frame. Some scholars characterize the emergence of bhakti as a revival of tradition; if revivalism is taken to mean active selection and recontextualization of tradition, then it fits in with the scholarly perspective on bhakti that I discuss in chapter 1. Usually, however, this is not the case: The persistent image of revivalism in contemporary scholarship points to the emotionalism of bhakti in contrast to the "cold" religions of Brahmanism, Jainism, and Buddhism. In response to this image, I review theories of bhakti as a movement in chapter 2 and provide a detailed case study of the relationship between bhakti and Jainism in medieval Tamilnadu in part II. It is the case that the emotional aspect of bhakti is crucial, and it does serve as a frame for interpreting received tradition, but this was done in relation to emotional responses that had already been defined and discussed by tradition. In chapter 1, then, after considering the nature of bhakti as a frame for received tradition, I turn to a consideration of the oft-used translation of *bhakti* in English, "devotion."

ONE

Bhakti as Devotion

Scholarly consensus today tends to view bhakti as a post-Vedic development that took place primarily in the watershed years of the epics and purāṇas, literatures that are credited with a primary role in the cultural transition from Vedism to Hinduism. The scholarly periodization of texts within Vedism and Hinduism is based on a view of tradition reworking itself, but its relentlessly linear nature probably obscures contemporaneous and competing formulations, rather than elucidating them. Since the *Bhagavad Gītā* is the first text to thematize bhakti overtly and it is contextualized in the *Mahābhārata* epic, we must acknowledge that the first self-consciously bhakti text does appear in a post-Vedic milieu, in spite of a minority scholarly position that bhakti can be found in the Vedas.[1]

Madeleine Biardeau, who has done much to revise scholarship on the early history of bhakti, states that bhakti "englobes" the earlier traditions of Vedism (including the Brāhmaṇas and Upaniṣads), a process that is characteristic of cultural change in India:

> Historically, the conquests of the great sovereigns did not, in general, lead to the substitution of one power for another, but to a subordination of the vanquished to the victor—which prepared the ground for a possible reversal of the situation, always theoretically conceivable since this took place in the limited domain of artha. But reversal is no longer possible when it is a question of imposing socio-religious norms which structure the whole of society. The superior has to remain superior, but his hierarchical vision precisely enables him to integrate almost anything with a minimal change in structure.[2]

The perspective of the *Bhagavad Gītā* seems to support this characterization of change; in that text, bhakti was the frame for understanding traditions that could be traced to earlier textual sources and ritual practices. The example of the displacement of Vedic sacrifice, which was atomized through subsequent interpretation, never to reappear as a dominant community ritual activity, illustrates Biardeau's notion of the irreversibility of socioreligious norms. Did bhakti ever possess the kind of cultural hegemony that the Vedic sacrifice once possessed? Biardeau suggests that it did, in her thesis of "the universe of bhakti" and her identification of bhakti as *the doctrine* of the mythological epics.[3] With this image, Biardeau revisions the idea of the epics and purāṇas as a cultural watershed to understand them as full-blown bhakti treatises.

Biardeau suggests that, within Vedic tradition, the *Yajurveda* may have provided a cornerstone for the development of bhakti. She makes the case strongly, indicating that bhakti's "structures are unintelligible so long as they are cut off from Vedic Revelation." According to her, the *Yajurveda* provides a model for the importance of action for salvation, which is a major thread in bhakti: "There is no doubt that the *Yajurveda* was particularly at the centre of the speculations of bhakti, both in its ritualistic part and in its *Upaniṣads*, and this cannot be a pure accident; the *Yajurveda* is the Veda of the *adhvaryu*, the priest who, in the sacrifice, is charged with all the ritual manipulations, the actor *par excellence*, whose every gesture must receive a symbolic interpretation. This will be one of the threads to guide us through the labyrinth of bhakti."[4] In particular, the Taittirīya school of the *Black Yajurveda* may be most directly influential; for example, it is this school's version of the *Śatarudrīya-stotra* that appears to have been quoted in Tamil Śiva-bhakti poetry.[5] The *Yajurveda* is a manual of praxis in a ritual context, and the *Śatarudrīya* is a liturgical prayer; both are part of the Vedic worldview, which understands community activity in the world to be religious activity. Indeed, most scholars have noted the this-worldly nature of the Vedic worldview. Bhakti's positive valuation of action in the world, which is a constitutive premise of bhakti's thesis on embodiment, resonates with practical aspects of the Vedic worldview. The selectivity on the part of agents of bhakti may have been grounded in such resonances.

Biardeau further points to two Upaniṣads as especially significant for the development of bhakti: the *Kaṭha* and the *Śvetāśvatara*.[6] For Biardeau, the sectarian aspects of these texts (Viṣṇu in the former; Śiva in the latter) are less important than the texts' representation of the cosmic force as active: "But the fact that the divine is no longer a neutral principle also changes its relationship to the still empirical man who aspires to liberation. Nor is it an accident that the *Kaṭha* and *Śvetāśvatara* bring into this relationship an element of election, grace. . . . The disciple's knowledge and his assiduity in his exercises do not suffice to ensure the success of his undertaking if the Puruṣa himself does not call him."[7] One of the most famous images of an active God promoted in bhakti literature is the descent of Viṣṇu in the form of avatāras to help humanity. Not only is God amid humankind as an active agent but also there is a relationship (bhakti) between them. God "calls" humankind to partake (bhakti) of him. In the poem-songs of Tamil Śiva-bhakti, both the cosmic and local deeds of Śiva are celebrated, in the context of the poets' emotional engagement with the Lord.

Biardeau identifies this selection of elements from Vedism, primarily the this-worldly focus and the action of God in the world, as part of a worldview that balanced the practical and speculative dimensions of tradition in a "tension characteristic of the world of bhakti."[8] One manifestation of this tension is the interaction of two competing worldviews in bhakti: the perspective of renunciation and that of affirming life in the world. They are brought together in a bhakti theory of salvation. Biardeau views this interaction as constitutive of the transformation from Vedism to Hinduism: "Neither the world of the renouncers nor secular life remained unscathed, and what is called 'Hinduism' rather than 'brahmanism' emerged from the process."[9]

This negotiation was played out across the developing schema of the puruṣārthas —the four goals of humankind, being ārtha, kāma, dharma, and mokṣa. According to Biardeau, the key term is kāma. Kāma had been "readily" used in the *Bṛhadāraṇyaka Upaniṣad* as a term that denoted love of ātman, the highest goal of spiritual knowledge and the love for which all else was abandoned.[10] Yet the term was also used in the same Upaniṣad with the meaning of a selfishly constituted love, involving the rise of the ego and resulting in ignorance.[11] Ultimately, in an increasingly polemical context, the language of kāma as representing connection to the ātman was dropped, and kāma became understood by the speculative renouncers, or sannyāsins, as representing the egoism and ignorance of the world, "the all-encompassing value in this world." According to Biardeau, the sannyāsin perspective presented the problem to which bhakti proposed a solution:

> Whereas the starting-point of the sannyāsin's speculations was karman, the analysis he conducted, parallel to that of the Brahman, on human actions and goals, has shifted the focus of interest. It is this notion of kāma—in the all-encompassing sense which the renouncer attributes to it—together with the whole constellation of associated ideas, which comes to constitute a golden thread that runs through all speculations about true universal salvation. Bhakti would seek a solution in the abolition of kāma in the very heart of man's ordinary activity. In other words, it would seek to imbue secular life with the sannyāsin's ideal.[12]

There is a tension in bhakti, then, between encompassing the critical stance of the yogic renouncer toward the world and affirming life within the world. In Biardeau's terms, the former, representing the sannyāsin ideal, was englobed by the latter, representing the ideal of bhakti; what made this possible was the banishment of kāma. Certainly the *Gītā* endorses bhakti-yoga, the discipline of bhakti, with its main teaching that this discipline involves relinquishing attachment to the fruits of action in favor of dedicating them to the Lord. Biardeau views this as the sannyāsin ideal embedded in everyday life: to live life in the world but eschew desire or passion for the fruits of action.

The bhakti of the *Gītā* did respond to the physical and emotional sequestering of those on the religious path as represented by the sannyāsin ideal. In its emphasis on embodiment in the ordinary social world, the *Gītā*'s vision of bhakti presented an alternative to dominant forms of religiosity, both the asocial sannyāsin and the temporally defined practice of ritual. In the former, religious experience was engendered by physical separation from society; in the latter, time was the mechanism by which religious experience was set apart from social formations. In contrast, bhakti represented the possibility of religious experience anywhere, anytime.

However, if bhakti sought to "abolish" kāma, why privilege a term (*bhakti*) that had, and continued to have even in the epics, meanings of love and affection?[13] The move toward using bhakti in place of kāma suggests that the sannyāsin-inspired redefinition of kāma did not take root as a viable meaning. Kāma continued to denote erotic love, and it remained necessary to acknowledge that it was part of human social life as distinct from human religious life. Bhakti had to chart a new course with respect to emotion and experience. Nor was it necessary to distinguish bhakti from kāma alone; it also had to be distinguished from other well-defined terms, notably *śraddhā* (reverence).[14]

The tension in bhakti is between emotion and intellection: emotion to reaffirm the social context and temporal freedom, intellection to ground the bhakti religious experience in a thoughtful, conscious approach. This tension was missed by orientalist scholars, who even in the earliest definitions stressed what they viewed as the uncontrolled emotion of bhakti: "The whole religious and moral code of the sect is comprised in one word, *Bhakti*, a term that signifies a union of implicit faith and incessant devotion, and which . . . is the momentary repetition of the name of KRISHNA, under a firm belief, that such a practice is sufficient for salvation."[15] For Monier-Williams, the full realization of bhakti's potential for uncontrolled emotion occured in the "abuses" of the followers of the sixteenth-century bhakta Vallabhācārya.[16] But the orientalists were mistaken in their analysis; in bhakti texts, emotion is freed from social and temporal constraint, not moral principles.

As a religious perspective, bhakti is not to be understood as uncritical emotion but as committed engagement. Bhakti as a religious perspective encourages a critical stance, a distance not usually associated with the bonds of emotion (which was the criticism raised by the sannyāsin ideal). The tension—or, perhaps, balance—between emotion and intellection can be seen in the *Gītā* itself. The *Gītā* identified four types of bhakti salvation, which include, and are not opposed to, jñāna (higher knowledge). These types are related to the condition of the person practicing bhakti: ārta, one who is in distress; jñāsu, a seeker of knowledge; arthārathī, a seeker of worldly success; and jñānī, a person of higher knowledge. The *Bhagavad Gītā* favors the jñānī, who thinks of God single-mindedly: the jñānī is *ekabhakta*.[17]

Modern scholarship on regional bhakti traditions also illustrates the tension between emotion and intellection; for example, Edward Dimock discusses the importance of prema (love) to the Bengali Vaiṣṇava Sahajiyās: "In his attitude and in his worship there can be no trace of kāma, of carnal desire, of desire for the satisfaction of self; kāma, unless it is transformed into true love, prema, leads not to joy, but to misery and hell."[18] David Haberman has identified methods of aesthetic theory in the Gauḍīya Vaiṣṇava tradition of drama (associated with Caitanya): "This study is intended to stand as a conscious contradiction and challenge to those who claim that means and methods have no place in Hindu *bhakti*. . . . *Sādhana*, an intentional method or technique designed to realize the ultimate goal, does occupy a prominent position in the type of religion known as Hindu *bhakti*."[19] And Norman Cutler discusses Tamil Śaiva and Vaiṣṇava bhakti poetry as defined by a poetics of communion among poet, God, and audience; the emotion of the poetry is expressed within an efficacious poetic structure.[20]

A problem for modern scholars is whether the language we use in discussing bhakti acknowledges the tension between emotion and intellection that proponents of bhakti carefully developed.[21] One of the most pervasive phrases used to describe bhakti in contemporary literature is "devotion to a personal deity."[22] As Krishna Sharma has argued at length—the argument runs through her entire book, *Bhakti and the Bhakti Movement*—this definition of *bhakti* reproduces the orientalist agenda of monotheism, as well as its emphasis on Vaiṣṇavism, by privileging the saguṇa (with attributes) imagination of God. Sharma criticized the early orientalists for their development of this definition of *bhakti*, as well as modern scholars who reproduce it, by appealing to the religious perspective of Kabīr, whom she views as a proponent of nirguṇa bhakti, which envisions God as formless or without attributes. The orientalists had only loosely connected Kabīr, as well as Rāmānanda and Guru Nānak, with bhakti.[23] In contrast, the current scholarly consensus, developed primarily by scholars of bhakti in regional languages, holds that Kabīr's religious vision is bhakti.

Today, scholars tend to understand bhakti as comprising independent nirguṇa and saguṇa ways of imagining God. In particular, this division within bhakti has been used to group the bhakti literatures in regional languages, although we are now more aware that nirguṇa and saguṇa distinctions were related in complex ways throughout Sanskrit literatures.[24] In an early parallel to the nirguṇa and saguṇa distinction, the orientalists had noted that there were what they identified as theistic and pantheistic tendencies in the *Gītā*, but they attributed this to the composite nature of the text and in general believed that the theistic strands were original.[25] In the modern schema, the Tamil Śaiva and Vaiṣṇava bhakti poets are classified as imagining a saguṇa god, as are the north Indian bhakti saints Surdās, Mīrābāī, and Tulsīdās. The Vīraśaivas of Karnataka, plus the north Indian saints Ravidās, Kabīr, and Nānak, are all held to imagine God as nirguṇa.

The first academic use of this schema was by a Hindi scholar of the 1920s, who applied it to the poems of Hindi sants.[26] He attributed a different source to each: The poetry of the nirguṇa bhaktas was "rooted in knowledge" (*jñānāshrayi*), whereas the poetry of the saguṇa bhaktas was "rooted in love" (*premāshrayi*). He understood both of these methods to be *śakhās*, or branches, of bhakti. The early orientalists had opposed jñāna to bhakti, just as they had implicitly opposed two theistic perspectives, pantheism (*advaita*) and monotheism (*bhakti*), whereas scholars now distinguish nirguṇa and saguṇa perspectives within bhakti. Thus, in the contemporary understanding of bhakti through poets' images of God, scholars include elements that the orientalists tended to distance, yet the opposition between knowledge and emotion is retained.

In a fascinating article, John Stratton Hawley has questioned whether the nirguṇa-saguṇa distinction prominent in contemporary scholarship on bhakti actually has any grounding in the poetry, hagiographies, and anthologies of Hindi bhaktas up to the seventeenth century. He concludes that the distinction "survives with only mixed success" in the poetry and hagiographies; yet, the distinction is part of an organizational strategy in later sectarian anthologies. Hawley derives a cautionary perspective from his research: "Each of these yardsticks teaches us to exercise caution when we speak of the great contrast between *nirguṇīs* and *saguṇīs* in the early or 'classical' period of North Indian bhakti, the *bhakti kāl*."[27] So the idea of nirguṇa-saguṇa, which is increasingly coming to define bhakti in contemporary scholarship (whether or not this is intended), actually comes from a very localized tradition: sectarian anthologies of bhakti poetry in Hindi produced in north India in the sixteenth and seventeenth centuries.

Furthermore, A. K. Ramanujan has denied the usefulness of the distinction, viewing it as a limitation on our understanding of the bhakti poets' creativity. His analysis is similar to Biardeau's in that he views bhakti as holding in tension elements that other religious traditions would tend to keep separate:

> The distinction iconic/aniconic is a useful one, as *nirguṇa/saguṇa* is not. All devotional poetry plays on the tension between *saguṇa* and *nirguṇa*, the lord as person and the lord as principle. If he were entirely a person, he would not be divine, and if he were entirely a principle, a godhead, one could not make poems about him. The former attitude makes *dvaita* or dualism possible, and the latter makes for *advaita* or monism. . . . It is not either/or, but both/and; myth, *bhakti*, and poetry would be impossible without the presence of both attitudes.[28]

It is surely part of the dynamic of crafting definitions that the impetus is toward collapsing distinctions made in many traditional or sectarian interpretations of a given term or phenomenon. The nirguṇa-saguṇa distinction addresses this issue: It supersedes the orientalist definition of "devotion to a personal deity," and it affirms an indigenous classificatory perspective. However, its applicability to bhakti generally is put into question by Hawley's reflections, and its usefulness in doing so is challenged by Ramanujan's. Nor is it simply an issue of Sanskrit as against regional-language bhakti formulations. As Sharma demonstrates, the *Bhagavad Gītā*, the *Bhāgavata Purāṇa*, and the *Bhakti Sūtras* of Nārada and Śāṇḍilya do not present a unified picture of bhakti; even within Sanskrit traditions, interpretations of bhakti changed over time.[29]

Some scholars today, rather than reduce bhakti to a single term or phrase, have opted to compile a list of characteristics for bhakti, with the caveat that each element "may or may not" apply to each interpretation of bhakti in the Indian context.[30] This is helpful for comparison, but it does not relieve us of the problem of conceptualizing the various bhaktis as bhakti, which is part of the scholarly agenda. What we need to establish in an understanding of the term *bhakti* is an inclusive definition within which the many voices of bhakti can speak to us.

A possible solution, as Sharma recognized, is to define *bhakti* generically as "devotion," rather than as "devotion to a personal deity." "Devotion" has been successfully discussed cross-culturally, as an encyclopedia article by David Kinsley demonstrates.[31] In addition, the religious meanings of devotion, including praise, prayer, meditation, and self-discipline,[32] are relevant to the study of bhakti, although it is noteworthy that self-discipline was rarely a characteristic the orientalists associated with bhakti.

Yet, how much does the term *devotion* tell us about bhakti? According to the *Oxford English Dictionary*, the term originated in Latin and in its oldest sense denoted that which was consecrated to something either good or evil. Then the term took on the more positive sense of devotion to something good, implying loyalty; it was in this sense that the term passed into Christian usage, meaning specifically devoted to God, piety, service, or religious zeal. Significantly, only the Christian meanings of devotion originally came into the Romance languages from ecclesiastical Latin, proceeding from Old French to Middle English. So our use of the term in English is historically derived from Christian usage. But the specificity of the term as religious piety did not last in the Romance languages, for during the sixteenth century its semantic range became expanded to include reference to secular persons and things. In contemporary usage, "the action of devoting or applying to a particular use or purpose" is an equally common meaning for devotion as "the action of devoting or setting apart to a sacred use or purpose; solemn dedication, consecration."

The liberation of the meaning of devotion from its original ecclesiastical usage has consequences for our understanding of the word as a religious term. Some of the issues are broached in the contemporary study of the term; for example, Charles Hallisey has eloquently described the term's long and difficult history in the scholarship of history of religions. He notes that two main streams of academic thought have developed to explore the meanings of devotion. One is to emphasize an esoteric context for devotion, equating it with mysticism. The other is to stress a popular context, in which devotion is the religious response of laypeople. In both cases, the image is one of devotion bleeding through the borders of established religion; it is not a central premise for organized religious worship.[33]

With the aim of providing a redescription of devotion, Hallisey turns to the pragmatics of devotion "to describe devotion as a strategy for relating religious systems to men and women in particular contexts." His argument attempts to recentralize devotion as a religious strategy and to invest the term with a sense of the conscious activity of agents. He turns to the analogue of devotion in medieval Sinhala, *mamāyana*, "which refers to a complex attitude recognized by the linguistic action of calling an object, 'mine'." It is this notion of "I am involved" that Hallisey sees as the core of devotion.[34]

Hallisey's emphasis on active self-involvement is important and directly relevant for the study of bhakti. Poets who write or sing bhakti poems in regional languages are involving themselves; they are making God theirs. This does involve emotional commitment. For example, there are images of unbridled love for God in the Tamil poems, which convey a sense of the bhakta's longing or even madness for God. At the same time, however, these poems situate this state of mind in the context of knowing about God: who God is, where God is, and how we can participate in God. In their bhakti poems, the poets play with the conventions of both social behavior and poetry itself, in the interest of transforming aspects of the known world (for example, social mores and literary works) into a world that puts God at the center of existence and participation in God at the center of human life.

I believe that Hallisey's redescription of devotion more accurately conveys the ideas that form the complex of bhakti, including the sense that bhakti is a serious religious path—a strategy—and that it includes the sense that people are conscious agents. But in ordinary usage, as Hallisey notes, the term *devotion* suggests exaggeration in terms of both emotion and action, and this, in turn, is associated with agents who are not religious specialists, that is, laypeople. In its ordinary sense, devotion connotes neither authority nor profundity. The orientalists were very aware of these meanings, and their language conveys it, from Wilson's "incessant devotion," to Barth's assessment that "from one exaggeration to another, *bhakti* came at length to be sublated. As the result of ascribing the most surprising results to a minimum of intention, they came at length not to require any intention at all."[35]

It appears to be the case that the terms *devotion* in English and *bhakti* in Sanskrit may have developed in reverse ways: as *devotion* took on more secular meanings, *bhakti* increasingly became a technical religious term. Bhakti poets in both Sanskrit and regional languages associated bhakti with knowledge of God and a religious path to salvation. Philosophers who wrote in both Sanskrit and Tamil in medieval Tamilnadu attempted to analyze the knowledge within bhakti and to relate it to other ways of being religious. Thus, the English word *devotion* does not accurately convey the issues at stake in bhakti. And yet we cannot perform a redescription every time we translate the term into English. Increasingly, the term *participation* is appearing in scholarship as a gloss for *bhakti*.[36] This gloss can be derived from the Sanskrit root of bhakti, *bhaj*, meaning "partake, participate." Participation signifies the bhaktas' relationship with God; it is a premise of their poetry that they can participate in God by singing of God, by saying God's name, and in other ways. As a representation in English of the bhakta's relationship with God, the term *participation* has the advantage of not resonating with something we think we already know but encourages us to understand the relationships of bhakti as represented by its promoters and interpreters in history.

TWO

Bhakti as a Movement

Not all scholars who were interpreting bhakti at the turn of the century accepted the idea that religious reformers, much less those influenced by Christianity, were the primary representatives of bhakti. Some, amplifying the idea that a kṣatriya had founded bhakti, imagined that the medieval streams of bhakti in north India were initiated by nonbrahman religious figures as well as "the masses."[1] An example of this perspective is found in the work of Mahadeo Govind Ranade, a brahman, judge, founding member of the Prarthana Samaj reformist religious group, and leading nationalist, who understood bhakti to have been a populist movement:

> Like the Protestant Reformation in Europe in the sixteenth century, there was a religious, social and literary revival and reformation in India, but notably in the Deccan in the fifteenth and sixteenth centuries. This religious revival was not brahmanical in its orthodoxy; it was heterodox in its spirit of protest against forms and ceremonies and class distinctions based on birth, and ethical in its preference of a pure heart, and of the law of love, to all other acquired merits and good works. This religious revival was the work also of the people, of the masses, and not of the classes. At its head were saints and prophets, poets and philosophers, who sprang chiefly from the lower orders of society—tailors, carpenters, potters, gardeners, shop-keepers, barbers, and even *mahars*—more often than Brahmans.[2]

In emphasizing nonbrahman agents, Ranade was creating a new type of radical other for reform, one that could effect major social changes. Indeed, orientalist scholars had noted that the reformist brahman medieval ācāryas (spiritual leaders) had failed to overcome caste boundaries in religious practice, even though they were able to attract and accept followers of all castes.[3]

This social aspect of reform, rather than the religious aspect, has had a continuing presence in contemporary scholarship on bhakti. As with Ranade's analysis, the contemporary research on bhakti as a movement of social protest focuses on bhakti traditions in regional languages.

One manifestation of this trend is the description of bhakti as a "popular" movement. This idea does involve reform, but it is of a political nature, more widely construed than the religious reformation of the orientalists. Many of the scholars who view bhakti as a movement for social and political change have themselves been considered "Marxist-oriented."[4] The agents in this case are nonbrahmans, but instead of the kṣatriyas described by Bhandarkar and Grierson, here they are imagined to be from the lower castes. The dominant portrait of bhakti in this kind of scholarship can be summarized as follows: The surrounding political structure is feudal, the bhaktas are low caste or peasants, their poetry is in the vernacular, their movement is popular and protest. Often scholars, such as Zvelebil, have countered this image of bhakti with evidence that many bhaktas were, in fact, brahmans, not low-caste peasants. For example, the poet-saint Campantar in Tamil Śaiva tradition identifies himself as a brahman: "In the closing verses of his hymns, Campantar identifies himself as a Kavuṇiyaṉ (a brahmin of the Kauṇḍinya *gotra*) from Cīrkāḻi."[5] But the issue is also one of ideology. If bhakti is divested of its religious content, as many of the populist images encourage, then the grounding is lost for its critical perspective; according to bhakti, only through participation in the worship of God can one evaluate one's self and surroundings. Bhakti cannot be reduced to the pursuit of ārtha. Although bhakti reinforces the value and validity of embodiment, it also encourages a critique of embodiment, which applies to brahman and untouchable alike, nuanced by the particularities of each individual's life history. To explore such issues of embodiment, authors of bhakti in regional traditions wrote volumes of hagiographical literature that detailed the life stories of celebrated bhaktas.

Many scholars have interpreted the use of regional languages for bhakti literature as a protest against Sanskrit formulations. Throughout India's history, Sanskrit, the "well-formed" language, has been the preeminent medium for religion, philosophy, commentary, poetry, epics, and even for the gods to speak to one other. As A. K. Ramanujan succinctly puts it: "Sanskrit was culture."[6] Although this idea of protest is supported by remarks made in the regional-language bhakti poems, it serves as only one aspect of bhakti's encompassing frame of participation.

The regional language bhakti poems have in common their nature as religious poems that highlight the voice of the poet. This is in contrast to the prominent bhakti texts in Sanskrit. The *Bhagavad Gītā* and the *Bhāgavata Purāṇa* both use a question-and-answer format in which the interlocutors are distinct from the author, and the *Bhakti Sūtras* of Nārada and Śāṇḍilya can be described as aphoristic in nature, seemingly omniscient rather than authored. In the bhakti poems, the author and thus the language of the author are prominent. A. K. Ramanujan has eloquently attributed meaning to this use of regional languages in his discussion of a Tamil Viṣṇu-bhakti poet: "To Nammāḻvār, god is not a hieratic second language of Sanskrit to be learned, to be minded lest one forget its rules, paradigms, and exceptions; he is one's own mother tongue. In his view, god lives inside us as a mother tongue does, and we live in god as we live in language—a language that was there before us, is all around us in the community, and will be there after us. To lose this first language is to lose one's beginnings."[7] Through the use of regional languages, the author is localized in a language and in a place where the language is spoken. Bhakti is represented to be as natural as a mother tongue; just as no one lacks a first language, no one is incapable of bhakti. By implication, God is also in that place, inside us or near us, for bhakti is a theology of participation in God and the ability to reach God, whether God is imagined as nirguṇa or saguṇa. The Tamil Śiva-bhakti poets said that the Lord himself loves "sacred Tamil" (tirunēriya tamil̲), which implies that he would especially hear the praise and pleas that were offered in that tongue.

The poets not only constructed their theology of bhakti in regional languages but also they offered reflections on the surrounding world. Their poetry tends toward the observational, with images of everyday life and their responses to it, including folklore, as well as the more institutionalized religious images such as God, temple, and ritual. Their interpretive observations are expressed in their own voices, often by a first-person "I" in their poetry (such as the Tamil Śiva-bhakti poets), and sometimes referring to themselves in the third person in their poetry (such as Kabīr). Female bhakti poets in regional languages often use images of their own bodies to comment on the world around them. From our perspective, it may sound like a truism to suggest that the bhakti poets used what they knew and what they observed to forge their poetry, but these poets wrote from 500 to 1,300 years ago. Whatever the variation in their poetic styles, the regional-language poets all responded directly to their historical contexts.

Scholarship on bhakti as a movement has explored the nature of the poets' responses through the classification of nirguṇa and saguṇa. In contradistinction to the populist studies, this line of inquiry is explicitly focused on discerning ideologies within the poets' response to their religious contexts. "The Saguna bhaktas had strengthened the existent sects, and had supported the established socio-religious norms. As against this, the Nirguna bhaktas had taken a radical position, and their teachings had led to the formation of new and unorthodox sects. The Bhakti movement, therefore, embodied the conservative and the liberal, as well as the revivalist and reformist trends. It contained both conformism and dissent."[8]

Evidence from bhakti poems, in both language and content, tends to support such a position. Although bhakti is a critical perspective, the bhakti poets of regional languages differ from one other in the degree of criticism represented in their poetry. In all cases, bhakti poets respond to the world around them; at issue is how much their vision of bhakti overlaps with the norms of the surrounding culture. In terms of language, the ideological distinction between nirguṇa and saguṇa is suggested from the tone of the poetry; for example, saguṇa poets, including the Tamil Vaiṣṇavas and Śaivas, as well as the Hindi poet Tulsīdās, use polished poetic language that emphasizes the beauty of their respective languages, whereas nirguṇa poets, including the Kannada poetry of the Viraśaiva poet Mahādēviyakka and the poetry of the Hindi poet Kabīr, are willfully choppy, in keeping with their caustic critique of aspects of the surrounding culture.[9]

Imagining God, language, and evaluation of the world are connected in the poetry of all of the bhaktas, and the content they give to this nexus determines the ways of participation in God that constitute their visions of bhakti. Bhakti is the frame within which the bhakti poets determine appropriate acts of participation. For the saguṇa bhakti poets, rituals that are associated with the elements of worship represented in the epics and purāṇas, such as offering flowers and lighting an oil lamp, are illustrative of the path of bhakti. They acknowledge their connection with these traditional methods by using epic and purāṇic images in their poetry. For the nirguṇa bhakti poets, ritualized actions performed outside the ritual context, such as the recitation of the mantra of God's name at any time or place, are illustrative of the bhakti path.

The emphasis on the nirguṇa and saguṇa ideological distinction in scholarship is complicated by considerations of how bhakti has been understood over time in the Indian context. Most of the recent essays on bhakti as a movement emphasize subsequent interpretations of the literatures in regional languages, in an effort to understand whether the themes of socioreligious criticism in bhakti poetry were, in fact, realized. There are conflicting images of bhakti's success in this realm in contemporary scholarship.

Jayant Lele, for example, focuses on the dialectic of tradition and modernity in understanding bhakti as a "living tradition" that has revolutionary potential if it is approached through a hermeneutics that affirms both the experience of bhakti in the world and the critical approach of bhakti to the world.

> If an authentic, conscious upsurge towards the attainment of communal ideals is to engulf the masses, it is unlikely to come from the transplants of symbols of alien or dead traditions. Symbols of liberation will have to be rediscovered from within, by those who will carry the burden of revolutionary action. These symbols, while common to both sterilised philosophical abstractions and ritualised everyday practice, cannot be rediscovered in either of these isolated settings. That has always been the message of *bhakti*. Therein lies its modernity.[10]

By way of example, he characterizes Jñāneśvar's thirteenth-century Marathi rendition of the *Bhagavad Gītā*, the *Jñāneśvari*, as a "discursive and conscious return to tradition" that yet must "result in a revolutionary transformation of society" insofar as it manifests the liberating aspects of tradition. The text's affirmation of embodiment, emphasis on the unity of community through dialogue, and investment of authority in members who engage in selfless social action encourage "a revolutionary and critical productive activity within social practice."[11] Thus, Lele assures us that bhakti is a modernizing force by virtue of its negotiation of tradition and liberation through criticism.

In contrast, Ranajit Guha tells us that bhakti is neither a liberating force nor a modernizing force. For him, bhakti is a map of power relations that promotes and maintains the opposition between dominance and subordination. "Bhakti, in other words, is an ideology of subordination *par excellence*. All the inferior terms in any relationship of power structured as D[ominance]/S[ubordination] within the Indian tradition, can be derived from it." Guha criticizes the attempt of the nineteenth-century intellectual Bankimchandra Chattopadhyay to restore bhakti from its disenfranchisement in the colonial period. Chattopadhyay had sought to represent bhakti as an indigenous model of relations of honor, which, if restored with some modifications, would, in turn, counter the indignities of the colonial experience. One of the major modifications Chattopadhyay made to bhakti, according to Guha, was to understand it as "conditional on *gun*, in the sense of virtue or spiritual quality, rather than on *jati*, that is birth into any particular *varna* or caste"; thus, a śūdra who demonstrated religious values, nonattachment to worldly matters, and educated by example, was worthy of bhakti, whereas a brahman who lacked these qualities was not.[12] But Guha remains unconvinced that the structure of bhakti would allow such modernization:

> But, for all its sophistication, this "modernized" Bhakti was still unable to overcome the older tradition. This was so not only because western-style education and liberal values were so alien to the subaltern masses that they could hardly be expected to take much notice of such positivist-liberal modifications of their cherished beliefs. The reason, more importantly, was that these modifications did not go far enough to question the premises of traditional Bhakti. . . . It is the weight of tradition which undermined Bankimchandra's thesis about *gun* rather than *jati* as the determinant of Bhakti. Whatever promise there was in this of a dynamic social mobility breaking down the barrier of caste and birth, came to nothing, if only because the necessity of the caste system and the Brahman's spiritual superiority within it was presumed in the argument. It was only by emulating the Brahman that the Sudra could become an object of Bhakti. In other words, Bhakti could do little to abolish the social distance between the high-born and the low-born, although some of the former's spiritual qualities might, under certain conditions, be acquired by the latter, without, however, effecting any change of place.[13]

Indeed, the failure of not only low-caste but also especially untouchable peoples to "effect any change of place" through bhakti has been noted in contemporary scholarship. For example, Burton Stein discusses the failed experiment of the Śrivaiṣṇavas in allowing untouchables into temples in medieval times; Lynn Vincentnathan notes that contemporary untouchable youths in Chidambaram look to the social activist Ambedkar as a hero rather than the classical untouchable bhakti saint, Nantaṉār; and Eleanor Zelliot tells us that the poetry of the classical untouchable bhakti saints Chokhāmeḷā and Eknath is remembered and recited on pilgrimage today but that "the living *bhakti* sect in Maharashtra today is not a force for change."[14]

Contemporary scholars who insist on the nirguṇa-saguṇa divide would probably identify each of these examples as within the tradition of saguṇa bhakti and then attribute their lack of success in realizing social change to the conservativism of saguṇa bhakti. It is worth noting that this perspective has much in common with the orientalist images of the medieval ācāryas (understood now to be in the saguṇa camp) as partial reformers, whereas Kabīr and the Gurus of Sikhism (both in the nirguṇa camp) were the "real" reformers. However, the nature of people's aspirations—which is the context of attempts to relate classical bhakti's problematizing of social issues to both past and contemporary situations—is rarely so straightforward. In a sophisticated article, Philip Lutgendorf notes that the Hindi bhakti poet Tulsīdās is ostensibly in the saguṇa camp, yet the poet "put his ultimate faith in an abstraction: the divine name"; similarly, there are two major streams in interpreting his epic, the *Rāmcharitmānas*, in support of contrasting images of the rule of Rām (Rāmrāj): "For Rāmrāj has been viewed both as a harmonious but hierarchical order, in which the privileged confidently enjoy their status and the dispossessed keep within their limits, or conversely, as a kingdom of righteousness, in which the possibilities of freedom are made accessible to all." Using alternative language, Lutgendorf tends to associate specific elements of the epic, such as language, personalities, and places of pilgrimage, with the "real" community—including fundamentalists who understand Ayodhya literally—while the "imagined community" of Tulsīdās includes all "good people": "The limits of this constituency were not determined by geography or time, and no territorial claims were made for it."[15]

Lutgendorf's analysis tends to equate Tulsīdās's ultimate message with the abstraction (nirguṇa) within his epic, suggesting Lutgendorf's sensitivity to the intellectualist counterarguments that dispute the literalism of the fundamentalist-nationalists' arguments.

> Tulsīdās's "imagined community" (to borrow Benedict Anderson's useful phrase)—constantly evoked throughout the *Mānas*—was neither linguistic nor regional, nor even "religious" in the twentieth century sense (since *yavanas*, i.e. Muslims—were also said to be saved by the power of Rām's name); rather it was the boundless circle of "good people" (*sujan samāj, sant samāj*) who were devoted to the Lord's name and acts. The limits of this constituency were not determined by geography or time, and no territorial claims were made for it. For although pilgrimage places such as Ayodhya, Prayag, and Chitrakut were indeed celebrated as gathering places, such locales ultimately served (in the poet's well-known metaphor) to connote the faithful themselves: "'a Prayag circulating throughout the world . . . accessible to all, everyday, in every land" (1.2.7, 12).[16]

Yet bhakti tradition plays on the relationship between the real and the imagined, the local and the universal, the specific and the abstract. If the fundamentalists have transformed the local into the literal in an attempt to realize the "imagined community," then we can criticize them for both a flawed method and an improper understanding of the ideal, but the local remains important in bhakti epics and bhakti poetry as a manifestation of bhakti's thesis on embodiment. Bhakti is not so much an attempt to "effect any change in place" as to define place.

In their definitions of place, the bhakti poets did not just provide images of religious experience through the details of embodiment—their longing for God, their forgetfulness, their sense of intimacy, their joy, their ritual worship, their observations and criticisms of people around them—they also identified with geographical place through their use of regional languages and through their use of regionally specific imagery in their poetry. Since texts that extol bhakti in regional languages were, according to extant textual evidence, written earliest in south India (Tamil, seventh century) and only later in the north (sixteenth century), can bhakti be understood as both a geographical and social movement? In language that reminds one of Grierson's wave, the introduction to a recent volume of translations from the poetry of medieval Hindi-language bhaktas represents bhakti as such: "Despite the division between these two sets of saints [characterized as nirguṇa and saguṇa]—with the Protestants, so to speak, on one side and the Catholics on the other—they all inherited a single, massive *bhakti* movement that had been gathering force in other parts of India for a millennium."[17]

The source for this pervasive scholarly image lies in an oft-cited Sanskrit verse: "I (Bhakti) was born in Dravida; and grew up in Karnātaka. I lived here and there in Mahārāshtra; and became weak and old in Gujarat."[18] Ironically, the image of bhakti in this passage is not of a strong, unified movement but instead of an exhausted woman, stumbling on foot through the regions of India. Although often quoted without proper citation, the source of the passage is the *Bhāgavata Māhātmya*, verse 48 of the first chapter.[19] I understand why it is convenient to cite this passage: It seems to explain bhakti as a movement, to declare the south as the place of its origin, and to provide a continuity between bhakti in the south and bhakti in the north. In addition, bhakti is personified as an image of self-determination: The "I" of bhakti makes its own way through time and space. This last feature diverts our attention from the question of the plurality of agents of bhakti and their relationships.

For all of its seeming explanatory value, the couplet is not as objective as scholars appear to assume. Although we do not know who its author was, we must assume there was (at least) one. To understand who the author might be, plus other aspects of this passage, it would help to put it back into the context of the story from whence it was taken. Next, I give a summary of this story.[20] In both the *Bhāgavata Māhātmya* and the *Padma Purāṇa*, this story is framed by the sage Śaunaka requesting the sage Śuka to narrate the *Bhāgavata Purāṇa*.[21] It is then said that formerly Nārada was taught the purāṇa by the sage Sanaka. When the story of bhakti begins, the sages of that earlier time, including Sanaka, are asking Nārada why he looks distressed.

Nārada's reply to the sages is that although he knows the earth to be the "best of regions," and he has visited the most famous places of pilgrimage on the earth, including Puṣkara, Prayāga, Kāśī, the bank of the Godāvarī, Haridvāra, Kurukṣetra, Śriraṅgam, and Rāmeśvaram, he could find no happiness anywhere because humanity had turned to bad actions. On his journeys, he had witnessed selfish people, heretical men, ascetics who pursue enjoyment, families who quarrel, and foreigners (*yavanas*) at holy places and sacred rivers; he found truth, purity, pity, and charity nowhere.[22] At Vṛndāvana, on the banks of the Yamunā River, where Kṛṣṇa once sported, he saw a puzzling sight: A dejected young woman sat there, crying over two old men who were unconscious beside her. She was attempting to rouse them to consciousness. Although she was attended by heavenly ladies, she approached Nārada, asking for assistance in relieving her worried mind.

When Nārada asked her who she was, she identified herself as Bhakti and the two men as her sons Jñāna (higher knowledge) and Vairāgya (freedom from all worldly desires), who were worn out by time.[23] Bhakti tells him she is waited on by gods but from this gets no bliss, and she begs him to listen to her life story. She relates: "I was born in Dravida; and grew up in Karnataka. I lived here and there [or: I was respected in some places] in Maharashtra; and became weak and old in Gujarat. There, during the terrible Kali age, I was crippled by heretics, and I became weak and old along with my sons. But after reaching Vṛndāvana I have become young and beautiful again; yet how is it that a mother is young when her sons are old? I am worried; please tell me the cause of these things."

Nārada tells her that with his wisdom he can understand her plight, and he knows that Viṣṇu (Hari in the *Māhātmya*) will bring her bliss. He says that the present age is governed by Kali and suggests that the kind of reversal she is experiencing is characteristic of the era. For example, people neglect the paths of yoga and austerities, dishonest men become deified, and saintly people suffer; the earth is burdened with wickedness, and auspiciousness is not to be found. Men are full of attachments and have abandoned Bhakti; only because of contact with praiseworthy Vṛndāvana has she been revived. The sons also lack support from the populace, but their slumber preserves them.[24]

Bhakti asks why Viṣṇu allowed the Kali age to become dominant. Nārada answers that, at the time Kṛṣṇa left the earth, Kali came to power, conquering the four corners of the world. When King Parīkṣit saw Kali, the latter became submissive, and the king accepted him, knowing that it is only in the Kali age that one can obtain fruit by reciting the deeds and names of Viṣṇu, without practicing penance. However, the Kali age takes its toll in other ways: The essence has gone out of things and left them like husks without seeds; the brahmans recite the *Bhāgavata* to those worthy and unworthy, out of greed for fees, thus weakening the Purāṇa; sinful men reside at the holy places, which reduces their efficacy; passionate people practice penance; and householders are obsessed with sex but indifferent to salvation. Participation in Viṣṇu is found nowhere; this is no one's fault but simply the Kali age. In the *Māhātmya*, Nārada says that lotus-eyed Viṣṇu is close to humanity (as the indwelling Lord), yet he endures; in the *Padma*, Nārada says that remembering lotus-eyed Viṣṇu will lead to happiness.

Nārada explains that Bhakti is dear to Viṣṇu; if she calls, he will come to the houses of even lowly people. In the former ages, knowledge and detachment accomplished salvation, but in the Kali age, Bhakti alone brings about the absorption into Brahman. In order that she should nourish his bhaktas, Viṣṇu gave her Mukti (liberation) as a handmaiden, and Jñāna and Vairāgya as sons. Bhakti remained in Vaikuṇṭha, but appeared as a reflection on earth, accompanied by the three during the Kṛta through the Dvāpara ages (the first three ages). Then in the Kali age, Mukti fell ill and returned to Vaikuṇṭha, reappearing on earth only when Bhakti thinks of her. And then Bhakti's sons grew old.

Nārada vows to promote Bhakti as a servant of Hari. He repeats that Bhakti is paramount in the Kali age and delineates the nature of bhaktas: They will go to Vaikuṇṭha; they will not experience death because they are pure of heart; they will never be molested by demons because their minds are full of God; they do not attain Viṣṇu through study of the Vedas, performance of rituals, or possession of knowledge, because he is reached through Bhakti, as evidenced by the gopīs; and they have achieved bhakti through thousands of existences. Toward the fulfillment of his vow, Nārada attempts to rouse Jñāna and Vairāgya by the recitation of the Vedas, the Vedānta, and the *Gītā*. The sons wake up but are still too weak to rise. Then a voice from the heavens tells Nārada that he must perform a right act (satkarma).

But Nārada does not know what constitutes the appropriate satkarma. After much wandering in and around Vṛndāvana to speak with various sages, with the result that many of the best brahmans are stumped, Nārada finally comes upon the group of sages led by Sanaka (the Kumāras). These sages inform him that the "right act" is neither the sacrifice of oblations, the sacrifice of penance, nor the sacrifice of yoga; it is, instead, the ancient jñānayajña, or knowledge sacrifice. Recitation of the *Bhāgavata Purāṇa* is the knowledge sacrifice that will bestow happiness on Bhakti and her sons. The *Bhāgavata* is the essence of the Vedas and Upaniṣads, but it is separate from them; its subtlety in comparison to them is represented by the sweetness of the sap when it is extracted from the rough sugarcane.[25]

Nārada then holds the knowledge sacrifice for the benefit of establishing Bhakti, Jñāna, and Vairāgya. As the sages advise, it is held on the banks of the Gangā River, and it is to last for seven days. Many categories of religious people, gods, and also the personifications of the texts recited earlier, along with other purāṇas and the śāstras, are present. As the lengthy discourse on the merits of the text and of Kṛṣṇa-bhakti comes to a close, Bhakti, bedecked with ornaments of the meaning of the *Bhāgavata Purāṇa*, appears with her two now-youthful sons. She then asks the sages where she should reside. They answer that she should reside in the hearts of the Vaiṣṇavas, and she does so. The sages say that when bhakti is in the hearts of people, even if they are poor, Viṣṇu will leave Vaikuṇṭha to come to their hearts. As Bhakti enters into the hearts of the Vaiṣṇavas, Viṣṇu descends from his heavenly domain to be among the bhaktas. At this wondrous vision of Viṣṇu, who is handsome and ornamented and carrying a flute, Nārada begins a lengthy praise of the *Bhāgavata Purāṇa*.

This story is about the excellence of a text, its ability to inspire bhakti, and its efficacy in bringing Viṣṇu/Kṛṣṇa to earth. The passage that everyone quotes on Bhakti beginning in Dravida suggests the transmission of the *Bhāgavata Purāṇa* and provides a comparison that serves to highlight the efficacy of Vṛndāvana in the context of a hierarchical arrangement of places where bhakti has resided. As the story's name, *Bhāgavata Māhātmya* (the latter term denoting glorification), and the information at its conclusion suggest, the story is in praise of the *Bhāgavata Purāṇa*. The *Māhātmya* picks up where the framing story of the purāṇa left off: The *Bhāgavata Purāṇa* opens with a dialogue between Nārada and Vyāsa, the latter the alleged author of the text, who suggests that the hearing of the text will please (the personified) Bhakti. This is fulfilled in the *Māhātmya*.

According to the story, Bhakti comes from the south and arrives in the north, to Vṛndāvana, the birthplace of Kṛṣṇa. Who is Bhakti? At the end of the story, she is identified as the meaning of the *Bhāgavata Purāṇa*. What is the *Bhāgavata Purāṇa*? In the story, it is an efficacious text whose recitation causes the heart to be filled with bhakti and Kṛṣṇa to appear. Historically, the *Bhāgavata Purāṇa* is a Vaiṣṇava bhakti text that was written around the ninth or tenth century, in south India.[26] In the text, Bhakti and the *Bhāgavāta Purāṇa* are images of each other. Just as Bhakti came from the south, so did the text. Just as Bhakti was appreciated—and thus revived—in Vṛndāvana, so was the text. This story is not a general statement about bhakti as a movement: It is a story of the efficacy of Vaiṣṇava bhakti at Vṛndāvana, in contrast to bhakti in other places.

In the course of its narrative, the story debunks a few of the pop-scholarly images of bhakti. The story is set in the Kali age, the last period of time before destruction and, as such, the time when dharma is weakest. The popular image of bhakti, based in part on popularized interpretations of the *Bhagavad Gītā*, is that it is the only religious path appropriate to the Kali age because it is "easy." But here, the text says that bhakti also suffers. Bhakti, like dharma, must also be cared for to flourish. Bhakti is accompanied by her sons, Jñāna and Vairāgya, but this is not recognized by people (including the orientalists, who divorced bhakti from jñāna). So instead of bhakti being the "easy" way in opposition to the "hard" ways of knowledge and right action (sometimes translated as "asceticism"), these two are born from, and dependent on, bhakti. But it is the case that she is revived faster; she becomes young again, merely by being in Kṛṣṇa's place. Her sons remain old, however, until additional activities that demonstrate their powers (that is, the satkarma of sacrifice and the hearing of the text) are performed.

Although some general characteristics of bhakti can be extrapolated, the story is not about bhakti in general. The bhakti of the text is Kṛṣṇa-bhakti. The text sets up a hierarchy that argues the superiority of this form of bhakti. One of the elements in its schema is that of region. The *Bhāgavata Mahātmya* tells us of the primary importance and sacredness of Vṛndāvana, as the place where Bhakti is revived and where Kṛṣṇa later appears. Its polar opposite is Gujarat, where Bhakti (aka the *Bhāgavata Purāṇa*) and her sons have been abused; the story implies that in Gujarat people did not listen to the text. Certainly, the narrative presents the southern areas of Dravida and Karnataka as the places where bhakti originated, and historically it is in this region that the Purāṇa was written. But Bhakti did not remain in the south; she wanted to go to Vṛndāvana, Kṛṣṇa's place in the north. There, as the only one who can bring about mukti (salvation), she lives in the hearts of the Viṣṇu-bhaktas. By implication, Vṛndāvana is also the best place for the *Bhāgavata Purāṇa*, where it is most efficacious. Both bhakti and the Purāṇa should, and do, remain there.

The schema is also played out in terms of texts. First, in the interest of reviving the sons Knowledge and Passionlessness, Nārada recites the Vedas, Vedānta, and *Gītā*. This awakens but does not revive them, which suggests that these classical texts are somewhat effectual yet incomplete. In addition, a satkarma must be performed, which is none other than the recitation of another text, the *Bhāgavata Purāṇa*, which the sages call "the best among texts." The context of the recitation is a sacrifice at which all are present. The image of sacrifice as a great meeting place for the gods and assorted hosts, culminating in the special appearance of a particular god, is relatively common in purāṇic literature. In this case, the text additionally endows "sacrifice" with new meaning, insofar as what is "consumed" is the *Bhāgavata Purāṇa* itself; its meanings then take the form of ornaments that decorate Bhakti. It is this new kind of "sacrifice" that effects the stability of the world, indicated by one of the results of the recitation, the restoration to youth of Knowledge and Passionlessness. Her sons restored, Bhakti enters the hearts of the bhaktas; once she is there, they are fit for Kṛṣṇa's presence. The *Māhātmya* celebrates the *Bhāgavata Purāṇa* as "the greatest" because it moves the hearts of its listeners and brings Kṛṣṇa to them. The message is that when the *Bhāgavata Purāṇa* is recited, everything is right with the world.

The *Māhātmya* thus not only endorses a specific place, bhakti, text, and deity but also is actively polemical against Gujarat. Thus, it is not appropriate to use this text as an unbiased history of bhakti or to reproduce it as a neutral statement. Moreover, although scholars have been particularly apt to use the passage from the *Bhāgavata Māhātmya* to describe the historical course of bhakti in regional languages, the author(s) of the *Māhātmya* distinguished themselves from bhakti in regional languages by their composition of the text in Sanskrit. The text does not represent itself as within the ranks of regional-language bhakti; in promoting a certain region, it uses a lingua franca that transcends identification with a specific region. Thus, in contrast to the specificity of the text on aspects of bhakti, it tends to obscure the identity of its author(s). Given the gap in time between the purāṇa and the *Māhātmya*—the former may have been written around the ninth century, the latter around the sixteenth—the wandering Bhakti in the *Māhātmya* may represent the transmission of the Purāṇa.[27] However, the *Māhātmya* does not specify the agents of this transmission; instead, it embodies bhakti in the personage of a young woman. By the implied allegory between purāṇa and bhakti, the *Māhātmya* diverts attention from the issue of authorship and transmission. This diversion accords with the Sanskrit tradition that the author of all purāṇas is assumed to be the mythical Vyāsa ("arranger"), not specific historical agents. Although much religious knowledge in Sanskrit was localized in specific groups that were ritual specialists who promoted its transmission across regional boundaries, such as the Vedas with brahmans and the āgamas with traveling philosophers who were members of certain lineages (gotras), other religious knowledge, especially that of the epics and purāṇas, tended not to be localized in this way.[28] As the glorification of a Sanskrit text, it is appropriate that the *Māhātmya* would also be in Sanskrit, yet its concern with the promotion of a pilgrimage site at the expense of other regions is in keeping with the concerns of regional-language bhakti poetry.

It may be the case, then, that the *Māhātmya* was written by a member of a regional-language bhakti group. Based on the text's explicit connection with Vṛndāvana, K. Sharma has suggested that the followers of Vallabhācārya or Caitanya may have composed the *Bhāgavata Māhātmya*.[29] Vṛndāvana is located near Mathurā and is known as the setting of Kṛṣṇa's youthful pranks, heroic deeds, and play with the wives of the cowherds, or gopīs. Both of these leaders are said to have traveled to Vṛndāvana. Vallabha (1479–1531), a Gujarati, is said to have experienced two visions of Kṛṣṇa while on pilgrimages to that place, which inspired him to found a Vaiṣṇava sect in Gujarat upon his return. Caitanya (1486–1533) is credited with the promotion of Vṛndāvana as a place of pilgrimage through the establishment of a Caitanyite temple, Madan Gopal, there. In addition, a commentary on the *Bhāgavata Purāṇa* is attributed to Vallabha, and Caitanya is said to have used the text as a guide to identify many of the places of Kṛṣṇalīlās (places of Kṛṣṇa's play) he experienced in visions. In the life stories of both religious leaders, Vṛndāvana is important as a place where bhakti was stimulated, which is similar to the *Māhātmya* portrait. There are various ways to interpret the polemic against Gujarat, including incidents in the lives of the two religious leaders. More generally, it may allude to the prominence of Jains in that location.

The embodiment of bhakti in the personage of a wandering woman also highlights the phenomenon of pilgrimage, which is an important theme in regional-language bhakti poetry. The travels of Bhakti from the south to the north of India through named regions results in her restoration and permanent residence at an increasingly significant—augmented by the *Māhātmya* itself—place of pilgrimage, Vṛndāvana. Her movement does not have the figurative sense of a sociopolitical movement but the real sense of pilgrimage. Instead of an image of "a single, massive *bhakti* movement that had been gathering force," the text advances an image of pilgrimage and distinguishes among various places based on their ability to care for the personified Bhakti through their residents' embodiment of bhakti in their own hearts.

Pilgrimage is especially stressed in biographical texts of regional-language bhakti leaders. Often the pilgrimages are transregional, but the texts tend to suggest that one particular region is most efficacious. The stories of regional-language bhaktas also include tales of bhaktas who meet each other on the path of pilgrimage and on the path of bhakti. They are kindred spirits, and in some cases the texts suggest a lineage of bhakti saints. For example, the Tamil *Periya Purāṇam* (Great Story, ca twelfth century) tells of bhaktas on pilgrimages, mainly the area traditionally associated with the Tamil language and somewhat in the neighboring areas of Kerala and Karnataka. The three most famous Tamil Śaiva bhaktas, Campantar, Appar, and Cuntarar, are described in the later biographies as meeting en route in the Tamil lands; for example, it is from the child saint Campantar that Tirunāvukkāracu is said to have been given the name Appar, "Father." The Hindi *Bhaktamāla* by Nābhādās (ca seventeenth century) describes the meeting of bhaktas in various areas. For example, Rāmānanda (fourteenth or fifteenth century) is said to have studied under his guru, Rāghavānanda, who was himself a guru in the Vaṭakalai (northern) school of Rāmānuja's Śrī Vaiṣṇavism. Rāmānanda became the fifth leader and teacher of this school and is said to have proceeded from south to north India, where he began to write bhakti texts in Hindi. In the north, he had twelve disciples, including Kabīr. Caitanya is said to have made the trip from Bengal through the south and back to Purī in Orissa; he brought with him from the south two influential texts, the *Brahma-Samhitā* and the *Kṛṣṇa-karṇāmṛta*. The biographies of Vallabha and Caitanya describe pilgrimages they took across northern India, including Gujarat, Banaras, Vṛndāvana, Nadīya (or Navadvīpa, Caitanya's birthplace in Bengal), and Purī in Orissa. Other texts that tell of the lives of the bhaktas include the Marathi *Bhaktavijaya* and the *Bhaktalīlāmṛta* by Mahipati (ca eighteenth century). From these biographical texts, we get a sense of movement by bhaktas in and among various regions, but we do not get the sense of a movement, meaning a unified agitation for reform.

The biographies of regional-language bhaktas elaborate on the sense of active participation that is emphasized in their poetry. The biographies embody the "I" of the poetry by providing details of identity, pilgrimage, discourse, and interaction with other bhaktas. The regionalism of the bhakti formulations thereby assumes greater prominence. For example, transregionalism is not highlighted by the Tamil bhakti poets; they emphasize their own and God's Tamilness. The language of their poetry is the mother tongue of Tamil, but their sense of the language is elevated, as they self-consciously insist that the Lord loves "sacred Tamil" (tirunēriya tamiḻ) and that active participation in God (through the Tamil language) fulfills human life in all of its vicissitudes. The biographies support the regional identity of the bhaktas in that they themselves were written in regional languages.

Analysis of the Tamil region has been historically underrepresented in past scholarship on bhakti. The orientalists tended to disregard south India as a locus for important ancient religious developments. In their search for the "original," they privileged antiquity, and antiquity was associated primarily with Sanskrit texts.[30] The Tamil texts with which the orientalists were acquainted, including the *Tirukuṟaḷ* and the *Nālaṭiyār*, both dated to the second or third centuries A.D., were categorized as "wisdom" books that did not focus on a deity. But textual evidence, or lack thereof, was only a part of the orientalists' thinking about south India and was blended with geographical and racial arguments that created a disparaging portrait of the Dravidians of the south in comparison with the Aryans of the north.[31] The observable physical differences among the people were, for the orientalists, most clearly demonstrated in the tribal peoples of south India. From observation of these people, they concluded that the earliest religion in south India had been a mixture of superstitious beliefs, animism, and shamanism, which involved "ecstatic frenzied dances, amid which the votaries, drugged and foaming at the mouth, are held to be in communion with some demon or goddess, and to become soothsayers of the deity thirsting for unholy rites and blood sacrifice." It was this context that produced the "pre-historic primitive Dravidian religion, known as some form of Śaivism, or worship of Śiva."[32]

South India quickly became identified in scholarship as the preeminent locus of Śaivism, and Śaivism did not, for the orientalists, represent "true" religion or even "good" religion; for that matter, its nature as "religion" was an implicit question. In an extension of the pervasive characterization of Christianity as the religion of love of God and Judaism as the religion of fear of God, Vaiṣṇavism was viewed as the religion of love and Śaivism as the religion of fear. Monier-Williams had noted that Śaivism "still held sway" in south India, whereas north India had "evolved" toward Vaiṣṇavism. H. H. Wilson had discovered bhakti in north India, and that is where it remained in orientalist scholarship. When Śiva-bhakti, understood as southern, was acknowledged, as in Grierson's encyclopedia article, it was attributed to the influence of Vaiṣṇava formulations:

> It may be stated as a broad rule that all the followers of the Indian *bhakti-mārga* are Vaiṣṇavas. Śiva, the other great deity of Indian worship, is associated with ideas too terrible to suggest loving devotion. There are, however, in Southern India, Śaiva sects which practise a *bhakti* cult . . . [this is due to the influence of Vaiṣṇavism]. Śiva was even provided with incarnations, such as Virabhadra, in imitation of those of Viṣṇu, to whom the love and devotion could be directed. . . . Regarding the true Śiva-*bhakti*, which is professedly a cult of Śiva or his incarnations, very little is known, and the subject deserves more study than it has hitherto received.[33]

Although the orientalists knew that southern ācāryas wrote philosophical treatises in Sanskrit in the medieval period, they did not connect these treatises to Śaivism. However, ten years before Grierson wrote his article, a large volume of Māṇikkavācakar's poetry, translated by G. U. Pope, had been published.[34] His work is a model of thoroughness. Pope translated the "fifty-one poems" of the *Tiruvācakam*—each poem more than a hundred lines of versified Tamil—into a rhyming (but stilted) English; included a translation of the *Tiruvaruṭpayaṉ*, a Tamil Śaiva

Siddhānta text from the fourteenth century; provided extensive notes to the poems and the philosophical text, plus a lexicon; and gave the legendary history of the saint, also with extensive notes. Why was this encyclopedic volume ignored by the author of "Bhakti-mārga"? Because Pope himself did not make the connection between the *Tiruvācakam* and bhakti. The scholarly context at the time of Pope's work was not particularly receptive to the idea that bhakti existed in south India, and his own introduction did not help to change that view. In the context of his sensitive hopes for an East-West rapprochement (among other things, there are title pages in both Tamil and English), Pope labeled the poems as Śaiva Siddhānta philosophy: "For, under some form or other, Çaivism is the real religion of the South of India, and of North Ceylon; and the Çaiva Siddhānta philosophy has, and *deserves to have*, far more influence than any other." Otherwise, he had only a brief note on bhakti.[35]

The main reason that Grierson did not seem to know about this marvelous text, however, is that he relied almost exclusively on Bhandarkar's reflections, for the latter was one of the first to describe Śaiva sects in detail and to identify them as bhakti. A drawback and possibly a source for Grierson's hesitancy was Bhandarkar's relegation of Śiva-bhakti to a "popular" status. To Bhandarkar, Śaivism is an ordinary (that is, popular) religion of "fervent devotional feeling," not a locus of knowledge that can be analyzed and understood. On this latter point, he posited that there "must be" other, philosophical works within Śaivism: "The Śaivism that prevailed in the Tamil country seems to have been generally of the ordinary kind, since the hymns in the Dēvāram sing the praises of Śiva and exhibit fervent devotional feeling, but there must have been some Darśana or system of philosophy also. . . . The last species of the Śaiva literature detailed above is . . . called Siddhāntaśāstra composed by Santāna-Ācāryas. These must be philosophical works on Śaivism."[36] Ironically, Bhandarkar only hypothesized that the texts of Śaiva Siddhānta were philosophical, yet Pope had already translated one from Tamil into English and provided detailed notes.[37]

After the publication of Grierson's article, scholarship continued to designate religion in south India as primitive. This scholarship was primarily written by missionaries who spent much time in south India and who thus were credited with knowing the culture there intimately. Their writings were determined not only by an agenda of saving people from the worst excesses of their religion but also by their wish to present examples of religious behavior that seemed most to challenge their ideas—not only as missionaries but also as scholars—of what religion is. So, for example, the Englishman Reverend Whitehead and the American Wilber T. Elmore had a running debate about whether the south Indian buffalo sacrifice was an example of totemism (as Whitehead believed) or of a conquest ritual originally symbolizing the victory of the Aryans over the "mad gods" of the south Indians.[38]

Important though the question may have been, given the academic presuppositions at that time, this type of scholarship reproduced a series of related images of south India, especially Tamilnadu, that portrayed the culture not only as primitive but also as terrifying. Some of the major elements in this view of Tamil culture were society at the village-level stage in development (that is, rural), malevolent goddesses (who were not consorts but agents of illnesses), blood sacrifice (held to be non-Vedic), and primitive iconography (involving sticks and stones, not anthropomorphism). The portrayal of India as primitive was played out not only in scholarship on the south, of course, but also in that on north India. But there was a big difference. North India was implicitly or explicitly compared to Europe, and found lacking; south India was compared to north India and found lacking. In essence, the following analogy was operative: south India : north India :: north India : Europe.[39]

These images have remained with contemporary scholarly discussions of south India. For example, both David Shulman and George Hart argue that images of blood and other bodily fluids are at the core of Tamil culture, as the "underlying" stratum of the later Aryan-Dravidian synthesis. In a similar vein, Friedhelm Hardy describes the emotionalism of Tamil religion as a distinguishing element.[40] Although these influential scholars may seek to rectify past scholarly images of Tamil culture by recognizing the distinctive contributions that Tamil culture has made to Indian culture more broadly construed, this project requires much more discussion of orientalist scholarship than has taken place thus far. Lacking such discussion, some of the images they present unfortunately resonate with orientalist images of south Indian religion. Moreover, there are other ways to discuss the Tamil contribution than through phenomenologically based studies; for example, Brenda Beck has identified processes that contribute to the making of Tamil identity through her anthropological study of ritual and social structures.[41] In my own attempt to understand how historical Tamil agents themselves sought to define Tamil culture and identity through Tamil Śiva-bhakti, an increasingly important component of their culture, I have found that the poets, kings, ritual specialists, and philosophers all demonstrated a concern with defining Tamilness in their writings, while they worked with a diversity of materials that may be outside those elements that some scholars have identified as the essence of Tamil identity. I thus focus on how the Tamil agents themselves defined their Tamilness as an aspect of their understandings of bhakti as a religious perspective. The critical examination of ideas and images in past scholarship informs my study of Tamil Śiva-bhakti that follows, in which I consider "the prolix series of subtle and unmeaning obscurities" of bhakti (as described by H. H. Wilson) meaningful and well worth the effort.

Scholars of the nineteenth and early twentieth centuries were correct in associating bhakti with change and with a critical perspective; that they characterized bhakti as "reform" in naming these changes depended at least in part on the comparison with Christianity that provided the context for scholarly writings on all other religions at that time. Later scholars have been critical of the tendency to use Christianity as a yardstick, yet many of the early ideas are important and did provide a catalyst for issues discussed in contemporary scholarship. In any case, their excesses should not prevent judicious and carefully thought-out comparisons with Christianity.

For Biardeau, bhakti played a major role in the transformation of socioreligious norms from Vedism to Hinduism. This transformation permanently changed the nature of religious life in India. However, an observation by Krishna Sharma would argue against Biardeau's suggestion that bhakti achieved a cultural hegemony: "The Hindus never used the term bhakti to denote any *mata* (school of thought), *siddhānta* (doctrine), or *sampradāya* (sect)."[42] When the meanings and context of religious practice changed, the field was open to many new formulations; bhakti was just one of them. Bhakti did not appear to wield the kind of systemic power associated with other religious perspectives and formulations, such as the āgamas. Instead, bhakti became embodied in numerous different perspectives. Subsequent to the *Gītā*, which established *bhakti* as a technical religious term, bhakti appeared in texts with different purposes. For example, the Tamil nāyaṉmār (Śiva-bhaktas) used bhakti as a frame for understanding all aspects of the world. Medieval authoritative philosophers interpreted the *Gītā* through commentaries, thus raising the text to the status of prasthānatrayā, the three texts (*Gītā*, *Brahma Sūtra*, and Upaniṣads) that are authoritative for religious and philosophical questions. For example, Rāmānuja supported bhakti as special knowledge in the service of Viṣiṣṭa Advaita philosophy; in contrast, Śankara tended to associate bhakti with those uninitiated in his Advaita philosophy. Bhakti also became embodied in living gurus, each with his own religious vision.[43]

Biardeau's analysis draws attention to the selectivity of the bhakti authors, and it is this question of selectivity that I examine in my study of transformations in Tamil Śiva-bhakti. The details of my analysis follow in the next three parts of the book; here, let me briefly present two models of change, in response to the selections that Biardeau suggests informed the early bhakti of the *Gītā* and to the notion that bhakti is a popular social movement.

One model highlights the tendency of religions to pick up on less emphasized aspects of the religion(s) that they concede were prior to, and even foundational for, them. For example, Christianity emphasized the Prophets, a significant part but not the core of the Hebrew Bible; they were not part of the Torah, and the New Testament reordered the books of the Hebrew Bible in its appropriation of them. Similarly, some of the key stories of the foundation of Islam drew upon Ishmael, not Isaac; the Hebrew Bible explores the life and progeny of Isaac, whereas Ishmael's line appears to die off within a few chapters in Genesis. It may have been the case that because proponents of the sannyāsin perspective advocated a revision of the meaning of kāma, the effect was to marginalize emotional responses to God that were recognizable as such in the religious and social contexts. Bhakti recentralized considerations of the nature and efficacy of emotional response.

Another model of religious change postulates that a religion transforms key elements to localize its message. For example, Avalokiteśvara was an important male bodhisattva in south and southeast Asian Buddhism, yet this figure of compassion became female in China, where her story was connected to preexisting legends of the Princess Miao Shan. The bhakti poets in regional languages all present bhakti as a distinctive religious path with explicit ties to regional culture, with some poets more self-consciously than others identifying the role of the *Gītā* in transforming *bhakti* into a technical religious term. A common feature of all of the regional-language expressions of bhakti is this localization, in terms of poetic voice, region, regional language, pilgrimage, and saints. Their interest is in the local embodiment of bhakti.

As a religious perspective, bhakti (participation) includes images of God (whether nirguṇa or saguṇa) and images of the social world (through cultural critique and embodiment) and elaborates on the relationship between them. In acknowledging the reality of both God and embodiment, bhakti suggests that the two are distinctive. However, the exact nature of the relationship between the two is not necessarily evident from the *Gītā* or bhakti poetry in regional languages because both leave the door open to interpretation. Such interpretation was undertaken by later thinkers—many of whom profoundly disagreed with one another—who wrote commentaries on the *Gītā* as major components of their developing philosophical schools. Similarly, the Tamil Śiva-bhakti poetry was engaged by people involved in the creation of authoritative worldviews, including kings, temple authorities, and philosophers.

With this said, it is also the case that the distinctions bhakti makes have philosophical implications that bear on the scholarly understanding of the relationship among regional-language bhaktis. Since bhakti affirms embodiment as the locus for religious experience, it must take a position on the meaning of distinctions among people, such as caste, gender, regional identity, and language. It may be the case that, in the "imagined community" of bhaktas, there is no distinction, as pointed out by Philip Lutgendorf. And yet in bhakti's theology of embodiment the accessibility of God to embodied humanity is represented precisely in the details, including the names and life stories of special bhaktas, the language of the bhakti hymns, and the efficacy of certain named regions. These qualifications are determined by intellection, in which the mind creates and maintains distinctions. Counterpoised with this emphasis on detail is the central metaphor for bhakti—not a certain image of God or a certain community (real or imagined), but the belief that the human heart is the same everywhere. It was this tension between the difference and sameness of embodiment in bhakti that appealed to various agents across India's lands and history, giving bhakti a fluidity that made it, rather than any authoritative systematization of it, one of the most influential perspectives in Hinduism.

PART II

Bodies of Poetry

The famous and prolific nāyaṉmār poets in Tamil Śiva-bhakti tradition are familiarly known as Campantar, Appar, and Cuntarar; they are often referred to simply as "the three" (mūvar).[1] A loose scholarly consensus locates Campantar and Appar as contemporaries whose lives partially overlapped during the hundred years between the late sixth and late seventh centuries A.D. Cuntarar, who mentions both Appar (Nāvukkaracaṉ) and Campantar (Campantaṉ) in his classic poem, *The List of the Holy Servants* (*Tiruttoṇṭattokai*), is thought to have lived around the beginning of the eighth century. Generally, Tamils of today primarily understand the mūvar through a series of later developments in Tamil Śiva-bhakti, including the canon of their hymns (*Tēvāram*), the hagiographies of their lives (*Periya Purāṇam*) and their elevation to sainthood (as nāyaṉmār, leaders), and the speculative interpretations of Śaiva Siddhānta philosophy.

The *Tēvāram* canon as we have it today includes 383 hymns composed by Campantar, 313 by Appar, and 100 by Cuntarar.[2] Each hymn, if it has been preserved in its entirety, comprises ten or eleven verses.[3] These hymns are thus numerous, filling the first seven volumes of the Śaiva canon, the *Tirumuṟai*. Although the poetic voice of the hymns is in the first person, the hymns themselves provide little detail of the life stories of the mūvar. Indeed, the subsequent composition of narrative stories concerning their activities involved an intensive selection from among their numerous hymns. For example, different hymns of Campantar on Ālavāy (Madurai) that mention the queen of Pandyanadu, flames "kindled by the crooked Jains to burn me," and Campantar's desire to defeat the Jains in debate became woven together into a story that relates the queen's total support of Campantar, the miracle of Campantar's curing the king's fever, the Jains' provocation of Campantar by burning his house and challenging him to debate, and Campantar's eventual victory over them.[4] The poems provide one- or two-line allusions to events or personalities but do not hand the reader or hearer a story. Nor does the canon of hymns provide such a narrative; it organizes the hymns by musical structure, thus breaks up hymns that focus on one place, such as Madurai, and in many cases prevents the reader from viewing them consecutively.

Although Tamils today understand the mūvar's hymns through the later biographical narratives, I focus on the worldview of the hymns themselves in chapters 3 and 4, with little reference to these influential narratives. The Tamil hymns appear to be the first in Hindu literature to use the first-person singular voice, conveying that the author is speaking from experience. What are the nature and the method of their experiences? The experience of the mūvar conveyed throughout the collection of their hymns is active participation in the worship of Śiva, or Śiva-bhakti. Their Śiva-bhakti is realized through the method of traveling to, and singing about, places where they claim Śiva resides. Praise is the content and pilgrimage the context of their hymns. The *Tiruttoṇṭattokai* hymn of Cuntarar provides support for this characterization, through its brief descriptions of Appar and Campantar as embodiments of bhakti. In verse four, he says of Appar: "Of blessed Nāvukkaracaṉ, 'Lord of Speech,' who took for his glory nothing other than the good Lord's name in which all blessings abide, I am the servant." In verse five, he says of Campantar: "Of the servants of my master Campantaṉ who worships nothing but the feet of the Lord who wears in his hair fragrant flowers swarming with humming bees and the good *koṉṟai*'s honey-filled blossom, I am the servant."[5] These are the two prongs of worship according to the mūvar's hymns: speech in praise of the Lord, through saying the Lord's name and evoking his image in hymns; and reverent humility in the presence of God. These are not two separate ways of worship, such as the scholarly nirguṇa-saguṇa perspective on bhakti would necessitate. They are two aspects of worship united in a single mode of bhakti and recognized as such in Cuntarar's assurance that he is "the servant" of both poets. Cuntarar's identification of himself in the hymn characterizes the third important aspect of the mūvar's bhakti, localization: "I am the poet Ārūraṉ, servant of our Father in Ārūr."

In the historical context of Sanskrit as the preeminent language of religion, the use of Tamil as the language of the bhakti poems is intentional; Tamil itself is celebrated in the hymns as a sacred language, worthy as speech offerings to God, and, as with Tamil language, Tamil towns and lands are celebrated in the Tamil bhakti hymns. The poets urge their audience to pilgrimage with them as they travel from town to town to "see" Lord Śiva there. In this dynamic, the poets localize the Lord—who is celebrated in their poetry as a transcendent, cosmic overlord through images drawn from Sanskrit purāṇas—in the Tamil lands. Yet, it is not simply the case that Tamil represents the particular and Sanskrit represents the transcendent in the bhakti poems. The major sources the poets draw on would suggest otherwise. For example, the Sanskrit *Śatarudrīya-stotra* is a long liturgical list of detailed features of God—from head to toe—giving the Lord a "physicality" or literal nature. In contrast, the Tamil sources, including the Caṅkam poems, suggest a sublime emotional and psychological landscape that is developed as a response to God in the bhakti hymns.

The theme of local-transcendent or literal-sublime is played out in the poets' representation of human communities in the Tamil lands. Through their hymns, the mūvar define a bhakti community. Significantly, they do not draw on caste identification in describing people of this community. For example, although the *Tiruttoṇṭattokai* does mention the brahmans of Tillai and does identify some of the nāyaṉmār by their occupations (a potter, a prince), the hymn emphasizes the names and deeds of Tamil bhaktas. In exploring this realm, I draw on images from Appar's poetry. He understands the bhakti community to be focused on God, with a disciplined, spiritual approach to life.

The mūvar were not accepting of everything they encountered in the Tamil lands, however. In particular, they thought it impossible that all people could join them on the path of bhakti; the contrast presented in the hymns is of the sanctity and harmony of the Tamil community through bhakti as opposed to members of non-Hindu traditions, particularly Buddhists and Jains. There are many negative references to Buddhists and Jains in the mūvar's hymns; for example, Campantar ends most of his sets of eleven verses (patikam) with a verse denouncing these non-Hindu people. Beyond these short, polemical statements, Appar has a hymn in which he presents a critique of the Jains in every verse. An analysis of this hymn reveals the moral force of the mūvar's invective against these groups. The hymnists sought to map a moral landscape through the details of pilgrimage and praise in Tamil towns and left nameless the settlements of Buddhists and Jains in Tamil country.

THREE

Pilgrimage and Praise

Pilgrimage is a prominent feature in Indian religious traditions. The pervasiveness of pilgrimage, whether in honor of a natural site, a founder figure, or a god, has prompted many to consider it a pan-Indian phenomenon; for example, Stella Kramrisch asserts that "the sacred geography of India recognizes the whole country as a field of more than human activity. It is carried by the rivers, from the celestial region where they have their prototype and origin, down to the earth."[1] When traditions of pilgrimage are taken collectively, this is an accurate impression. However, even a brief review of the literatures of pilgrimage reveals images of profound and overwhelming regionalism. In the eyes of any given pilgrim, then, all parts of India are not equal; it matters where one stands.[2]

In the classical Sanskrit tradition, the earliest use of the word *tīrtha*, which eventually came to designate pilgrimage, occurs in Vedic and Upaniṣadic sources. In these ancient ritual and philosophical texts, the noun *tīrtha*, which is derived from a verb meaning "to cross over," is associated with both material and symbolic properties and powers of rivers. Diana Eck suggests a threefold image of efficacy: the "nourishing and purifying power" of the river as a place to drink and to bathe; the river as a symbol of crossing over, where "one launches out on the journey between heaven and earth"; and the power of ritual, suggested in the homologies between the falling river and the falling Soma, and between the sacrifice and a tīrtha as "a crossing place where all the elements of this world are brought together in symbolic microcosm for the vertical crossing of the sacrificer to heaven."[3] In this context, the river is understood to have purifying, perhaps even expiatory, powers; it is an auspicious place to begin a spiritual journey; and it is a microcosm, containing all efficacious elements within it.

These three meanings were continued, and added to, in the transition from tīrtha to tīrthayātrā (journey to a tīrtha; that is, pilgrimage), which can be glimpsed in the classical purāṇic literature of Hinduism. Many purāṇas have a section on sacred places; the *Mahābhārata* epic has a special section devoted to pilgrimage, the "Tīrthayātrā Parva." In this phase of the development of pilgrimage, the efficacy of journeying to a sacred place is described in terms of the known, ancient ritual idiom of sacrifice:

> A man of good fortune will visit in the world of men the famous ford of the God of Gods, renowned in the three worlds, which is called Puṣkara. At the three joints of the day ten thousand crores of sacred places are present in Puṣkara. The Ādityas, Vasus, Rudras, Sādhyas, and the band of the Maruts are always present there, lord, as well as the Gandharvas and Apsarās. It is there that the Gods, Daityas, and brahmin seers mortified themselves and, possessed of great merit, achieved divine yogas. . . . The man who, devoted to the worship of Gods and ancestors, does his ablutions there attains, the wise say, to ten Horse Sacrifices. If he visits the Puṣkara wood and feeds but a single brahmin, he rejoices because of his act both here and hereafter. . . . A man who offers the *agnihotra* for a full hundred years and the man who stays in Puṣkara one full-moon night of Kārttika are equal. Puṣkara is hard to reach, austerities in Puṣkara are hard, gifts in Puṣkara are hard, to live there is very hard.[4]

To convey and affirm the importance of pilgrimage, the author(s) describe the efficacy of ritual journey in terms of efficacy of ritual sacrifice. The passage suggests that there is a dual structure of efficacy involved in pilgrimage. On the one hand, ritualized actions that can be performed elsewhere (that is, at home) are more efficacious when performed at a tīrtha; on the other hand, one short stay at a place of pilgrimage is dramatically more effective than performing another ritual many times. The epic also emphasizes that pilgrimage is not easy: All aspects of it, including the approach to and stay at the site, are difficult. This difficulty not only contextualizes rituals performed at Puṣkara, but also suggests that the journey itself becomes part of the ritual.

There is another important move signaled by the epic's praise of Puṣkara. This is the naming of pilgrimage places. A name is a sign of individuality, and each place can be praised for its own special efficacy. So, for example, the epic continues by describing the fruits one gains from traveling to the River Narmadā: "When a man bathes in that eminent ford, pure and of humble mind, he obtains the fruit of both the Laud-of-the-fire and the Overnight Sacrifice."[5] In addition, the name of a place of pilgrimage can be invoked. In the case of Puṣkara, this invocation somewhat ironically obviates the undertaking of pilgrimage to that place: "A man of spirit who, even if just in thought, has a desire for Puṣkara is freed from all sins and honored on the rooftree of heaven."[6] Each pilgrimage place is thus distinguished by its geographical location, its name, and its special qualities of efficacy.

The texts that describe pilgrimage tend to link many individual places of pilgrimage together into a route, such as the route(s) described in the later sections of the Tīrthayātrā Parva.[7] Here, pilgrimage is a network made up of a series of ritual actions performed at a series of efficacious places. The epic and purāṇic texts plot pilgrimage routes all over India. However, the texts do not equally privilege all places of pilgrimage but emphasize those within a certain region (*kṣetra*), creating a concentrated zone of efficacy. Thus, the *Matsya Purāṇa* devotes six chapters (189–194) to pilgrimage places on the River Narmadā yet has no chapter devoted exclusively to the Gaṅgā; as Surinder Mohan Bhardwaj suggests, the *Matsya Purāṇa* privileges the region of the present state of Maharashtra.[8]

None of the Sanskrit texts that describe places of pilgrimage, including the *Mahābhārata* and the *Garuḍa*, *Matsya*, and *Agni Purāṇa*s, focuses on south India.[9] There is disagreement among them on the number and location of pilgrimage places in the south; however, they have in common mention of the sacred Kāvēri River in Tamilnadu and the sacred site of Rāmeśvara, associated with the legend of Rāma.[10] The reasons given by scholars for the scant mention of the south in these texts are varied, including probable place of authorship and degree of knowledge about south India. Often these factors are subsumed under an appeal to Sanskritization in literature on Indian pilgrimage.[11] But, based on the pilgrimage texts themselves, we should view their emphasis on certain regions as opposed to others as more than just a "sectarian" impulse.[12] Rather, there seems to be a pattern of constituting pilgrimage as regional, so that the grand pilgrimage of the *Mahābhārata* is less a unified pan-Indian statement than a linking together of known regions of religious efficacy. Religiously, culturally, and, for most of its history, politically, India has been constituted by regions of efficacy rather than by a notion of pan-Indianism; to put this another way, there would not be a rhetoric of pan-Indianism unless various regions had chosen to share in a known religious language (including, for example, sacrifice and gods) while reconstituting it on their own terms. Epic and purāṇic literatures attempt to create a loosely connected network of religiously potent regions, suggesting a pan-Indian religious idiom, but the regional base of these imaginative activities is clear.

The Tamil bhakti poets highlighted Tamil pilgrimage by naming the towns in which they found Śiva in their hymns, as in the following example:

> The Lord at Puḷḷirukkuvēlūr
> has the form of lightning;
> He is one in the heavens
>   two in the blustering wind
>   three in the flames of the red fire
>   four in the flowing water
>   five in the earth,
> a refuge that does not diminish.
> His form is a great coral flame,
> a pearl,
> bright light,
> a diamond,
> gold without blemish.
> I dismiss as in vain all days not spent worshipping Him!
>
> Appar (1.12/6.54.5)[13]

This hymn, like the majority of the mūvar's hymns, locates the poet's imagination of Lord Śiva in a named town—here, Puḷḷirukkuvēlūr. The presence of named towns in their verses and the Tamil language of the hymns are the most consistent markers of their Tamilness, their inextricable ties to the land and culture of Tamilnadu. That most of these towns can be located today, many concentrated in the Kāvēri

River delta region within some ten kilometers of one another, strengthens the impression that the mūvar visited these places on pilgrimages and composed their hymns in what they believed to be the presence of God in each town.[14] Indeed, some of the hymns describe the poets' desire to go to a certain place or otherwise indicate that they are traveling.[15]

It is not surprising that the nāyaṉmār chose to link their worship of Śiva inextricably to pilgrimage, for pilgrimage is a preeminent example of the public demonstration of one's individual decision and commitment to participate in worship. Pilgrimage is a social act that creates social space, often through transforming peripheral and uninhabited places.[16] Victor Turner, the most influential theorist of pilgrimage, would agree that pilgrimage is a social act, although he tended to portray it as an antistructural component in a process that challenged social structures but nevertheless ultimately led to a reaffirmation of social norms. Elsewhere I have critically evaluated Turner's image of pilgrimage and largely rejected his language of structure and antistructure in favor of an image of pilgrimage as that which makes the unfamiliar familiar, in contrast with worship in a local church or temple, which renders familiar surroundings unfamiliar.[17]

The pilgrimages of the Tamil hymnists contribute a distinctive perspective on the dynamics I have identified. Their pilgrimages, as represented in their poems, brought what is inside out, and what is outside in. The internal component is the poets' love for Śiva, their constant meditation upon him, and their desire to be in proximity to him; these are brought out through their words and through their travels. The external component is the autonomy of Lord Śiva, who is portrayed in purāṇic mythology as a transcendent God with cosmic powers and a kingdom high in the clouds on the Himālayan Mountains. Śiva is brought inside the poets' hearts and minds and the Tamil lands, by the poets' love for him, by their use of the Tamil language to praise him, and by their portrayal of him as One who lives in Tamilnadu and who is concerned with people there. Thus, the poets are embodied as bhaktas of Śiva, and Śiva is embodied in all things Tamil, including the poets. The poets sing from experience; the range of their emotions encourages identification with them as imperfect people, bound by the limits of the human condition. They are embodied and thus are ordinary human beings working against numerous limitations in order to reach God. The theme of human inadequacy is most prominent in Appar's poetry, to a lesser extent in Cuntarar's, and still less in Campantar's poetry. When these internal feelings become expressed in the poetry, however, transformations occur: The feelings of anguish become words in praise of Śiva, and the familial language becomes sacred, *tiru tamiḻ*.[18]

The poets address their very human problems by doing more than participating in the praise of Śiva; significantly, they also assume that God comes to them. Śiva is embodied in a number of different ways, all of which are grounded in the theme that he is Tamil. The poems do use the Sanskrit purāṇic portrayals of Śiva's cosmic powers and emphasize his transcendent overlordship and association with the Himālayas. These images of Śiva are placed in Tamilnadu, however, through a variety of techniques, including the naming of Tamil towns to localize the vision; the juxtaposition of cosmic and local acts in the poetry, which Indira Peterson has identified as a "blending technique" in which the hymnists "alternate, in the ten verses of the song, the cosmic acts of Śiva with those that he performed out of compassion for a particular Tamil devotee"[19]; and the first-person voice of the hymns, as in the following example, which brings together a cosmic image of Śiva, the poet, and the Tamil town of Ārūr.

> The Lord who burned the cities
> drawing against His body
> the mountain as the bow, the strong cobra as the bowstring,
> and Agni and Hari as the arrows—
> I am a fool not to think of Him first.
> Bearing this body,
> How long can I remain separate
> from my Lord of Ārūr?
>
> Cuntarar 7.2/7.51.6

This poem and many like it raise the issue of the real and the imagined in the Tamil bhakti hymns. In this case, it appears that the Tamil elements, including the body of the poet, the language of the poem, and the town of Ārūr, are all real components of the hymn, whereas Sanskrit elements, included in the mythological allusions to several Hindu gods, are imaginative. The Tamil elements are local, whereas the Sanskrit elements are universal. Since it is supportable through the poems to suggest that the three most famous nāyaṉmār actually went on pilgrimage, the physical aspect of the journey is a factor that is represented. Yet the description of Śiva in Cuntarar's poem seems an imaginative vision, seen in the mind's eye. Pilgrimage itself combines the real and the imagined into a single experiential mode; this is the context of Cuntarar's hymn.

Or were the hymnists actually seeing artistic representations of the Śiva of the purāṇas, perhaps on temple walls? This is the position taken by the influential scholar of *Tēvāram*, M. A. Dorai Rangaswamy: "The three great Śaivite saints of Tēvāram, along with their hosts of followers, went round the whole of the Tamil country and composed and sang their beautiful and original musical compositions in every one of the temples they visited. The cult of temples and pilgrimages was thus unconsciously laying its deep foundations in this country."[20] Several factors contribute to the impression that the mūvar were traveling to temples in which there were actual images of Śiva for worship. Indeed, the word *kōyil* (temple) does appear on occasion in their hymns.[21] Scholars are aware from historic inscriptions on temple walls that temples in brick preceded stone structures and often served as models for them. From this evidence, it is possible that there were even earlier temples in nondurable materials that provided models for the brick structures, although art historians have not come to a definitive conclusion on this point. Another factor in possible support of Dorai Rangaswamy's thesis is an old Tamil saying to the effect that a town is defined by the presence of a temple.[22] In addition, the focus of the mūvar's hymns is on "being there" before Śiva as the preeminent experience, suggesting darśan (seeing and being seen by God) within the pūjā (offering) ritual.[23] Finally, the extant artistic representations of Śiva in Tamil temples draw mainly on Sanskrit purāṇic images.

Yet, it cannot be concluded from this evidence that "the three" were making pilgrimages exclusively to temples. All three of the hymnists compiled classificatory lists of places they visited; many of the terms denote open, unstructured places. For example, one finds *kāṭu* (forest, uncultivated land), *tuṟai* (port or refuge), *kuḷam* (tank of water), and *kaḷam* (field) among the terms they used.[24] Thus, both natural (yet social) and constructed places are included in the poets' places of pilgrimage; only some are specifically religious buildings. In addition, there are some ritual places that are not temples at all; for example, the "post" in which Appar "sees" Śiva (10.12/6.61.3).

It is more in keeping with the pilgrimage model to assume that the poets identified several different types of places as sacred and that built structures, which in the history of pilgrimage sites are often a secondary development, need not have been the preeminent locus of religious experience or symbol of the social world in the poems. The poets traversed natural place and social space, designating all types as the home of Śiva.[25] Significantly, in general the poems do not represent social space as contested space; the poems give the impression that the hymnists were free to wander and to offer their songs of praise to Śiva. Tradition, supported by the hymns' use of some colloquial terms, their intimate tone, and their emotional intensity, suggests that the hymns are spontaneous emotional responses to God, within a context of pure accessibility to him. Is it believable that temples would be uncontested space? It is more likely that designated ritual space would have a community of ritual specialists, perhaps brahmans, to attend to it. And yet we do not hear of those persons at specific sites in the hymns, save for scattered references to the brahmans at Tillai (Chidambaram). As I discuss in parts III and IV, temples in the imperial context (which was both contemporaneous to the nāyaṉmār and later than them) represented negotiated space; when the bhakti hymns found a place in the temples, different meanings of bhakti were developed, some of which directly challenged the intimacy and accessibility of God that are described in the hymns. This distinction should make us cautious in assuming that the mūvar simply traveled from temple to temple on their pilgrimages. In contrast, as I discuss later in this chapter, the hymns themselves created an image of contested space in their invective against Buddhists and Jains; their authors made it quite clear that they did not want to share Tamil space with these groups.

The hymnists imagined Śiva as one with the Tamil lands and culture. They see Him everywhere: Śiva is in the hearts and minds of the Tamil people, Śiva is in the stories of cosmic deeds and local bhaktas, Śiva is in Tamil towns and lands, and Śiva is in temples. In keeping with the practice of pilgrimage, the mūvar created a region of efficacy based on a network of diverse places that embodied bhakti. The variety of images and ideas in the hymns suggests that, during the course of pilgrimage, the mūvar drank in the people, places, and ideas they came across. It has often been said that the poets used everything and anything they could in their poems. In this way, they wove fragments of ancient and contemporary, esoteric and exoteric, mundane and sacred, and bits of realism and imagination together to create a cohesive discourse of bhakti. Along with observation on pilgrimage, the hymnists related their bhakti discourse to prior literatures in Tamil and Sanskrit in complex ways; in this sense, the hymns are not unlike compendia of culture. What held the fragments together was a representation of bhakti. The message of bhakti that underlies their representation is not only that Śiva is the source of everyone and everything but also the converse: that all elements of reality and imagination should make one think of Śiva, actively taking him into one's mind or heart (expressed by the same Sankrit-derived word in Tamil, *ma<u>n</u>am*). The poets' insistence on the path of bhakti—the specific way that they constituted that path—means that although they drew upon many intellectual heritages (Tamil and Sanskrit, textual and ritual, and so on), none of these perspectives was simply adopted in its own right. They used pieces to create their own distinctive whole, Śiva-bhakti.

Many scholars have noted that Tamil is the great exception to the apparent rule that the first literatures originally composed in regional languages were those of bhakti. Scholars have acknowledged, however, that the mūvar's hymns contributed to the classical Tamil intellectual heritage, through their conscious relationship to the Caṅkam poetry (ca second century B.C. through second century A.D.). The bhakti hymns play with the classical poetic division of akam (interior) and pu<u>r</u>am (exterior), although the pu<u>r</u>am poems, which praise a human king or patron, may have been more widely influential in the bhakti hymns.[26] However, the bhakti hymns transform the nature of praise from the Caṅkam pu<u>r</u>am poems. In the style of the earlier poems, the mūvar praise Śiva with images of kingly power, of heroic deeds, and of a benefactor's generosity.[27] Yet, in the bhakti hymns, the discourse often becomes focused on the poet by the end of the poem; for example, in the poem from Cuntarar I quoted previously, the image of Śiva as a cosmic archer leads to the author's lament that he has separated himself from Śiva by not thinking of him (which is, in turn, rectified by his pilgrimage to Ārūr).

The hymnists seem to use akam poems as models less frequently than they do the pu<u>r</u>am genre, but when one does come across a poem that plays with these conventions, it is compelling. The akam genre describes love relationships of varying types. In this example, the poet describes the persona of a young woman (talaivi) who is mad for her lover (talaiva<u>n</u>). It evokes the kuriñji category of classical akam poem, in which the lovers are unmarried, so their love is illicit at the time of the poem, but there is an implied expectation that they will be married, for their love is well matched.

> First, she heard His name
> then she heard about His color and form
> and His Ārūr.
> Though dissuaded, she became mad for Him
> and left her mother and father that very day,
> abandoning the customs of the world.
> Losing herself
> forgetting her own name
> this girl placed her head at the Lord's feet.
>
> Appar 7.1/6.25.7

This poem plays with the classical Caṅkam conventions in that the central figure is a young woman in passionate love with a distant hero. Her love appears to threaten social conventions, and an attempt is made to dissuade her; not only is this impossible but also it increases her love such that it becomes akin to madness. This sense of love that is uncontrolled yet compelling for its truth and honesty pervades the classical poems and this bhakti example, as well. The compelling nature of the passion indeed causes the girl to abandon protocol, as she leaves home to find her lover. She even abandons the simplest of conventions in forgetting her own name; this is similar to a major theme in akam poetry, that the girl in love cannot bring herself to eat and grows thin. Yet, in the bhakti poem, the heroine does not flee to the hills for amorous embrace with the hero, as in the classical poems; instead, she pilgrimages to Ārūr, prostrates herself before Śiva in a gesture of submission, and places her head at the Lord's feet. In the bhakti poems, the feet of the Lord signify both his grace and release (mukti) from the world. Whereas in the Caṅkam akam poems the implied culmination of the situation is marriage and thus proper life in the social world, this bhakti poem can be interpreted as illustrating the young girl's path to, and attainment of, religious release from the world.

The Caṅkam poems are fairly clear-cut examples of sources that the hymnists were likely to have quoted in their bhakti hymns. Their use by the bhakti poets is uncontroversial, not only because the connections between their structures and contents are a good match but also because the Caṅkam poems are not religious texts, and thus it is relatively straightforward to suggest that the mūvar contributed a religious perspective to known poetic conventions. The early Caṅkam poetry, like the early Tamil grammar, the *Tolkāppiyam*, does mention gods, but it does not focus on them; the gods are part of a constellation of characteristics that signify particular landscapes.[28] More difficult and controversial is the possibility that the mūvar looked to precedents in Tamil religious literature.

Four categories of religious works in Tamil appear to have emerged in what amounts to a watershed period between the flourishing of the Caṅkam poems and the rise of sectarian bhakti literatures. Recent scholarship on Tamil poetry tends to assign the dates of fifth or sixth centuries (although usually with a question mark) to four types of religious poetry: the *Paripāṭal*, an anthology of poems containing seven to Tirumāl and eight to Murukan̲; the *Tirumurukār̲r̲uppaṭai*, a praise poem to Murukan̲; early bhakti poetry, including the poems of Kāraikkāl Ammaiyār in praise of Śiva and those of three early Vaiṣṇava bhakti poets; and the *Tirumantiram* by Tirumūlar.[29] Scholars usually discuss the first two together as "late classical Caṅkam" poetry; the poems of Kāraikkāl Ammaiyār are considered to be part of the canon of nāyan̲mār Śiva-bhakti (the author was designated a nāyan̲ār); and the *Tirumantiram* is discussed either as sui generis, as part of bhakti, or as part of Śaiva Siddhānta. The *Tirumurukār̲r̲uppaṭai*, the hymns of Kāraikkāl Ammaiyār, and the *Tirumantiram* were eventually incorporated into the canon of Śaivism, now known as the twelve-book *Tirumur̲ai*.[30]

The various texts use distinctive elements that are associated with bhakti. The *Paripāṭal* poems to Tirumāl describe the uniqueness and fertility of the Lord's mountain, urging listeners to go seek him there for worship.[31] The *Tirumurukār̲r̲uppaṭai* poem to Murukan̲ populates the god's hill with his earthly retinue of ritual specialists and devotees and gives the listener a vivid picture of his ritual worship.[32] This text also uses the language of "setting your mind upon god's red feet"[33] and of the Lord "granting divine boons out of love." The poems by Kāraikkāl Ammaiyār speak of her undying love (iravāta a͟npu) for the Lord, in the context of her gaining release and watching the Lord dance at Tiruvālaṅkāṭu.[34] The *Tirumantiram*, a complicated and dense text, appears to be the first example of a Tamil text using the transliterated word *patti* for the Sanskrit word *bhakti*.[35] The *Tirumantiram* also emphasizes some of the purāṇic stories that find emphasis in the mūvars' hymns, such as Śiva as the destroyer of the three cities, Śiva as the fiery liṅgam, the blue-necked Śiva, and Śiva the conqueror of Rāvaṇa.[36]

It is notable that these early Tamil poets draw attention to themselves (and others) as participants in the worship of God, which is the premise of bhakti. In contrast, the Sanskrit *Bhagavad Gītā*, which has been viewed as a major precedent for all of bhakti literature, presents the main characters (Kṛṣṇa and Arjuna), and not the author, as speaking in the first person. In the course of the *Gītā*, the reader or hearer learns of the nature of bhakti from overhearing their conversation. The early Tamil poets, by contrast, highlight their own knowledge through experience; they actively urge others to see the Lord by making pilgrimages to his special ritual places, and they encourage the hearer to experience love for God. The author of the *Tirumurukā͟r͟ruppaṭai* says, "I speak what I truly know," and Tirumūlar claims that his knowledge has come from Śiva himself, through a lineage of seers. These early Tamil poets thus appear to have introduced the idea of the author as bhakta, who is participating in the worship of God through poetry.

The mūvar developed the emerging tradition of the first-person voice in Tamil praise poems to God by imbuing the poetry with intensive experiential and emotional themes, based on their own experiences of love for God and the problems of being human, especially the tendency to forget God. As part of this development, they not only highlighted their emotional experiences but also sought to engage the hearer emotionally as well, in marked contrast to the perhaps simpler goal of urging others to worship that was characteristic of the *Tirumurukā͟r͟ruppaṭai*. Norman Cutler, in analyzing the poetics of bhakti, emphasizes the importance of this emotional engagement in the poetry:

> The model of bhakti poetry developed here is rhetorical insofar as it concerns the interaction between author and audience and the ways that interaction is articulated in sectarian discourse. However, this is a special kind of "rhetoric" because the performance and reception of bhakti poetry involve not so much the *communication* of a message from author to audience as a profound *communion* between the two. The hymns themselves are the instrument of that communion. The communion between author and audience, which, as I have emphasized, is a communion between devotee and god (with each taking both roles), has profound theological significance. The aesthetic/rhetorical process, as described here, is, in the final analysis, a process of divination, and the hymns fuel that process.[37]

It is this sense of communion, or sharing (which is another meaning of *bhakti*), that distinguishes the bhakti hymns from other religious Tamil poetry of this early period.

Cutler notes that bhakti poetry is involved in sectarian discourse, and this raises the important issue of what constitutes such a discourse and whether it is present in the poetry of the mūvar. Like the late Caṅkam poetry and the *Tirumantiram*, bhakti poetry is oriented around the praise of one God, though this God differs from one poem to another: Tirumāl, Murukaṉ, Śiva. This is one definition of sectarianism: to have a common focus. In ordinary understanding, however, the term connotes opposition, as groups try to distinguish their common focus from that of others. In this sense, the Tamil poetry of the watershed era does not appear to have much sectarian consciousness. In contrast, the bhakti poetry of Campantar, Appar, and Cuntarar appears to engage in three types of polemical discourse: that Śiva is superior to other Hindu gods (this is encoded in many of the purāṇic images they use), that bhakti is the correct way of worship in contrast to other Hindu ways, and that Buddhists and Jains are immoral. The frequency of these three aspects of polemical discourse in their poetry should not be overstated. These themes appear occasionally and are not necessarily main themes in the poetry—with the possible exception of Campantar's invective against Buddhists and Jains in the final verse of virtually every one of his poems. But they do have implications for the mūvar's sense of "Hinduism" and Śiva-bhakti's encompassment of it.

The hymnists praise Śiva in the strongest possible language; Śiva is the Source, he is Everything, and so on. This praise implies that Śiva is greater than any other Hindu god, but it does not explicitly involve the negative comparison that constitutes a polemic. It is significant that when Śiva is explicitly compared with other Hindu gods in the bhakti hymns, the polemic occurs in the allusions to Sanskrit purāṇic mythology. For example, Śiva is in the heart of Viṣṇu lying on the primordial ocean (1.13 in Appendix A); Śiva defeated Viṣṇu and Brahmā as the fiery liṅgam (4.7, 6.10); Śiva rules locally, in Ārūr, as opposed to Indra, who rules in heaven (6.1); Śiva's arrow against the evil triple cities is composed of Viṣṇu and Agni (7.2); and Śiva is Absolute over Brahmā on the lotus and Viṣṇu (8.2). The mūvar primarily draw on images of Śiva from the purāṇas to praise his beauty and his cosmic deeds in their poetry; in so doing, they at times choose images that reflect the very developed sectarian consciousness in the Sanskrit purāṇas, but this is not a technique they seem to develop, as they do the poetics of experience, in their hymns.

Thus, the bhakti hymns do not criticize other Hindu gods overtly; rather, through purāṇic imagery they describe other gods as less powerful than and thus subordinate to Śiva. Indeed, by claiming Śiva as the Source for everything, the poets are able to encompass Hindu ways of worship within their view of bhakti. For example, in one poem Appar is critical of performing tapas (austerities) in the wrong way (7.10); in another, Campantar praises knowledge of the Vedas (10.5). What the two have in common is the hymnists' insistence that every act of worship and every type of religious knowledge must be grounded in love for Śiva, often described as the worshiper's desire to meditate on or reach the Lord's feet. The bhakti poems make it clear that if Śiva is not acknowledged as the Source, then neither traditional ritual practices nor traditional religious knowledge is efficacious.

The effect of this argument is both to preserve traditional structures of Hinduism and to transform the foundation of their potency.[38] Campantar, Appar, and Cuntarar locate bhakti within the Hindu fold by their acceptance of the Vedas, their worship of the god Śiva, and their acceptance of traditions of worship, including prostration and the offering of flowers, among other features. But the hymns invite the hearer to reconsider the meaning of religious actions and knowledge and to value the structure of them less, in favor of a greater realization of their source in Śiva. The poems insist over and over again that the real danger is in forgetting Śiva; the poets pilgrimaged throughout the Tamil lands while singing of him, reminding people of Śiva, asserting his presence in Tamil country, and encouraging their participation in his praise and worship.

It is within this framework that they appeal to a variety of Sanskrit religious formulations in addition to the purāṇic images in their poems. Sanskrit texts other than the *Gītā* may have more directly provided source material for the bhakti hymns, both in terms of their nature as poems of praise and in terms of the way they characterize the human condition. For example, the *Śatarudrīya-stotra* (Hymn to the Hundred Rudras), a Sanskrit hymn in praise of Rudra, has been identified as a source for the mūvar's hymns. The *Śatarudrīya* is extant in several recensions: as the sixteenth chapter of the *Vājasaneya-Saṃhitā*, within the *White Yajurveda*; and as four versions within the *Black Yajurveda*—namely, the Saṃhitās of the Taittirīyas, the Kaṭhas, the Kapiṣṭhala-kaṭhas, and the Maitrāyaṇīyas.[39]

The *Śatarudrīya*'s connection with the bhakti poems was perhaps first postulated by K. A. Nilakanta Sastri, in the 1950s.[40] He observed that the five-syllable invocation to Śiva (the pañcākṣara-mantra), namaḥ Śivāya (Hail to Śiva), first found in the *Śatarudrīya*, appears in the mūvar's poem-songs. In the example he cites, Appar creates a parallelism between the Vedas' enormous worth to the brahmans and the pañcākṣara's worth to Appar and his followers.[41] In several hymns, Appar links the presence of Śiva specifically with the mantra; in the following example, the poet urges people to recite the mantra, even if they do not understand the meanings of its syllables:

> For those who recite even though they lack knowledge of anything
> and for those who understand the five syllables
> the Lord of Māṟpēṟu and His Lady
> will happily enter their minds
> without distinguishing between them.
>
> Appar 9.4/5.60.1

This poem endorses recitation of the mantra, yet it is reluctant to link the mantra with any one intellectual heritage; instead, both those who understand the meanings of the mantra, as well as those who do not, will receive the Lord's presence—a mental epiphany of the Tamil-based Śiva and his wife. Śiva will come inside the bhakta.

Appar's hymn highlights the nature of the liturgical role of the pañcākṣara mantra as an invocation of the Lord. In this dynamic, the Lord is invoked to come to the worshiper. The ritual context of the mantra was emphasized in the many texts that drew upon the *Śatarudrīya*. The five-syllable mantra did not stand alone in the *Śatarudrīya*; the hymn is a litany of names, deeds, and images in praise of the god Rudra, and the pañcākṣara mantra is a refrain within that list. The entire hymn was originally performed in the context of Vedic sacrifice, and J. Bruce Long notes that the *Śatarudrīya* was the spoken equivalent of the actions that were performed to effect the sacrifice: "The hymns of praise, the visible movements of the rituals and the sacrificial oblations are three different aspects of a *single mode* of religious veneration."[42] The *Śatapatha Brāhmaṇa* gives the greatest details of the performance of the *Śatarudrīya* in the sacrificial context. It speaks of ritual transformation: The body of the fire (Agni), constructed through the ritual building of the fire and offerings, and the body of Rudra, orally constructed through recitation of the hymn, are homologized. This is the essence of the ritual: "He then performs the Śatarudrīya sacrifice. This whole Agni has here been completed; he now is the deity Rudra."[43] The function of the hymn, then, was to create an efficacious ritual body for Rudra, which could then be activated by homology with Agni. The body of Rudra was created through the specific modes of naming, praise, and image; the mantra provided the mysterium in refrain.

A sense of perfection and completion pervades the performance of the Śatarudrīya sacrifice; the several types of food offered to Rudra make him the primary recipient of the sacrifical food, in contrast to the dominant image of Rudra as the one who receives merely the remainder of sacrificed food.[44] The *Śatarudrīya* hymn is a list that the Vedists believed completely encompassed the many aspects of Rudra. For example, he is said to be both benign and horrible, a woodsman clad in an animal skin, the master of animals, the deity of artisans, the archer of the bows and arrows of illness and death; he is pictured as having a blue neck, a copper-brown-purple body, and he is both tall and dwarfish.[45] The text can be understood as the complete praise of Rudra because the many bodies by which human beings imagine him are all brought together to constitute an efficacious ritual body.

The *Śatarudrīya* was an important source from which later traditions reconstituted both images of Śiva and the worship of him. The *Atharva Veda* (XI.2) extended the list to include every part of the god's body. The hymn was further quoted in the *Śvetāśvatara Upaniṣad* and the *Kaivalya Upaniṣad*, among others, and the *Mahābhārata* included a "Hymn of a Thousand Names" (sahasra nama stotram) addressed to Śiva, which was quoted in several purāṇas.[46] According to Jan Gonda, the hymn became linked with bhakti in the *Rudrārthāsārastavah* of Arunādri, which he considers to be a bhakti-inspired paraphrase of the *Śatarudrīya*.[47] The technique of his paraphrase is *samasyāpūrana*, by which the author selectively retains some phrases from the original hymn while inserting his own phrases, some of which tend toward explanation of the original text.[48] In its conclusion, this text enumerates the immediate benefits to one who reads the hymn, including the removal of sins, freedom from illness and affliction, and spiritual liberation.[49]

Thus, over time, the liturgical nature of the *Śatarudrīya* was preserved, even while the ritual contexts and meanings given to the text were changed. The liturgical role of invocation through praise from the *Śatarudrīya* does have a place in understanding the bhakti hymns. The hymns appear to recognize the function of the mantra as invocation, particularly in obtaining Śiva's presence. In addition, the hymns create lists of praise fragments, like the *Śatarudrīya*, as in the hymn from Appar quoted previously, "The Lord at Puḷḷirukkuvēlūr" (1.12 in Appendix A). In that hymn, Appar likens Śiva to a series of luminous objects (a flame, a pearl, a light, a diamond, pure gold) in praise of his luminosity. Like the Vedic text, the Tamil hymns recognize many bodies for Śiva; the difference is that the bhakti hymns do not exclusively promote a ritual context requiring invocation but, instead, hold in tension the religious modes of invocation (Śiva comes to us) and pilgrimage (we must go to him).

The pañcākṣara mantra is also associated with another stream of tradition that emphasizes invocation, the Śaiva āgamas, which are ritual and philosophical manuals that became a prominent mode of worship in Tamil country possibly during the time of the mūvar; however, not much is known of the texts during this period. One of the Pallava kings, Mahendravarman I, suggests in an inscription at Kāñcīpuram that he is a follower of Śaiva Siddhānta (though he was fulsome in his epithets), and he also uses the pañcākṣara mantra to begin some of his inscriptions, but overall we do not know much about this āgamic-based ritual and philosophical tradition before the tenth century or so, when attempts were made to systematize the āgamas.[50] The hymnists, however, did appear to have some knowledge of āgamic methodology and meaning. For example, the hymns refer to the Vedas as *Vētam*, *maṟai*, or *mantiram*; often the word *tantiram* follows this last term, and it is this word that may refer to the āgamas.[51] In addition, on occasion the hymns use terminology associated with the āgamas, as evidenced by the following hymn by Appar:

> I prayed:
> Oh my Perumāṉ of the curly matted hair
> who destroys the sorrow of births
> that are like a whirlwind,
> Oh my Guide of the purest clear water
> who destroys the births
> arising from pacu and pācam
> that are difficult to go beyond,
> Oh my great Lord,
> Mother!
> Light that blameless Tirumāl and Ayaṉ could not see,
> Strong pillar of Maḻapāti
> who wears the Vedas on His crest
> who guides us on the path!
> Then I melted, weeping.
>
> Appar 6.10/6.40.7

In this poem, Appar is clearly using the terms *pacu* and *pācam* to describe something negative: As elements that give rise to birth, they, or the resulting births, are "difficult to go beyond." One of the many descriptions of Śiva in this short poem is that he is the pure One who will destroy such births. Pacu and pācam are thus stumbling blocks for ordinary people, but they are obliterated for those guided on the path by Śiva. These two Sanskrit terms, *paśu*, transliterated as *pacu* in Tamil, and *pāśa*, transliterated as *pācam*, represent concepts central to āgamic philosophy, as does the term *pati* or Lord. Though there is some distinctive nuancing of these terms according to various philosophical schools, generally in āgamic thought *pacu* is "cow" or "creature," and *pācam* is "bond" or "affliction." In describing the nature of the human condition, the āgamas postulate that these are both negative conditions resulting from birth and must be transcended for salvation. The attachments formed by human beings as embodied beings are often labeled as desires or sorrows.

Since āgamic philosophy was probably being developed during this period, contemporaneous with the composition of the Tamil Śiva-bhakti hymns, it would be unwise to suggest that the hymnists inherited a mature system of āgamic philosophy, especially not the system of āgamic temple worship, which became the primary domain of the āgamas in the medieval era. For the hymnists, the source of āgamic ideas on the nature of the world, especially the threefold division of pati, pacu, and pācam, probably came from the *Tirumantiram*, whose author, Tirumūlar, is praised by name in Cuntarar's *List of the Holy Servants* (*Tiruttoṇṭattokai*, v. 5). The *Tirumantiram* is a highly speculative text, in contrast to Sanskrit āgamic texts, which link themselves directly to the practice of temple rituals. In a few verses, the Tamil hymnists, especially Appar, used language from the āgamas to describe the problem of embodiment, yet bhakti posed a distinctive solution to this inherited way of viewing embodiment, one that contrasts with the elaborate ritual system of bodily transformation found in Vedic liturgy (which creates a ritual body of Rudra) and the āgamas (which transforms the body of the priest into a ritual body).

In keeping with their emphasis on embodiment, the bhakti hymnists display little sustained interest in such bodily transformations. For them, it is not a ritual transformation but a reorientation of one's mind and heart through pilgrimage and praise. The hymnists advocate a path for actualizing the positive value of embodiment in the world: keeping one's mind on Śiva (invocation) in tandem with appropriate action to glorify him (pilgrimage). The main focus of Appar's hymn is the image of Śiva as the mythological Lord of the Gaṅgā, a motif that appears frequently in the poems. Just as Śiva guided the Gaṅgā River through his matted locks to prevent her from destructively crashing to earth, so, too, he will guide his bhaktas through the obstacles of life, foremost among them births arising from pacu and pācam, to save them from destruction. In the myth and in the poem, Śiva's hair is divine and therefore a positive obstacle, for it guides the water of Gaṅgā; in the poem, the pacu and pācam are negative obstacles that block humankind's path toward salvation and necessitate the guidance of Śiva. The images of Śiva in the poem as a mother, a light, a pillar of strength, and one of great knowledge represent different ways of envisioning him as a guide. The hymn encourages its hearers to recognize Śiva as a guide, with special emphasis on his preservation of the world through his control of the nourishing waters of Gaṅgā. Only when he fully realizes the Lord's powers does the poet melt, weeping.

FOUR

Defining a Community

Many of the bhakti hymns suggest that there are three major components of good Tamil society: the presence of Śiva, Tamils who meditate upon him, and the prosperity of the Tamil lands. The three are intimately related. Sometimes a hymn is thematically split: Half extols the beauty of Śiva, and half emphasizes the beauty of the Tamil lands. In these cases, the poets are suggesting that the power of Śiva and the productivity of the land are mutually related, as center to periphery. Śiva's presence makes the land potent, and fertile land is an attractive home for Śiva. Between these two are the Tamil people, who meditate on Śiva and who live in and from the land.

It was perhaps to facilitate people's remembrance of Śiva that the mūvar sang in their mother tongue of Tamil. They gave their listeners short Tamil phrases to remember; for example, *neñcu iṭai ni<u>n</u><u>r</u>u* (he remains in my mind), and *u<u>n</u> pātamē kāṇpatarku uruki<u>r</u><u>r</u>u* (melting for the sight of Your feet), along with well-chosen images of Śiva. The hymnists gave their hearers many ways to meditate on Śiva and to experience love for him. According to the hymnists, with Śiva in Tamilnadu, the world was a good place. The presence of Śiva in Tamil towns forms the basis for a moral society, while his goodness is embodied by people who worship him. Several types of people are favorably described by the hymnists, all with the common denominator of actively worshiping Śiva. The hymns provide us with portraits of happy people at festivals, good servants of Śiva who wear the Śaiva marks in ashes on their foreheads, and people who worship Śiva with flowers and sandalwood paste; in a remarkable poem from Appar, agricultural labor is used as a metaphor for spiritual development that culminates in the bliss of Śiva (3.1, Appendix A). These groups of people are not named, nor are groups of people praised as classical religious adepts, for example, "those who know the Vedas" and "those who perform tapas (austerities)." Some personages are, however, named in the hymns; this is an application of the "blending technique" Indira Peterson has identified as a strategy by which the hymnists portray Śiva as both cosmically and locally concerned. The cosmic personages include, among others, the daughter of Himālaya, Arjuna, Gaṅgā, and Rāvaṇa; Tamil personages include Cantīcar, Kōccenkaṇāṉ, and Kaṇṇappar.[1] The named Tamil personages were gathered together by Cuntarar in his famous hymn, the *Tiruttoṇṭattokai* (List of the Sacred Servants), which very briefly alludes to the identity of these personages.[2] The poems suggest that, just as there were many forms in which God could be embodied, there were many forms in which those who participated in his worship could be embodied. However brief the allusions in the *Tiruttoṇṭattokai*, the poem presents an image of the diversity of the bhaktas, yet in presenting them as a collectivity, it frames their diversity with an implied assertion that they are united on the same religious path.

Many of the individuals on Cuntarar's list represent paradigms of activity inspired by bhakti. In a very few cases, their actions as exemplary bhaktas are explored in more detail in other poems by the mūvar; for example, Cuntarar describes Campantar, Appar, Pukaḻttuṇai, King Cenkaṇāṉ, Kaṇṇappar, Ēyarkōṉ, Cāṇṭi, Cākkiyaṉ, and Kaṇampullaṉ; and Appar describes Naminanti, Amarnīti, Kōccenkaṇāṉ, Caṇṭīcar, Cākkiyaṉār, Kaṇṇappar, and Kaṇampullar.[3] In the main, these more detailed descriptions are presented in the length of a verse. Although a diversity of bhaktas are celebrated in the mūvar's hymns, the poets did offer some paradigms on the nature of a true bhakta, based on their own experiences. For example, a hymn from Appar provides a more detailed representation of paradigmatic actions in bhakti. In this hymn, Appar uses the first-person plural pronoun, *we*, the specific form of which in Tamil (*nām*) denotes the inclusion of both the speaker and the hearer.[4] It is thus a vision that the poet imagines to apply generally to bhaktas. Moreover, although the brief examples of bhaktas serve to define ways of active participation in the worship of Śiva, Appar's hymn defines the nature of a toṇṭar, or servant to the Lord.

1. We are slaves to no man,
nor do we fear death.
Hell holds no torments for us,
we know no deceit.
We rejoice, we are strangers to disease,
we bow to none.
Joy alone is ours, not sorrow,
for we belong forever
to Śankara, who is the supreme Lord,
our King who wears the white conch earring on one ear,
and we have reached his beautiful, flower-fresh feet.

2. The wide world is our home;
generous householders in every town
give us food.
Public halls are our only shelter; we sleep
in Goddess Earth's loving embrace—
all this is true.
The Lord of the warlike bull has taken us.
We lack nothing, our trials are over now.

Why need we listen to the words
of men who parade themselves in silk and gold?
We are innocent men.

3. We do not consort with women;
we rise before dawn to bathe
and chant Mahādeva's name,
our sole ornament is sacred ash.
Tears, welling from our eyes like monsoon rains,
proclaim the melting of our stony hearts.
Why need we obey the commands
of kings who ride on elephants?
We are free from bonds.

4. Śaiva devotees are our only kin,
we wear nothing but the waistband and the loincloth.
Even our enemies cannot harm us;
all evil is turned into good for us,
and we will never be born again.
Our tongues chant "Hail Śiva!"
good name of the Lord
with the sweet, golden *ko<u>n</u>rai* wreath.
We are devotees of the Lord
whose blazing forehead eye
reduced crocodile-bannered Kāma to ashes.[5]

This hymn explores the nature of the servant or slave (toṇṭar) status of the bhaktas, an important image that pervades the poetry of the mūvar. Foremost, the hymn claims that the bhaktas belong forever to Śiva; this is the defining factor in each individual's status as a toṇṭar, as well as the unifying force that defines them as a group. The status of the toṇṭar has social, political, and religious meanings and implications. The defiant tone of the hymn suggests that being a toṇṭar is chosen, not an endowed status. It is a voluntary association, and the tone of the hymn and its language of "we" and "kin" encourage its hearer to participate in the toṇṭar group.[6] The seriousness of the committment to Śiva is emblazoned on the bodies of the toṇṭar through sacred ash, which provides the only ornament to their minimalist clothing. Their actions are disciplined, conducive to sustaining a life dedicated to Śiva. They rise before dawn, eschew the company of women in favor of "Goddess Earth's loving embrace," and chant the Lord's name. These visible gestures are symbols of their emotional response to the Lord, expressed as "the melting of our stony hearts."

Acceptance by the Lord is assured: He has "taken us." Both iconographic and purāṇic images of the Lord convey the power and certainty of salvation. As the king, Śiva wears an emblem of religious and social aristocracy, the earring; his feet, adorned with fresh flowers, convey the image of him as the Lord of salvation; in contrast to kings who ride elephants, Śiva is Lord of the warlike bull (Nandi); and, finally, he is the powerful vanquisher of desire, kāma. These images of Śiva are appropriate to the tone of the poem, which portrays the bhaktas as conquerors of all human problems, through their love of Śiva. As a result of his acceptance of them, they are joyful in the world, freed from sorrow.

The toṇṭars' commitment to Śiva marginalizes all other relationships that may compete with it, especially all social relationships of exchange and obligation. In the hymn, the figure of an earthly king provides a contrast, in the sense of both one who demands allegiance and one who embodies worldly aspirations, signified by "men who parade themselves in silk and gold." Both aspects, embodied not only in the king but also by implication in anyone who is understood to have interests that compete with service to the Lord, are rejected by the toṇṭar. The later biography of Appar in the *Periya Purāṇam* invests this hymn primarily with political meaning and understands it to be the saint's defiant reply (maṟumāṟṟam) to a Pallava king in Kanchipuram who was persuaded by the Jains to punish Appar for his rejection of them. In the hymn, the defiant tone is grounded in the bhaktas' commitment to Śiva, each other, and the certainty of salvation.

The hymnists were defining a Śiva-bhakti community within a pluralistic religious context. At stake was how they would define their community in relationship to others, primarily Hindus, Buddhists, and Jains, and their hymns invite comparison with these groups. Although it is clear from the sources and content of their hymns that the mūvar viewed themselves as Hindus, on closer examination a paradox emerges. Within a frame of appealing to Hindu tradition, the hymnists defied the structure of relations among classical categories within Hinduism, yet they criticized the heterodox communities for defying established boundaries.

The portrait of the bhaktas in Appar's hymn evokes the image of the sannyāsin from classical Hinduism, through its emphasis on constant meditation on God, the disciplined lifestyle, and the sense of detachment from worldly concerns. The sannyāsin, or world renouncer, is the culmination of the fourfold stages of human life, known as the *varṇāśramadharma*. It is preceded by the student stage (brahmacāri), the householder stage (gṛhastha), and the forest-dweller stage (vānaprastha). Later traditions of Śiva-bhakti tend to liken the mūvar to these stages: Campantar was a child, Cuntarar was a married man, and Appar was an older unmarried man. Appar's vision in the hymn, then, became a way of characterizing him as a bhakta. However, in the hymn it is clear that Appar thought the image applicable beyond himself; indeed, many of the themes in the hymn are representative of dominant themes in the poetry of all three Tamil Śiva-bhakti composers.

The hymn focuses on an image of bhaktas that appears to be similar to the sannyāsin. The other categories of people mentioned in the verse are householder (although the poem does not call this type gṛhastha) and king. Veena Das has explored the relationships among these traditional categories of Hindu society, including householder, king, sannyāsin, and brahman, in her influential study of the *Dharmāraṇya Purāṇa* (a caste purāṇa) and the *Gṛhya Sūtras*. She states that these categories constitute a "grammar of structural relations" and that the "nature of relations between the four categories . . . [is] essential in defining the structural order in Hinduism."[7] What is at issue, then, is the extent to which Appar's image of the bhaktas overlaps with an established structure of relations in Hinduism.

A critical part of Das's analysis is her assertion that the brahman is a category that mediates between the physical and social realms. In the purāṇa, this is achieved by the creation of a tīrtha: "Thus the creation of the Brahmans transforms a mere physical space into a tirtha, which is a category of social space."[8] At a very basic level, then, the category of brahman is associated with the creation of culture. Within the social order, the brahman is the arbitrator of proper relationships, standing between sannyāsin and householder and between king and gods; this latter involves a relation of exchange between king and brahman. For Das, then, householder and sannyāsin are opposing categories, two ends of one of the spectra within which brahmans are defined. Das interprets these categories as the opposition between social (householder) and asocial (sannyāsin), respectively. Of critical importance is her suggestion that asocial does not mean "not socially constituted"; rather, "it is meant that the sannyasi is above the structural distinctions operative in society."[9] The sannyāsin stands outside the structure of exchange that defines all of the other categories and embodies the most spiritual power, which is acquired through his own agency; in contrast, the householder is dependent on all, having neither the temporal power of a king nor the inherent spiritual power of a brahman.

Das's discussion of the traditional, structural definitions of the brahman, householder, king, and sannyāsin lends support to the suggestion that Appar's vision of the bhaktas implies a comparison between the category of bhakta (or toṇṭar) and that of sannyāsin. She extrapolates a list of the sannyāsin's characteristics from relationships described in the *Dharmāraṇya Purāṇa*; by extension, this list is applicable to images of sannyāsa in the wider purāṇic corpus.[10] Some of these characteristics are:

1. Sannyāsa is a voluntary category, meaning that its spiritual power is acquired and not inherent (as with brahmans).
2. Sannyāsa is an asocial category, in the sense the sannyāsin is above the structural distinctions operative within society.
3. The category of householder status is in a relation of opposition to the category of sannyāsa.
4. The power of the sannyāsin is constituted by a boon from God, whom the sannyāsin often forces to come into relationship by his austerity.
5. The power of the sannyāsin is expiatory (in the purāṇa, the lake at Dharmāraṇya—a tīrtha—is given expiatory powers by the sannyāsin and purificatory powers by Śiva).

The first two characteristics resonate with the image of the toṇṭar in Appar's hymn. Like the self-made sannyāsin, the spiritual power of the toṇṭar is acquired, and not inherent. Appar describes a number of methods by which the toṇṭar acquire and maintain their spirituality, including meditating on the Lord through chanting his name, emotionally responding to the Lord, rejecting ownership of material goods (a shelter, fine clothing) in favor of being owned by Śiva, practicing sexual chastity, and rising before dawn to bathe and chant the Lord's name. These activities are voluntarily undertaken by a community of bhaktas, and, indeed, the hearer of the hymn is encouraged to join them. The community's relationship with Śiva marginalizes all other relationships, which is why the most intimate term, *kin*, is used to characterize the connection among bhaktas. Kin is usually restricted to biological ties in common usage, which connotes caste in the Indian context. Appar's use of *kin* rejects such criteria—though not its associations of fundamental similarity among the group members—and thereby supports the principle that one acquires spiritual power and does not inherit it.

In acquiring such power, the bhaktas do not rely on obligatory relations of exchange, as do kings and householders, but rather on their own disciplined actions that focus on the Lord. The bhaktas pilgrimage through towns, sleep in public spaces, and consider the "wide world" as their home. They possess no personal wealth and have only simple cloth as clothing and sacred ash as ornament. The food that nourishes their bodies comes from others, namely, the householders in each town that they visit. The gift of food does not appear to engage the bhaktas in an exchange obligation with the householders (unlike the brahmans, who traditionally performed services in exchange for food); rather, the food is given by "generous" householders. Rather than receiving self-sustaining material and symbolic gifts from sources of power—that is, brahmans and kings—the bhaktas maintain direct and daily relations with householders of the Tamil lands. The food they receive is not a permanent gift recorded on stone for the adherence of many generations but a daily act of generosity. The toṇṭar are thus above the structural obligations operative within society and their implications, especially those relating to karma.

However, the toṇṭar are not necessarily asocial, as is the sannyāsin in Das's analysis. In Appar's hymn, they appear to have very much a social presence, in contradistinction to the classical sannyāsin. The bhaktas take the wide world as their home; their travels span a diversity of places, including urban and rural, developed and natural, as is characteristic of pilgrimage. Yet, their overwhelming focus is on the social world, demonstrated in the hymn by their contact with householders and their taking refuge in public halls and more generally demonstrated in the structure of the mūvar's hymns, including their consistent reference to named Tamil towns, their capacity to engage an audience through communion, and their medium of the Tamil language. The toṇṭar have a religious community identity that has a social presence, more like the brahman than like the sannyāsin.

Das also explores the asocial nature of the sannyāsin in the sense of "ultramundane." This designation raises the issue of the sannyāsin's relationship with God. As described in her list, this relationship involves three types of power: the power of the sannyāsin in terms of austerities (tapas); the ultramundane power of God, which becomes challenged by the increasing power (usually described as heat) of the sannyāsin in tapas; and the ultramundane power that God bestows on the sannyāsin, in recognition of the latter's achievements in the performance of austerities. As Das notes, the purāṇas tell many stories of a sannyāsin forcing God to grant him a boon. In Appar's poem, ultramundane power is implied by the bhaktas' freedom from mundane problems, including disease, death, birth, and desire, which is understood as signifying the release from karma, both by the poets' own activities and those of God. Thus, the disciplined simplicity of a life spent in the worship of Śiva results in the release from religiously defined problems of embodiment. In its configuration, the relationship between bhakta and God in Appar's poem is markedly different from the classic purāṇic image of the sannyāsin. Śiva-bhakti does not revolve around performing penance to receive a boon. The goal of attaining Śiva in the bhakti sense of being proximate to him is not a definable, temporally isolated event but rather an ongoing, daily aspiration. Appar describes austerities, or things that are given up, but he does so in the assertion that the bhaktas have attained the feet of Śiva; there is no sense of accumulation of power or that they are striving to be anything other than what they already are in that they "have reached his beautiful, flower-fresh feet."[11]

The attainment of Śiva is not viewed as static in bhakti poetry; the hymns describe the dynamic of estrangement from and attainment of Śiva as an oscillation, both intellectually and emotionally. For example, the chastisement of Śiva is a feature in the mūvar's hymns, to a greater or lesser extent, depending upon the poet. Cuntarar, in particular, is known for challenging Śiva through harsh words, just as the sannyāsin challenges God through deeds. However, the bhaktas' admonishment of Śiva is predicated on their intimacy with him, as opposed to the image of two disputing powers, as in the case of the sannyāsin figure. In the intimacy of bhakti, the weaknesses of the bhaktas as well as their strengths are appropriate responses to Śiva, for both types of response are grounded in purity of heart. In contrast to the sannyāsin, the bhaktas' motives are pure. Similarly, the bhaktas' actions are pure in contrast to brahmans', especially in their resistance to exchange relationships.

The power struggle between ascetic and God in the sannyāsin model continues even in the contest's resolution, as the sannyāsin gains enough power to challenge God. According to Das's model, the ascetic gains expiatory powers, while God retains purificatory powers. In later interpretations, the mūvar and their poems are understood to have expiatory powers, but Appar's hymn emphasizes the bhaktas' purity of deed and motive and the expiatory powers of Śiva. The bhaktas are free from karma and its effects, yet they are actively engaged as servants to Śiva. As toṇṭars, the bhaktas work for Śiva; in Appar's hymn and the mūvar's hymns more generally, the primary example of their work is to remind Tamils of Śiva through hymns, although the later biographies develop this theme in many ways. More than a simple expression of servitude, this work symbolizes the participation of the bhaktas in Śiva. As toṇṭar, they partake of his nature, which is another root meaning of *bhakti*. In contrast to the sannyāsin, who takes God's power, the bhaktas share God's nature, as another hymn from Appar makes clear.

> The Lord of Kaṉṟāppūr
> is seen in a post
> and in the hearts of His servants,
> who worship not only Him
> but also whomever they should see
> who bears the sacred ash on the forehead
> and other Śaiva marks.
> When the servants see such persons
> they are glad, thinking them also servants,
> and joyfully look upon them.
> They say, "This one is a deva, that one is a deva,"
> without separating the two.
> They honor them as having the nature of the Lord,
> without distinguishing the two.
>
> Appar 10.12/6.61.3

Appar's vision of the nature of bhakti and the toṇṭars draws on established images of religious people, including the social presence of the brahman and the discipline of sannyāsin. To some observers, this may represent the brahmanization of bhakti, especially in that Appar is identified as a nonbrahman Vēḷāḷa in the *Periya Purāṇam.* In the theory of brahmanization, Appar would be viewed as attempting to elevate bhakti through his use of Sanskrit images and terms in his poetry and also his appeal to brahman ways. However, such a perspective obscures the poet's vision that bhakti encompasses other traditions within Hinduism by providing a frame for understanding them through bhakti. When Cuntarar's *Tiruttoṇṭattokai* begins with praise for the brahmans at Tillai (Chidambaram), one is invited to view them first and foremost as bhaktas, performing service to Śiva and partaking of his nature. For the poets, bhakti was not an alternative way of being religious but one that encompassed on its own terms the classical structural distinctions that defined Hindu culture.

As the key to defining a good Hindu, bhakti could not encompass everything the poets encountered in their travels across the Tamil lands. As many scholars have noted, the bhakti hymns engage in a vitriolic polemic against Buddhists and Jains. These polemical statements appear variously in the hymns: They are a frequent feature of Campantar's poetry, in which they regularly constitute the last verse in a set of ten or eleven verses; Appar denounces them in closing verses and, on occasion, devotes an entire set of verses to their censure, as I discuss later; and the polemic appears in Cuntarar's work as well, though much less frequently. The poets use harsh language and cruel imagery in seeking to exclude definitively the Buddhist and Jain communities from their vision of bhakti. An obvious reason for the polemic is that these religions do not focus on God, therefore preventing the possibility that they would praise Śiva. Indeed, both Appar and Cuntarar portray Cākkiyaṉ, the nāyaṉār who was formerly a Buddhist, as one who threw stones at Śiva.[12] Yet, as the examples of Cākkiyaṉ, a former Buddhist, and Appar, a former Jain, demonstrate, individuals from these traditions could become bhaktas.[13] Indeed, in an amusing twist, Cākkiyaṉ is said in later tradition to have continued to wear his Buddhist robe and to throw stones at Śiva *as an expression of bhakti*; Appar, however, bitterly resented his time spent with the Jains.

The criticism of Buddhists and Jains is, then, not on the level of individuals but on the community level. Like the Buddhists and Jains, the bhaktas were creating a voluntary association in which the primary identity of its members was their religious worldview instead of their caste. Appar emphasized the sameness of the bhaktas through the shared essence of kinship and partaking of Śiva's nature. The mūvar crossed over boundaries within Hinduism in their effort to identify the bhaktas of Śiva as the best Hindus. The image of shared essence also had an ethnic dimension: Since Śiva is the Lord of the Tamil lands and language, the bhaktas share their Tamilness with each other and with Śiva. The issue of defining a good Hindu informed the poets' negotiation of received tradition. As the poets sought to distinguish their voluntary association from others around them, the issue of defining a good Tamil assumed greater prominence as a way of creating a boundary that would distinguish the bhaktas from Buddhists (Cākkiya in the poems) and Jains (Camaṇ).

As we have seen, orientalists tended to view bhakti as reform—sometimes grudgingly, for many of them preferred to locate true reform in Buddhism or in the verses of Kabīr. In contrast, scholarship today, particularly that which concerns south India's history and religion, is more likely to characterize bhakti as revival rather than reform. The image is of a wilted Hinduism in the powerful presence of Buddhism and Jainism.[14] Hinduism thus needed to be, and was, revived by bhakti (just as Bhakti herself needed to be revived in the *Bhāgavata Māhātmya*). The revival of Hinduism provided by bhakti then turned the tables on Buddhism and Jainism, and they became dry and decayed religions. Note the parallelism here:

1. Sanskrit Hindu traditions were dry and/or cold because they were too formalistic.
2. Sanskrit Hindu traditions were dry and/or cold because of increasing numbers of Buddhists and Jains.
3. Bhakti revived the dry and/or cold Hinduism with a flood of emotion.
4. The popularity of bhakti dried up support for Buddhism and Jainism.

In an interesting twist to this image of revival, Kamil Zvelebil asserts that Buddhism and Jainism were the "cold" religions: "So, in comparison with the decayed, deteriorated Southern Buddhism and Jainism we see in the Tamil Hindu revival the triumph of emotion over intellect, of the concrete over the abstract, of the acceptance of life over its ascetic denial, of something near and homely against something alien and distant, and, above all, the acceptance of positive love against cold morality or intellectually coloured compassion."[15]

Part of the emphasis—explicit or not—in the determination that Hinduism, Buddhism, and Jainism were "dry" religions is on language. The canonical works of these three religions were written in Sanskrit or in the related languages of Prākrit and Pāli. There is evidence to suggest, however, that Buddhists and Jains were very active in writing literature in Tamil that was informed by religious concerns. The Jains translated Sanskrit texts into Tamil and also wrote original compositions such as the *Tirukkuṟaḷ* and the *Cilappatikāram* epic, both of which scholars cautiously attribute to them. The Buddhists wrote a sequel to the *Cilappatikāram*, the *Maṇimēkalai*, and other texts in Tamil, most of which are not extant.[16] Buddhists and Jains were thus actively contributing to Tamil culture. Moreover, there is evidence to suggest not only that these groups were vital in the Tamil lands well into the Pallava dynastic period, when the mūvar composed their hymns, but also that they were patronized by the Pallavas and, at least in the case of the Jains, had developed a style of worship that drew upon Hindu practices.

Jains had been present in south India for perhaps as long as six hundred years before Appar's time. There are two main sects within Jainism: Those who settled in south India are called the Digambara (sky-clad) sect, and those associated with north India are the Śvetambara (white [cloth]-clad) sect. The split between the two groups of Jains may have been created by the southward migration of some Jains to the Deccan-Karnataka region in the centuries just before the millennium; texts of the Digambaras claim that Chandragupta Maurya was a Jain and accompanied the great saint Bhadrabāhu in a southward migration (for example, the *Tiloyo-Paṇṇatti*, ca A.D. 600, and the *Bṛhatkathākośa*, ca A.D. 931).[17] From the references to the nudity of the Jains in the mūvars' hymns, including one from Appar I discuss later, the Digambaras are indeed targeted by them.

In Tamilnadu, the first Jain monuments—which are most likely the first lithic structures in the region—were caves probably used for monasticism.[18] These were cave dwellings created in the Eastern Ghats, with concentrations in the Madurai and Tiruchirapalli regions. The caves were prepared by uncomplicated but highly significant modifications of the natural stone hills, including the cutting of a ledge to carry rainwater away from the sheltered portion of the cave and the cutting of beds, followed by chiseling to make them smooth. Holes were made in the rock, probably to hold palm frond awnings in front of the cave openings. These cave constructions also contained the earliest inscriptions in Brāhmī and in Tamil, engraved into the beds or on the overhanging rock above the rain ledges. They list the names of the occupants or donors and include such descriptive terms as *pāḷi*, *paḷḷi*, *atiṭṭāṉam* (seat or bed), *kañcaṇam* (bed), *kūra* (roof), *piṇa-ū* (fronds), and *mūśagai* (covering).[19]

Later, around the seventh century, Jains in south India began to change this system and give greater priority to visual images, resulting in a great production of Jain images.[20] In the seventh to ninth centuries, the monastic caves were embellished with carved Jain sculptures on the surface of the rock near the cavern, accompanied by inscriptions in Vaṭṭeluttu that give the names of famous Jain teachers and sometimes the names of the donors.[21] The sculptures represent Mahāvīra, other Tīrthaṅkaras such as Pārśva, various Yakṣīs including Ambikā and Ajitā, and the names of teachers such as Ajjaṇandi.

Roughly contemporaneous with these developments was the excavation of cave temples of a simple maṇḍapam type, with a central rectangular maṇḍapam (hall), pillars, and a square shrine behind projecting somewhat into the maṇḍapam. The cave temple at Sittannavasal (near Pudukkottai in the Tiruchirapalli district), dated to the late seventh or early eighth centuries, is an example. Called Arivar-kovil of Aṇṇalvāyil (temple of the arhat at Annavāśal) in an inscription, the temple boasts sculptures of ācāryas and Tīrthaṅkaras accompanied by explanatory inscriptions. Jain structural stone temples were also built during this period, such as the Jain temple complex at Tirupparuttikkuṉṟam, near Kāñcīpuram and better known as Jina-Kāñcī. The Candraprabha temple, dated on stylistic grounds to the reign of Narasimhavarman II Rājasimha (ascended 691), features sculptures of Tīrthaṅkaras in minature shrines on its top story, plus a śikhara (tower) that has Tīrthaṅkara figures on its four faces.[22]

The sculptures in various places of worship, plus the inscriptional evidence, suggest that in later Pallava times image worship became a common practice in south Indian Digambara Jainism. This impression of change from the stone monuments is supported by textual descriptions of transformations in religious practice. Early texts in the Jain canon describe a fourteen-stage path of purification (guṇasthāna, or stages of essence) from bondage (various forms of karma) to liberation.[23] The fourth stage, samyak-darśana (having the correct view) represents the first achievement that allows one to call oneself a Jain. Described as an awakening or insight, samyak-darśana is a redirection of the soul's energies (vīrya) away from delusions (darśana-mohanīya), passions (anantānubandhī-kaṣāya), and karma toward liberation (mokṣa or bhavyatva).[24] This is a profound internal transformation that results in the state of perceiving the self within (antarātman). Some texts suggest that external events, such as encountering a Jina or his image, hearing Jain teachings, or recalling past lives may function as catalysts for this awakening.[25]

The central system in the Jain canonical texts is meditational and concerned with internal transformations: Darśana was understood as a mental process, although it could be aided by the sight of a Jina or his image. Later, Jain ācāryas began to write texts that located the worship of images in a frame of meditational practices, thus developing the idea of seeing a Jina as conducive to spiritual awakening. In particular, texts of the Jain ācāryas Jinasena (ca 840) and Somadeva (tenth century) sought to clarify the relationship between the image worship and meditation, in part by developing a new list of six obligational duties for laypeople:

1. Devapūjā, worship of the Tīrthaṅkaras
2. Guru-upāsti, venerating and listening to the teachers
3. Svādhyāya, study (of the scriptures)
4. Samyama, restraint (including observance of the mūlaguṇas, the anuvratas, the guṇavratas, and the first śiksāvrata, sāmāyika)
5. Tapas, austerities (especially fasting on holy days, as in the second śiksāvrata)
6. Dāna, charity (giving alms to mendicants).[26]

Here, devapūjā is a category unto itself, represented as a legitimate way of worship by an authoritative list. It is as much a part of a Jain layperson's path as meditation. Importantly, devapūjā also became legitimized through the creation of a new category of Jain specialist to perform the pūjā. In his *Ādipurāṇa*, Jinasena calls these figures *deva-brāhmana*, often translated as "Jain brahmans."[27] The text locates the "brahmans" as part of the creation of the social world by Bharata, son of the primordial king Ṛṣabha (who is called prajāpati and ādi deva). Specifically, they are laypeople whom Bharata promoted because, according to him, they were committed to the principle of ahimsā (nonviolence). As "brahmans," they became negotiators of lay and ascetic statuses, who practiced some of the lay stages of renunciation (pratimās), were called twice-borns, and were invested with sacred thread at each stage undertaken.

In offering explanations for these developments in Jainism, P. S. Jaini emphasizes the Jain need to adopt a course of social acceptability, given the circumstance of their regular social proximity to the Hindu majority.[28] He suggests that this conformity was achieved by the Jain appropriation—or Jainization—of traditional Hindu rites and customs. These developments hardly present a picture of the Jains as a dying group that was effectively eclipsed by the mūvar's bhakti. In contrast to the distance that scholars presuppose existed between Hindus and Jains in this period, the two were actually becoming more similar in ritual practice and cultic life. The Jains were able to reconstitute themselves in a changing cultural environment and subsequently garnered patronage for their temples (called paḷḷi), recorded in the inscriptions of Nandivarman Pallavamalla (ca 745 and later).[29] In south India, the incorporation of image worship into the Jain system was a response to changing imperial claims to power and to the role of religion in constituting that power, which I discuss in the next chapter.

It is in this context of similarity that the hymnists sought to denounce the Jains. One of Appar's poems illustrates the nature of the polemic:

1. The Jains, who expose their skulls,
Conceal Śiva with their minds.
But is it possible to conceal him?
Meditate on the feet
Of the One who resides at Pa̲laiyā̲rai vaṭataḷi
    enclosed by groves and ocean waves
And gain release.

2. The god who uprooted
    the group that bears waterpots
    and recites mantras through their noses
Reveals the temple at beautiful vaṭataḷi
As his own;
No dread diseases will afflict those who
Gaze fondly upon this temple.

3. The hands of your humble servant
    who worshiped the One at Pa̲laiyā̲rai vaṭataḷi
Are saved.
He is the cosmos, the blue-necked One
    who destroyed the arrogant and fat Jains,
    lacking in both virtue and clothing.

4. How cool is my mind,
Meditating
Upon the master of Pa̲laiyā̲rai vaṭataḷi who,
    bearing as weapons fire and a white axe,
    drove away the stinking, debased Jains,
    who pluck their heads bald.

5. Sorrows will wither
When we praise the benefactor of Pa̲laiyā̲rai vaṭataḷi
    where the ground is flooded
    with sweet sugarcane juice
    and turned to mud;
He destroyed the Jains
    who rob propriety
    by eating while undressed
    before young women who have red lines of beauty
    in the corners of their eyes.

6. Afflictions will cease instantly
For those who pray to the
Source and Light of life itself at Pa̲laiyā̲rai vaṭataḷi;
He destroyed the Jains
    who ruin the order of life when they eat thus.

7. The fire of karma is extinguished
When we worship the One who illuminates

pleasing Pa<u>l</u>aiyā<u>r</u>ai vaṭataḷi
which is full of grace
Cleaving from there the deceptive Jains
who cram riceballs into their mouths.

8. All karma will perish
When we worship the One who endures at Pa<u>l</u>aiyā<u>r</u>ai vaṭataḷi;
His foot kicked cruel Yama
And caused such trouble for the Jains
who are ignorant of the five holy syllables
recited by the kin [bhaktas].

9. All karma will fall away
When we say:
"He who favors Pa<u>l</u>aiyā<u>r</u>ai vaṭataḷi
where the river flows
Destroyed one thousand Jains
who remained unenlightened
despite their study
of Tamil, the truth itself."

10. When we pray to the One
who restored Pa<u>l</u>aiyā<u>r</u>ai vaṭataḷi
who is form and meaning
who broke the neck and body of Rāvaṇa,
infamous in heaven as a war-monger
with the slightest pressure from His little toe

All our karma is erased.

Appar 5.58.1–10 Tiruppa<u>l</u>aiyā<u>r</u>ai vaṭataḷi

Appar begins his attack with an apparent reference to a physical symbol of the Jain monks' discipline—the bald head, which has been ritually shaved or plucked—which can be taken as an ironic reference to the nature of the poem itself as an exposé of the Jains. The chain of associations in this polemical rhetoric begins with the opposition between the Jains' exposure of their skulls and their concealment of Śiva. This motif appears in two of the verses (1 and 4), which contrast the Jains' concealment of Śiva with the Lord's revealing himself to drive them away from Pa<u>l</u>aiyā<u>r</u>ai vaṭataḷi. According to Appar's hymn, the Jain approach to spiritual life is strictly literal; their bare skulls do not symbolize a renunciation of attachments and thus an escape from karma but, instead, delusion in their minds. In contrast, the bhaktas of Śiva adopt the right internal state of meditation on Śiva's feet and immediately gain release from karma.

In Appar's poem, the nudity of the Jains is not only an illustration of incorrect practice and attitude but also an offense to morality. Appar condemns the Jains' exposure of their bodies as a signifier of their lack of virtue and their destruction of the Tamil moral order (vv. 3, 5, 6). In particular, the poet is outraged by the image of naked Jains, standing and eating before young women, from whom they have presumably just received food. Whereas the bhaktas in Appar's poetry are represented as moral people who are fed by generous householders, here he implies that the Jains abuse the householders' kindness. To underscore the point, he represents the Jains as greedily cramming riceballs into their mouths, instead of eating in a detached and disciplined manner. At stake is the moral fiber of Tamil society.

Indeed, through his remarks on language, Appar implies that Jains are not Tamils at all and thus can hardly be understood as representatives of Tamil morality (vv. 2, 8). He criticizes them for reciting mantras through their noses and suggests that the mantras are incomprehensible, either because they do not understand what they are reciting or because they lack the articulation necessary for language, like the ancient Greek definition of a *barbarian* as one who makes the confused sounds of ba-ba-ba. The passage may also be referring to the Jains' use of Prākrit in some of their religious works. In particular, the Jains are ignorant of the pañcākṣara mantra, which is recited by the kin of bhaktas in keeping with good Hindu tradition. The efficacy of the five-syllabled mantra is contrasted with the indistinct mumblings of the Jains when they recite their mantras.

Appar acknowledges that the Jains know Tamil (v. 9); yet he creates a distance between them by indicating that the Jains have studied (paṭittu) Tamil; thus, their knowledge of Tamil is contrived, in contrast to the bhaktas, for whom Tamil is a mother tongue. Moreover, in spite of their study, they remain unenlightened, for Tamil is the truth itself and appropriately sacred for the praise of Śiva; the Jains are ignorant of the truth of Śiva as the truth of language. For Appar, knowledge of Tamil should lead to love for Śiva, for the truth of Śiva is contained in the poet's Tamil verses. Even if the Jains speak Tamil, they do not speak the language of the poet; from the poet's tongue, Tamil is sacred, whereas it is debased when spoken by the Jains. And if the Jains are outside the poet's mother tongue, they are outside his culture and thus outside the pale of goodness and virtue.

These very human indictments are intensified by Appar's assertion that Śiva himself destroyed the Jains. They were uprooted, destroyed, and driven away in great number, given as one thousand according to verse nine. These images of the Jains' destruction can be taken in two senses: first, that the truth of Śiva destroys the premises of Jain knowledge and practice; second, that Śiva's destruction of the Jains is one of his heroic acts on the local, as opposed to the cosmic, level. Indeed, the images of Śiva in these passages underscore the violence of the act: He is the One who swallowed poison, who kicked Yama, and who broke the neck of evil Rāvaṇa. The Jains are defeated by the presence and power of Śiva; in contrast, the bhaktas benefit from proximity to him. By destroying the Jains, Śiva took Pa̲laiyā̲rai vaṭataḷi as his own and "restored" it for the bhaktas.

The mūvar's insistance that Tamil country was the home of Śiva carried with it several implications. They encouraged Tamils to participate in the worship of Śiva and to partake of his essence. The regional identity of Tamilness, as celebrated in their poetry, was a manifestation of bhakti's thesis on embodiment. For the hymnists, being a good bhakta included being a good Tamil citizen; appreciation of Śiva meant appreciation of things Tamil. Thus, the details of Tamil land and culture were harmonized with both the cosmic Śiva and his powers of freedom and the local presence of the Lord. Bhaktas enjoyed a special relationship with Śiva, demonstrated by Appar's appeal to the sannyāsin ideal in the context of a community defined by voluntary association and the language of kinship. Kinship reinforces a natural sense of obligation within the community, as all participants are bound to a shared ethic of honor to Śiva and a reciprocity to one another. In the mūvar's vision, the bhaktas are a moral community that pervades the Tamil lands.

Given this image of the community, it is difficult to escape the impression that the hymnists viewed Jains (and Buddhists) as foreigners in their midst. The mūvar represented themselves as proponents of the best of Tamil and Hindu tradition. In contrast, in Appar's representation the Jains are ignorant of both Tamil (they remain unenlightened despite study of Tamil) and Hindu (they do not know the five-syllabled mantra) traditions. The hymnists drew a clear distinction between their sense of moral order and that of the heterodox religions of Buddhism and Jainism. According to the mūvar, members of these religions were not, nor were they ever able to become, participants in good Tamil society; in fact, their presence was actually detrimental to Tamil morality.

The language of Appar's hymn and others that denounce the Jains and Buddhists is a vitriolic polemic composed of cruel and violent images. In Appar's hymn, the indictment of the Jains culminates in Śiva's destruction of them, which allows a restoration of Pa<u>l</u>aiyā<u>r</u>ai vaṭataḷi for the bhaktas. Rather than conveying a sense of revivalism, this virulent creation of "otherness" in one's midst bears much similarity to the fighting mentality that Martin Marty and Scott Appleby have identified as distinctive to fundamentalism.[30] Fundamentalism is mainly discussed as a contemporary phenomenon; for example, studies of fundamentalism in India have focused on events centered around Ayodhya in the last ten years. Hindu fundamentalism has generally been understood as an urban, political revival of Hinduism in the service of nationalism. In keeping with the inherited image of bhakti as a warm Hindu revival in contrast to the cold religions of Brahmanism, Buddhism, and Jainism, there are attempts in recent scholarship to distinguish bhakti from fundamentalism. For example, Daniel Gold contrasts "devotional movements" with fundamentalism in contemporary India:

> Fundamentalism is not the only new religious phenomenon that has emerged in Indian cities. Gurus, yogic centers, and devotional movements also flourish—all, moreover, appearing as adaptations of Hindu tradition to an urban environment. . . . The new phenomena offer alternative ways of being religious that are more practicable in an urban environment. Devotional movements give intense, temporary experiences in which caste distinctions can lose significance. Gurus and yogic centers present the same type of unorthodox inward religion in Indian cities as they do in Western ones. As religious traditions, Hindu fundamentalisms offer another alternative, one demanding no devotional enthusiasm or yogic inwardness. Hindu fundamentalisms appeal instead to what may be urban Hindus' lowest common denominator: a Hindu identity. If personal religion entails among other things the identification of the individual with some larger whole, then the Hindu Nation may appear as a whole more immediately visible and attainable than the ritual cosmos of traditional Hinduism. For some urban Hindus, fundamentalist groups may offer the most viable personal religion available.[31]

I agree with Gold that there should be a distinction between phenomena that define themselves through a religious goal (Gold's language is "inwardness") and those that define themselves as having primarily another goal, which in the case of contemporary Hindu fundamentalism in north India may be defined as cultural purity and political power. Yet, contemporary fundamentalism does seem to draw on bhakti themes, including pilgrimage, identity, participation, and the hostile creation of an "other."

It is difficult to separate the spiritual and material aspects of the mūvar's hymns; by linking Śiva-bhakti to liberation and to the Tamil lands and Tamil identity, they combine the two approaches in an encompassing message that Śiva-bhakti is both constituted by, and representative of, Tamils. It is clear from Appar's hymn that he viewed the Jains to be encroaching on resources—exactly what resources are left unstated, but the *Periya Purāṇam* later interprets the resources as a temple—that more properly belong to the Śiva-bhaktas. If the context of the hymns was a competition for recognition by ruling kings, the mūvar developed an ingenious argument by connecting Śiva-bhakti to Tamil identity. By presenting Śiva-bhakti as a representation of Tamilness, the need to articulate a solicitation for patronage from kings (besides Śiva), who were engaged in promoting themselves as representatives of the region, was mitigated; indeed, this sort of appeal is eschewed in the mūvar's hymns. Ultimately, the mūvar's glorification of things Tamil did have an impact on the patronage of kings: The Pallava dynasty incorporated it; the Chola dynasty built an empire on it.

PART III

Contours in Song, Sculpture, and Story

The history of Tamil Śiva-bhakti is interwoven with the development of imperial stone temples. In the medieval period, the imperial temple became a center of culture, it legitimized and actualized the dynamics of kingship, it represented the evolution of Hinduism, and it served as an economic nucleus for imperial donations, taxes, and trade. Given the importance and magnitude of these developments, it was not assured that the emerging religious perspective of Śiva-bhakti would have a role in them. Although the nāyaṉmār had represented the religious path of Śiva-bhakti as regional, though not provincial, there was a question whether their poetic vision, grounded in the personal, would have public meaning in a religious institution, and, if this were the case, how it would relate to the centralizing forces of the imperial temple culture.

The medieval imperial temple embodied the coalescence of sacred power, political authority, and material wealth. With few exceptions, the hymns of the mūvar represented a worldview mistrustful of such connections. In addition, the poets were agreed that Śiva himself constituted the center, yet they had resisted localizing him in any one type of religious place, such as a temple. Temples were mentioned in the nāyaṉmār's hymns, probably indicating very early temples in brick or nondurable materials, but they did not represent the preeminent locus of bhakti. Instead, there were many other geographical places mentioned more frequently as homes of Śiva in the nāyaṉmār's hymns—all of them united by their nature as Tamil places. Indeed, the poets believed that the most profound locus of Śiva was also the most ephemeral: the human heart.

In a seeming irony, the regionalism of the mūvar's hymns was a key to their acceptance within these grand developments. The rhetoric of the kings who built and patronized these temples was matched by the magnitude and permanence of their granite creations, as they claimed universal overlordship in their inscriptions on the walls. And yet, a king was ultimately defined by the land he possessed, which provided the regional foundation for nearly cosmic claims of power. In addition, a temple would have to be built either within an existing local community, or it would have to create one, thereby creating a condition in which local concerns could be expressed. In chapter 5, I discuss the specific nature of changes in the construction of imperial power that precipitated the evolution of Hinduism from the classical traditions of Vedism and Buddhism. As this emerging imperial temple culture developed in the sixth to eighth centuries, a space was created for regional voices to participate in both the significance and the authority of the temple. In this context, the hymns of the mūvar began to be sung in the temples as part of an emerging liturgical formulation.

When Tamil Śiva-bhakti became part of imperial temple culture, it entered into a context of competing religious visions. If Tamil Śiva-bhakti sought to "englobe" other traditions, such as Vedic prayers and āgamic philosophy, the imperially constituted Hindu temples sought to "englobe" all the known traditions in a centralized, demonstrative arena. In this process, some religious traditions were given priority in a hierarchy that was designed both to manifest and to testify to a king's access to, and embodiment of, divine power. In chapter 6, I analyze further developments in imperial temple culture during the ninth and tenth centuries to understand the embodiment of Śiva-bhakti during this period. The liturgical performance of the hymns was continued through a group of professional temple singers, who evoked the performances of the mūvar themselves. In turn, the evocation of their image through song provided a connection to the possibility of creating their image through the arts. Attention turned toward the lives of the mūvar, as well as the other sixty bhaktas mentioned in Cuntarar's *Tiruttoṇṭattokai*. Allusions to the stories of bhaktas from the hymns of the mūvar provided sources for the imaginative elaboration of personalities for these bhaktas, transforming them into religious exemplars or saints (nāyaṉmār). Paintings and sculptures that represented the essence of a bhakta's story or personality were made and housed in the imperial temples, for it was through their life stories as much as through their hymns that people could relate to them as models of the bhakti path to Śiva. In the imperial temple context, song, story, and sculpture represented ways that Tamil people could participate in the worship of Śiva.

Readers familiar with south Indian history will note that I emphasize developments during the Pallava (sixth to eighth centuries) and Chola (Cōḻa; ninth to twelfth centuries) dynastic eras in these chapters. Tamil south India has traditionally been defined by three dynasties, known as the triple kingdoms: the Pallavas, Cholas, and Pandyas; they were primarily located in the north, middle, and south of the Tamil lands, respectively. This image is most influentially represented in the Tamil epic the *Cilappatikāram*, though it can be noted from inscriptions as well. The era of the Pallavas is significant because it yields the earliest extant inscriptions that mention the singing of the nāyaṉmār's hymns in temples. In addition, the legendary story of Appar meeting a Pallava king looms large in scholarly discussions as a reference point for determining the date of the nāyaṉmar. At present, it is assumed that the nāyaṉmār lived during the early years of the Pallava dynasty. The era of the Cholas is significant because the area of the nāyaṉmār's pilgrimages, though extending all over south India (into regions that are not presently defined as Tamil), is concentrated in the center of what is now the state of Tamilnadu, along the sacred River Kāvēri, which is the traditional kingdom of the Cholas (though not without contest from other dynasties). It is also the case that the Chola inscriptions provide us with the most detail on the development of Tamil Śiva-bhakti in medieval imperial stone temples.

There are several reasons that I do not focus on the Pandya region in this discussion. Pandyan inscriptions and art historical evidence concerning the nāyaṉmār do exist, but they are usually later than the Chola inscriptions, making it difficult to reconstruct from them the point of transition in which I am interested.[1] In addition, the Pandya capital of Madurai was saturated with numerous traditions centered there, including the legend of the three Caṅkam (academy) conferences, the *Cilappatikāram*, and the legends of Māṇikkavācakar—the author of famous bhakti hymns to Śiva in Tamil, including the *Tiruvācakam*—which place him as a resident of Madurai. Thus, the legendary biography of Campantar (which has some support from his poetry), which describes him on a mission to Madurai to establish Tamil Śiva-bhakti there, must be understood within the context of a number of distinctive traditions of Madurai. Exploring these traditions is beyond the scope of this book. In particular, the relationship between the group of sixty-three nāyaṉmār and Māṇikkavācakar must be sorted out; whereas Māṇikkavācakar is a Tamil Śiva-bhakta, he is not listed by Cuntarar, and thus he is not one of the sixty-three nāyaṉmār. Nor does Māṇikkavācakar mention the nāyaṉmār in his poetry. Both tradition and scholars tend to date Māṇikkavācakar either before or after the mūvar, in the fifth or the ninth century.[2] By the fourteenth century, their respective works were brought together in the Śiva-bhakti canon, and they were called the four "leaders of religion" (camayācāryas) by Tamil Śaiva Siddhānta; by the sixteenth century, stories of all four were included in the *Tiruviḷaiyāṭal Purāṇam* (which is centered in Madurai), and at least by the nineteenth century the mūvar and Māṇikkavācakar were thought of as "the four," which is the way the works of Saint Irāmaliṅkar (Rāmaliṅga) represent them. In these chapters, I focus on the early period, when the traditions of the mūvar and Māṇikkavācakar appear to have been kept distinct.

FIVE

Regional Voices through Song

Tradition and the scholarship that draws on it have identified the conversion of a Pallava king from Jainism to Śaivism as an important moment of transition in the history of Tamil Śiva-bhakti.

The *Periya Purāṇam* narrates a story about Appar, who undergoes and miraculously survives numerous trials of torture that lead to the conversion of the king who had ordered the trials.[1] In the larger narrative of the "Appar Purāṇam," the emphasis is on the conversion of Appar himself, which precedes his trials with the king. According to the story, Appar used to be a Jain and then finally saw the light of Śiva through the persistent intervention of his sister; his own conversion is a theme found in his bhakti hymns and developed in the biographical account. Thus, the story of the king's conversion in the *Periya Purāṇam* mirrors Appar's own conversion in the bhakti poetry. The converted king is generally thought to be the Pallava ruler Mahēndravarman I (ca A.D. 580–630), a famous monarch understood through inscriptions and literature to be creative in the arts; he is credited with building the first imperial, free-standing stone (as opposed to brick) temples in south India.[2] This quasi-historical understanding of the *Periya Purāṇam* story plays upon two images: that if anyone were to innovate, it would most likely be Mahēndravarman, and that if anyone were to have the drive and persistence to challenge a king single-handedly, it would surely be the older and long-suffering Appar.[3]

Scholars have sought independent corroboration for this religious story, and they have seemingly found it in an inscription attributed to Mahēndravarman I. The inscription is found at the Lalitānkura Pallavēṣvara-gṛha rock-cut cave temple at Tiruchirapalli.[4] This rock-cut temple appears to be the farthest-flung of Mahēndravarman I's excavations; most of the rock-cut and free-standing temples attributed to him are located in the Kāñcīpuram area, which was the Pallava capital for centuries. The temple is situated on a hill overlooking the Kāvēri River, which the inscription refers to as the "wife" of the king, and it faces the territory beyond the river, which the text explicitly refers to as belonging to the Cholas. Thus, the location of the temple and certain references in the inscription suggest that Mahēndravarman I was making an imperial claim to ownership of the coveted and sacred River Kāvēri, while conceding that the land on the other side of the river belonged to the Cholas.[5] The inscription may thus allude to a dispute between two neighboring dynasties in Tamil country. To understand the inscription as signifying a dispute may be the more straightforward and less controversial interpretation of the inscription than the story of the king's religious conversion; the language of the inscription is convoluted because, as with all good Sanskrit inscriptions, this one involves extensive wordplay.[6]

The *Periya Purāṇam* attempted to answer questions, not provoke them, and to ask how imperial formations changed in the Pallava era and what the mūvar's Śiva-bhakti contributed to these changes, we will have to move beyond legend and dubious inscriptional support and into a broader survey of changes in the ritual legitimation and practice of kingship.[7]

In a provocative article, Ronald Inden has argued that configurations of kingly legitimation and ritual practice characteristic of medieval Hindu temple culture developed from Vedic and Buddhist precedents in the context of changing power relationships.[8] Inden agrees with Madeleine Biardeau that these developments in ritual practice represented a reworking of the prominent Vedic tradition of sacrifice but adds that there were "two major transformations . . . rather more sudden than gradual" that took place in the Buddhist kingdom under Aśoka in the third century B.C. and in five Hindu kingdoms, including the Pallavas, starting from the eighth century A.D.[9]

His argument is highly schematic and difficult to summarize. One of the key points he makes, however, is that despite the triad of formations—Vedic, Buddhist, and Hindu—the relations among them were not triadically construed but were, instead, two sets of parallel oppositions: Buddhist-Vedic and Hindu-Vedic. In Inden's argument, this alignment conveys the displacement of Vedic sacrifice in the context of distinctive notions of cosmic power: "To a large extent I read this contrast, whether Buddhist/Vedic or Hindu/Vedic, as essentially a contrast between religions of the imperial and regional levels, the one concerned with a world where cosmic power is concentrated, the other with a world wherein it is dispersed."[10] As I understand the contrast, in Vedic formulations—primarily sacrifice—cosmic power is dispersed in various autonomous regional levels and thus lacks a center, whereas in Buddhist and Hindu formulations, cosmic power is concentrated into an overarching imperial schema that operates through a center.

According to Inden, the imperial power that defines the center in Buddhist and Hindu formulations is the kingly prerogative to give a major gift; this is the mahādāna (great gift) ceremony, which originated in the Buddhist ideal of making gifts to monks. Both the Buddhist mahādāna and the Hindu mahādāna (which is chronologically the latest and thus displaced both Vedic sacrifice and the Buddhist version) functioned as key ritual practices in constituting the imperial power of their respective kings. Increasingly, the imperial power of the king was represented as universal overlordship, in which his ritual action of giving gifts aggrandized his power as a ruler and provider who ensured his subjects sustenance and stability.

The transformation and displacement of Vedic imperial formulations took place in the context of competing claims for kingship, unfolding along the interface of center and periphery. King Aśoka of the Mauryan dynasty (ca 272–232 B.C.) peripheralized the brahman performance of Vedic sacrifice through his establishment of the Buddhist mahādāna ceremony as the central imperial ritual of the kingdom; Inden states that "so long as the Aryan states were included in [the Buddhist imperial kingdom], they were confined to the performance of vegetarianized, simplified domestic forms of the Vedic sacrifice."[11] According to Inden, the Vedic regional centers had been "domesticated" by Buddhist overlordship, which precipitated the creation of an important distinction between śrauta (revealed) and smārta (traditional) rituals. The former included such preeminent Vedic imperial rituals as the aśvamedha (horse sacrifice), whereas the latter included versions of a mahādāna ceremony that prefigured the later Hindu pūjā rituals (offerings to God).

During the eight hundred years of Buddhist rule that followed (through the reign of Harṣa, A.D. 606–647), the marginalized Vedic practitioners rethought their tradition. In Inden's argument, this is the period that represents the rise of Hinduism, which is defined in part by the introduction of regional elements into tradition and their transformation into elements of the mahādāna ceremony: "Side by side with the reformulations of the sacrificial tradition in the *sūtras* were the efforts made, beginning in the Mahābhārata, to transform regional deities, sages, or heroes, e.g. Kṛṣṇa, of the various Aryan states into ecumenical deities of the Vedic pantheon whose icons eventually came to be 'honored' (*pūjā*) in much the same way as the symbols of the Buddha, enshrined as Cosmic Overlord of the imperial state."[12] This move involved a fundamental change in worldview: "To summarize, the feeding of the god in the Vedic mode was held to be literal and effective in maintaining the sociocosmic order (*dharma*) while the feeding of the god in the Hindu mode was considered figurative, having as its objective liberation (*mokṣa*) from the sociocosmic order itself."[13]

The other image of center and periphery in Inden's article concerns the nature of the Buddhist and Hindu polities. A key factor is the differing "modes of integration" of their imperial rule. Inden characterizes the Buddhist imperium as a "horizontal" mode of integration, which is predicated on a distance between the imperial center and the hierarchized regional centers, which were located primarily on trade routes and composed of ethnically diverse peoples. It is a model of expansion. The situation changed, however, with the onset of Muslim incursions, which limited expansion and directly influenced the evolution of the Hindu imperial center. As the Hindu kingdoms developed in this environment, they turned to a model of "vertical" integration. This is a model of consolidation, emphasizing concentrated power and a universally hierarchized channel of imperial influence: "The vertical integration of the Aryan cults of the regional level into new Hindu cults of the imperial level, effected here in condensed, ritual form, was echoed in a multitude of cultic, political, and social contexts throughout the subcontinent."[14] As I understand the argument, the Buddhist imperial polity comprised a royal center, to which all satellite groups—ethnically diverse and organized around regional structures that were local centers in their own right—paid tribute. There was thus ample room for regional variation within the model. In contrast, the Hindu imperial polity integrated regional structures into a central temple structure that provided a model of hierarchical relationships that were reproduced in smaller, subordinate temples within the kingdom. The Hindu model thus represented a drive toward unification by reproducing relationships of the center in the periphery.

If the Hindu imperial model as described by Inden is the context for religious developments in medieval India, and I believe that it is, then it provides a way of understanding how the structure of the Hindu center hierarchically integrated regional variation. Exactly how the regional voices were brought into temples—in particular, what agencies were involved in this dynamic—is the subject of an important article by Nicholas Dirks on the Pallava dynasty.[15]

The origin of the Pallavas has long been a conundrum for scholars, although it now seems likely that they were vassals of the Satavāhanas before striking out to establish their own kingdom in the north of Tamilnadu, a region they called Toṇḍaimaṇḍalam, in the sixth century A.D.[16] Because of its location in the far north of Tamil lands, the Pallava dynasty can be seen as a mediator between northern and southern cultures, insofar as it participated in the developing Sanskrit imperial idiom (in which the Guptas played no small role) and served as a model for groups farther south that eventually established powerful kingdoms in their own right, that is, the Cholas and Pandyas.[17]

The Pallava imperial rule is seen as a consolidated, effective, and, for much of its history, stable period in the history of south India, in spite of the dynasty's constant rivalry with the Chalukyas of the Deccan. However, Dirks cautions us against viewing the Pallava hegemony as a "unitary" phenomenon. Instead, he calls attention to "the importance of differential modes of the constitution of sovereign authority for this period."[18] In its broad outlines, the structural changes Dirks recognizes are similar to the transformations in Inden's schema. The Pallavas may have constituted their initial claims to imperial hegemony with the performance of the Vedic-inspired aśvamedha, agniṣṭoma, and vājapeya sacrifices,[19] but later in their dynastic rule they established their authority through the developing culture of Hindu temple worship, in which pūjā is offered to an image of God. In a detailed fashion, Dirks's essay explores the nexus of relations appropriate to each movement within this broad dichotomy. As in the case of Inden's analysis, the result is not a simple notion of the later system inverting the former but is rather a complicated process of developing certain relations at the expense of others to create and maintain an efficacious imperial ritual system.

The medieval Hindu kings in south India did not inherit a fully developed system of ritual legitimation; they cultivated new ideas for their own ritual idiom. The image of process is evident even within one dynastic lineage. According to Dirks, a decisive break in the Pallava idiom of authority came with Nandivarman Pallavamalla (ca A.D. 731).[20] His innovations in defining the nature and basis of authority for his rule distinguish his vision of kingship from that of his ancestors. Similarly, King Rājarāja I (ca A.D. 985) is prominent in Chola dynastic history. The Pallavas began the consolidation of kingship and ritual that eventually culminated in the Chola dynasty's rule over the Tamil lands; thus, Inden's idea of the establishment of "vertical," concentrated power was most fully realized by the powerful Cholas, beginning with Rājarāja I.

According to Dirks, the Pallava rulers prior to Nandivarman Pallavamalla had operated in a "mode of self-reference" in which the king was the "ritual principal," both ultimate patron and recipient of the benefit from the performance of sacrifices and the donation of gifts. In most cases, the inscriptions included an explicit statement that the grant had been undertaken for the life and success of the king. In addition, members of the king's circle, including family and officials of the court, performed subsidiary rituals along these lines, participating in the king's aura of sacred potency: "One of the primary roles fulfilled by this group had to do with royal dānas, gifts that were often themselves unrelated to particular sacrifices but rather linked in a more general sense to the sacrificial arena by royal substance, which in turn worked to orient the nature and distribution of the merit accruing from them."[21] Along with attention to the specifics of the royal family, these early Pallava grants detailed the type of gift offered. The vast majority of gifts in the early Pallava period were land grants for brahmadēyas, settlements of brahmans. These settlements did not necessarily overlap with the centralized imperial area; several of the grants are issued from Kāñcīpuram but pertain to areas in the Guntur district, Andhra Pradesh.[22] In this period of Pallava rule, the performance of various Vedic sacrifices, especially the aśvamedha, and the issuing of brahmadēyas appear to be parallel constructions, illustrating what Inden suggests is the diffused nature of Vedic-based kingship.[23] Both the horse sacrifice and the land grants to brahmans were the means by which the king marked off territory; the emphasis was on the kingdom's borders, the most controversial of its aspects.

One of the major changes Dirks sees from early to late Pallavas is the increased emphasis of the latter on their divine origins, which were expansively detailed in Sanskrit in their inscriptions. The effect of the claimed direct line to the gods was a decreased emphasis on the king's identity as a ritual participant in favor of an image of his own divine nature. Dirks explains:

> The Pallava kings continued to describe themselves as munificent givers. However, the kings no longer identified the particular purpose of each grant, as they did earlier when they proclaimed that the gifts would add to the welfare, merit, and general prosperity of their race and family. Rather, their welfare and prosperity were predicated principally on their divine origin and their inherent noble conduct. The particular grant now appeared more as an expression of their sovereignty than as the generative principle of it, and yet as an expression it was still thought to promote prosperity.[24]

The shift in focus from the king as participant to the king as divine presence opened the door, at least in theory, for another person to become the official participant-donor. This is what happened but with a crucial modification: The official participant-donor was, in essence, petitioning *the king himself*, because the king was the representation of divinity on earth, on behalf of the residents of the official's stipulated region. Gift giving remained a kingly prerogative,[25] but the actual donor was a new category of person, the vijñāpti (petitioner). The role of the vijñāpti was to "provide the impetus for gift giving." In three of Nandivarman Pallavamalla's major inscriptions (the Kāśakkuḍi plates, the Udayēndirum plates, and the Paṭṭattāḷmaṅgalam plates), the vijñāpti is lavishly praised, suggesting that "these personages represented an order of magnitude previously embodied only in the king and his family."[26] This was, then, an entrepreneurial person, one who was not from the royal family but who entered into relations with the royal family and gained honor from his role in facilitating royal gift giving. The vijñāpti fashioned a donative link between the residents in his territorial region and the king. For example, in the Paṭṭattāḷmaṅgalam grant, the vijñāpti is called Maṅgalarāṣṭrabhārti (lord of the rāṣṭra of Maṅgala) in the Sanskrit beginning of the grant and Maṅgalanāṭāl̲vān̲ (lord of the nāṭu of Maṅgala) in the Tamil part of the grant; he petitioned on behalf of the residents (nāṭṭar, from *nāṭu*) of Ārvalakūr̲r̲am in Chola country (Cōl̲anāṭu).

At the regional level, the vijñāpti was an official position, to be filled by a local spokesperson. In this manner, all regions were brought into the hierarchy of the imperial center, which was unique, as was the king. This dynamic is an illustration of Inden's Hindu model of imperial polity. It is also an example of the negotiation between local and imperial powers in the developing imperial temple culture, in which the vijñāpti stood as mediator. The language of the imperial inscriptions themselves revealed the negotiation, with the sacred genealogies and summary of the transactions that begin the record written in Sanskrit, whereas the subsequent details of the donative transactions were recorded in Tamil. On the one hand, the inscriptions presented the rhetoric of a divine, imperial dynasty that transcended specific regions; on the other hand, the inscriptions read as decidedly local documents, specifying detailed arrangements for named groups of people. The developing imperial system allowed—possibly for the first time—the dynasty to hear the many voices in the kingdom, through the petition of the vijñāpti. Some of the voices for whom the vijñāpti petitioned included village residents, local sabhās, brahmans, and women, all of whom played a role in constituting the Pallava political hegemony.

Significantly, these voices seem to have come from within a variety of religious communities. The Pallavas appear to have patronized many religious activities, including Hindu, Buddhist, and Jain. They gave brahmadēyas, land grants for brahman communities; they built temples to Śiva and Viṣṇu; they made donations to Jain temples and schools; and they probably supported Buddhist schools at Kāñcīpuram. The combined comprehensiveness of the monarch's power and his demonstration of that power in his building activities appear to have fostered a thriving pluralistic religious environment in the northern Tamil country. The possibilities for patronage and participation in the king's power were opened rather than closed.

According to contemporary scholarly dating of "the three," Campantar and Appar lived before Nandivarman Pallavamalla, whereas Cuntarar's lifetime may have overlapped with that of this illustrious ruler. The historical context of the mūvar, then, was a period in which imperial kings were increasingly turning from the performance of Vedic rituals as constitutive of their ruling power toward the performance of Hindu rituals. Dirks identifies the reigns of Pallava kings Paramēśvaravarman I (ca 669–690) and Narasiṃhavarman II (ca 690–728), the period in which some scholars locate the mūvar,[27] as a period of transition in which both Vedic- and purāṇic-inspired sovereign rituals were performed, according to inscriptions.[28]

Representing the mūvar as a catalyst for the establishment of Śaivism during the Pallava period, however, as in the legend of Appar and Mahēndravarman I, is problematic. First, the Pallavas never had control of the Kāvēri delta, the main region where the mūvar pilgrimaged and sang, although they coveted it. Second, the political context of ritual changes went beyond the borders of the Pallavas' realm. When the Pallavas most clearly identified themselves as Śaiva (Narasiṃhavarman I, ca 630; Narasiṃhavarman II), they were engaged in active and heated warfare with their neighbors in the Deccan, the Chalukyas, who identified themselves as Vaiṣṇava: "Whereas the Chalukyas represented themselves as terrestrial emanations of Vishṇu, the imperial Pallavas depicted themselves as royal devotees of Siva, as manifestations of Skanda, son of Siva and youthful general of the gods, and, on occasion, as Siva himself."[29] For political and religious reasons, the early Pallavas of the Siṃhaviṣṇu line promoted the worship of Śiva; thus, the Pallava kings established the context for the mūvar, not the other way around.

In general, kings do not feature largely in the mūvar's hymns, which identify Śiva as the king. Hymns that do mention kings generally tend to emphasize the bhakti of the earthly kings for Śiva, downplaying their earthly military might and ruling skills, such as those simply mentioned by name in Cuntarar's authoritative list of bhaktas, the *Tiruttoṇṭattokai*. And the hymnists do not privilege the Pallavas; for example, King Kōccenkaṇāṉ, who was claimed in Chola inscriptions to be one of their ancestors, is praised by all three of the hymnists as a bhakta,[30] whereas Campantar praises the Pandya queen (and Chola princess) Maṅkaiyarkkaraci[31] ; a possible exception to this trend is Cuntarar's praise of the Pallavas as righteous rulers.[32] For the mūvar, the focus of bhakti was not the royal family; only later did the relationship between the nāyaṉmār and human kings become important in the development of Śiva-bhakti. The Chola kings held the Kāvēri delta within their kingdom and constituted themselves as Śaivas in the manner of the Hindu model described by Dirks; it was this dynasty that capitalized on resonances with the mūvar's hymns. The *Periya Purāṇam*, composed during the Chola era, contextualized the lives of "the three" in the imperial temple culture, at times imaginatively elaborating on, and at times departing from, their poetry. Some of the best known stories of the mūvar are, in fact, from the *Periya Purāṇam* and do not exist in the hymns: for example, Campantar's invitation by the Pandya queen to rescue Madurai from Jain influence in order to restore it as a place of Śaivism; Appar's trials by the king to prove his bhakti for Śiva; the identification of Naraciṅka Muṉaiyaraiyar as a local Pallava chieftain and Cuntarar's foster-father; and the story of the Chera king's participation in Cuntarar's ascent to Kailāsa.

The evidence of the hymns does, however, suggest that the mūvar undertook pilgrimages, mainly in the central Tamil lands, within a context of the established worship of Śiva. Historically, the context was probably the (Siṃhaviṣṇu-line) Pallavas' allegiance to Śiva. The hymns would have been conducive to the worship of Śiva in that they are in praise of Him. The hymns also highlight a distinctly Tamil religiosity and would have been remembered if not recorded by local people, especially in the towns of which they sang. Later, after the era of the mūvar, Śiva-bhakti would find a place in the developing imperial temple culture, which became more open to hearing local voices during the reign of Nandivarman Pallavamalla. Although the sacred genealogies in the inscriptions of Nandivarman Pallavamalla relate this king to Viṣṇu, not Śiva,[33] as part of the later Pallavas' increased claims of overlordship, they patronized many religions in their realm as a demonstration of their encompassing power. It was the role of the vijñāpti to communicate the local religious variations to the king for inclusion in the regional temples that represented his rule. The hymns of the mūvar were included in these regional temples; there are inscriptional records extant from the late Pallava era that mention provisions for the "singers of the tirupatiyam" (singers of the sacred verses) in temples, although these inscriptions are not many in number. Dorai Rangaswamy refers to some half-dozen inscriptions mentioning the tirupatiyam that he claims date to the reign of Nandivarman Pallavamalla (ca A.D. 731).[34] Yet, at least three of the inscriptions he cites are dated by the epigraphists who recorded them to the reign of the Cholas, not the Pallavas.[35] The evidence is thus scarce but significant.

One of the inscriptions that is datable to the Pallava era and that does mention the singing of the tirupatiyam illustrates some possibilities and problems in understanding the Śiva-bhakti hymns as a part of Pallava imperial temple culture. The inscription is from the Bilvanatheśvara temple at Tiruvallam, a town near Vellore in the modern North Arcot district.[36] Dating this inscription is problematic. The text says that it is a copy of an earlier record of a grant that existed before the maṇḍapam of the temple was taken down and then restored. In this regard, the inscription is like some half-dozen other inscriptions found here.[37] All of these inscriptions are now reportedly on the walls of the maṇḍapam. Several of the inscriptions are from the kings of the Bāṇa dynasty, vassals to the Pallavas and then the Cholas. Other inscriptions are attributable to the Cholas, who probably renovated the temple and eventually erected the Tiruvaiyya Iśvaram temple on the south side of the Bilvanatheśvara; many of the Pallava inscriptions could have been lost in such renovations. However, the inscription that mentions the tirupatiyam appears to belong to the Pallavas and thus was preserved in subsequent renovations. The text says that it was written in the seventeenth year of Vijaya Nandivikramavarman. Although some scholars suggest that this was Nandivarman II, S. R. Balasubrahmanyam has suggested that the king was probably Nandivarman III, which would put the inscription roughly a century later, at about A.D. 852.[38]

The inscription includes several features consistent with the late Pallava inscriptional idiom identified by Dirks; for example, there is a petitioner, and a theme of the grant is to establish proper amounts that the villagers should give to the temple.[39] In the inscription, the role of vijñāpti is played by Māvalivāṇarāyan̲, alias Vikkiramādittavāṇarāyan̲, whom Hultzsch suggests is a Bāṇa chieftain.[40] It records the grouping together of three villages into one village, called Viḍēlviḍugu-Vikkiramādittacaturvēdi-maṅgalam, and specifies that this new settlement should be given to the temple of Paramēśvara as devadāna. The use of the term *caturvēdi* (four Vedas) suggests that at least part of the new village included a settlement of brahmans. In this inscription, the members of the assembly (cavaiyār) of this new community are required to pay the amounts of rice and gold to the temple formerly supplied by one of the three villages.[41]

The distribution of the required gifts to the temple by the villagers is itemized. Various amounts of the annual rice crop (paddy) were specifically allocated to a number of designated agents at the temple; they included food for the god (in this case, Śiva) and food for the variety of religious agents performing services at the temple. The gold was to be used for obtaining sundry necessities for the temple, including oil lamps and repairs to the building. The breakdown of the gift was as follows:

> Of this paddy, six hundred *kāḍi* of paddy [are allotted] for offerings; five hundred . . . to the *Śiva-Brāhmaṇas* who desire to be fed, beginning with those in charge of the store-room [or: sanctum] of the temple; five hundred . . . to those who beat [drums before] oblations; four hundred . . . to those who pick [flowers for] temple garlands, and to those who perform various service, including the singers of the *Tirupatiyam* [*tirupatiyam pāṭuvā-uḷḷiṭṭa palapaṇi*]; and twenty *kalañju* of gold for the perpetual lamps, for anointing the image, for bark, and for repairing breaks and cracks, etc.[42]

This inscription makes it clear that by the late Pallava period there was a category of singers of the mūvar's sacred verses included in annual provisions made for the temple. Although the term *tirupatiyam* could, in theory, denote any sacred verse, many factors point to its signification of the mūvar's hymns, including the temple's dedication to Śiva, the mūvar's own references to their work as sacred Tamil verses (tirupatikam), and the inscription's explicit designation of the singing as great (in the sense of strong, powerful) service (palapaṇi), evoking the mūvar's image of a bhakta as a servant (toṇṭar) to Śiva. Simultaneously, the inscription suggests that it is not the mūvar themselves who are singing but rather an established group of singers (pāṭuvār), who are related as partners or even family, which is the meaning of the word *uḷḷiṭṭār*, from the root *uḷ* (interior). This again evokes the language of the hymnists in defining the Śiva-bhakti community. Although these singers may be less important than God, the brahmans, and others who perform service in the inscription's hierarchy of payment (in the absence of specific numbers of people involved, however, this is inconclusive), they are, along with the drummers, portrayed as significant participants in temple worship who provide important service to Śiva.

It is difficult to extrapolate from this example to determine how widely the hymns were sung across Tamil country during the Pallava era. On the one hand, the singers are presented as a normative category, as with the Śiva-brahmans, in an imperial grant. On the other hand, the grant is locally concerned and details the specifics of land redistribution and temple maintenance in Tamil, at the petition of the local vijñāpti. In addition, Tiruvallam is significant (but not exceptional) in that Campantar composed a hymn to Śiva there. Campantar's patikam (set of ten verses), of which I translate a selection here, stresses in the refrain of each verse that Śiva lives in Tiruvallam:

1 He is the Destroyer who bathed the triple cities in fire
the Source in whose matted locks Gaṅgā flows
the Exegete of the Vedas
the Knower of this and that—all things;
and Tiruvallam is where He lives.

2 He is the Leader of the world
the Ascetic without equal, crowned with the white moon
the Shepherd of all
the Youth of the muṉis and celestials;
and Tiruvallam is where He lives.

3 He is the Starer who destroyed the essence of Kāma
the Warrior who wears the tiger skin
the One who severed the head of the four-faced one,

then put it back;
and Tiruvallam is where He lives.

5 He is the Bestower of ways
that make love grow among relations;
He belongs to knowers and seekers
whom He makes search in proper ways;
and Tiruvallam is where He lives.

7 He shines for pilgrims and desirers who seek Him
His foot pressed down on the strong demon
    who excavated, then haughtily lifted the sacred mountain;
and Tiruvallam is where He lives.

9 He conquered the hateful Jains and depraved Buddhists
    who by custom do not speak virtuous words
    and who obey the five senses;
He goes everywhere to spread light;
and Tiruvallam is where He lives.

Campantar 1.113 Tiruvallam

This hymn embodies most of the themes that I identified in chapter 3 in its depiction of a moral universe through the microcosm of a hymn. The first three verses carefully list the cosmic images of Śiva from purāṇic mythology, while simultaneously asserting that he lives in Tiruvallam in Tamil country. Thus, the two identities of Śiva, both universal and local, are not opposed but are mutually possible. Verses five and seven focus on the people who desire Śiva, the bhaktas, and suggest that the Lord can be sought—and found—at Tiruvallam. The final verse castigates the Buddhists and the Jains, whose language and customs lack virtue because they are guided only by their senses rather than by an ideal morality; Śiva conquers these agents of darkness by spreading his light everywhere.

Is it possible that the tirupatiyam mentioned in the grant was, in fact, this hymn of Campantar? The hymn's consistent assertion that Śiva lives in Tiruvallam provides a rationale for why the hymn would have been remembered there, why its performance would be a regular feature in the temple, and why the vijñāpti would have included provisions for the singers in his petition. The Pallava era, then, may have been the period in the history of Tamil Śiva-bhakti when the hymns began to be transformed into temple liturgies or regular offerings of song to God, based on the recognition of certain places as important *because* the mūvar sang about them. This was perhaps the beginning of the awareness that later led to every such place being designated as *pāṭal peṟṟa talam* (a place that obtains singing, meaning a sacred spot sung by the mūvar), as they are now known.[43] It may be that other temples in northern Tamil country, where the Pallavas definitively ruled, also had such provisions, although this region was not the major area of the mūvar's pilgrimages.

With the Tiruvallam temple, we have evidence that the mūvar's verses were sung by a defined group of people who were officially and regularly paid for their service to God. The conjunction of song and place in the mūvar's bhakti supports the idea that Campantar's hymn would have been particularly meaningful to those who worshiped Śiva in Tiruvallam, and served to compel the community to institute the hymns as liturgy and request support for this program's maintenance. In the case of Tiruvallam, the singing of the hymns represents not only the community's bhakti for Śiva but also the local voice of the community in a grant imbued with the increasingly universal significance of the king's rule. Just as Campantar's hymn maintains that the universal power of Śiva is manifested in his local presence, the later Pallava inscriptions, as illustrated by the one at Tiruvallam, maintain that the king's claims to universal power are supported by his local authority.

SIX

Images of Tamil Bhaktas

The hymns' insistence that Śiva lives in Tamil towns, their praise of the rivers and fertility of Tamil country, and their context of pilgrimage all point to the significance of land in the poets' vision. In a beautiful hymn, Appar transforms an agricultural scene into a message of bhakti.

> Using the plow of truth
> sowing the seeds of love
> plucking the weeds of falsehood
> pouring the water of patience;
> They look directly into themselves
> and build fences of virtue.
> If they remain rooted in their good ways,
> the Bliss of Śiva will grow.
>
> Appar 3.1/4.76.2

Was Tamil Śiva-bhakti a religious path primarily directed toward, or embraced by, peasant peoples? One influential scholar suggests that it was. Many scholars of south Indian history have undertaken important research on the allocation and production of land, particularly that of the fertile Kāvēri delta region, to obtain information on economic, social, and political developments in early medieval times. Among them, Burton Stein envisioned a specific role for bhakti in these developments, primarily by linking bhakti to the peasant population. In his widely influential book, *Peasant State and Society in Medieval South India*, Stein locates bhakti within the context of what he calls the "segmentary state," a dynamic image of state formation in the context of competing groups. Although scholars have criticized his idea of the segmentary state on many issues, especially his depiction of the village, my interest here is specifically the way he locates bhakti in his model of the developing social and political order in early medieval south India.[1]

According to Stein, bhakti arose among peasant people on the Tamil plains at a time when the region was in political turmoil. The Kaḷabhras of the infamous Kaḷabhra interregnum were being challenged by other groups who defined themselves in relation to Hindu formulations, as opposed to the Kaḷabhras, who supported Buddhism and Jainism.[2] The Pallavas and Pandyas finally achieved a stable prominence over the plains region, through two main factors: "Durable power was facilitated by the adoption of the two elements rejected by the Kalabhras: respect for and support of Brahmanical institutions and Hinduism as well as recognition of locality chiefs who were, in most cases, members of the dominant peasant group of the locality."[3] Victory was thus possible through a network of power relations: Those with the widest influence were members of the imperial dynasty, then the brahmans, then the "locality chiefs." The meaning of this latter phrase depends on both status and territorial claims; for example, in the Tamil lands there were numerous "little kingdoms," whose rulers constituted themselves as both divine and imperial, yet who paid tribute to the more powerful and encompassing imperial dynasty through a vassal system. Here, Stein suggests that the locality chiefs were spokesmen of the peasants; their role in the network would presumably be to represent the concerns of the peasants to the imperial and brahman communities.

Stein characterizes the worldview of these peasants as bhakti: "*Bhakta*s of the hymnal tradition presented a religion apparently suited to the peasant society which was achieving supremacy over the non-peasant peoples. Theirs was a religious tradition well-rooted in the devotional faith of peaceful people of the plain."[4] Thus, bhakti was both popular and peaceful, mirroring the gentle peasant society. Even the nature of the bhakti poets' devotion was representative of the peasants' connection to the land: "Bhakti hymnists in the Kaveri did not so much contend against the Aryan heresies of Jainism and Buddhism—though their judgements of these sects was often harsh; it was more the vigour of devotion to female tutelary deities that moved them."[5]

Unfortunately for Stein's thesis, I know of nothing in the mūvar's hymns that supports the identification of "devotion to female tutelary deities" as a major theme, although I did note in chapter 2 that the theme of the feminization of "indigenous" south Indian culture prevails in much of the classical scholarship.[6] Stein's interest in representing bhakti as such is to emphasize it as a chthonic religion in contrast to brahmanic Hinduism. The dichotomies between male and female, intellectual and chthonic, and nonpeasant and peasant are important for Stein because he wants to suggest that a brahman–peasant alliance (again, two opposites) was formed during this period, one that had a durable stabilizing force. The implication is that these forces were extreme on their own yet became a potent balance of culture when combined through an alliance. Correspondingly, Stein is less interested in the mūvar's polemic against the Buddhists and Jains, in spite of the fact that this is a genuine and highly visible concern in the poetry. The bhakti hymnists may not have sought to "contend" with Buddhists and Jains—although later biographies claim that they did—as much as agree with the kind of polemic that the Pallava and Pandya dynasties were spouting against the Kaḷabhras at that time.

Since the brahmans and peasants were two powerful groups with very different worldviews, Stein indicates that each side would have to see the relationship as advantageous if the alliance ("a voluntary association to achieve particular ends") was to be not only forged but also maintained. In this part of the discussion, Stein hastily alludes to an intellectual side of bhakti. In addition to being a peaceful and popular religion, bhakti "had other advantages as well. It was congenial to Brahman leaders in its philosophical presuppositions, and it offered a powerful theological and ideological counter to Jainas and Buddhists." In Stein's view, the alliance yielded to brahmans control of a large number of people who could provide a base of support—particularly important because the Jains and Buddhists were threatening at their boundaries—as well as a means of economic maintenance. Meanwhile, the peasants received an ideological coherence and a hierarchical strategy that recognized them as moral people who could keep social order among the lower castes. In other words, the brahmans (or "nonpeasant peoples") maintained their status above peasant peoples (or bhaktas) while the peasants gained influence through brahman recognition and approval. Ultimately, it was the largess of the brahmans that made the alliance work: "Changes in prevailing Brahmanical religious forms to those more congenial to the devotional religion of peasants made the alliance easier to achieve and sustain—a factor which should perhaps be given greater weight in our understanding of the *bhakti* movement."[7]

I agree with Stein that the development of imperial temple culture precipitated the negotiation of powers, though I do not agree that it is clear who had a stake in the ensuing discussion. It is difficult to determine who the proponents of bhakti were in this early period after the lifetimes of the mūvar. For example, we do not have much information on the identity of the "singers of the tirupatiyam" from the Pallava inscriptions. Yet, to assume that they are peasant peoples and that bhakti primarily represents the peasant perspective seems in conflict with the worldview of the bhakti hymns. The bhakti hymns of the three poets mention the names of several bhaktas to the Lord; this trend culminated in Cuntarar's *Tiruttoṇṭattokai* hymn and was later expanded in Cēkkiḻār's *Periya Purāṇam*, of which Stein is aware. In contrast to Stein's image of a unified peasant group, the poets and those who continued the tradition of Tamil Śiva-bhakti named many different people and emphasized the diversity of their participation in Śiva: For example, brahmans, a queen, a king, a hunter, a merchant, and a potter, to name just a few types, are all praised as bhaktas in the mūvar's hymns. They are considered kin to each other not through a peasant status but instead through their participation in Śiva and their Tamil identities. For the mūvar, local means Tamil, not a class or caste.

Imperial temple culture brought both brahmanic and bhakti modes of religiosity into the pattern of devadāna (gift to god), which demanded that they share the same ritually defined space—the temple—where devadāna was performed. The vijñāpti was the mediating figure in the temple context, responsible for negotiating among the brahmans who performed the pūjā (offering), the structures of the imperial mode of gift giving, and the proponents of regional traditions, of which Tamil Śiva-bhakti was one group. Bhakti can thus be understood not so much as a kind of social glue as a religious perspective that had meaning for Tamils, through the hymns' specificity of place and celebration of things Tamil. This and the hymns' praise of Śiva encouraged their recitation in temples as a Tamil liturgy. The process did involve negotiation because the presence of bhakti in the temple precipitated important and controversial questions of participation: If the brahmans held their hereditary hegemony in ritual performance, what place would be allocated for singing the Tamil Śiva-bhakti hymns? Would the hymns' image of "being there," or standing before God, be compromised or enhanced in the temple context? How were the mūvar to be understood or represented? These important questions cannot be answered from the paucity of references to the singing of the tirupatiyam in extant inscriptions from Pallava times. Much more numerous are the inscriptional references relating to Tamil Śiva-bhakti during the Chola dynastic era.

In a manner similar to other imperial dynasties, the Cholas' claims to universal overlordship, as manifested in their inscriptions, were based on images of victory over their rivals and prosperity in their lands. Victory supported their proclamations of power, while prosperity manifested their avowed virtue. Yet the Cholas were able to amplify these assertions considerably as they rose to become perhaps the greatest imperial power in south Indian history. The hymns of the mūvar, tied as they were to the traditional homeland of the Cholas, proved significant in the early dynasty's real and imagined maps of influence and affluence.[8]

The power of the Chola dynasty was initiated by the reign of Vijayālaya around A.D. 850. His claim to power is thus roughly contemporaneous with the Pallava inscription that mentions the singers of the tirupatiyam at Tiruvallam. At this foundational stage in the Cholas' hegemony, there was more of an emphasis on victory (obtaining land) than on prosperity (developing land). Vijayālaya is credited with establishing a political base for the Cholas in Tanjavur (Tañjāvūr, Tanjore), located on the Kāvēri River west of their traditional capitals at U̲raiyūr and Pa̲laiyā̲ru. In one of his early inscriptions, he is called *Tañcai-koṇṭa parakēcari* (Parakēcari who took Tanjavur).[9] The use of this conquest motif in titles was continued by later Cholas, who identified themselves as "the one who took Madurai" or "the one who took the head [crown] of the Pandya" (Parāntaka I, reiterated by many subsequently); as "the one who extended [his territory to] Toṇḍai-nāṭu"; as "the one who brought the Gangā" (Rājēndra); and as "the one who took Madura, Karuvūr, and Ilam, and who was pleased to take the crowned head of the Pandya" (Rājarāja I). Vijayālaya's initial act of conquest was fondly remembered by later kings; in language that recalls the Pallava Mahēndravarman's claim to the Kāvēri, the Tiruvālankāṭu plates of Rājēndra Chola poetically describe Vijayālaya's conquest as "laying hold of Tanjavur as if the city were his lawful wife" and specify that he set up a temple to the goddess Niṣumbhasūdinī (Durgā) there.[10] Along with this temple, which marked his capital, Vijayālaya built other temples to mark the boundaries of his new kingdom, including a temple in Nārttāmalai to the south and a temple at Vikkanāmpunti to the north.

The theme of conquest persisted in the subsequent Chola rulers' identification of themselves as universal overlords. To this, they added a program of prosperity within their traditional homeland of the Kāvēri Delta: Specifically, they embarked on an ambitious agenda of temple building. Later rulers remember Vijayālaya's successor, Āditya I (ca 871–907), as a prolific builder of temples; the Anbil plates of Sundara Chola (Parāntaka II, ca 956–973) state that he built temples in honor of Śiva all along the Kāvēri River from the Sahyādri mountain to the sea.[11] Following this lead, S. R. Balasubrahmanyam has dated temples in Tirukkaṇṭiyūr, Tiruvaiyā̲ru,

Tiruppalaṉam, Tiruvētikuṭi, Tiruppūnturutti, Tiruccatturai, and Tiruvilakkuṭi, among others, to the reign of Āditya I.[12] The first five are places of which the mūvar sang, which suggests that the building program of Āditya I was informed not only by his desire to own the sacred Kāvēri River delta but also by his desire to tie the established sacrality of sites to his rule. The mūvar's hymns provided a template of sacred places for the Chola imperial building program.

The significance of these links for the early Cholas distinguished them from other dynasties, such as the Pallavas. The Pallavas had begun the impetus toward transforming the mūvar's hymns from spontaneous and unique events to planned and permanent liturgical performances in temples. But it was the Cholas who controlled the lands where the mūvar pilgrimaged and perceived Śiva's greatest presence. As if to underscore the connection, the Cholas increasingly used the linguistic structures common in the Tamil Śiva-bhakti hymns to refer to Śiva in their temple inscriptions, either by using the formula "the One of [place name]" ([place name]-uṭaiyār) or by adding the term *nāyaṉār* to this formula ([place name]-uṭaiya-nāyaṉār).[13] By building temples on sites sung by the mūvar, the early Chola rulers were not just acknowledging the poets' insistence that "Śiva lives here;" they were also providing Śiva with an appropriately glorious home. The mūvar spoke of his constant presence; the Cholas enshrined him in permanently endowed temples across the Tamil lands. The Chola kings drew upon the map of sacrality created by the mūvar in representing their own sacred power.

Perhaps the most important early Chola patron of Śaiva temples was not a king but a queen: Queen Sembiyan Mahādevī, wife of the Chola ruler Gandarāditya (ca 949–957), the second son of Parāntaka I.[14] The extensiveness of her patronage—she even founded a town named after herself, though now desolate, some forty miles from Tanjavur—provided the foundation for additional grants by later kings and perhaps even prefigured the enormous building and patronage activities of Rājarāja I. Leslie C. Orr has presented Sembiyan Mahādevī's patronage activities as a critique of the familiar triangle of relations—namely, king-temple-brahman—discussed by Dirks and Stein.[15] She noted that scholarly discussions of this classic construction of power relations either omit women completely or simply designate women as attributes of kings according to a mythological model that limits them to this role. In fact, according to inscriptions, women and men both contributed to the creation of imperial temple culture; Orr has noted, however, important distinctions between the public reputation of royal men and that of royal women. Although inscriptions describe kings as valorous and victorious in warfare along with other qualities such as temple building, they describe women virtually exclusively as agents of religious beneficence through building and gifting activities. Thus, religious endowments were royal women's primary means to a positive public reputation.[16]

Sembiyan Mahādevī created her lasting reputation through some sixty years (ca. 941–1001) of active religious endowments.[17] She may have been widowed at an early age, which traditionally precipitates seclusion, not greater public activity.[18] Her patronage activities may thus be attributable to her great personal courage, stamina, and religiosity. Yet royal lines ran deep on her husband's side: Her father-in-law and her husband had both ruled, and the next three kings were her husband's brother Arinjaya (957–958), who immediately assumed the throne after her husband's death (possibly by suicide), followed by his son Sundara Chola (958–969), and then finally Sembiyan Mahādevī's own son Uttama Chola (970–985). It was perhaps to offset the bad associations of widowhood and assert her ongoing connection to auspicious power that the queen was consistently described in inscriptions as the wife of Gandarāditya and the mother of Uttama Chola. Yet in those same inscriptions, she is unequivocally said to be responsible for the building and patronage activities. Consistently through the reigns of some seven kings, Sembiyan Mahādevī was represented in inscriptions as a complex public persona; although her identity and authority were inextricably linked to male relatives, her initiative and work on religious structures were definitely her own.

Sembiyan Mahādevī built or rebuilt temples on sites sung by the mūvar. In some cases, it is clear that she rebuilt the temple—in stone, replacing a brick structure—because inscriptions specifically mention that she has carefully copied prior inscriptions; for example, the temple at Āvaṭuturai, a place sung by all three hymnists, has at least one earlier inscription.[19] In other cases, such as the Cōḻiśvarar temple at Kuṟṟālam, a place sung by Appar and Cuntarar, an inscription specifies that the queen built the temple.[20]

Sembiyan Mahādevī's grants to sites about which the mūvar sang provided material supplies for Tamil liturgists, like the Pallava grant at Tiruvallam, and provided a foundation for later grants. For a detailed example of her activities, we turn to one of her most important temples, the Umāmahēśvarar temple in the town now called Kōṉērīrājapuram but formerly known as Tirunallam. Both Appar and Campantar sang of the Lord at Tirunallam.[21] The inscriptional records here identify the queen's auspicious power as the wife of Gandarāditya and the mother of Uttama Chola.[22] Two of her inscriptions are located around stone images on the south wall of the central shrine; these are descriptions of both her and the images.[23] The first inscription informs us in careful and precise language that Sembiyan Mahādevī "caused to be constructed" (*eḻuntaruḷuviṭṭu*) in stone a temple to the Lord of Tirunallam (*tirunallamuṭaiyārkku*) in the sacred name (*tirunāmattāl*) of her husband Gandarādityadeva. Thus, she simultaneously activated the sacrality of a place claimed by the hymnists to be endowed with the presence of Śiva and memorialized the sacrality of her husband. The inscription also tells us that the building was done during the reign of her son, Uttama Chola; thus, inscriptions linked the queen to sacred power in several ways. She also embodied it through bhakti. In a graphic image near the inscriptions, both she and the former king are commemorated in an image that pictures a female figure in a kneeling posture of worship, with attendants behind her and a much smaller male figure close to a liṅgam.[24] The liṅgam is an aniconic representation of Śiva, but the language of the inscription is iconic because it describes the male figure, Gandarādityadeva, as worshiping the holy feet of the Lord of Tirunallam (*tirunallamuṭaiyārait-tiruvaṭit-toḻukiṉṟārāka*). The worshipful aspect of the queen, the proximity of the king to the image of Śiva, and the language of "worshiping the holy feet" all suggest that this is an image of bhakti (*bhaktipratiṣṭhā*). The queen and king are represented as actively participating in the worship of Śiva.

Chola inscriptions continued at Tirunallam for approximately two and a half centuries, beginning with Sembiyan Mahādevī's son and extending through the period of Rājarāja I's rule to Rājarāja III's reign. An inscription during Uttama Chola's reign is important because it gives us a detailed look at the workings of the temple and a glimpse of the types of people who performed the duties of temple worship there.[25] This massive two-part Tamil inscription, totaling some 238 lines, begins with a description of Sembiyan Mahādevī's original construction of the temple and purchase of lands for a flower garden and then describes her extension of her gift to include greater funds for servicing the God of the temple, a feeding house (*śālā*) for twenty-five brahmans, and funds to purchase food and hire cooks, all accomplished through elaborate renegotiation of the lands constituting the devadāna. Particularly interesting in this inscription is the description of the residents of the district (*nāṭṭār*), who see the royal order coming (by bearers), go to meet it, worship it, place it on their heads, and mark out the boundaries by circumambulation with a female elephant, all in accordance with Sembiyan Mahādevī's orders. What follows is an elaborate description of the boundaries of the grant, which are marked by villagers' constructions, such as channels and flower gardens in the four directions.

Within these boundaries, the land was further divided so that specified portions of the paddy would go to support specific temple requirements. The itemization of these requirements appears to follow, at least initially, a hierarchical order. First among the necessary items is food for the god, in various types and various amounts specific to the time of day worship is held. Also included are substances such as tamarind and sandalwood paste for smearing on the god and other substances used in the ceremony, including incense, oil, and lamps. Then several people, including the wife of a brahman and a headman, along with the king, are credited with giving lamps.[26] Next, paddy is granted for the celebration of Sembiyan Mahādevī's astral star of Jyēshthā, in the month of Chittirai. This is followed by food provisions for brahmans, forty in total after Uttama Chola increased their number by fifteen. A separate amount is reserved for the worshiping priest and for other brahmans who perform various services, including crushing the sandalwood paste, repairing the sacred interior of the temple, and holding the canopy over the god.

What these elements appear to have in common is a relationship to the sacred interior, or garbhagṛha (sanctum; lit., womb house), of the temple. At first, the list delineates things that are necessary for God. The first few items are constituents of the pūjā (honoring) ritual, which require handling by officiants (for example, food that is placed before God; sandalwood paste that is smeared upon the Lord's image; lamps that are lit and waved before the Lord). The next mention is of important donors to the pūjā, including the largest donor, the king. Then the inscription highlights the role of the queen by providing for a special type of pūjā to celebrate the queen's natal star. The last component is a provision for the feeding of brahmans, with the worshiping priest singled out and others mentioned by tasks that entitle them to be in the sacred interior of the temple.

The next group of provisions appears to involve people who are described only by their services, not by name or other official title, in contrast to the specificity of those whose gifts or actions take place in the center of the temple. The inscription appears to suggest a hierarchical schema in which some attendants are presented as performing auxiliary services for the pūjā but not necessarily directly connected to its performance. They are thus primarily located outside the sanctum. The inscription lists those who pick flowers and string them, those who sweep the sacred temple floor and smear it with cow dung, musicians, two people who blow the conch, three men who guard the sacred images, and two singers of the tirupatiyam. Additional miscellaneous servants listed include two brahmans who perform the duty of kōyilvāriyam (perhaps guarding the temple), potters, a brahman who brings sacred water from the Kāvēri, a superintendent who is under orders from the king, an astrologer, three men who water the flower garden, a builder, a carpenter, and a blacksmith.

The inscription also describes three images, probably bronzes, indicating that they are for festival processions outside the temple: Tripuravijāyā (the goddess victor of the three worlds, consort to Tripurāntaka), Vṛṣabhavāhana (Śiva as the rider of the bull), and Gaṇapati (Ganesh).[27] It provides funding for their feeding, bathing, and clothing.

Finally, the grant provides separate houses for various temple agents, including the two tirupatiyam singers, temple priests, musicians, and the temple manager. At this point, well on the periphery of the temple worship area, the grant concludes.

It seems clear that this inscription is concerned with a hierarchy of temple space. The Cholas' heightened sense of place was expressed not only through victory, prosperity, and sacred heritage but also through proper procedures in their temples. Although the Tirunallam inscription in some ways resembles the Pallava grant at Tiruvallam, especially in terms of including the singers of the tirupatiyam as liturgical performers on a permanent basis, this inscription articulates relationships among the various elements and groups them together or separates them on the basis of place and performance. The schema of payment is based on this as well: The brahman priest gets 120 kalam (a unit of measurement) of paddy per year, the two singers get 180 kalam (90 apiece), and the brahman who gets water from the Kāvēri gets 30 kalam of paddy per year. There are three spheres in this schema, representing the major distinctions in the grant: the center, middle, and periphery of temple space. In the inscriptions from Tirunallam, the singers of the tirupatiyam are located in the middle, which distinguishes them from ritual experts and in the process distances them from the temple images.

The map of sacrality drawn by the mūvar may thus be seen as adding a dimension of sacred meaning to an emerging dynasty that initially possessed only a myth of conquest. The Cholas built temples in specific towns sung by the mūvar, yet they also understood the hymnists' map to apply more generally to their lands. Their inscriptions included provisions for temple singers of the tirupatiyam, even at shrines in places not sung by the mūvar. For example, inscriptions of Parāntaka I (ca 907–925) at Andanallur detail the building of the temple and gifts to it by his vassal, Sembiyan Irukkuvel alias Pūdi Parāntakan.[28] One of these inscriptions, dated to Parāntaka's fourteenth year, provides a list of temple servants, including four attendants to the priests (*māṇis*), two conch blowers, two flower gardeners, and one person to sing tirupatiyam.[29] Another inscription from Parāntaka I, plus one from Sundara Chola (ca 960) and Uttama Chola (ca 974), provides further evidence for the singing of the mūvar's hymns as a regular temple feature.[30]

The Śiva-bhakti of the mūvar continued to be primarily represented in the temple by the singing of their hymns, now standardized by the early Cholas. There is little evidence of other manifestations of Śiva-bhakti from the inscriptions of the early Chola period. However, the Tirunallam temple's image of the king and queen as bhaktas, bowing before the liṅgam with the caption specifically explaining that they are "worshiping the holy feet of the Lord of Tirunallam," is significant. The language of bhakti allowed the royal family and others to express their religiosity through a path of participation and engagement beyond the protocol of donations. This identification with bhakti was developed during the middle Chola period, and it involved an increased interest in the stories of the nāyaṉmār.

In part, Rājarāja I returned to the conquest model of Vijayālaya when he made Tanjavur his capital and built there his great Rājarājeśvaram temple, finally completed in the twenty-fifth year of his reign (1009–1010). Evoking the great power of the king—he is portrayed in inscriptions as an internationally influential figure, from his conquest of Sri Lanka (actually achieved by his son) to his statesmanship toward Indonesia and Cambodia—this massive temple (its base and tower combined are more than sixty meters high) embodied his claims to universal overlordship and established him as the first Chola who could seriously make such claims.[31] Tanjavur was most appropriate for Rājarāja I's self-important and encompassing imperial identity; whatever it lacked in sacred history, it more than made up for in political significance.[32]

At Tanjavur, Rājarāja I inherited the temple to Durgā built by Vijayālaya, according to the Tiruvālangāṭu plates of his son Rājēndra Chola. This early temple celebrated the goddess who, in a variety of forms, conquered an all-powerful demon that proved too great a challenge for the gods. When Rājarāja I turned toward building his own capital temple, he did not follow this lead. Largely eschewing the symbology and participation of the powerful feminine (goddesses, royal women) in the temple, Rājarāja I instead turned to Śiva and a male-dominated ritual system that was governed by the āgamas.[33] Brahman priests were the officiants; the king gathered some three hundred brahman priests from two hundred villages to conduct pūjā to this liṅgam in the center (garbagṛha) of the temple.[34] The central image of his temple was the aniconic liṅgam. According to the āgamas, the smooth, aniconic liṅgam of Śiva represented the highest essence of the Lord, the undifferentiated, encompassing, and transcendent aspect of Paramaśiva. The liṅgam thus represented a more comprehensive power than the tejas or fiery energy represented by the image of Durgā in Vijayālaya's temple. The āgamas understood tejas to be simply one aspect of Śiva, and thus it did not represent his complete power. Therefore, the most appropriate place to represent the tejas of Śiva was not at the center but on the walls inside and outside the Rājarājeśvaram temple, surrounding the central liṅgam. The forms of Śiva in these locations were iconic, each symbolizing an aspect of his power; for example, the Liṅgodbhava image of Śiva as the fiery liṅgam is represented on both the eastern and western walls of the temple, and the Tripurāntaka image appears thirty times within the temple.[35] Rājarāja I also brought to his capital temple images of the dancing Śiva that evoked earlier Chola patronage of the famous Chidambaram temple by Āditya I and Parāntaka I. At his great temple, there was a supplementary shrine for the dancing Śiva, a replica of the Chidambaram temple carved in relief on one of the walls, and carvings of the 108 dance poses from the *Natya Śāstra*: "It would seem to appear that Rājarāja I's policy was to bring the power of the Dancing Image to Tañcavūr, rather than to further the development of Citamparam itself."[36]

The āgamas formed the core of sacred meaning in Rājarāja I's large temple; they were the heart around which other ways of worshiping Śiva circulated. From the perspective of the temple center, worship of Śiva according to other methods, including Śiva-bhakti, would play only a supporting role. The centralization of the liṅgam did not preclude developments in understanding Śiva-bhakti within the temple context, which suggests both that Śiva-bhakti was established as an approach to Śiva and that it had enduring meaning to worshipers. However, it did influence the development of other forms of worship, including Śiva-bhakti, in directions that were not competitive with its aims and goals. I discuss these directions of development later; for the purpose of comparing the āgamic system to the Tamil Śaiva Siddhānta philosophical school, I defer detailed discussion of the āgamas to part IV.

The Rājarājeśvaram temple was a forum for encompassing and ordering ways of worshiping Śiva, in the interest not only of veneration but also of constituting the Chola king's material and symbolic claim to rulership. As part of his scheme of grandeur, Rājarāja I continued the tradition of having singers of the tirupatiyam in his temple, though on a much larger and more organized scale than ever before. In his great Rājarājeśvaram temple, provisions for the recitation of the hymns were made on an elaborate scale; these are detailed in an inscription from the king's twenty-ninth regnal year.[37] Some fifty people were employed; their wages were paid in paddy from the treasury. These fifty included forty-eight singers, one person to play the small drum (*uṭukkai*), and one to play the large drum (*koṭṭi-mattaḷam*) in accompaniment. Further, the inscription gives each singer's name: Some have the name of a temple, suggesting the location from which they were brought into the large Chola temple, and others have the name of one of the mūvar (Campantaṉ, Tirunāvukkaraiyaṉ, Nampi Ārūraṉ).[38] In all cases, they were given a second name that ended in Civaṉ (Skt. Śiva), which can be interpreted as an attempt to create a distinctive group of ritual specialists in the temple: those who sang or accompanied the singing of the mūvar's hymns. Further, the inscription specifies that in the case of death or emigration of one of the singers, his place should be taken by one of his relations. Only if no relative was qualified would the members of the group (*nyāyattār*, "those by right or equity") select another qualified person.

The inscription represents the musicians as a distinctive community, unified by name and endowed with the right to sing the hymns. This image suggests that the occupation of singing the tirupatiyam had come to resemble a jāti (subcaste defined by occupation). In the temple context, Appar's language of a kinship shared by all worshipers of Śiva had been transformed into a language of rights to perform the hymns in the pūjā ceremony. Was this jāti linked to a caste? The inscription does not specify what constituted a "qualified" person. However, another inscription of Rājarāja I may provide a clue to this question. It mentions the *composition* of a tirupatiyam to the Lord of the temple at Tirumāṟpēru (modern-day Tiṟumālpuram).[39] It was composed by the father of one Kuḷakkuṭaiyāṉ Arunilai Śri Kriṣṇaṉ, alias Mūvēntappiṭavūr Vēḷār; his son made endowments for the regular singing of this hymn in the temple. The identification of this man as a Vēḷār (or Vēḷāḷa, also Śaiva

Piḷḷai), a high-ranking though nonbrahman agricultural caste, reopens the question of bhakti and a peasant identity raised by Burton Stein. It is likely that the singing of tirupatiyam became definitively identified with the Vēḷāḷa caste during this period.[40] If this was the case, let us first note that it represents a change from the worldview of the mūvar as expressed in their poetry; they did not define the practice of Śiva-bhakti as appropriate to only one caste. Second, the association of the singing of the hymns with a nonbrahman caste had the advantage of eliminating a possible avenue of competition between groups of brahmans—or those who aspired to represent themselves as being of brahman status.[41] It was the least controversial of the options possible in the competitive temple culture. Stein misses these dynamics because he views bhakti as innately a "religion of the peaceful peasants," thereby collapsing the historical distance and change of context between the composers of the hymns and the Chola temple singers.

The designation of those who had the right to perform the mūvar's hymns did not preclude others being interested in the mūvar. Just as there was a concern to define the embodiment of the singers, there was a concern to define the embodiment of the mūvars and the other nāyaṉmārs themselves, through iconographic representation of them. The emulation of the mūvar through song was expanded to an emulation of their lives through painting and sculpture.

A vestibule surrounding the garbhagṛha in the Rājarājeśvaram temple is the site of several mural paintings, including panels that depict scenes from the life of Cuntarar. The vestibule is a slender corridor between two thick stone walls:

> To support the large mass of the thirteen tiers [of the temple tower or vimāna] and the śikhara [the eighty-ton single granite block in an octagonal shape that crowns the tower], all made of stone, the device of widening the load-bearing surface of the walls of the garbhagriha has been conceived. But, instead of presenting the requisite surface in one compact stretch, the sthapatis [builders] have struck upon an utilitarian and, at the same time, aesthetically satisfying arrangement of two unicentric parallel walls on all the four sides, removed from each other by a width of about 1.68 metres. This gap . . . serves to form an art gallery invaluable to the student of Dravidian art. . . . This mode of broadbasing the wall is known as the Sāndhara type, the outer and the inner walls being known as the bāhya bhitti and the antara bhitti respectively. This architectural feature is no innovation in the case of the Rājarājēśvaram temple; there have been illustrious precedents for it, as for instance in the Vaikunṭha Perumāḷ temple at Kānchi, built during the Pallava days.[42]

The vestibule intersects four entrances into the square garbhagṛha structure. One of these is the main, public entrance leading from the pillared porches into the sanctum. By this route, a priest or worshiper can approach the sanctum in a straight line, without entering the vestibule. The other three entrances, on each side of the square sanctum, lead directly from outside the temple into the vestibule and, because of this directness, would probably have been reserved for priestly or royal persons. By these entrances, one must walk along several of the vestibule's fifteen chambers to reach the entrance on the east side, into the center of the sanctum where the liṅgam rests. How many people had the right to walk along the vestibule remains an open question; certainly the royal family did, and the friezes of the dance poses and the murals on the walls represent images that had special meaning to the king.[43]

Chamber seven, on the western side of the vestibule, contains images of Cuntarar on its east wall and jamb. The rendering is in mural form on three panels, which take up the entire space from floor to ceiling.[44] The lowest panel depicts Cuntarar's marriage at the point of its interruption by Śiva in the guise of an old man. The middle panel depicts Cuntarar ascending to Kailāsa on the elephant Airāvatam and the Cēra king following him on horseback. The upper panel illustrates the heavenly realm of Śiva at Mount Kailāsa, where the Lord's heavenly servants (gaṇas, devas, and so on) perform a procession while Śiva and Pārvatī look on.

The murals thus present Cuntarar through a highly selective chronology of his life. Today we know the stories of both Cuntarar and the Cēra king (Cēramāṉ Perumāḷ; the Cēra lands were located in what is today the state of Kerala) from the *Periya Purāṇam*, but the mural depiction predates Cēkkiḻār's epic by more than a hundred years. Since the mural presupposes an understanding of Cuntarar through narrative, stories of the lives of the mūvar were circulating orally at this time. The mural represents an intermediary stage between the composition of the hymns and the writing of hagiographies of the mūvar and the other sixty nāyaṉmār. In this stage, narratives were developed that creatively departed from the autobiographical references given in the hymns in favor of a story line that situated the bhaktas in a living context. For them to become examples to others, the actions of the bhaktas would have to be understood. Thus, the murals of the vestibule represent more than a confirmation that stories of the nāyaṉmār were in circulation; they point to an understanding of the nāyaṉmār's stories (in this case, that of Cuntarar) as resonating with human experience and identity (in this case, those of a king).

For example, Cuntarar says in his hymns that Śiva took him as a servant (*toṇṭar*) at the Aruṭṭuṟai shrine at the town of Veṇṇeynallūr.[45] The mural situates the call of Śiva in the context of a public gathering, which B. Venkataraman identifies as a marriage scene: "Śiva in the guise of the old man is aggressive and angry, confidently flaunting a palm leaf as documentary proof. While he fusses over his rights over the brahmanical slave, a frightened and perhaps somewhat sullen Sundarar is cowed down before him. Consternation is writ large on the face of the guests at the unexpected turn of events."[46] The *Periya Purāṇam* expands on this theme, for its author Cēkkiḻār frames his entire narrative of the lives of the nāyaṉmār with the story of Cuntarar, beginning with Śiva's call to him at the time of his marriage.

The mural is not a shorthand version of the *Periya Purāṇam*, however; although there is great continuity between the two, a seeming diversion occurs in their respective treatments of Cuntarar's ascent to Śiva on Mount Kailāsa.[47] In the mural, Cuntarar is riding on an elephant, accompanied by the Cēra king on horseback. Cuntarar carries a tāḷam or cymbal in his hand, and the king wears his hair in a side bun (a traditional hair style in Kerala) and is adorned with pearl necklaces, armlets, anklets, and a girdle.[48] In the hymn *Tirunoṭittāṇmalai* (this title is Tamil for Mount Kailāsa), which is traditionally understood to be his final hymn, Cuntarar concludes nearly every verse with a reference to a heavenly elephant that the Lord gave him to ride. However, there is no mention of "Cēramāṉ Perumāḷ" in any of Cuntarar's hymns. The *Periya Purāṇam* links this figure to one Kaḻaṟiṟṟaṟivāṉ, who is mentioned in the sixth verse of Cuntarar's *Tiruttoṇṭattokai*, where he is described as being as generous as a rain cloud. The identification of Kaḻaṟiṟṟaṟivāṉ was further developed by tradition, which understood him to be an author of poems in praise of Śiva.[49] Both the mural and the *Periya Purāṇam* imagine that the two ascended together to Mount Kailāsa. The mural depicts the two as passing through the ocean, represented by frothy waves.[50] This image evokes Cuntarar's hymn, in the final verse of which he asks the Lord of the ocean to carry his poem to Śiva at Añcai (Añcaikkaḷam, which is in Cēra country, thus providing a link to the story developed by later tradition). In contrast, the *Periya Purāṇam* asserts that Cuntarar flew through the heavens on his white elephant.[51] These differences between the two stories, while inconclusive, do illustrate the complex relationship between autobiographical hymn and hagiographical narrative in the selection of elements to represent the mūvar's personalities and their Śiva-bhakti over time.

The presence of the Cēra king in Cuntarar's story would have been important to the Chola king Rājarāja I and probably informed the choice for its representation in the vestibule. Powerful images of Śiva as a conqueror were selected for representation on the walls in other chambers of the passageway: Śiva as the ascetic master of the senses and illusion (Dakṣiṇāmūrti, chamber five) and Śiva as the destroyer of the three cities (Tripurāntaka, chamber eleven). There were also portraits of the king in these chambers: Rājarāja I and his three queens worshiping Śiva as the king of dance (Naṭarāja, chamber nine) and a portrait of Rājarāja I with his spiritual guru, Karuvūr Tēvar (chamber ten). With the story of Cuntarar and the Cēra king, Rājarāja I could combine these images of cosmic spiritual power (the representations of Śiva) and earthly power (his own portraits) in one scene, as the two bhaktas—one a spiritual leader and the other a king—ascended to Mount Kailāsa. Even within the Cuntarar panel, certain additions suggest the king's special identification with this story. For example, to the left of the middle panel is a small, detailed portrait of a king worshiping a Śiva-liṅgam. In the uppermost panel, the mural depicts a crowd of heavenly spectators, drummers, and dancing women. Two of the dancing women are in classical dance poses, which was of special interest to Rājarāja I, who had 81 of the 108 classical dance poses carved in relief in chambers above the sanctum. In contrast, Cuntarar imagined in his hymn that he would be greeted by the gods, including Indra, Māl, and Brahmā, while the Vedas, āgamas, and hymns of the brahmans were recited.

The mural panels illustrate the beginning and end of Cuntarar's story; the call by Śiva and the attainment of Śiva. The "being there" quality of the mūvar's hymns may be evoked when the hymns are performed in the temple, but the mural emphasizes the *results* of bhakti. In other words, the experience of song and pilgrimage has been displaced in the mural, which has distilled the practice and message of bhakti into a brief linear narrative of call and attainment. All three panels point to salvation in bhakti as an overwhelming theme. The lowest panel depicts the beginning of salvation as the call of Śiva. The middle panel depicts the ultimate pilgrimage to Śiva, displacing the earthly pilgrimages in the Tamil lands of the mūvar's hymns (but drawing on Cuntarar's hymn to do so) with an image of heavenly pilgrimage to Śiva at Kailāsa, yet retaining the hymns' sense of proximity to God as a key element of bhakti. The upper panel lacks images of Cuntarar and the Cēra king, prompting Venkataraman to explain: "The panel brings the sequence to an end with the absorption in the Ultimate of Saint Sundarar and his devoted friend Chēramān."[52] Here, the pilgrimage results in *samādhi*, complete absorption in God. The term represents a classical way that Indian religious thought imagines the end of human life for the religiously adept. The mural includes Cuntarar in this category of being. From the poet, we have words of departure; from the mural, a statement on salvation.

It is significant that the king accompanies Cuntarar to samādhi. The story, as represented in the mural, posits an important connection between ruler and nāyaṉār, in that both eventually reach the feet of Śiva in the ultimate pilgrimage. Cuntarar reaches Śiva through his love; the king reaches Śiva through his love of both God and the nāyaṉār. A king who provides for Śiva can surely follow the path of the nāyaṉār to him; by creating the mural and placing it in an inner chamber of the temple, the Chola king appears to have appropriated this story as representative of his own rule as service to God. He, too, was participating in Śiva, and he, too, would someday reach Kailāsa.[53] The Chola king's painting of Cuntarar represents his approval of the bhakti path, his identification with a preeminent bhakta, his own status as a bhakta, and his certainty of salvation.

Through the embodiment of the mūvar and the other sixty nāyaṉmār, Śiva-bhakti provided a mode of participating in the veneration of Śiva. This was especially important in the imperial temple context. In imperial temple culture, the mode of kingly participation in religious activities was primarily dāna, or gift giving. The king provided the foundational act of gifting a temple, both in its creation and in providing for its continued functioning. It was a system of honor (*pūjā*), and the king both displayed honor to the God and received honor from his subjects in the temple context. Yet, it was bhakti and not the system of dāna that provided the language of emotional commitment to God, the knowledge that one's heart and mind were actively engaged. Dāna and honor provided the context; bhakti specified the correct attitude.

It is perhaps in this vein that the king and one of his ministers donated images of the nāyaṉmār to the temple. Inscriptional records show that the king himself donated metal images of the nāyaṉār Chaṇḍēśa and his father.[54] Like the Chera king, Chaṇḍēśa is not one of "the three," yet both were understood to have been designated as toṇṭar in Cuntarar's list, and from this they came to be known as nāyaṉmār. Also similar to the Chera king, Chaṇḍēśa's story provides an image of bhakti that can be understood as resonating with kingly power. The donated images of him might have been placed in the temple as a selective telling of his story, rather like the painted mural, for the inscription mentions two images of Chaṇḍēśa that represent two major events in his story: "one solid image of Chaṇḍēśvara with two arms, five *viral*s and five *tōral*s in height from 'foot to hair' (*pātāti kēśāntam*); one solid image of his father, with two arms, depicted as having fallen and lying on the ground . . . one solid image of Chaṇḍēśvara, having two arms, represented as receiving a boon (*prasādam*) from the God . . . one *puṣpa-mālai* (flower garland) given to Chaṇḍēśvara as a boon.[55]

The story, as we know it from the *Periya Purāṇam*, has a number of different elements, but the ones relevant to the metal images are the following: Chaṇḍēśa was a brahman who decided to help cows mistreated by cowherders. Due to his care, the cows became healthy, and Chaṇḍēśa used their milk to worship a liṅgam he fashioned out of mud. One day while he was worshiping the liṅgam, he was interrupted by his father. Without looking up, Chaṇḍēśa took his staff, which was transformed into Śiva's axe, and cut off his father's legs. Here, the metal image as described in the inscription differs from the story, insofar as the former depicts the father as missing his arms, not his legs. It may have been too difficult for the artisans to render the father without legs, because the image would have to be supported in some way; therefore, they substituted the upper limbs for the lower. It may also be that the story differed at the time the metal image was made. The story continues that Śiva, pleased with his bhakta, crowned Chaṇḍēśa with a garland of flowers and bestowed his grace upon him.

It is not too much of a leap to see that this story might have especially appealed to the Chola king. The king constitutes his power as a worshiper and protector of the liṅgam, and he is crowned by Śiva and receives his grace. In addition, the crowning of Chaṇḍēśa indicates that he is understood to be the head of all bhaktas, much as the king is head of all his subjects when he is crowned. There is a parallelism here: While the nāyaṉār is a bhakta, he is also a righteous leader; while the king is the ruler, he is also a bhakta. The differences between the king and Chaṇḍēśa in the story would be downplayed by such an interpretation, but they are significant. Chaṇḍēśa was out in open space, fashioning a liṅgam from mud, which perhaps required daily construction, but the king built a permanent multistoried temple in stone, and installed a fixed liṅgam in the very interior of its space. Each was a bhakta appropriate to his embodiment; unlike rural Chaṇḍēśa, the king in his capital was able to provide an elaborate home for Śiva.

Evidence of other images of the nāyaṉmār in this temple supports the idea that, increasingly, people other than the king were identifying with the stories of the nāyaṉmār. The donor of the largest number of images to the temple, many of which represent the nāyaṉmār, was, in fact, not the king but a manager of the temple. The inscriptions call him Āditya Sūryan, also known as Taṇṇavaṉ Mūvēndavēlāṉ, and identify him as a headman of Poykai nāṭu and a manager of the Rājarājeśvaram temple.[56] As a donor, he was part of a larger group of people in the king's circle, including some female relatives of the king and ministers to him, who participated in Śiva by gifting images of God and his bhaktas.[57] But unlike the royals, who mainly donated images of Śiva, Ādityan gave thirteen images, nine of which were either nāyaṉmār or participants in the stories of the nāyaṉmār. The nāyaṉmār images included the mūvar plus the wife of Cuntarar, a nāyaṉār who is a ruler, and a nāyaṉār who is a minister, plus his wife and child and the form of Śiva that appears in his story. Again, the choice of images resonates with the status of the donor. As an agent of the king, Ādityan would have been interested in representing him in the donation; thus, images of both the king and a nāyaṉār who was a king constituted part of the donation. In addition, Ādityan donated the image of a minister nāyaṉār, which resonated with his own status.

One inscription describes a group of six images: Nampi Arūraṉār (Cuntarar), Naṅkai Paravaiyār (wife of Cuntarar), Tirunāvukkaraiyar (Appar), Tiruñāṉa (Campantar), Periya Perumāḷ (the king himself), and Lōkamahādevī (his chief queen).[58] This grouping suggests that the king is like the mūvar, who are the greatest among the bhaktas. Each image in this set was a pratimam—that is, a human likeness, distinguished from images of gods by their smaller size, two arms, and ornamentation. Each stood on a metal base; the mūvar measured between seventeen and twenty-two inches.[59] The images of the mūvar were adorned with golden flowers, threads, jewelery, rudrākṣa beads (108 beads for reciting the names of Śiva), and, in the case of the child Campantar, a golden girdle, part of which was donated by the citizens of two devadāna villages, Veṇṇi and Ku̱ruvāniyakkuti.[60]

Another inscription describes Āditya̱n's gift of two more images. One is of Chandraśēkharadēva, "set up as Dēvāradēvar of Periya Perumāḷ," as the inscription explains.[61] This image is distinguished from the others by being a divine form (*tirumēṉi*) and would have been visually encoded as such by having four arms. Chandraśēkharadēva is a form of Śiva, standing usually in the samavanga pose while holding the axe and the deer in his two upper arms.[62] It is tempting to agree with Venkataraman that the inscription labels this image as "the Lord of Dēvāram, the Tamil Śaivite hymns, deified," but Dorai Rangaswamy has raised important questions that challenge the idea that the term *Tēvāram* was used to refer collectively to the mūvar's hymns before the fifteenth century.[63] According to Rangaswamy, the inscription means that Chandraśēkharadēva was the Iṣṭa Dēvata or "favored deity" of the king, the form of Śiva that he preferred, and the one to whom the king offered personal and private worship.[64] I tend to be convinced by the latter's arguments because of the iconography and the sheer awkwardness of translating the relevant portion as "the Lord of Tēvāram of Periya Perumāḷ."

The other image mentioned in this inscription is one of the nāyaṉmār, Milātu-Uṭaiyār, also known as Meyporuḷār.[65] Like the scenes from the life of Cuntarar depicted in the wall mural and the sculptures of Chandēśa, this story involves a kingly theme, insofar as Meyporuḷār is a chieftain. However, this story is controversial; although it portrays the ruler as a bhakta and a patron of Śiva-bhaktas, it also describes his assassination. The story, again from the *Periya Purāṇam*, is that Meyporuḷār was the ruling chieftain of Tirukōvilūr and a devout Śaiva. His rival from neighboring lands was unable to defeat him in open combat, so the rival disguised himself as a Śiva-bhakta, wearing ashes on his body but concealing a sword. In this way, he got past Meyporuḷār's guard, Tattaṉ, who had been instructed to allow any and all Śiva-bhaktas into the inner palace. When Meyporuḷār bowed to the "bhakta," the latter stabbed him fatally. As the guard moved to apprehend the impostor, the ruler cried: "Oh, Tattaṉ, see—he is one of us!" and he made the guard take the culprit safely to the border of the city. The image is identifiable by the inscription, which includes the chieftain's words (*tattā, namarēkāṇ eṉṟa milāṭuṭaiyār*). The story is thus of a ruler who sacrifices both kingdom and life in his bhakti for Śiva. Incongruously, this image was installed in the massive temple of a flourishing king, as if to suggest that, were the events in the story to occur, then the king would respond as the bhakta, even while the power and the overlordship of the Chola king, as represented by the temple, ensured that there would, in fact, be no rival.

The last inscription details a gift of five images, one of Kṣētrapāladēva with eight arms and a group of four images representing the story of the famous nāyaṉār Ciṟuttoṇṭar.[66] This bhakta, as described by Cēkkiḻār, was a military commander who later renounced royal service to worship Śiva and provide for other bhaktas. Śiva came to the home of Ciṟuttoṇṭar disguised as a wild beggar (the Bhairava form, described in the inscription as dancing) to test his devotion. Eventually, the "beggar" agreed to eat at his home only if the meal would be a young child cooked as a curry; he then specified that it had to be their own child. Ciṟuttoṇṭar and his wife killed their son and prepared him thus. In the end, the child was restored to life after Ciṟuttoṇṭar and his wife had proved their bhakti for Śiva. Metal images of the Bhairava form of Śiva and a set of three images of the family members on a single pedestal were donated by Āditya<u>n</u>, who perhaps identified with the minister Ciṟuttoṇṭar in that both were agents of the king.

The number of images of the nāyaṉmār created for the temple suggests that both the bodies and the stories of the bhaktas were becoming increasingly important as emblems of religious salvation. Both the path of bhakti and the nāyaṉmār as preeminent proponents of that path were given prominent roles in Rājarāja I's temple, mainly through the king's identification with the status of the mūvar and selected stories of the nāyaṉmār. As composers of the hymns and the greatest among the Śiva-bhaktas, the mūvar were honored, but the stories and images of other nāyaṉmār that captured the imagination of Rājarāja I had to do with kings who were portrayed as bhaktas. These stories resonated with and reinforced the idea of the Chola king as a preeminent participant in the worship of Śiva, as a servant whose royal power was dedicated to and constituted by service to the Lord, and as one whose salvation was assured. Individually, these stories could be understood in other ways, as well; for example, the story of Meyporuḷār conveys the absolute sanctity of the Śaiva marks, in addition to the king's sacrifice. However, when taken as a group, they demonstrate that there was a perceived resonance between the temporal king and the king as bhakta of the stories.

The density of these bhakti stories increased as they became, along with the hymns, the primary ways of representing and understanding Tamil Śiva-bhakti, a development that reached its culmination in later tellings of these stories in Nampi Āṇṭār Nampi's *Tiruttoṇṭar Tiruvantāti* and especially Cēkkiḻār's *Periya Purāṇam*. Although the hymns contain personal references and names of the devotees, during Rājarāja I's rule we see these hymns greatly expanded into stories with which people could relate to bhakti. Increasingly, the "I" of the poems became the "I" of such interpreters because the making of images of the nāyaṉmār in pigment or bronze connected the donor, the nāyaṉmār, and Śiva in a salvific relationship.

Moreover, there are indications that these images and stories became a locus for many people—not just agents in the royal circle—to participate in Śiva-bhakti. I noted before that citizens of two villages contributed some of the gold for a girdle for Campantar's image. The decorations on the images, which required donations of various amounts of gold, were a way for ordinary people—perhaps not individually wealthy but with enough means collectively to donate an ornament for the sculpture—to participate in Śiva-bhakti. Even the casting of the images was an opportunity for creative participation, for the iconographic representation of the nāyaṉmār was not fixed; the texts that mandated their construction in a certain way, such as the *Kantapurāṇam* (Tam.), the *Śiva Rahasya* (Skt.), and the *Śiva Bhakta Māhātmya* (Skt.), date only from the thirteenth century and later.[67] Depicting them allowed for artistic creativity in a way that other images did not; even in later periods, the canons were not necessarily followed for constructing images of the nāyaṉmār.[68] Both the bodies and the stories of the nāyaṉmār became avenues for people to know, experience, and interpret Śiva-bhakti, as they constituted themselves as bhaktas.

The attention to specific, named nāyaṉmār and allusions to their stories in graphic depictions of them in Rājarāja I's temple provide evidence that the nature of embodiment became a preeminent way of understanding the bhakti of the nāyaṉmār. Acknowledging the samādhi of the nāyaṉmār, various people in the Chola realm of the early eleventh century, including royal agents, temple staff, and villagers, sought to reembody them in the here and now. Developments later in the eleventh century demonstrate this interest as well; for example, Rājarāja I's son Rājēndra Chola (ca 1012–1044) had a stone panel-in-the-round of the crowning of Chandēśvara (Candēśānugraha) carved into his temple at Gaṅgaikoṇṭacōḻapuram.[69] By the middle of the eleventh century, interest in the nāyaṉmār appears to have been represented not only by the highly selective choices of individual stories and images—especially of the mūvar, who had gained enduring prominence as the composers of bhakti hymns—but also increasingly by the donation of images of all sixty-three of the nāyaṉmār.[70] For example, there is an important inscriptional reference to images of all sixty-three saints, to a festival of these saints, and to a recitation of Cuntarar's *Tiruttoṇṭattokai* (Collection of Sacred Servants, *Tēvāram* 7.39), a hymn that lists all the nāyaṉmār's names.[71] This inscription, plus textual evidence from the latter part of the eleventh century, which I discuss later, suggests that the nāyaṉmār were becoming collectively identified as a specific category of religious person, and certain aspects of their lives were deemed most representative of bhakti. In other words, there was a move toward recognizing them as a distinctive and authoritative group in Tamil religious history.

These developments in Tamil Śiva-bhakti can be thought of as a process of transforming the nāyaṉmār into saints. Several recent books have used the term *saint* as a cross-cultural category for the comparative discussion of religious exemplars in many religious traditions.[72] This discussion—largely phenomenological as distinguished from historical—demonstrates similarities and differences between and among images of religious exemplars from a variety of religious traditions, including Christianity. For example, a major distinction between the nāyaṉmār and Catholic Christian saints is that the former are not viewed as intercessors.[73] My interest is in highlighting sainthood as a historical process of representation, not only biographical but more broadly as reembodiment in image, art, and text.[74] Saints are characterized by a dialectic between their actions during life and their reembodiment in peoples' imaginative constructs upon their deaths. There are identifiable historical processes that contribute to the joining of liturgy to hagiography, and these have importance in understanding the relationships among the *Tiruttoṇṭattokai* list of Tamil saints, the recitation of that list, and the formation of a canon of saints.[75]

By the mideleventh century, a list of Tamil Śiva-bhaktas' names was recited, and there were images of and a festival to these bhaktas at a temple in Tiruvoṟṟiyūr. This temple is located eighteen miles from Madras; as such, it is one of the northernmost towns sung about by Campantar and Cuntarar. The fact that Cuntarar probably composed the *Tiruttoṇṭattokai* at Tiruvārūr in the Kāvēri delta region, which is quite a distance from the Tiruvoṟṟiyūr temple, suggests that it may have been widely sung as a liturgical list.[76]

Cuntarar's *Tiruttoṇṭattokai* is a list of names. Its rationale seems clear: Cuntarar begins his list with "I serve the servants" (*aṭiyārkkum aṭiyēn*), and this continues as a refrain throughout.[77] Thus, through Cuntarar's humility, the hymn identifies and praises the bhaktas, whose names and, for some, their actions were culled from the hymns of Campantar, Appar, and Cuntarar.[78] If the rationale for the list as the naming of bhaktas seems clear, its order does not. I quote a portion from David Shulman's translation:

> (4) I am the servant of the servants of the King of the Holy Tongue
> (Tirunāvukk'araiyaṉ), who took for himself that excellence
> that is imbued with splendor;
> of the great prince Kulacciṟai's servants;
> of the great Miḻalaikkuṟumpaṉ and of the Demoness;
> of Nilanakkaṉ from Cātamankai,
> surrounded by roaring water;
> of the servants of the rare prince, Naminanti—
>
> I, Ārūraṉ, slave
> to the lovely lord in Ārūr.[79]

As is typical of a list, the order of the elements appears random and open-ended.[80] For example, most scholars now agree that Kāraikkāl Ammaiyār (the Demoness in the passage quoted) is one of the earliest of the nāyaṉmār; she is almost certainly earlier than Tirunāvukkaraiyaṉ (Appar), who is listed first in this verse of the hymn. Nor does the list provide us with many details of these servants, much less a classificational schema for understanding them. Like the mūvar's poems to Śiva, the list alludes to stories greater than it can tell. An additional consideration is the orality and meter of the hymn, which may have governed the placement of names to a greater extent than any idea of completion.[81] Completion is not intrinsic to the genre of list.

Completion is, however, characteristic of a canon: "The only formal element that is lacking to transform a catalog into a *canon* is the element of closure: that the list be held to be complete. This formal requirement generates a corollary. Where there is canon, it is possible to predict the *necessary* occurrence of a hermeneute, of an interpreter whose task it is continually to extend the domain of the closed canon over everything that is known or everything that exists *without* altering the canon in the process."[82] Through its liturgical performance in temples, the *Tiruttoṇṭattokai*, as well as other hymns of the mūvar, would have gained authority and stability of form (though this is disputed by a later text, the *Tirumuṟaikaṇṭa Purāṇam*), indicating a move toward completion. But because we possess scant evidence concerning its performance, it is impossible to tell whether the performers or audience viewed the *Tiruttoṇṭattokai* as complete.

More solid evidence for discerning a perspective of completion comes from written works. An important figure in this regard is Nampi Āṇṭār Nampi, who lived during the reign of the Chola king Kulōttunga I (1070–1122) and authored ten texts that were later included in the eleventh book of the Śiva-bhakti canon, the *Tirumuṟai*. A late-eleventh-century date for this author makes sense because his writings, which focus on the mūvar, fit in well with the general movement toward embodying the nāyaṉmār as saints.[83] Ten texts are attributed to Nampi: one on Vināyakar, one on Chidambaram, one on Cuntarar's *Tiruttoṇṭattokai*, six on Campantar, and one on Appar.[84] Tradition associates Nampi with the act of making a canon; he is credited with the creation of the *Tirumuṟai* canon. However, this attribution, which is based on information in the fourteenth-century *Tirumuṟaikaṇṭa Purāṇam*, is historically problematic. Based on the evidence of his own writings, Nampi canonized Cuntarar's list of saints.

In his writings, Nampi developed poetic techniques that were related to those in the mūvar's hymns yet distinctive enough so that he could be considered a founder of what Kamil Zvelebil calls a "revolution" in Tamil prosody.[85] Specifically, the revolutionary technique was the purposeful and skilled blending of Tamil and Sanskrit metrics to achieve new genres in Tamil verse, an equivalent in meter to what the mūvar had achieved in verse imagery. This technique is evident in Nampi's compositions in the antāti meter. Zvelebil says of the form it takes in Aruṇakiri's work: "Each line has a double organisation: in terms of *acai* [basic metrical unit] organised into feet (*cīr*), which is the original Tamil metrical structure; and in terms of syllables organized into regular rhythmic groups purely on the basis of quantity, whether short or long, which represents the impact of Sanskritic metrical structure." As with the mūvar's hymns, this form of meter is closely associated with music: "All this is part of the process whereby the connection between poetry and music, which began with the adoption of fixed melody-types (*paṇ*) for poetry identified with devotional singing of Śaiva and Vaiṣṇava *bhakti* hymns, becomes closer and closer, more intimate, more organic, until centuries later, the Tamil *kirttaṉai* is born."[86] In addition, one of the meters in which Nampi composed was viruttam, possibly derived from the Sanskrit vṛtta meter, which is today especially connected with the singing of the mūvar's hymns.[87]

Nampi's text, the *Tiruttoṇṭar Tiruvantāti*, is of particular importance because it relates itself directly to the *Tiruttoṇṭattokai* of Cuntarar. Nampi's text follows the exact order of the nāyaṉmār in Cuntarar's list.[88] He even preserves a sense of Cuntarar's self-referential refrain by interweaving Cuntarar's name and deeds in his praise of "the sixty-three" (*aṟupattumūvar*). In using Cuntarar's list, Nampi transformed an open-ended list into a closed list or, to use more provocative language, into a canon. In Nampi Āṇṭār Nampi's *Tiruttoṇṭar Tiruvantāti*, we have the simultaneous suggestion that Cuntarar's list is closed, yet its domain can be extended by interpretation. What Cuntarar accomplished in eleven verses takes eighty-nine in Nampi's work. Nampi used the frame of Cuntarar's list to elaborate on the character of each nāyaṉār, to fill in the stories alluded to in the original list, and to elaborate on the attributes and greatness of Śiva.

For example, Cuntarar's hymn begins with the line, "I am the servant to the servants who are the brahmans of Tillai." Nampi's composition begins with the verse: "I will tell about those who perform hereditary service to the One of coral hue who bears the crescent moon, to the One of the ambrosial sacred dance, to the Father who burned the cities of the heavenly asuras and the three worlds, who is enjoyed by those who know the excellent Vedas at the place of Tillai, whose fame is fit to declare." In this verse, Nampi uses Cuntarar's line as a frame for the fulsome praise of Śiva through description of his purāṇic embodiment. He chooses to elaborate on the nature of Śiva and leaves the nature of the brahmans' service unstated, perhaps indicating its status as a cultural presupposition.

The situation is different when Nampi describes a named bhakta. Of Appar, Cuntarar says, "I am the servant of the servants of the King of the Holy Tongue (Tirunāvukkariyaṉ), who took for himself that excellence that is imbued with splendor." Nampi writes, "This is the pure gem called Nāvukkaracu, who was born in Āmūr. [His sister] beseeched the Lord of Vīraṭṭaṉam [who gave him] medicine that dispelled the poison [the Jains] had given him. After this, he went to many places; then at Nallūr Śiva placed His holy feet on his head." Nampi emphasizes Appar's turning toward the Lord and his attainment of the Lord's acceptance. Again, we see that an early representation of the life of one of the mūvar stresses the themes of call and salvation.[89]

In addition, Nampi provides information on other bhaktas that makes it clear they are a diverse group, including both women and low-caste servants. Cuntarar says, "I am the servant . . . of the Demoness [*pēy*]." Nampi writes, "Thinking, 'I will not tread upon my Lord's mountain,' she walked on her head with her two legs high above. Umā smiled when she saw it, but the Lord whose body is copper in color called the lady 'my Mother.' She is the treasure of the town of Kāraikkāl, where the tree branches drip with honey." In this case, Nampi describes the moment of the lady's salvation, when she ascends Mount Kailāsa and is recognized as a bhakta by Śiva. The author chooses to represent her ultimate act of service; omitted are other details of her service, including ones that might explain Cuntarar's use of the term *pēy* to refer to her.[90] Evoking the hymns of the mūvar, he includes a reference to her Tamil hometown and emphasizes its fertility.

One of the servants is an untouchable of the pulai community; the term *pulai* is associated with everything vile, including uncleanliness, vice, adultery, and animal food, and also designates an outcaste. Cuntarar says of this bhakta, "I am the servant . . . of Tirunāḷaippōvāṉ, who goes straight to the god." Nampi writes, "It is said that Nāḷaippōvāṉ became a sage (*muṉi*) worshipped by the 3,000 [brahmans at Tillai/Chidambaram] after he left his lowly pulai [status] as a holy servant (*tiruttoṇṭaṉ*) and gained the grace (*aruḷ*) of the Lord of the hall (*ampalam*) at Tillai, which is praised by all. His hometown is a region called Ātaṉūr, which is famous among people." Here again, Nampi stresses the salvation of the bhakta through Śiva's grace while he localizes the event in a named Tamil town.[91]

As these examples demonstrate, Nampi uses Cuntarar's list as a structure through which he emphasizes the certainty of the bhaktas' salvation while evoking the mūvar's emphasis on the praise of Śiva and things Tamil. Through his prioritization of salvation as a major theme, Nampi assures us that the bhaktas are truly nāyaṉmār; they are saints. His work represents a transitional stage in the process of canon: establishing a fixed and authoritative list accompanied by interpretive elaboration yet lacking an impulse "to extend the domain of the closed canon over everything that is known or everything that exists." That impulse would come later, with Cēkkiḻār's *Periya Purāṇam*.

In early medieval times, the central imperial temple and its network of satellite temples were demonstrative components of the imperial assertion that everything in the king's domain was a manifestation of his embodiment of power, from fertile lands to peaceful social existence. In contrast, the vision of the three hymnists represented a distinctive perspective: Everything in the Tamil lands signified Śiva's embodiment of power. The two perspectives came together in the emerging imperial temple culture of dāna, in which the king became both donor of materials to God and in essence his representative on earth, while the mūvar's Śiva-bhakti was brought into the temple as a regional voice in the worship of Śiva. Certain elements of the mūvar's bhakti became de-emphasized in that context, especially pilgrimage, because the imperial temple was a stationary center; in this context, the pilgrimage of the hymnists to see Śiva in the Tamil lands became displaced by an ideal of salvation as the ultimate pilgrimage (samādhi) to Śiva in Kailāsa. As a result, the proximity to Śiva celebrated by the mūvar became problematic in the here-and-now, influenced by the hierarchy of temple ritualists and the emphasis on samādhi as the model for proximity to God.

Yet Śiva-bhakti did not become disembodied in the temple context; instead, the temple served as a locus for new interpretations of bhakti. These developments involved two distinctive perspectives on the issue of embodiment. On the one hand, the performance of the mūvar's hymns became a regular, liturgical aspect of worship in imperial temples, rendered by a group of singers. Increasingly, the singers of the hymns were defined by heredity, tending toward a homogeneous class of Tamil ritual specialists. On the other hand, stories of the nāyaṉmār were being told and referenced in paintings and sculpted images of them. These stories tended to highlight their diversity as embodiments of bhakti yet assert that they were all destined for salvation. These stories were a way for people to relate to Śiva-bhakti, to understand and engage with the praxis of participation. Although the status of temple singer was limited by right, the stories of the nāyaṉmār opened the path of bhakti to everyone and made participation possible however, and wherever, one found oneself. Ironically, the temple singers represented limitation; the canonized saints did not.

PART IV

A Corpus of Hymns

In building the Rājarājeśvara temple at his capital in Tanjavur, Rājarāja I aspired for it to be paradigmatic: The capital temple was the largest and most complex representative of a model of relations that would be institutionalized in all other temples in the kingdom. The capital city and its temple constituted, above all, a center, and the choices and methods operative therein were to be emulated within regional temples within their capacity. Burton Stein suggests the complexity of such an arrangement in medieval south India in his remarks on brahmanical ritual kingship:

> It is a transactional and redistributive process involving priests, kings, gods, and a multiplicity of ranked groupings (castes) capable of being replicated in territorial segments of larger political systems as an ideology of homologies. Local chiefs, e.g., the heads of dominant agricultural groups, are homologized to great kings, as their tutelary gods are homologized to great vedic gods. The method of incorporation is the technical medium of ritual carried out by trained priests—increasingly within the special context of temples.[1]

The purpose of having a center was that other temples built by the Cholas in their kingdom, while maintaining an autonomy of honor and redistribution within their own circumscribed areas, all participated in the centralized imperial formation emanating from the capital city.

Stein's emphasis on trained priests is apt, for whatever the king's ambitions, it was the religious authorities in the temple who would furnish and maintain the integrity of his system. When Rājarāja I built his temple in Tanjavur, the town was already associated with conquest. The king established the sanctity of this site by his selection and support of a distinctive school of Śaivism: "The temple of Rājarāja reflects the teachings of one particular *āgama*-based school of Śaivism, the Śaiva siddhānta."[2] The Śaiva Siddhānta school, whose name translates as "the culmination of knowledge of Śiva," represented itself as an authoritative tradition; it was pan-Indian in scope, with established centers all over India.[3] The school possessed ritual specialists and Sanskrit texts (āgamas) that were simultaneously philosophical treatises and ritual manuals. Śaiva Siddhānta was a system, and Rājarāja I used the school's coherence and organization to define the center of his imperial temple system.[4]

As I explore the logic of the Śaiva Siddhānta system in chapter 7, it will become clear that this school envisioned embodiment in a manner altogether different from the bhakti perspective. The Śaiva Siddhānta system understood ritual as a detailed enactment of complicated philosophical presuppositions, the main presupposition being that the most subtle essences were of the highest value. This principle applied to the forms of Śiva: The smooth liṅgam at the center of the temple was most subtle, and the anthropomorphized forms of Śiva represented his heroic deeds of mythology and were comparatively gross aspects of his concentrated power in the liṅgam. This principle also applied to the worshipers of Śiva. Those on the most correct religious path would be heading toward reabsorption (*samhāra*) in the Lord's subtle essence, resulting in mokṣa; those on a lesser path would remain in the world of gross distinctions, or the emission (*sṛṣṭi*) of Śiva, resulting in bhoga, or worldly enjoyment. Worshipers of Śiva were thus not all on the same religious path. Nor did they all have access to the higher path, for the Śaiva Siddhānta school's version of the appropriate body for the worship of Śiva was carefully and rigidly defined by both caste and privileged knowledge of ritual transformations.

As we have seen, pilgrimage and praise were the main ritual actions undertaken and encouraged by the mūvar. Every one of their hymns is an act of praise, and the vast majority of hymns locate the poet in a named town to which he has pilgrimaged. Sometimes the hymnists mentioned other acts of ritual worship. Indira Peterson has classified these in two ways: as "spontaneous, unstructured ways that are characteristic of emotional *bhakti*," including dancing and weeping, and as "structured, ceremonial acts," including offering flowers and lighting a lamp before the image of God.[5] Just as the mūvar imagined a variety of ways of "seeing" Śiva through his embodiment in prayer, in one's mind or heart, as an image in a temple, and as a presence in the Tamil lands, they evoked a variety of ways to worship him.

Many scholars today would identify the structured ways of worship with pūjā, a ritual offering of substances to God. Today, pūjā is the main way of worship in Tamil south Indian temples, and it is performed according to the āgamas as understood by Śaiva Siddhānta. This fact leads many scholars to assume that the pūjā performed earlier in history must have been performed in the same way, according to the same āgamas: "The dominant scholarly viewpoint has regarded *pūjā* as an undifferentiated ritual form. If you've seen one *pūjā*, according to this perspective, you've seen them all."[6] Richard Davis takes an opposing position, asserting that pūjā was a locus of contesting viewpoints: "*Pūjā* became a common ritual form in which contesting schools of thought could enact, display, and (they each hoped) constitute the shared world of medieval India in ways consonant with their own metaphysical premises and soteriological aims. As a central ritual of temple Hinduism, *pūjā* acted as a ceremonial arena for philosophical as well as ritual debate."[7]

In Tamilnadu today, pūjā in temples is performed according to Śaiva Siddhānta philosophy and practice. Furthermore, bhakti and āgamic styles of worship are tightly joined together, making it nearly impossible to imagine one without the other. Their mutual acquaintance has its roots in medieval times: The bhakti songs of the Tamil saints betray a knowledge of āgamic motifs, even as authors of āgamic texts do of bhakti. However, their awareness of each other and seeming compatibility today should not obscure each perspective's premise that the other, while it could support the worshiper's approach to Śiva, lay squarely within its own encompassing worldview. Thus, for the saints, bhakti alone would ensure the worshiper's salvation in Śiva, whether one's bhakti was actualized in performing a pūjā, singing the Lord's praises in Tamil, or feeding a bhakta of Śiva. All of these actions were to be performed with the active engagement characteristic of bhakti, and as such, they were examples of worship grounded in the same religious path. For āgamic ritualists, bhakti could be an important component of ritual worship, insofar as it encouraged a mind completely focused on Śiva, but bhakti alone could never replace the formal philosophical premises enacted in elaborate temple rituals. Richard Davis's viewpoint encourages us to understand that different approaches to pūjā *constitute different pūjās*, and to recognize that there is a tendency today to overlook past conflicts in the interest of creating a seamless contemporary identity, in this case, Hindu.

In the medieval imperial temple context, the philosophy and practices of the Śaiva Siddhānta school were central. For the priests of Śaiva Siddhānta, bhakti could complement their program of detailed ritual transformations; an attitude of engagement would not contradict their work to effect such transformations. But bhakti was not the foundation.

I view Cēkkiḻār's hagiographies of the nāyaṉmār in the *Periya Purāṇam* as a response to the centralization of the Śaiva Siddhānta school in Tamil Śiva temples during the Chola era. I thus highlight his role as an interpreter of Tamil Śiva-bhakti, a role that is a necessary corollary to the closure of canon. The *Periya Purāṇam* is dated by most scholars to A.D. 1135, during the reign of Kulōttunga II (ca 1133–1150), some hundred years after the completion of the Rājarājeśvaram Temple. More than a logical extension of Nampi Āṇṭār Nampi's work or an imitation of the Jain hagiography, the *Cīvakacintāmaṇi*, the *Periya Purāṇam* boldly contextualizes the lives of the nāyaṉmār within imperial temple culture, acknowledging its own historical circumstance.[8] Yet the *Periya Purāṇam* remains insistent that the diverse bodies of the nāyaṉmār—which are detailed in every way, including caste—are each appropriate to the worship of Śiva. Thus, in spite of their diversity of embodiment, all of the nāyaṉmār are on the same religious path, that of Tamil Śiva-bhakti. And their practice of bhakti results in salvation, or mokṣa.

The stories of the *Periya Purāṇam*, which detail the lives of the sixty-three nāyaṉmār in a total of 4,281 verses in viruttam meters, are difficult to classify. Most of the stories involve actions at temples or actions that by the time of the volume's composition would have been viewed as involving āgamic-based worship. Since I view the *Periya Purāṇam* as a response to āgamic-based temple worship and because a general discussion of such a large text is nearly impossible, in chapter 7 I discuss two examples that highlight the nature of that response: a scene from Appar's story and a more controversial story, that of the untouchable saint Nantaṉār, or Tirunāḷaippōvār, "He who will go tomorrow." Through text, philosophy, and practice, the Śaiva Siddhānta school carefully defined the placement of people in temples by basing its assessment largely on caste. Untouchables were left out of the discussion, as even below the śūdra level of caste, which was the level at which the nonbrahman singers of the mūvar's hymns were placed. What would bhakti have to say on the placement of an untouchable? Could even this category of person be part of the recentralization of bhakti in the *Periya Purāṇam*? Nantaṉār's story throws these questions into high relief.

In chapter 8, I discuss a chronologically later response to Śaiva Siddhānta that, although not made from within the bhakti fold, viewed itself as an heir to the bhakti vision of the mūvar. Late in the thirteenth century, philosophers from both brahman and Vēḷāḷa castes, many of whom were fluent in both Sanskrit and Tamil, began to write texts in Tamil that authoritatively explored topics in Śaiva Siddhānta philosophy. These texts were not Tamil translations of the Sanskrit Śaiva Siddhānta texts or necessarily in agreement with the earlier texts' tone or perspective. The Tamil texts themselves constituted a distinctive Śaiva Siddhānta canon.[9] One canonical author of the Tamil Śaiva Siddhānta school, Umāpati Civācāryār, is of particular significance because of his interest in the hymns of the mūvar. In his effort to create an authentic Tamil lineage for Śaiva Siddhānta philosophy, he undertook several organizational and interpretive works with respect to the nāyaṉmār: He compiled the first anthology of the mūvar's hymns, which he keyed to foundational philosophical categories explored in one of his own canonical works (both these texts are translated in the appendixes to this book); he wrote a number of short texts on stories of the nāyaṉmār; he created the Śiva-bhakti canon that is now known as the *Tirumuṟai*; and he distinguished Śaiva Siddhānta philosophy from temple culture by his emphasis on the guru, a category he applied to both the mūvar and Tamil Śaiva Siddhānta philosophers. In viewing both the saints and the philosophers as gurus, Umāpati sought to define the nature of religious leadership. Yet, in spite of their shared status as leaders, Umāpati does not understand the mūvar and the philosophers to be the same. In drawing a distinction among the nāyaṉmār, Tamil Śaiva Siddhānta philosophers, and āgamic ritual practitioners in the temple, Umāpati represents the Tamil Śaiva Siddhānta philosopher as the apotheosis of the interpreter of all things religious. The influence and significance of both the *Periya Purāṇam* and Umāpati's perspective are demonstrated by the fact that Tamil Śiva-bhakti is understood today through Cēkkiḻār's stories of the nāyaṉmār and also through the canon that Umāpati Civācāryār established.

SEVEN

Defining the Center of the Temple

The temple manager Ādityan Sūryan, who, it wiḷl be recalled, donated several images of the nāyaṉmār to the Rājarājeśvaram temple, was not the only temple authority to be mentioned in inscriptions or the most significant. There were, in fact, two other religious figures of greater importance at the temple. One was Karuvūr Tēvar, the "spiritual guru" of the king.[1] The king and his guru were depicted together in a mural and possibly in stone, and Karuvūr Tēvar is credited with composing a poem, the *Tiruvicaippā*, in which the king is praised.[2] Perhaps more important from an institutional point of view was Guru Iśāna Śiva Paṇḍita, the chief priest of the temple and a Śaiva Siddhāntin. This priest is often mentioned in inscriptions and even donated a metal image of himself to the temple.[3] He was a Śivācārya (priest of Śiva) in the Śaiva Siddhānta āgamic lineage of those qualified to approach God in the temple to perform pūjā to him.[4] This proximity to God, which included access to the sanctum sanctorum, was the special prerogative of those of a certain lineage and approach to the āgamas, and it did not extend to those lower on the āgamic spiritual hierarchy.[5] And, indeed, eventually this pandit was succeeded by other Śivācāryars in his lineage.[6]

The āgamic texts asserted a special relationship between followers of the āgamas, primarily Śaiva Siddhāntins, and the king. They made it a duty of the king to protect their religion, and they provided the king with ritual "blueprints" for the construction of the preeminent medieval sacred place, the imperial temple. These texts focus attention on ritual placement of both the images outside and within the temple and the ritual specialists who perform the worship of Śiva. Richard Davis explains: "The primary focus of the texts . . . is clearly on religious practice. The *āgamas* spell out in detail the organization of the temple cult, from the ritual procedures and architectural guidelines needed to construct and animate Śaiva temples, through the regular program of daily worship and subsidiary rites, to the much larger occasional festivals."[7] The āgamas were the primary guide to Rājarāja I in making his new temple at Tanjavur sacred.[8] Unlike the mūvar's hymns, the āgamas gave detailed information on how to make a place sacred and how to keep it functioning as sacred.[9]

Generally speaking, there was a presumed homology between the king and God. Just as the imperial temple system manifested the overlordship of the king, the defined space of the temple itself manifested the overlordship of God:

> The Hindu perspective . . . envisioned a concentration of cosmic power in one divine overlord and his earthly replica, the imperial ruler, dual axes of a unicentric structure of hierarchic and irenic relationships. The *pūjā* offerings made to the Cosmic Overlord and to other gods of the Hindu pantheon, all of whom were subordinate and partial aspects of Him, were not considered part of a cycle of exchange, at least in textual exegesis. Nor were gifts made to Hindu ritualist (*guru*) and temple. The Cosmic Overlord was thought to be completely independent and did not, therefore, need the food of men. The benefits bestowed by Him were granted by his "grace" or "favor" (*prasāda*) and not out of any obligation to return a gift previously proffered. Similarly, offerings to the Overlord and gifts to Brāhmaṇas and temples were to be made not in expectation of any immediate return gift, but because the honoring of superiors and altruistic giving were in themselves positive goods and helped the worshiper toward the ultimate goal of liberation and penultimate goal of paradise.[10]

Temple architecture, according to the āgamas, maximized the presentation of God as overlord. From outside the temple, one gets the impression of an "intensely closed space."[11] For example, the sculptures on the outer walls are carved to emphasize the surface of the temple, and the eye is drawn across the sheer massiveness of the walls. At Rājarāja I's temple, perforations in this surface are few; there are small windows at each level of the vimāna (tower), which soars above the earth and is ultimately crowned by a heavy stone, the śikara. On the ground level, there are six entrances to the temple, a small number for its massive size of approximately thirty by fifty-five meters. The main entrance, which is the largest, has a stairway that leads to the maṇḍapa, a pillared hall. This entrance is at the opposite end of the temple from the garbhagṛha and is the most distant and public entrance to the temple. Two smaller entrances intersect the antarāḷa, which is the antechamber between the ardhamaṇḍapa (a closed maṇḍapa, with pillars represented in relief) and the garbhagṛha. There are also three entrances directly into the garbhagṛha that lead from the vestibule, which I discussed in the last chapter. These entrances are not public and were probably reserved for priestly and royal use.[12] An imposing structure of heavy stone occasionally punctuated by entrances and windows, the temple gives the impression of virtual impenetrability. It is a place of sacrality, demonstrated especially in the tower that reaches some thirteen stories into the sky and in the carefully channeled access to the temple's interior.

Around the outside of the temple, just above a spectator's height, are magnificent stone sculptures carved in the round. They are located in dēvakōṣṭas or niches, which number sixteen at Rājarāja I's temple, increased from the nine niches standard in Sembiyan Mahādevī's temples. The sculptures are gods familiar from Sanskrit purāṇic stories, mostly various forms of Śiva.[13] Although the purāṇas indicate that these many forms of Śiva (Liṅgōdbhava, Gaṅgādhara, Dakṣiṇāmūrti) are Śiva himself, in the logic of the āgamas the placement of these forms of Śiva on the walls of the temple represents a different understanding of their relation to him: "The temple complex forms a structure of hierarchically ordered spaces, and Śaiva texts carefully prescribe which divinities should occupy which positions. As in the court of a human king, subordinates must arrange themselves around their overlord in a definite and determinate order, expressive of their political relations of respective inferiority and superiority. For this reason the Śaiva temple, viewed as a community of divinities, acts as a topography of Śiva's cosmic lordship."[14] Davis continues: "What emanates through the temple, in the siddhānta view, is Śiva's lordship (*aiśvarya*); what brings these other deities to be present in the Śaiva temple is their shared, hierarchized participation in his rule."[15] One sense of this subordination is thus imperial: The forms of Śiva around the outside of the temple visually represent his deeds to the observer. For example, Liṅgōdbhava challenged both Viṣṇu and Brahmā, whereas Gaṅgādhara carried the Gaṅgā River in his matted locks from heaven to earth, and Dakṣiṇāmūrti is a teacher. On the same level as Śiva's forms are dvārapālas (doorway guardians), humanesque figures that are particularly large and ferocious looking (although at this temple their expressions are mild) and who guard the entrances to the temple. The anthropomorphic sculptures on the outside walls of the temple symbolize the mythological figures' participation in and protection of the ruling Lord, and allude to that of humankind.

Another dimension of subordination in the temple context is philosophical in nature. The temple is itself a representation of Śaiva Siddhānta cosmology and ontology, which revolve around the dual notions of emission (*sṛṣṭi*) and reabsorption (*samhāra*). The garbhagṛha is the conceptual center of the temple, the place where the superior image of Śiva, the liṅgam, is permanently installed. In Rājarāja I's temple, it is a very large (*bṛhat*) liṅgam, some three meters high. The liṅgam is the source of all emission, which radiates out initially as pure, subtle, and intangible but becomes increasingly impure, gross, and tangible the farther it gets from the center. The liṅgam enclosed in the garbhagṛha is more (but not the most) pure and subtle, and the anthropomorphic images of gods around the outside of the temple are gross in comparison to it. The metal images of the nāyaṉmār and others that I discussed in the last chapter would be still grosser because all metal images are for processional (*utsava*, "festival") purposes, for which they are carried outside the temple and even the temple premises. Indeed, a temple built by Rājarāja I's son Rājēndra included carved reliefs of the nāyaṉmār around the outside of the temple that depicted scenes of their lives from the *Periya Purāṇam*.[16] The walls of this temple graphically illustrate the nāyaṉmār's service to Śiva, in both narrative and symbolic dimensions.

It becomes clear from the analysis of the Śaiva Siddhānta perspective on the embodiment of Śiva that this philosophical school tends to view embodiment as problematic, insofar as the body represents that which is farthest from the true and pure nature of Śiva. Indeed, the organizing principles of sṛṣṭi and samhāra apply to human ritual worship as well as to ritual space.[17] The āgamas divide Śaiva worshipers in the temple into two main categories: bubhukṣu (one who desires worldly enjoyments) and mumukṣu (one who seeks liberation). The goal of the former is bhoga; of the latter, mokṣa. This distinction of categories of layperson and religious adept is made in many religions. As in other religions, these groups have different ritual responsibilities. The āgamic texts describe these divergent rituals as either emission oriented (going out from Śiva) or absorption oriented (going into Śiva); the former are for laypeople, and the latter, for religious adepts: "The householder seeks worldly benefits, things that come about through the differentiation of the cosmos. The renouncer pursues liberation through a purification of himself, a decreasing involvement with the material aspects of his being, and a reunification of his soul as similar to Śiva."[18] In other words, laypeople are on the differentiated periphery of Śiva's emission, whereas religious adepts are near the center, close to the source of emission. Thus, the liṅgam must be approached only by people who are qualified to do so—those who are in the mumukṣu category and who therefore represent purity of aim in worship. The anthropomorphic images of Śiva may be approached by anyone in that they are vigraha (body) and thus able to be grasped by the mind.

For the purposes of priestly worship of the liṅgam, the Śaiva āgamas redefine embodiment as "ritual transformation." In the ritual context, both Śiva and the priests must take on appropriate "bodies"; Śiva temporarily takes on the body of the liṅgam, while priests take on the "body" of Śiva.[19] Such is the significance of these processes that the liṅgam and the body of the priest are "the two material focal points of daily worship."[20] Both of these transformations are accomplished by the placing of mantras on the respective bodies. Prior to the invocation of Śiva, the priest begins his ritual sequence of self-purification (*ātmaśuddhi*) by imposing mantras on his hands (*karanyāsa*). This makes his hands "Śiva-like" and fit for performing all subsequent rites.[21] The priest continues to purify his entire body by equally complex mantric rites. He thus transforms his body to be parallel but not equal to Śiva's own. In this state, he is fit for worship. The priest then invokes Śiva to come down from the *dvādaśānta* (location of the undifferentiated Paramaśiva) into the form of Sadāśiva, a "differentiated divine body comprised of mantras, yet infused too with the presence of Paramaśiva."[22] The priest establishes Śiva in the liṅgam with ritualized hand gestures (*mudrā*s), then welcomes him with an oral greeting, which initiates the rites of service to the liṅgam that the priest will perform in the pūjā ceremony.

Whereas material embodiment itself represents distinction and thus distance from Śiva, necessitating the transformation of the priest's human body into a body of mantras that "becomes a Śiva," the āgamas actually make a provision that people from several castes within Śaivism can worship the liṅgam. Like Śiva-bhakti, the āgamas suggest that correct worship of Śiva is that which is practiced in a manner appropriate to the embodiment, or socially defined body, of the worshiper. Unlike Śiva-bhakti, the āgamas hierarchically arrange the type of worship done by various agents appropriate to their embodiment; at the top is the āgamic worship of the liṅgam, which is the most important, efficacious, and influential type of worship. At the other end of the spectrum is worship, including bhakti, that is perceived by the āgamas to be limited in scope and efficacy.

The āgamas describe the division of Śaivas into five groups: anādiśaiva, ādiśaiva, mahāśaiva, anuśaiva, and antaraśaiva. Although there is no unanimous agreement among āgamic texts as to the meanings of these categories, often they correspond to Śiva, the higher brahmans, the lower brahmans, the kṣatriyas and vaiśyas, and the śūdras.[23] The āgamas thus evoke the Vedic varṇa categories, yet they give those categories their own specific meaning in an effort to define the proper worship of Śiva. Hélène Brunner suggests that the two categories most often discussed in the āgamas are ādiśaiva and antaraśaiva, which correspond to the two extremes of the Vedic varṇa system, brahmans and śūdras, respectively.[24] This means that the texts are most concerned with defining the limiting cases of human participation in Śiva.

The ādiśaivas are a privileged group, for they are the ones who are pure enough to be priests by virtue of their birth in one of five gotras (lineages).[25] As priests, they have the authority and capacity to perform āgamic rituals in temples for the benefit of all other categories of Śaivas.[26] The āgamas make the specific point that this category ritually encompasses all other categories of Śaiva worshipers: "Worship on behalf of others must always be done by a Śaivabrāhmana. A pious *ādiśaiva*, best among the brahmans, does worship regularly, but if others should perform worship other than for their own behalf alone, the worshipers will be destroyed."[27] Thus, the Śaiva āgamas invest a certain category of brahmans with the preeminent role of worship in the temple, where they perform pūjā to Śiva on behalf of a public audience.

As Brunner notes, the inclusion of the class of śūdras in āgamic texts is itself remarkable, although they are limited in their sphere of activity.[28] For example, although they can be initiated (*nirvāṇadikṣā*), they can act as ācārya (teacher) or perform worship only in a semiprivate world well outside temple culture.[29] As examples of a śūdra's ritual domain, Brunner suggests that they can initiate other śūdras only and that they can have their own private worship (*ātmārthapūjā*) of an impermanent liṅgam, for example, one that they construct out of sand, in contrast to the permanent stone liṅgam in temples. The domain of śūdra ritual worship is thus limited in scope, materials, and efficacy.

This conceptual hierarchy governed all worship activities in the temple, where it was played out in terms of space. Each place within the temple was encoded with a hierarchical order that was enacted at every pūjā offering. The ādiśaivas exclusively were allowed to enter the sanctum as ritual officiants. Entering the temple and going to the sanctum is an act of reabsorption; as such, it is reserved for those who have the partly inherent and partly constructed capacity to handle such power.[30] All other categories of Śaivas remained outside the sanctum. One āgamic text, the "Jātinirṇayapūrvakālayapraveśavidhi," attributed to Rāmakaṇṭha, a dualist Śaiva Siddhāntin from Kashmir who probably lived during the eleventh century, gives us precise details on exactly where the other Śaivas stood in the temple, including the singers of the mūvar's hymns.[31] Although we do not know how authoritative Rāmakaṇṭha's discussion was, translator Pierre-Sylvain Filliozat suggests that the text has pan-Indian significance because it quotes major āgamas and mentions the Tamil hymns.[32] The text itself is evidence that Śaiva Siddhānta was a pan-Indian school with an emphasis on system.

In placing the reciters of the Tamil hymns, the text uses the five-class division of Śaivas. The singers of the Tamil hymns are located below the highest four categories, namely, Śiva (anādiśaiva), the higher brahmans (ādiśaiva), the lower brahmans (mahāśaiva), and the kṣatriyas and vaiśyas (anuśaiva). Corresponding to this hierarchical order of varṇa is a spatial orientation in the temple, proceeding from the sanctum out. In āgamic understanding, the closer one is to Śiva, the source of emission, the closer one is to salvation. The ādiśaivas are with Śiva in the sanctum, and they recite āgamic mantras. The mahāśaivas, "who have gone on the other bank [of the ocean] of the Vedas, must praise and make a mental representation of the God, avid for a view of Him." The anuśaivas stand at the forefront of the mahāmaṇḍapa, able to view the liṅgam directly. And the śūdras, who sing the Tamil hymns (*drāviḍastotra*), stand at the back of the mahāmaṇḍapa, able to view Śambhu (the source of happiness, a name for Śiva): "In the *mahāmaṇḍapa*, in the farthest region up to Nandi, the *avāntara sat-śūdras* [highest category of śūdras] are able to sing the Tamil hymns while looking at Śambhu, consistent with good practice."

Accompanying this spatial hierarchy is a hierarchy of religious knowledge, which also communicates the distinction between subtle and gross. The ādiśaivas in the sanctum have "become a Śiva" by invoking Śiva through recitation of mantras and visualization. The mahāśaivas, lacking the ādiśaivas' shared nature with Śiva, praise him and make a mental representation of him; their distance from him is signified by the text's characterization of them as "avid for a view of him." The anuśaivas lack the subtlety of mind and gaze upon the liṅgam. Last, the singers of the hymns see a purāṇic form of Śiva as Śambhu. Given the status of purāṇic representations in Śaiva Siddhānta thought, Śambhu, as "the source of happiness," would in this context be associated with bhoga, or enjoyment.[33]

In support of this schema, Rāmakaṇṭha cites evidence from āgamic texts that appear to characterize the lesser modes of worship of the anuśaivas and the śūdra singers. Devotion is characteristic of the former; he quotes the *Svāyambhuva* as saying: "At the exterior of the ardhamaṇḍapa the anuśaiva can view the God with devotion." Manual labor is characteristic of the latter; he quotes the *Kiraṇāgama* as saying: "In the space of the mahāmaṇḍapa the śat-śūdra can view [the God], sweep and wash, etc."

As the "culmination of knowledge of Śiva," the Śaiva Siddhānta school sought to encompass and order all other ways of worshiping Śiva, including Śiva-bhakti. The key is that in the Śaiva Siddhānta system, the purāṇic-anthropomorphic images of Śiva were a lesser form of the Lord. Such images of Śiva were placed around the outside of the temple, where all Śaivas had access to them, but it was the liṅgam, enclosed in strictly guarded space, that stood at the center. The distinction between imagining God as nirguṇa (the liṅgam; Śaiva Siddhānta) and as saguṇa (the purāṇic images; Śiva-bhakti) is one manifestation of what is essentially a difference in imagining the relationship between God and humankind. The Śaiva Siddhānta priests were capable of proximity to the Lord and undertook ritual transformations to "become a Śiva." In contrast, Śiva-bhakti represented distance from Śiva, according to Śaiva Siddhānta. This contrast was understood in terms of temple worship and in terms of philosophical presuppositions. Richard Davis characterizes the difference from the perspective of Śaiva Siddhānta:

> We have seen as well that bound souls are distinguished from Śiva by the fetters that constrain them. The passage of a soul to liberation gradually removes these fetters, and in so doing it effaces the differences between the soul and Śiva. The transformations of soul and Śiva performed in daily worship similarly decrease the discrepancy

that normally exists between the two. Purified Śaiva worshiper and embodied god approach one another as separate but relatively equal, unlike in the *bhakti* schools that presume and extol an eternal and unbridgeable hierarchy between the two. (Śaivas admit, however, that the condition of equality between soul and Śiva can only be relative, never absolute, in ritual and in liberation.) The ritual transformations effected through *ātmaśuddhi* [self-purification] and invocation enable the soul and Śiva to meet face to face in worship as in liberation.[34]

Śaiva Siddhānta may have represented Śiva-bhakti as presupposing an unbridgeable gap between God and bhakta, in contrast to its own system for ritual proximity to God, but the hymns of the mūvar suggest otherwise. In their vision, Śiva-bhakti possessed a distinctive sense of oscillation. This oscillation occurred in their worship of Śiva, at times invoking Śiva to come to them through song and at times seeking Śiva through pilgrimage. It occurred in the way they addressed Śiva in their hymns, at times praising him and at times rebuking him. And it occurred in the way they represented themselves, at times rejoicing in their shared essence with Śiva and at times berating themselves for forgetting him. For the mūvar, oscillation was common to all human beings as the nature of the human condition. It could not be permanently settled by virtue of one's embodiment or by the practice of ritual.

Cēkkiḻār's *Tiruttoṇṭar Purāṇam* (Old Story of the Holy Servants) or *Periya Purāṇam* relishes the oscillation in the mūvar's hymns and extends it to his detailed descriptions of all of the nāyaṉmār's lives. The frame Cēkkiḻār uses to present these stories, however, is the certainty of salvation from Nampi Āṇṭār Nampi's *Tiruttoṇṭar Tiruvantāti*. Throughout the bhaktas' trials and tribulations, Cēkkiḻār insists that they were constantly engaged with Śiva and thus had direct access to him. Cēkkiḻār's use of Cuntarar's story throughout his multivolumed work is a good example of this strategy. Cuntarar, traditionally called the "hard servant" (*vaṉroṇṭar*), is known for the argumentative tone in his poetry. Cēkkiḻār draws on this aspect of his poetry in presenting the saint's oscillation between intimacy with and rebuke of the Lord during the saint's pilgrimages across the Tamil lands, which the author situates in the midst of his multivolumed work. However, this oscillation is framed by Cuntarar's intimacy with the Lord, which Cēkkiḻār conveys in opening the *Periya Purāṇam* with the story of Cuntarar's life in heaven prior to his birth and then concluding the text with the scene of Cuntarar and the Cēra king reaching Śiva's Mount Kailāsa.[35] His strategy is to frame the saints' oscillation with the certainty of their salvation by their constant engagement with Śiva.

The *Periya Purāṇam* thus explicitly and self-consciously relates itself to earlier bhakti texts in several ways: It quotes verses from the hymns of Campantar, Appar, and Cuntarar in its telling of their stories; it reproduces the order of bhaktas from Cuntarar's list and Nampi Āṇṭār Nampi's *Tiruttoṇṭar Tiruvantāti*; and it draws on the biographical allusions of the mūvar and other bhaktas, as well as on the brief stories presented in the *Tiruttoṇṭar Tiruvantāti*.[36] The *Periya Purāṇam* is distinguished from these earlier texts by its size (including Cēkkiḻār's presentation of seventy-two stories, as opposed to sixty-three, because of his elaboration on groups in Cuntarar's list) and by its perspective from a different historical context.

Clearly, such a text, whose length gives substance to its authoritative perspective, can be understood in many ways. Today, many Śaivas regard the text as the last authentic voice from within nāyaṉmār bhakti, and thus the stories are a preeminent way of understanding the bhakti tradition; for example, its stories of the nāyaṉmār are inexpensively reprinted today in Tamilnadu and used in schools for lessons on history and literature, in temples for the presentation of their histories, and in programs sponsored by the Śaiva Siddhānta. The authority and popularity of the text have made it a focus of scholarship on Tamil Śiva-bhakti, with scholars suggesting different angles for studying the *Periya Purāṇam*; providing classificatory schemata,[37] reflections on biography,[38] and explanations for the violence in some of the stories[39]; and reading the text in light of Śaiva Siddhānta texts in Tamil.[40]

My own perspective is to understand Cēkkiḻār's emphasis on the nāyaṉmār's access to Śiva in the historical context of the twelfth century. For example, in contrast to the mūvar's hymns, the *Periya Purāṇam* presupposes imperial temple culture as it describes their pilgrimages. This presupposition allows Cēkkiḻār to assert that there were relationships between the mūvar and various kings and to explore the nature of those relationships. For example, in the stories of Campantar and Appar, the saints restore worship of Śiva in spite of kings and win them over to the Śaiva side in the process. In the story of Cuntarar, the saint is identified as an ādiśaiva who was adopted by a prince; he then meets Cēramāṉ Perumāḷ, who as a devout bhakta has eschewed kingly duties in favor of going on his own pilgrimage, and a friendship ensues, culminating in their ascent to Kailāsa.

A scene from the story of Appar illustrates the king's duties in promoting the worship of Śiva. The context of this excerpt is Appar's pilgrimage to temples along the Kāvēri River.

> In time he approached Paḻaiyāṟai where the One with red matted locks appears, and clasped his hands to pray to Śiva. But the temple was concealed by the Jains; therefore he could not see it. He inquired whether this was indeed the [Śiva] temple tower that the Jain sect had covered with their lies. Upon learning that it was, his mind became intolerant and indignant.
>
> Reaching the side of the tower, he meditated upon the red feet of the One who wears white jasmine with fragrant petals on His head. Appar worshiped, praying: "May you remove the deceit with which the ignorant Jains concealed the tower, and may you cause the Jains, who possess fetters, to flee." Vakīcar [king of speech, a title for Appar] finished his thought thus: "If I do not see and worship your divine form, I will go no further," and he began to fast.
>
> The Great Lord perceived this and, in order that the King [Appar] should worship Him there, He graciously manifested Himself palpably in a dream. He [Śiva] graciously manifested signs in that place, saying: "Though the ignorant Jains concealed Us yet We remained there," and He manifested His grace, saying: "King who prays to us, remove and destroy the improper Jains and then go!" And Appar awoke and arose, then joined his hands above his head and bowed.
>
> Amazed at the sight [of Śiva's signs], Appar told the imperial king's minister about it and quickly returned to the temple with him. They saw the signs that Perumāṉ, Lord of the Universe, graciously manifested, and Appar pointed out the deceit of the Jains. Then the royal king himself came and worshiped

the feet of the great servant who had brought the deceit to light, and he rooted out the assembled Jains.

After the great [royal] king destroyed 1,000 Jains who were beaten as a shrub [that is trampled] by elephants, and after he made Śiva's tower shine, he provided materials for image worship [*arccaṉai*], worshiped Śiva, and bowed. And Appar entered the temple, bowed, and sang praises before Śiva: "Even if the Jain sect, which eats after plucking the hairs from their heads, conceals, is it possible to conceal the state of those who are devoid of truth?" After declaring these verses which are invaluble and true, and circumambulating the temple, Appar continued on his journey to other places where He who holds the trident resides.

Tirunāvukkaracu Purāṇam, vv. 1559–1565

The story quotes from, and is an interpretation of, the poem by Appar (5.58) that I translated and discussed in chapter 4. What had been a rhetorical question in Appar's poem ("The Jains, who expose their skulls, conceal Śiva with their minds; / But is it possible to conceal Him?") becomes the setting for a dramatic encounter between Appar and the Jains in Cēkkiḻār's narrative. Whereas the poem implies that the destruction of the Jains was one of Śiva's heroic deeds, Cēkkiḻār understands the poem to be a record of a historical event undertaken by human agents.

A persistent theme in Cēkkiḻār's narrative is that Śiva appears to his bhaktas at any time and place in order to actualize the self-motivation of the bhakta and bring it to fulfillment. In this case, Appar's motivation is to restore the worship of Śiva at the temple. Reasons are not given in the narrative to explain how the temple, which was originally Śaiva, came to be overtaken by the Jains. But whether the alleged decline of Śaivism at the temple is to be attributed to an earlier king's patronage of Jainism, the "Jainization" of Hindu structures, the forgetfulness of the people, or the abandonment of those who used to worship in the temple, the bhakta Appar restores the worship of Śiva. Cēkkiḻār has transformed the hymnist's displeasure with sharing space with the Jains into an image of encroachment and retribution. If there is a revivalism at work in Śiva-bhakti, it better characterizes Cēkkiḻār's approach than that of the hymnists.

A king is not mentioned in Appar's poem, but in Cēkkiḻār's narrative two people are called king: Appar, the king of speech, and an imperial king. The historical reality in Cēkkiḻār's time was that imperial kings did establish temples, yet in the narrative, it is the king of speech who both enlightens and directs the imperial king.[41] The narrative provides a blueprint that specifies the king's responsibilities toward Śiva and his bhakta. The king should listen to the Śiva-bhakta because he communes with God (as evidenced by the "signs"); furthermore, he should also worship the bhakta. The king should work with force to reestablish Śaivism in the temple and even destroy people of another religion. The king should acknowledge the glory of Śiva and provide materials for his worship.

In the narrative, Appar's actions, performed out of bhakti for Śiva, make possible all future worship of Śiva in that temple; the king's contributions, while significant, are secondary to Appar's. The story suggests that, far from having a limited role, Śiva-bhakti was central to the establishment of Śaivism as a living tradition in Tamil country. Through his narrative, Cēkkiḻār himself restored the image of Śiva-bhakti as an encompassing tradition by challenging the impression of Śiva-bhakti's marginalization in the temples. Cēkkiḻār represented Śiva-bhakti as having a foundational role in temple worship and as making possible the bhakta's direct access to Śiva. Cēkkiḻār's identification of Appar as a Vēḷāḷa is also significant in this regard, for it provides an image of a śūdra hymnist who has direct access to Śiva.

Cēkkiḻār's narrative betrays a caste consciousness that is absent from the earlier texts on the names and identities of the bhaktas. Since caste was presupposed in Indian society, it would have been unusual for a detailed description of the bhaktas to omit such information, yet it was also a cultural presupposition, illustrated by the Śaiva Siddhānta categorization of people by caste for specific temple duties, that people who shared a religious path would also share the same caste identity. Cēkkiḻār does not accept this premise in his narrative. Through the details of caste, place, and action, he extends the canon of saints to all known features of life in the Tamil lands. What emerges is an image of a unity in diversity; people whom society would ordinarily view as having nothing in common share the same religious path of participation in Śiva.

An important story in this regard is that of Nantaṉār, whose saint-name is Tirunāḷaippōvār (the one who will go tomorrow). Emphasizing the saint's salvation, Nampi Āṇṭār Nampi's *Tiruttoṇṭar Tiruvantāti* asserted that Nāḷaippōvār left his untouchable status (pulai) through service to Śiva and the Lord's grace and became a muṉi (sage) worshiped by the brahmans of Tillai. Salvation was also evoked in Cuntarar's description of the saint as one who "goes directly to the Lord." In Cēkkiḻār's telling of the story, in which he reemphasizes the pilgrimage context, the route to the Lord is not all that direct.

> There is a town named Ātaṉūr that has an ancient fertility and beauty the world praises. It lies on the western bank of the shining river Koḷḷiṭam (Coleroon), whose water benefits the wide fields, and whose waves draw out concealed gold and precious gems from the lotus stalks on both of its banks.
>
> In this place, where the great light of Śiva's ashes shines, beautiful lotuses flourish, and black crabs that live in the mud walk in the furrows and ridges created by strong ploughshares of yoked oxen, with blades that resemble varāl fish.
>
> Crowds of trees flourish, stroking the maṇḍala of the sun with their dense branches full of fragrant buds. They shake with honeybees and embrace the clouds; rains of water, honey, and flowers shower down without cease.
>
> When the flowers have opened and yield fragrance, vālai fish leap, rising high from the large waterholes, to butt and shake the roots of the coconut trees laden with bunches of green fruits. When the ripe fruits fall, the fish play in their overflowing sweet juices.
>
> Prosperity was everywhere, in both the open fields and cultivated lands. Because of this there was great wealth. Shining houses rose almost without limit up to the clouds, and large families were settled closely together. Indeed, Ātaṉūr possesses the closeness of kin.

At the edge of the boundary of cultivated fields lay a pulai hamlet. It was densely populated by the kin of agricultural laborers who were devoted to their families, settled in many sturdy huts whose roofs were made of thatched grass, upon which clinging green gourd creepers spread.

A crowd of chicks with soft feet and sharp nails roams about there, while young children wearing black iron bracelets run seizing puppies. The children have bands made from iron and jewels around their waists, which make gentle sounds that satisfy the puppies.

Everywhere in the pulai community these things belong: coconut trees under which puppies rest their heads; mā trees from which hang drums made of leather; vañji trees whose thin branches shade the large pots on top of which hens incubate their eggs; and marutam trees which shade infants that the pulai women suspend in leather hammocks.

The rustic songs of the lowly pulai women with curly hair are heard everywhere. Under the fragrant shade of the kañji tree roosters with red combs call, rousing the strong laborers at daybreak to begin their ploughing.

In all corners of the village tank, water fowl bathe noisily in the cool water. The lowly pulai women spread ears of paddy in the fields, their legs jostling blue water lilies which open and flow with intoxicating honey. Drums beat harmoniously.

There was an incomparable one who came to stay in this world, named Nantaṉār. He lived in this agricultural milieu; he came into the world with prior knowledge due to his earnest desire for the feet of Śiva who is truth and love; and he was possessed of the hereditary nature suited to the pulai village in that place.

After his birth, his prior knowledge became evident and he undertook the path of service (*toṇṭu*) to the feet of Śiva, as one whose mind was straight due to his exceeding love for the king who wears the moon as his garland, as one who did not possess forgetfulness, and as one of religious virtue who followed the way appropriate to his birth.

Taking for his livelihood the suitable work of servant on paṟiah lands released to the village, he excelled in his service to Śiva. For every temple of the Lord who holds the sharp three-pronged trident he lovingly (*ārvattiṉuṭaṉ*) provided skins and straps as covering for drums and other instruments with faces, strings well suited to the lute and vina instruments, and bezoar stone for the worship of the Lord of the gods.

He made all these things to the extent possible in the course of his livelihood. One day while standing outside the entrance to the temple, he became greatly inspired by the exceeding love and truth of the singing and dancing therein, and he meditated on the holy feet of Civalōkaṉ, who appears at Tiruppuṉkūr. He experienced single-minded desire for performing service to Śiva, and set out from Ātaṉūr for that place, reaching the edge of town in a state of love.

At the temple entrance, the holy servant who sang distinguished songs thought about his desire to worship the Lord directly. The Lord with the eye in his forehead (*Kaṇṇutalār*), who resides at Puṉkūr, which is surrounded by a wall that rises to the clouds, then gracefully caused the fierce bull (Nandi) to move aside from in front of Him, and appeared for the one who thought thus.

He overcame his birth in this world standing before the entrance to the temple of Civalōkan̲. After he completed his service and worshiped there, he went with the leather straps he used to make instruments shaking on his back (in ecstasy). He saw a small depression in back of the temple, approached it, and began to scoop it out for a tank.

After digging the tank, circumambulating the temple where Perumān̲ resides, performing service, and dancing, he was granted leave by the grace of the Lord whose hair bears golden flower blossoms, and he returned to his own village.

He went to many such places where the Lord full of Grace appears for worship, living as a true holy servant, his love (*an̲pu*) growing more and more. His desire to worship at the court of Tillai (Chidambaram) became overwhelming.

He could not sleep that night. At dawn he thought: "The nature of that holy place is not suited to my heritage (*kulam*)." But then, reasoning that "this thought too is a command from our Perumān̲," he discontinued his efforts to go there. After this he said: "I shall go tomorrow," and his desire grew greater.

Many days passed with him saying "I shall go tomorrow" in this manner, and his mind was not at rest. Finally, he set out for Tillai, which is surrounded by ripened fruit, flowering betel nut, and fertile fields leaping with fish, as one who would be released from the fetters of his birth.

When he reached the boundary of that holy place, he stood without going further, confronted by the sight of smoke from the great sacrificial fire, and of the brethren of maṭh (religious) leaders reciting in their exalted state. He paused, reflecting on the lowness of his heritage.

He stood there, thinking of the greatness attached to that place: "If one goes through the entrance in the wall surrounding the town there should be 3,000 oblations on as many altars, reaching up from each house like mountains."

Thinking fearfully that "one must be of that same nature; it is not suitable that I approach," he remained outside the walls of that place and circumambulated its boundaries with hands clasped and heart melting, while his love increased.

Circumambulating in that manner night and day, while thinking of that rare nature one needs to approach and enter, the servant whose heart swelled thought longingly: "How can I worship the dance in the hall of the Lord with the black neck?" as he swooned with sleep.

In his sleep he thought: "This base birth is certainly a hindrance." But the Lord of the Dance in the sacred hall knew of his state, and appeared before him in a dream, smiling gracefully, in order to resolve all his troubles.

The Lord of the sacred hall gracefully told him: "When you bathe in the fire it will extinguish this birth and you will be as a brahman wearing the triple thread on his chest." The Lord then commanded the appropriate inhabitants of Tillai to light the fire.

All the knowers of the Vedas (*mar̲ai*) who heard the command of Perumān̲ came together fearfully before the entrance to the dance hall, and agreed that

"we will observe the command that Our Perumāṉ full of Grace made known."
The holy servant drew near to that side with his love increasing.

The sages said: "Aiyarē! We have come to you now by the Grace of the
Lord of the hall, to set the hot fire and give it to you." The holy servant re-
plied, worshiping with heart melting: "I am saved," and the muṉis who know
the Vedas went about discussing how to set the fire.

After the Vedists spoke thus he came through the entrance that rose to touch
the moon at the southern wall, and arrived at the pit where the Vedists had set
the fire. He circumambulated the fire holding the Lord in his mind.

Then, meditating on the dancing feet of the Lord, with hands clasped in
prayer, he entered the fire. At that moment his form which is associated with
falsehood due to māyā was shed in the fire, and he emerged with a muṉi's
form that is pure, with the three threads shining on his chest, and matted hair.

When he went on that intense fire, he appeared as a brahman going over a
red flower. Then a heavenly drum sounded in the world, the gods were full of
joy, and fresh petals from the heavenly mantāram tree showered down.

The inhabitants of holy Tillai clasped their hands and worshiped the praiseworthy servants with joy in their hearts. Tirunāḷaippōvār, the sage of the Vedas,
went to worship the feet that dance inside the ampalam (sanctum) that contains the rare Vedas.

All the inhabitants of Tillai approached, stopping at the gōpuram to worship Him who holds the deer and the trowel in His hands, then hastily entered
inside. But when they reached the place where the dance is performed for the
benefit of the world they saw no one.

The brahmans were amazed, while the rare muṉis praised. The Lord of
the dance appeared, full of Grace, so that the evil karma of the servants who
came and joined him would be destroyed, so that there would be continuous
worship of his protective lotus-like feet, and so that there would be great bliss
instead of spiritual ignorance.

Henceforth, we speak the honor of the servant who reached the feet of the
Lord of the hall as a muṉi without fault, due to his bathing in the fire to remove his impure body; and who conquered the bonds of this world as a servant with the mark of holiness, by praising the Lord's shining feet.

Tirunāḷaippōvār Purāṇam, verses 1041–1077

Cēkkiḻār begins the story of Nantaṉār with a portrait of a Tamil town and landscape morally constituted by Śiva's proximity and evokes the images and sentiments
of the hymns to Śiva composed by the mūvar. At the periphery of the social world
is the pulaiyār community. Nantaṉār's pilgrimages to local temples and to Chidambaram represent a journey from the periphery of society to the center of religious
worship.

The oscillation between proximity to and distance from the Lord that is characteristic of Śiva-bhakti is here expressed in terms of Nantaṉār's bhakti and his self-
consciousness of his pulai status. The issue of whether Nantaṉār achieves salvation
because of his status or in spite of it is left tantalizingly unresolved. Nantaṉār's prior

knowledge of Śiva suggests a twice-born status that is traditionally a characteristic of only the higher castes, yet he is embodied as an untouchable. He performs service to Śiva appropriate to his status, yet he longs to approach Śiva in temples, which are off-limits to him as an untouchable. He goes to Tillai even though he knows he does not belong there, which creates internal turmoil for him. As an untouchable, he is an exemplar of Śiva-bhakti, yet he is transformed into a brahman muṉi just prior to his ultimate union with Śiva.

The story clearly implies that an act of worship performed with bhakti transcends caste affiliation. The Śaiva Siddhānta method, which attributed different religious capacities to those of different caste identities performing within a given pūjā ceremony, would be unable to acknowledge this perspective, much less that an untouchable would be an exemplar of religious worship for all. According to traditional views, the beginning of the story confuses categories: How could someone bearing a body that signifies past mistakes (karma) be born with prior knowledge of Śiva? Some interpreters would find solace in the conclusion of the story, which they would understand to support the traditional wisdom that one can ultimately join the Lord only if one is embodied as a brahman, which signifies purity. Other interpreters, taking a perspective more in keeping with the mūvar's hymns, would suggest that bhakti does not view past mistakes of karma as the exclusive determinant of one's ability to approach the Lord in the present lifetime. Whatever the embodiment, consistent worship of Śiva with bhakti will result in the Lord's granting salvation to the worshiper. Nantaṉār was transformed into a brahman at the end of the story not because he or Śiva necessarily required it but because it was impossible to communicate the purity of his heart to the brahman onlookers in any other way.

The story of Nantaṉār questions the assumption that heredity is a manifestation of religious capacity. This question was posed by bhakti in medieval Tamil religious culture, and there is evidence that the Śri Vaiṣṇava community actively explored it with respect to untouchables and temple worship.[42] A major issue in considering the practice of untouchables entering temple space was the pollution of the place's sacrality, which had implications for the community of worshipers beyond the consideration of an individual's capacity for bhakti. It is notable that in the Nantaṉār story the sacrality of Chidambaram is preserved by the saint's purification by fire before he entered the sanctum.

There is evidence only from modern times that the story of Nantaṉār was interpreted in a way that politicized the message of the saint's salvation; for example, in the nineteenth century, the famous scholar-musician Gopalakrishna Bharati emphasized the social disabilities of the protagonist in his dramatic rendering of Cēkkiḻār's classic.[43] His story was told several times on film in the context of the emerging critique of caste hierarchies during the Tamil nationalism movement of the 1930s and 1940s.[44] In contemporary times, as Lynn Vincentnathan has observed, attempts to interpret the story of Nantaṉār as a call to social action are extremely problematic. According to her research, untouchables who today live in the Chidambaram area have internalized the message of Cēkkiḻār's narrative: "For untouchables, their versions of the Nandanar legend fit with what they know about themselves—that they are capable of religiosity comparable or superior to that of caste Hindus."[45] Yet they also acknowledge that this sentiment has not resulted in a change in social status. Ultimately, modern attempts to view bhakti as a radical social message that serves to change, rather than define, place have resulted in a failure. Perhaps these interpreters have tried to extrapolate too much from a story such as Nantaṉār's, for the story begins to question caste at a very fundamental level. The pulai status of untouchable was characterized by nonhuman traits; the term connotes vileness and animal food in addition to designating untouchables. In the context of such degradation, Cēkkiḻār's story endows Nantaṉār with a human status and argues not only that he has a heart but also that his heart is pure.

The problem of whether events depicted in the Nantaṉār story could or should have translated into social action is an issue endemic to hagiographies of saints, which draw on the real in the service of an ideal. Saints are represented as exemplars, yet they are difficult to understand as models. In Christian tradition, the pressure to relate the lives of saints to the lives of believers was alleviated by the development of doctrines addressing the power of the saints, including the criterion that to be considered a saint, the candidate must have performed miracles, the paradigm of a saint as a reformed sinner, and, perhaps most important, the idea that a saint served as an intercessor, more than a model, for believers. In contrast, the continuing tradition of Śiva-bhakti did not develop a set of criteria that defined the nature of a saint and was applicable to each of the nāyaṉmār, largely because the list of bhaktas was closed through canonization. Thus, the continued evaluation of candidates that led to official doctrine on their relationship to humankind, such as took place in Christianity, did not occur in Tamil Śiva-bhakti.

Paradoxically, the Tamil saints were "leaders" (*nāyaṉmār*) for everyone through their embodiment of bhakti in their distinctive biographical contexts. In elaborating on the nāyaṉmār's stories, Cēkkiḻār provided plenty of detail within the frame of assured salvation through bhakti to Śiva to ensure that people could relate themselves to aspects of the nāyaṉmār's efforts. According to Śiva-bhakti, the oscillation of the human condition, as well as the promise of salvation within this lifetime, was in such details. It was a still later interpreter of Tamil Śiva-bhakti, the philosopher Umāpati Cirācāryār, who attempted to define the nature of religious leadership as a general category and to apply it to the bhakti saints.

EIGHT

The Tamil Śaiva Siddhānta

Śaiva Siddhānta was an authoritative school in Tamil country during medieval times, especially in the philosophical meaning and ritual practice of worship in temples. With its texts in Sanskrit, a lingua franca, the school established a network of centers in Tamil country and across India. In the thirteenth century and later, several historical factors contributed to the compromise of the school's pan-Indian network, including the acceptance of Śankarācārya's monism across India and Muslim incursions in the north, which, in turn, fostered the development of the Tamil region as a major center of Śaiva Siddhānta. It was in this historical context that a Tamil Siddhānta school emerged, distinguished from the Śaiva Siddhānta by its own canon of original philosophical texts in Tamil. Historical circumstances may have created an environment conducive to the rethinking of tradition in the Tamil context, but they do not explain the reconstitution of the school as Tamil; this is why I consider the creation of a distinctly Tamil Śaiva Siddhānta school to be a response to the Sanskrit Śaiva Siddhānta school, which continued to thrive in Tamil country. The Tamil philosophers had their own agenda in creating the Tamil school, which at times brought them into conflict with premises of the Sanskrit school.[1]

Guided by an ethos that they were heirs to Tamil texts in praise of Śiva, the Tamil Śaiva Siddhāntins both codified Tamil Śiva-bhakti tradition in the *Tirumuṟai* canon and expanded the range of its philosophical meanings. Both of these actions were motivated by the school's attempt to establish a Tamil lineage for Śaiva Siddhānta philosophy. Their creation of the school's identity as Tamil, through the Tamil Śiva-bhakti hymns and other Tamil texts on Śiva (which they linked with bhakti) and through their own writing of authoritative texts in Tamil, justifies distinguishing a Tamil Śaiva Siddhānta school from the Sanskrit-based school, although the Tamil Śaiva Siddhāntins did write noncanonical texts in Sanskrit. Their premise that Śaiva Siddhānta philosophy had a Tamil lineage and a Tamil corpus served as counterpoise to the formerly pan-Indian Sanskrit philosophical tradition that became centralized in Tamil country because of historical circumstance in the late medieval period. In a highly original, intertextual discourse, the Tamil Śaiva Siddhāntins defined their own philosophy, refuted other schools, and brought the Tamil Śiva-bhakti poems into their purview as examples of their philosophy.

Instead of maintaining regional centers with a pan-Indian outlook, as had the Sanskrit Śaiva Siddhāntins, the Tamil Śaiva Siddhāntins were unabashedly regional, both in terms of location, because their primary canonical authors were all from the Chidambaram area in Tamilnadu, and in terms of the language of their philosophy, Tamil.[2] Their canonical texts in Tamil are not translations from the Sanskrit but are original texts; thus, it is not the case that Sanskrit Śaiva Siddhānta simply came to be expressed in Tamil.[3] Moreover, although the Tamil texts drew on many of the elements of the Sanskrit school, including philosophical concepts and the importance of a guru lineage, they were also critical of it.[4] Tamil philosophers actively made the decision to create a school to promote the glorification of Śiva through writings and teachings in their mother tongue.

One of the main differences between the Tamil school and the Sanskrit school of Śaiva Siddhānta is that the former did not connect its philosophy with a specific temple ritual tradition.[5] This may suggest that the Tamil Śaiva Siddhāntins accepted several of the premises of Advaita Vedānta, a philosophical perspective that is critical of the implied duality between God and humankind in ritual worship. In fact, many of the contemporary philosophers of Tamil Śaiva Siddhānta I have spoken with in Madras indicate that this school "leans toward" advaita philosophy.[6] Although the exact relationship between Tamil Śaiva Siddhānta and Advaita Vedānta is not fully understood, it appears clear that the Tamil school's rejection of a close connection between philosophy and temple ritual practice should be understood as a criticism of the Sanskrit school. This is not explicitly stated in the Tamil canonical texts. However, the texts' concern with pure knowledge (Tam. *cutta ñāṉa*; Skt. *śuddha jñāna*) is clear, which implies a contrast between the contemplative Tamil school and the political Sanskrit school, which had to contend with issues of priestly status and patronage in the temple context. Indeed, a traditional simile depicts the Tamil Śaiva Siddhānta as both distinct from, and purer than, the Sanskrit āgama tradition: "The Vedas are the cow; the true āgamas are its milk; the Tamil sung by the four is its ghee; the essence of the book in Tamil written by Meykaṇṭār of the famous Veṇṇey is the taste of the ghee of great knowledge."[7]

The writing of Tamil Śaiva Siddhānta—for this was very much a philosophical, written formulation—is traditionally considered to have begun in the midtwelfth century, with the *Ñāṉāmirtam* by Vākīcar or Vākīca Muṉivar, and to have continued for the next two hundred years.[8] Fourteen texts in Tamil, which were in the main (although not exclusively) written by philosophers who traced their lineage to Meykaṇṭār, himself one of the authors, were collected as a canon, known as the *Meykaṇṭa Cāttiraṅkaḷ*.[9] Though when this corpus was constituted as a canon remains an open question, the Tamil texts indicate that the authors wrote with a strong sense of intertextuality, related to their ideology of the Meykaṇṭa guru lineage, and that they considered their texts to be authoritative; that is, the texts display a collective coherence, which is always insisted on when a corpus is transformed into a canon but is not often found in fact.

Umāpati Civācāryār was the most prolific of the authors of Śaiva Siddhānta canonical texts in Tamil; he is credited with eight of the fourteen śāstras. In several of these texts, he locates himself within a lineage that extends back into cosmic time and forward into his own historical time. Calling his various predecessors "the ones who are by nature leaders of the cantāṉam [lineage]," he lists: Tiruṇanti, Cattiyañāṉ, Taricaṉikaḷ, Parañcōti, Meykaṇṭār, Aruṇanti, and Maṟaiñāṉa Campantar.[10] Tradition has divided these eight ācāryas (including Umāpati) into two groups of four, according to the division of "interior" (*akam*) and "exterior" (*puṟam*) known from classical Tamil grammar and poetry. The first four are called *akaccantāṉam*, which suggests that they are symbolically "inside" the center of tradition. Mythically, these preceptors are not of this world; they reside at the abode of Śiva, Mount Kailāsa. The latter four are called *puṟaccantāṉam*, the lineage of gurus that carries the inspired teachings out into the world and radiates them among the people. Tradition says that Meykaṇṭār and Aruṇanti lived just prior to Umāpati, whereas Maṟaiñāṉa Campantar was Umāpati's living guru. The abode of these mortal gurus was the region of Chidambaram.

According to the hagiographies about Umāpati, he was a temple priest at Chidambaram, among the group of hereditary Dīṭcitars (ones who are initiated), who alone had and have the right to perform worship in the temple, although we do not know his Dīṭcitar name.[11] The identity of the Dīṭcitars is a matter of some uncertainty. Although Chidambaram has been the focus of many scholarly books and articles that describe the mythology of the dancing Śiva, the temple's art and architecture, and the lore surrounding this renowned temple town, only recently has there been a detailed attempt to reconstruct its very complicated history.[12] A cornerstone of the temple's history is the origins and identity of the family of priests that has apparently been in continuous control of the ritual activities therein since medieval times. It is clear from both mythohistorical legends and discussion with present-day priests there that the Chidambaram priests distinguish themselves from other priests in Tamilnadu temples. They seek to differentiate themselves in several ways: by their ethnicity (as all members of a select group of interrelated families who are descendants of the original priests at the temple); by the exclusiveness of the dancing Śiva as their temple's main image; by their distinctive traditions of worship, different from those of the majority of other Śaiva temples, which follow the Sanskrit Śaiva Siddhānta tradition; and by the fact that their temple, unlike all others in Tamilnadu, is not under government control.

The bhakti tradition of the Tamil nāyaṉmār does specifically mention the brahmans of Chidambaram (Antaṇar, Tillai). In the hymns of the mūvar, these brahmans are praised mainly as ones who know and recite the Vedas and the Aṅgas (Limbs).[13] And tradition understands Cuntarar to have begun his list of the holy saints with the brahmans of Tillai. In their praise of these brahmans, the mūvar's hymns are distinguished from other perspectives on Tillai represented in texts that eventually became included in the *Tirumuṟai* canon. Specifically, Tirumūlar's *Tirumantiram* and Māṇikkavācakar's *Tiruvācakam* emphasize a more mystical and symbolic understanding of Śiva at Tillai and do not mention the priests at all.[14]

Although he draws upon the mūvar's hymns, Cēkkiḻār's image of the brahmans of Tillai is characterized by ambiguity. When he tells their story, he compliments them on their commitment to "perform service to the holy feet," their competence in "the Four Vedas and the Six Limbs," and their command of the āgamas: "Knowing faultlessly the four parts of the *Ākamam* [*Kriyā*, *Caryā*, *Yoga*, *Jñāna*], they are equally adept at sharing wealth and practicing austerity. They live as householders, and practice tolerance and sensitivity. Being fit for their task, they are free from sin hereafter."[15]

However, other portions of Cēkkiḻār's work preserve a sense of ambiguity toward them; in the narratives of other nāyaṉmār, Cēkkiḻār tends to suggest that the brahmans of Tillai represent obstacles to Śiva-bhakti. For example, Cēkkiḻār says that Campantar hesitated to go to Tillai until he had a vision in a nearby temple, in which he saw the Chidambaram priests as Śiva's gaṇas, or heavenly hosts. In addition, Cēkkiḻār's narrative of the time when Cuntarar was commanded by Śiva to compose a list in praise of bhaktas implies an ambiguity.[16] The scene of Cuntarar's composition of the list is as follows:

> As [Cuntarar] passes the Tēvāciriyaṉ pavilion at the [Chidambaram] temple's entrance, he sees Śiva's earthly devotees [*aṭiyār*] assembled. "When will he make me one of them?" he wonders as he enters the shrine. Śiva appears with a command: "Sing a garland of words in service to those devotees, who have won me as theirs; who have conquered the world through oneness (with me); who are without flaw, and filled with the happiness of love—and you shall join them in this way." But Cuntarar is tongue-tied, unable to commence until Śiva himself gives him the first words of "his" (Cuntarar's) poem—*tillai vāḻ antaṇar tam aṭiyārkkum aṭiyēn*, "I serve the servants of the Brahmins who live in Tillai. . . ." Now Cuntarar can sing, in the new awareness granted by the god; the famous *Tiruttoṇṭattokai* flows out of him.[17]

Is Cuntarar—or Śiva—actually praising the brahmans? It is unlikely, though not impossible, that the priests are the aṭiyārs assembled at the entrance to the temple, for whom Cuntarar has so much admiration. And the Tamil of the first line is ambiguous: The way it is read in the quoted translation distinguishes the servants (aṭiyār) from the brahmans and makes the former the object of praise.[18] In Cēkkiḻār's story of Nantaṉār, the priestly community of Chidambaram at first represents an obstacle to the bhakta; it is only on Śiva's command that they agree to let him into the temple. And in the story of Kūṟṟuva, the Tillai priests refuse to crown as king Kūṟṟuva, a chieftain of Kaḷantai, because of their loyalty to the Cholas; eventually, Śiva himself crowns him king.

This ambivalence toward the brahman priests at Chidambaram is also found in some of the texts Umāpati wrote in Tamil.[19] Umāpati's history of the Chidambaram temple, the *Kōyil Purāṇam*, is one of the most important sources for the history of the Chidambaram temple in general and the Dīṭcitar priests there in particular. His Tamil text has four of its six sections in common with the Sanskrit *Citamparamāhātmya*, perhaps of the thirteenth century, but even within these sections there are differences that reflect Umāpati's perspective and render the text as his own composition. For example, although the texts have in common many of the stories about Viyākirapāta, a legendary ascetic who settled in Tillai, and about Paṭañcali, a snake devotee who watched Śiva's dance, they differ in their stories of Hiraṇyavaramaṉ, a legendary king who settled in Tillai, especially in the second half of this story, which focuses on the origins of the priests.[20]

There are at least three stories of the priests' origins within the Hiraṇyavaramaṉ sections of the respective texts. Paul Younger has suggested that the priests themselves may have edited these sections and were concerned about how they would read because the stories concerned their own origins and thus their legitimacy. The Tamil and the Sanskrit texts have two of the stories in common. One story has the priestly group as the Mūvāyiravar, "three thousand," accompanying king Hiraṇyavaramaṉ from his hereditary kingdom in northeast India on his journey to Tillai in the south to establish his new kingdom. The other story locates the priests as hailing from the Antarvedī region in north central India, where they performed elaborate Vedic sacrifices. The king persuaded them to accompany him as he journeyed south. As Younger notes, the Antarvedī region of India (between the Gaṅgā and Yamunā rivers) is known from many stories as the place from which the highest status brahmans hail. This story thus emphasizes the high status of the priests and their autonomous existence as tenders of the sacred sacrifice.[21]

The third story is found only in Umāpati's text. This story places the other two stories in a new chronological sequence. Here, the priests were *originally* at Tillai, where they witnessed Śiva's sacred dance. Then they were requested to come to Antarvedī to perform one of the greatest sacrifices of all time. Afterward, they were brought back to Chidambaram by king Hiraṇyavaramaṉ, who was traveling south to establish his new kingdom. When they reached Chidambaram, a count of the priests determined that there were only 2,999 of them. At this moment, Śiva's voice was heard from the heavens announcing that he was one among them, thus making the total 3,000. The effect of Umāpati's telling is to place the other stories in the frame of direct contact with Śiva, which determines the priests' origins and identity. The sacrifice at Antarvedī demonstrates the priests' competence in their performance of Vedic sacrifices, an aspect of the story that confers a high value on them as practitioners in the world and presents this competence as a complement to their darśan (seeing) of Śiva's dance. The inclusion of the story in which they accompany Hiraṇyavaramaṉ gets them back to Chidambaram and sets the scene for another example of the priests' contact with Śiva. In Umāpati's text, the priests participate in Śiva in both Vedic (sacrifice) and bhakti (seeing Śiva and proximity to God) ways. This image resonates with the status of the Tillai priests as bhaktas in earlier bhakti literature.

Later in the text, however, in the section on Naṭarājaṉ (the dancing Śiva), Umāpati draws a distinction between the priests as bhaktas and knowledge of Śiva's dance. At the dance, the priests are observers, not practitioners. Along with the Sun and the Moon, sages, Viyākirapāta and Patañcali, and the Goddess, they watch the dance, which Śiva performs as a boon to Patañcali. They do not play the role of interpreting the dance: This task Umāpati takes on himself, describing Śiva's dance at length with Tamil terminology from Śaiva Siddhānta philosophy, such as *aruḷ* (grace), *pati* (lord), *paśu/uyir* (soul), and *pāśa/mala* (bond, fetter). In several verses, Umāpati puts the philosophy of Śaiva Siddhānta into the mouth of Śiva as teachings to the assembled multitude.[22] The distinction is that the priests are praiseworthy bhaktas, having the right participation in Śiva, but it is Śaiva Siddhānta that provides the right knowledge, which comes from Śiva himself.[23]

This implied distinction between Umāpati and the Dīṭcitar priests is given concrete expression in the hagiographical literature about Umāpati. Umāpati had been a Dīṭcitar and then left the group of his fellow priests to follow the Śaiva Siddhānta guru Maṟaiñāṉa Campantar. This guru, about whom information is known only from Umāpati's texts, was a disciple of Aruṇanti and thus is a member of the puṟaccantāṉam line of gurus in Tamil Śaiva Siddhānta.[24] Maṟaiñāṉa Campantar was a brahman and well versed in the Vedas (maṟai). After his initiation from Aruṇanti at Kāṭantai (Tiruppeṇṇākāṭam), he went to Chidambaram, worshiped Lord Naṭarāja, and then settled in Tirukkalāñcēri, where tradition holds that he eventually attained release. One day, Umāpati, who had finished worship at the Chidambaram temple and was riding home on a palanquin, passed by Maṟaiñāṉa Campantar on the road. The latter remarked, "The blind by day is riding on dead wood," referring to the palanquin and the torch customarily on the front of the vehicle.[25] Recognizing the stranger as his guru, Umāpati immediately got down from the palanquin and began to follow him.

Maṟaiñāṉa Campantar is said to have wanted to test the "ripeness" of Umāpati, that is, the readiness of his soul to be granted initiation into Śaiva Siddhānta. Therefore, he went down a lane populated by the low-caste weavers and drank from the rice water that was used to starch the warp. In a traditional show of subservience, Umāpati drank the water that ran down the guru's forearm. Although Maṟaiñāṉa Campantar was pleased, the Dīṭcitar community was not, however; it perceived Maṟaiñāṉa Campantar, though a brahman, to be of a lower status than themselves. As a result of his ingestion of water from the hand of a lower status brahman (and that from a low-caste weaver), Umāpati was ostracized by the Dīṭcitars and took up residence at Koṟṟavaṉkuṭi, on the outskirts of Chidambaram.[26]

This legend of his break with the priests represents Umāpati as one willing to abandon the idea that temple worship was the most efficacious way to reach Śiva. His rejection is supported by formulations in his nonśāstric texts, including the omission of the priestly role in his Tamil *Kōyil Purāṇam* and his famous *Śataratnasaṅgraha* in Sanskrit, which is a compilation of ślokas from well-known Sanskrit Śaiva Siddhānta āgamas, such as the *Svāyambhu*, *Mṛgendra*, and *Kiraṇa*, that carefully avoids passages that would contextualize the āgamic knowledge in temple praxis. His śāstras are in a number of literary genres, two of which underscore the point that knowledge comes through the relationship between guru and disciple: the *Viṉā veṇpā* (*viṉā* is "question" in Tamil; Umāpati asks questions directed to his guru, Maṟaiñāṉa) and the *Neñcu viṭu tūtu* (*tūtu* is "message;" Umāpati imagines himself and his teacher as beloved and lover and sends a heartfelt message to Maṟaiñāṉa). Other śāstras in the larger corpus of Tamil Śaiva Siddhānta also highlight the guru-disciple relationship, including the link between the texts of Meykaṇṭār, Aruṇanti, and Umāpati and other examples of the question-and-answer format (*praṣṇa-uttara*).[27]

Although Umāpati expressed a reluctance to link the Tamil Śaiva Siddhānta idea of knowledge with a specific temple tradition, this does not mean that he rejected temple praxis. In all three categories of his works, Tamil śāstras, Tamil nonśāstras, and Sanskrit works (nonśāstras), Umāpati can be seen to have a continuing concern for the Chidambaram temple as a locus of the dancing Śiva. One of his śāstras (the *Koṭikkavi*) is linked to the "miracle story" of his raising the flag at this temple, his *Kōyil Purāṇam* gives the history of this temple, and one of his Sanskrit texts

(*Kuñcitāṅghristava*) gives a philosophical interpretation of the image and temple and may additionally be evidence for donations he made to the temple.[28] However, the promotion of philosophical knowledge predominated in Umāpati's śāstraic texts and in the larger Tamil Śaiva Siddhānta corpus of śāstras as the most efficacious path to Śiva, and in the process it hierarchized other ways of reaching the Lord. In this context, Umāpati rejected membership in a family of priests in favor of membership in a "family" of teachers.[29]

Tradition associates Umāpati with another type of institutional organization in place of the temple. Monastic educational centers (Tam. *maṭam*; often translated as *maṭh* or *mutt* more colloquially) under the leadership of a guru were established in the Chidambaram area probably around the fifteenth century. At least two of these centers trace their lineage to Maṟaiñāṉa Campantar and to Umāpati; for this reason, later tradition considered Umāpati to be a link between the puṟaccantāṉam and the institutional phase of Śaiva Siddhānta, called the *abhisēka paramparai* (lineage of the initiated).[30]

In turning away from the temple praxis associated with Sanskrit Śaiva Siddhānta, Umāpati turned toward established traditions of Tamil religiosity, particularly nāyaṉmār Śiva-bhakti. Umāpati Civācārya demonstrated a special interest in nāyaṉmār bhakti; many of the nonśāstraic texts in Tamil that are attributed to him by tradition explore themes relating to the nāyaṉmār's pilgrimages and identities. For example, *Civaṭcētra civaṉāmak kaliveṇpā* details, in three hundred couplets, the 274 pilgrimage sites visited by the mūvar and names the presiding form of Śiva found in each. Two shorter texts, the *Tiruppatikkōvai* and *Tiruppatikakkōvai*, also enumerate the pilgrimage sites. Other texts explore the identity of the nāyaṉmār; for example, the *Tirunaṭcattirakōvai* gives the piṟantai naṭcattirankaḷ (the ascendant star when each achieved samādhi) of each, as well as those of the philosophical writers (cantāṉācāryas, including Umāpati). These stars were used to determine the correct time for festivals celebrating these religious leaders. Umāpati is also credited with a distillation of Cēkkiḻār's *Periya Purāṇam*, the *Tirttoṇṭarpurāṇacāram* (essence of the stories of the holy servants).[31]

One such text is the first known anthology of the mūvar's hymns, called the *Tēvāra Aruḷmuṟaittiraṭṭu* (anthology of the corpus of the *Tēvāram* full of grace).[32] This anthology is explicitly linked to Tamil Śaiva Siddhānta philosophy by its use of foundational philosophical concepts to group ninety-nine verses from the hymns into ten categories. The category headings—including God, soul, bond, grace, guru, methodology, enlightenment, bliss, mantra, and liberation—correspond to those in one of Umāpati's canonical works, the *Tiruvaruṭpayaṉ* (the fruit of divine grace). The *Tiruvaruṭpayaṉ*, which I translate in appendix B, is composed of ten sections headed by these philosophical terms, each with ten enigmatic yet provocative couplets that explore the nature of its heading. The progression of the text is from the nature of the human condition to salvific liberation. Since the *Tiruvaruṭpayaṉ* is a canonical text that, although not expository, nevertheless explores the nature and meaning of humankind's journey to salvation, it is probable that Umāpati composed it first and then used his understandings as a guide for selection of the bhakti hymns he included in *Tēvāra Aruḷmuṟaittiraṭṭu*.[33]

Umāpati's interest in nāyaṉmār Śiva-bhakti may be viewed in two ways. On the one hand, the bhakti poems and stories provided an important heritage of inspired writings on the nature of Śiva and humankind's relationship to him in Tamil for the Tamil Śaiva Siddhāntins. The hymns proved that religious questions of universal import (Who is God? How do we worship him?) could be asked and answered in the regional language of Tamil. On the other hand, the bhakti poems and stories projected a path of religiosity that the Tamil school found more compelling than the temple ritual worship of the Sanskrit Śaiva Siddhāntins. The Tamil bhakti tradition may have become institutionalized as part of ritual worship in the Chola temples, but the bhakti hymns themselves did not propagate a specific form of temple ritual worship.

However, the Tamil philosophers also sought to distinguish themselves from the bhaktas, a perspective that was crystallized into the respective titles given to each group. The philosophical authors are known as *cantāṉācāryas*, where *cantāṉam* means "progeny" or "succession" and *ācārya* means "leader"; the bhakti poets are known as *camayācāryas*, where *camayam* means "religion." These titles connected the two groups as Tamil ācāryas yet differentiated their domains of authority as a philosophical lineage and religion. What is "religion" in this context? It is not the śruti of the Vedas, which Śaiva Siddhānta understands as a revelation authoritative for and applicable to all. Nor is it the metaphysics that Tamil Śaiva Siddhānta understands as the āgamas. It is the experience or enjoyment (Tam. *anupavam*; Skt. *anubhava*) of the Lord or the Lord's grace (Tam. *aruḷ anupavam*).[34] Tamil Śaiva Siddhāntins understand the experience of the Lord's grace to be direct and unmediated. In their schema, the nāyaṉmār are the primary representatives of "religion" in this sense of direct experience. Capturing the conflict between experience and explanation, one of the Tamil Śaiva Siddhānta canonical authors asked rhetorically: "Even those who went earlier as a group of men to join [the Lord] could not say what [he] is like; How can I say what [his nature] is like today; [his nature] is such."[35]

Direct experience was understood to be manifest in Śiva-bhakti tradition in two ways, drawing on both the established singing of the hymns in temples and the hagiographical tradition. In the first instance, the hymns of "the three" were utterances made at the time of direct experience of Śiva; they not only communicated their experience as a present tense reality but also encouraged others to participate in the experience of communion. In the second instance, the life stories of the nāyaṉmār represented direct experience of Śiva within the context of the human life experience and demonstrated that the experience of the Lord's grace was possible within one's lifetime. Further, the stories of the other sixty nāyaṉmār demonstrated that direct experience need not be limited to "the three."

In the Tamil Śaiva Siddhānta perspective, the stories of the nāyaṉmār provided a way to explore the direct experience of Śiva; they were examples of embodied persons who had reached Śiva within their lifetimes.[36] Umāpati's concern with the stories of the nāyaṉmār is found in his noncanonical texts, yet even within the canonical śāstras of the Tamil Śaiva Siddhānta there is a text that uses the stories of the saints as examples, the *Tirukkaḷiṟṟuppaṭiyār* by Uyyavanta Tēva Nāyaṉār of Tirukkaṭavūr. The author is considered to have written before Meykaṇṭār, which is reflected in the traditional placement of his text second in the canon of fourteen, just preceeding Meykaṇṭār's *Civañāṉa Pōtam*. One example will demonstrate how the author affirms that the experience of Śiva-bhakti can result from hearing about the actions of the nāyaṉmār. When Maṅkaiyarkkaraci, a queen of Pāṇṭiya nāṭu, heard about Campantar, she became overwhelmed by love: "Being told of the child who drank the pure Śiva-jñāna that flowed from the holy breasts full of milk, this great queen of southern Pāṇṭi[ya nāṭu], who had breasts full of milk, became a lady whose heart was engrossed in the way which is love [aṉpu]."[37]

This text suggests that, based on the example of the nāyaṉmār, if actions are done with an attitude of selfless love (the love that "engrosses" one in Śiva, as per the example of the Pandyan queen), then they are the actions of Śiva himself.[38] The text explains the relationship between God and soul as one of knowledge and love leading toward their "union" that is "neither one nor two" (*oṉṟaṉṟu iraṇṭaṉṟu*, v. 58). In his discussion, the author analyzes the actions of the saints before citing stories of several of the nāyaṉmār as examples of those who have loved, served, and reached the Lord. The stories of the Śiva-bhaktas are interpreted as examples of selfless actions of love that both lead to the attainment of Śiva and are indicative of having reached that state. Aware that some actions do not look like love, the author offers an explanation that reconstitutes Cuntarar's distinction between *nal aṭiyār* (good servant) and *val aṭiyār* (harsh servant). Uyyavanta clarifies that this distinction applies to the actions of the bhaktas, *melviṉai* (soft actions) and *valviṉai* (hard actions), and that through both these types of actions the bhaktas abandon the misfortunes of their births and approach Śiva (v. 16). Stories of the nāyaṉmār illustrate the Tamil Śaiva Siddhānta path to Śiva, insofar as they detail the actions—right or wrong—that make up human life. In this connection, some Tamil Śaiva Siddhāntins especially favor Appar—who spent most of his life following the wrong path of Jainism and then rebuked himself for that mistake for the rest of his life, according to Śiva-bhakti tradition—as an illustration of the depths of the human struggle. In this view, the nāyaṉmār evolve from performing ordinary actions, which are defined as "one's own" and are karmically bound, to actions that are selfless by virtue of being imbued with God's grace through one's love of God. The experience of love of Śiva is the experience of Śiva's bliss, which symbolizes union with the Lord.

Yet, however compelling the hymns and stories of the bhaktas were as paradigms of direct experience, the Tamil Śaiva Siddhānta perspective understood them as examples of a process that could not be explained through hymns and stories. For such an explanation, one had to turn to philosophy. This is not to say that the canonical texts of the Tamil Śaiva Siddhānta are expository texts as the term is ordinarily understood. They are as enigmatic and elliptical as any philosophical text (that is not a commentary) in Indian tradition, beginning with the *Brahma Sūtra*. The nature of such texts acknowledges the limits of language when contemplating metaphysical realities. In comparison to philosophy, the texts of Śiva-bhakti are signifiers, not analysis. According to the Tamil Śaiva Siddhānta, it is philosophy that provides knowledge of the deep structure underlying the universal human trajectory from ignorance to salvation. The Tamil Śaiva Siddhānta thus considered its own teachings to be most important, as a culmination of Tamil Śiva-bhakti tradition, drawing from earlier tradition yet superseding it.

Part of the dynamic of succession involves the closing of that which came before. This can be accomplished by labeling a predecessor in a distinctive manner, yet one that implies a relationship, for example, the camāyācārya and cantāṉācārya designations. It can also be accomplished by gathering and codifying materials that embody the predecessor's worldview—in essence, creating a canon. This latter dynamic, I would submit, represented a primary interest of Umāpati Civācāryār in his approach to the hymns and stories of the nāyaṉmār. Two texts attributed to him, the *Tirumuṟaikaṇṭa Purāṇam* (the story of bringing together the holy collection) and the *Cēkkiḻār Purāṇam* (the story of Cēkkiḻār), deal directly with canonization motifs.[39] Significantly, both texts set the development of Śiva-bhakti in Chidambaram, where the Tamil Śaiva Siddhānta was created. The mūvar may have journeyed throughout the Tamil lands, and the nāyaṉmār may have lived in towns all across Tamil country, but according to Umāpati the manuscripts of the hymns were subsequently "discovered" in a room inside the Chidambaram temple, and Cēkkiḻār wrote his *Periya Purāṇam* within the dancing Śiva temple complex, in the thousand-pillared hall. The first feature to note about Umāpati's purāṇas is their suggestion that the texts of Tamil Śiva-bhakti provided a precedent for developing Tamil religious literature at Chidambaram.

The *Tirumuṟaikaṇṭa Purāṇam* describes the compilation of the Tamil Śiva-bhakti canon, the *Tirumuṟai*, in forty-five verses. According to the text, a king named Rājarājamaṉṉaṉ apayakulacēkaraṉ was emotionally moved ("melting" and "his hairs standing upon end") when he heard the mūvar's hymns sung to Lord Śiva at Tiruvārūr.[40] The text says that the king knew the hymns were being sung in an eclectic manner and so he worshiped Lord Śiva to request that the hymns might be sung in an organized manner. At that moment, an Āticaiva (Ādiśaiva) brahman, as precious and unique as a gem, was born on earth. This boy was Nampi (v. 29 credits him with authorship of the *Tiruttoṇṭattokai antāti*, identifying him with Nampi Āṇṭār Nampi), and after enduring several tests put to him by the king, he was commissioned to retrieve the lost hymns. Nampi prayed to his iṣṭadevāta (chosen deity), Gaṇapati, in the form of Pollāppiḷḷaiyār of Tirunāraiyūr. This Lord revealed to him that the hymns were locked in a room behind the hands of the dancing Śiva at the Chidambaram temple, so Nampi and the king went there.

However, the worshipers at the Chidambaram temple, including priests, servants (*toṇṭar*), and guardians, expressed reluctance to open the door right away; they required that the mūvar themselves be present. The king then held a festival for the Lord, during which images of the mūvar were processed through the streets surrounding the temple before being brought before the chamber. The door spontaneously flew open to reveal manuscripts of the hymns. Many of the pages had been destroyed by white ants, but a divine voice told the assembled people not to worry and that what was available was all that was necessary, and Nampi began his organizational tasks.[41] Using the "seven crores of mantras composed by Manu" as his model, Nampi collected the hymns of the mūvar in seven volumes. The first three volumes contained the poetry of Campantar, the next three that of Appar, and the seventh muṟai that of Cuntarar. The *Tiruvācakam* (of Māṇikkavācakar) formed the eighth muṟai, the "garland of Tiruvicaippā poems that dispel desires" the ninth, and the "mantras that impart the experience of Śiva's Bliss" (now known as Tirumūlar's

Tirumantiram) formed the tenth muṟai (v. 26). The eleventh volume comprised "holy mystical hymns that speak of the Lord who grants Bliss," concluding with a composition by Nampi on "the good service performed by each of the nāyaṉmār," for which he drew on the *Tiruttoṇṭattokai* and on information he had received from Gaṇapati (vv. 27–29). Then, with the help of a female musician, he set the mūvar's hymns to music, specifying a tune (*paṇ*) for each hymn.

The text describes the making of a written canon, emphasizing the themes of collection, systematization, and authority. Priority is given to the mūvar's hymns; the *Tirumuṟaikaṇṭa Purāṇam* begins with a scene in which they are heard and concludes with a detailed itemization of the tune appropriate to each. Thus, performance of the hymns frames the discussion of the canon's formation.[42] The term *tirumuṟai* may originally have referred to the mūvar's hymns only, and perhaps even Appar's hymns alone, but the terms *tirumuṟai* and *tēvāram* were used in a variety of contexts throughout the medieval period, none of which definitively confirms that they designated the Śiva-bhakti canon (*Tirumuṟai*) and the hymns of the mūvar (*Tēvāram*).[43] The *Tirumuṟaikaṇṭa Purāṇam* may be the first text to use the term *tirumuṟai* unambiguously to refer exclusively to the Śiva-bhakti texts; it uses the term *muṟai* to describe individual volumes and the term *tirumuṟai* to refer to the collection of volumes.

With one glaring exception, the canon described in the *Tirumuṟaikaṇṭa Purāṇam* is as we know it today, including its title and content, the order of its volumes, and its assignment of melodies to the hymns. The canon of today, however, ends with the twelfth volume, the *Periya Purāṇam*, whereas the canon described in the *Tirumuṟaikaṇṭa Purāṇam* ends with the eleventh volume, concluding with Nampi Āṇṭār Nampi's *Tiruttoṇṭtar Tiruvantāti*. If the attribution of the text to Umāpati is not accepted, then the text may have been written before Cēkkiḻār wrote the *Periya Purāṇam* in the twelfth century. If the attribution is accepted, then Umāpati purposefully historicized the *Tirumuṟaikaṇṭa Purāṇam* to make the text seem to chronicle events as they actually occurred.

Another text by Umāpati, the *Cēkkiḻār Purāṇam*, conveys a sense of the completion of the canon. This text, which is written in the same meter of eight feet per line as the first twenty-four verses of the *Tirumuṟaikaṇṭa Purāṇam*, describes a ceremony marking the completion of the *Periya Purāṇam*. During the ceremony, the text was placed on the back of an elephant and paraded around the temple environs. This image of the text's treatment evokes a coronation ceremony, in which authority is publicly invested and recognized. Indeed, in Umāpati's *Koyil Purāṇam* Paṭañcali's (Patañjali) grammar is carried in procession at Chidambaram in the context of a coronation ceremony. As the story goes, the legendary king Hiraṇyavaramaṉ was married and crowned in the Chidambaram temple. First, he provided for the ritual needs of the temple and built homes for the three thousand priests. Then he was taken in procession on the back of an elephant, he anointed an image of God, and finally he had the grammar of Paṭañcali taken in procession on the back of an elephant. This procession of the grammar, mentioned only in Umāpati's version of the text, may be intended as a classical precedent to symbolize the authority conferred on the *Periya Purāṇam*.[44] According to the *Cēkkiḻār Purāṇam*, on its completion, the *Periya Purāṇam* was officially read out to an assembly of important persons, including the king, at Chidambaram[45]; the king, priests, and festival goers celebrated the *Periya Purāṇam* as though it were the pinnacle of tradition.

Umāpati's attention to these critical events in the life of nāyaṉmār Śiva-bhakti represents more than a passing interest in Śaiva bhakti. He was, I would argue, successful in creating a canon of Tamil Śiva-bhakti literature that has remained as he described it (taking both purāṇas together) until the present day.[46] In general, scholars have overlooked Umāpati's likely role in conceptualizing the canon, although there is much agreement that he wrote a text that described the making of the canon. To take the *Tirumuṟaikaṇṭa Purāṇam* as a text that represents historical events is problematic, as it is to take as history the legendary story that Nampi Āṇṭār Nampi was motivated by a king to produce the canon. Nampi did play a role in canonizing Tamil Śiva-bhakti: He canonized the list of saints. His role in the canonization of the saints alone made him a good candidate for the dramatized role of organizer of the written canon in the *Tirumuṟaikaṇṭa Purāṇam*; in addition, his work was associated with the development of Tamil music. In Umāpati's text, Nampi is an agent of Śiva's grace. The purpose of his compiling the Śiva-bhakti canon and setting the hymns to music was the spread of Śiva's grace: "In this manner, he [Nampi] made [the hymns and stories] of the sixty-three [saints] exist on earth, flourishing without end in all places, even up to the ears of Lord Śiva. As the embodiment of Grace, he cleared the minds of the good people of the world, releasing them from the three *mala*s (bonds) by the Grace of Śiva" (v. 44).[47]

The creation of a unified and closed written corpus of Śiva-bhakti would have been important to Umāpati for several reasons. First, he was interested in creating a coherent Tamil lineage for Śaiva Siddhānta. Second, the Tamil bhakti poet-saints had emphasized the "purity" of Tamil (centamiḻ), transforming it into a sacred language suitable for metaphysical speculation.[48] Third, Umāpati sought to encompass the Śiva-bhakti worldview with Śaiva Siddhānta philosophical premises. For all of these reasons, he closed Śiva-bhakti through the creation of a canon. In the process, texts that originally may have had nothing to do with nāyaṉmār bhakti were framed by its texts; for example, Māṇikkavācakār's work constitutes the eighth book of the *Tirumuṟai*, and Tirumūlar's *Tirumantiram* is the tenth book. The strategy may be summarized as making wholes into parts of another whole. Each autonomous text now became part of a whole—the canon—which suggested that there was an intrinsic likeness or similarity to them, that they were in some way of a piece.

Similarly, Umāpati joined the hymns of the first three nāyaṉmār to one of his canonical texts, *Tiruvaruṭpayaṉ* (hereafter TP) to create an anthology of the hymns, the *Tēvāra Aruḷmuṟaittiraṭṭu* (hereafter TMT). The mode of joining the two was his application of ten essential philosophical categories (which he enumerates and explores through couplets in the former text) to the anthology as headings for ten groups of verses. We may assume that Umāpati read through the corpus of hymns—which he had compiled—to select the poems for inclusion in the TMT. For him, the hymns were a text to be mined for specific examples of Tamil Śaiva Siddhānta philosophy. The TMT is highly selective: Of more than eight thousand stanzas in the *Tēvāram*, Umāpati chose only ninety-nine to constitute the TMT. In the anthology, each of the ten sections under distinctive categories contains various numbers of verses; there is no suggestion that the stanzas within the categories could or should be continued indefinitely. Some of the verses he has chosen use language from the āgamas, especially the concepts of *pacu* and *pācam*, which suggests that, at least in some cases, Umāpati may have believed that the mūvar had direct knowledge of Śaiva Siddhānta philosophy. Most of the verses, however, have no such explicit connection. The TMT represents a selective illustration of how Śiva-bhakti may be understood through Tamil Śaiva Siddhānta philosophy.

By far the majority of the verses included in the TMT are from Appar's *Tēvāram*. The breakdown is Appar, 63 verses; Campantar, 26 verses; and Cuntarar, 10 verses. In contrast to the TP, which assumes a critical distance between author and reader through an omniscient narrative voice, the TMT largely represents the voice of Appar. Unlike Campantar, who was blessed with a vision of the Lord and the gift of Umā's milk when he was only a child, and Cuntarar, who as a young man was "enslaved" by the Lord, Appar came to the knowledge and love of the Lord through a long life of trying experiences, as represented in the *Periya Purāṇam*. It is possible to suggest that, for Umāpati, Appar represented the intersection of knowledge and experience that would work best as an example for humankind. Appar came to God the hard way. So do we.

Umāpati frames his anthology with the understanding, demonstrated in the *Tirumuṟaikaṇṭa Purāṇam*, that the mūvar's hymns spread the grace of Śiva. The ten categories he uses to head each section of selected hymns describe the progression of humankind from ignorance to enlightenment and salvation; this is the deep structure that philosophy provides and Appar exemplifies in Umāpati's anthology. Tamil Śaiva Siddhānta understands three fundamental realities: the Lord (pati), soul (uyir), and bond (āṇava mala). The nature of each of these three essential realities is explored in the first three categories of the TP and, correspondingly, the TMT. The rest of the categories explore the nature of the soul's quest for the Lord. The āṇava mala, which is often understood to be ignorance, presents a barrier between soul and Lord. Salvation can be achieved only by the soul's movement toward pati; although the āṇava mala cannot be destroyed, in that it is a fundamental reality, it can be submerged beneath the unity of soul and Lord, which renders it ineffectual.

However, Umāpati does not provide us with explanations for his choices of poems within each category of the anthology. This omission may be due to the Tamil Śaiva Siddhānta's emphasis on the guru, who teaches face to face and not from a written text. Umāpati is our guru insofar as he identifies for us which among the verses of the bhakti hymns are examples of a specific philosophical concept, but the more complicated task of understanding how they illuminate the philosophical concept is left unstated. It is, then, with all humility that I approach a discussion of both the TP and the TMT. For the purposes of this preliminary comparison, for each section I first provide a summary of the meaning of each category heading, based on Umāpati's *Tiruvaruṭpayaṉ* (more detailed analysis of these ideas can be found in appendix B, after the translation of the text). I then identify patterns in each group of selected hymns that seem to relate to Umāpati's philosophical understanding of the category heading.

Patimutu Nilai (The nature before pati): For Umāpati, there is an original Lord who provides the foundation for the Lord that humanity recognizes as pati. This Lord is svarūpa lakṣaṇa, the "self-form-quality" of the Lord, composed of his pervasiveness and power (*śakti*). The form of the Lord that is accessible to humankind is the tatastha lakṣaṇa, the "that-standing-quality" of the Lord, who performs five deeds for the benefit of humankind: creation, preservation, destruction, concealment, and bestowal of grace.

The poems of the mūvar that Umāpati has chosen for this category emphasize the cosmic powers of Śiva, especially his role as Creator and Lord of the universe. The Lord is the One who mentally creates and then reabsorbs all creatures into himself, who is within the elements of the universe but is wholly described by none of them, who cannot even be described yet is able to take on many forms, and who controls the forces of māyā and karma through his grace (*aruḷ-śakti*), often depicted as the goddess who is his half. In contrast to the majority of the mūvar's hymns, nearly half of the verses Umāpati selected for this category do not localize Śiva in a Tamil town. In addition, only one verse from Campantar, which was perhaps deemed appropriate for the beginning of the TMT because it is the beginning of the *Tēvāram*, provides a description of Śiva in iconographic detail from the purāṇas, whereas this type of description is amply represented in the *Tēvāram*.[49] In his choice of verses, Umāpati sought to suggest the svarūpa lakṣaṇa nature of Śiva; he did not maintain the balance between universal and local that characterizes the mūvar's hymns.

Uyiravai Nilai (The nature of categories of the soul): The Lord provides the foundation for the human soul; the soul "stands upon" the Lord. Yet the soul does not know this because the primordial bond of ignorance, called the *āṇava mala*, "stands upon" it in turn. In describing the progress that the soul in an embodied condition must make toward God, Umāpati suggests that there are three stages, based on the degree of the soul's submission to the malas (bonds or fetters). The *sakala*s experience the three malas of āṇava, māyā, and karma; the *pralayakala*s have gone beyond māyā only; and the *vijñānakala*s have gone beyond both māyā and karma and wrestle only with āṇava. Because āṇava mala is one of the three fundamental elements of the universe (besides pati and uyir), it continues to challenge humankind up to the final "attainment" of the Lord.

The verses from the mūvar's hymns that Umāpati has chosen to illustrate this section focus on the body. In particular, this section is dominated by the pitiful and graphic laments of Appar. Appar is vexed by a lack of self-control, which he implies is encouraged by the nature of embodiment; he identifies desire, passion, the five senses, impermanence, ignorance, and illusion. Appar pleads with the Lord to rescue him. The last two hymns in the section, which are from Cuntarar, offer a more positive outlook and demonstrate the Śaiva Siddhānta perspective that ignorance can never completely conceal the Lord from the soul. By engaging in practices that encourage self-control, such as meditating on the feet of the Lord, practicing yoga, and forsaking desire and passion, the soul will eventually reach the Lord.

Iruḷmala Nilai (The nature of the dark bond): The āṇava mala exists fundamentally, in that it is never completely destroyed; it influences yet is distinctive from, the soul. The āṇava mala generates suffering, from which the soul can ultimately gain release. The method of āṇava mala is treacherous concealment; it conceals both the truth and its own existence from the intelligent soul. In this condition of ignorance, māyā and karma are actually positive forces that offer a flicker of light to the soul because it is through practical experience and action that one can gain at least some knowledge of the Lord. The soul works toward salvation in the smallest of increments; the key at this stage is gaining a preliminary knowledge of the Lord.

The verses Umāpati selects for this section focus on the mind. Here, the possibility of wresting the soul away from āṇava mala is represented through concrete examples of right action and right knowledge; it is a weed that needs to be plucked, and good ways put in its stead. These good ways come from within, and they also are aspects of embodiment (as with the negative aspects identified in the previous section); they are patience, love, knowledge, and virtue. It is also at this stage that humankind can begin to move beyond the concrete to intuit the presence of the Lord. A dominant image in the poems is the mind that is focused on the Lord. However, the influence of the āṇava mala inhibits the mind from true understanding; thus, Śiva enters the mind without the bhakta's knowledge.

Aruḷatu Nilai (The nature of grace): The capacity for receiving grace is inherent to the soul, but grace is the śakti of the Lord and must be granted to humankind. Thus, salvation requires both that humankind desires God and that God grants grace in an appropriate manner to humankind, after humankind is ready to receive it. In the TP, Umāpati indicates that humankind does not necessarily know grace when it appears and issues a warning to those who have not realized grace, even though it is in their midst.

For this section, Umāpati has chosen four verses from Appar to demonstrate that grace must be granted to humankind. Although Appar longs for a vision of Śiva, the Lord determines that he is not ready to receive grace; thus, in two poems the Lord playfully confuses the bhakta and causes him to mistake the Lord for a thief. The other two poems affirm that the Lord will grant his grace to humankind, primarily through knowledge that makes the mind clear. The power of grace is illustrated by Śiva's cosmic act of grace in destroying the triple citadels of the demons for the benefit of the universe. In purāṇic mythology, Śiva is the archer who destroys demons of the triple cities with arrows of illness and disease (or Agni and Viṣṇu in the mūvar's hymns). In Tamil Śaiva Siddhānta, this image has yet another meaning. The three cities are the three forms of mala; āṇava, māyā, and karma. Grace destroys the malas that afflict humankind, and it bestows knowledge upon humankind.

Aruḷuru Nilai (the nature of the form of grace): Umāpati defines the guru as a visible form of grace. The guru comes as a teacher to dispel doubt and give the disciple what is needed to proceed on the path toward the realization of God. The verses in the TP particularly focus on the sakala category of souls; this group, afflicted by all three malas, especially needs the cure that the guru can provide, although as the embodiment of grace the guru's teachings are relevant for all categories of the soul.

The poems Umāpati has chosen for this section are all from Appar, who serves as the model for the human condition. Appar's story has special relevance to understanding the nature of the guru, for he was led from Jainism to Śaivism by his sister, Tilakāvati, who is considered by many to have acted as a guru to him. Through the guru, the soul and the Lord are joined together, never to be separated again. In most of the poems, Appar understands that the Lord has saved him from manifestations of the malas, including a sea of afflictions, alternative tenets or religions, evil diseases, and even his own ignorant nature. The entrapment by afflictions is replaced by enslavement by the Lord. Of note is the verse (5.3) that praises Śiva both for creating a "family of bhaktas" and for providing a "path of philosophy that says grace is the source of all virtues" and thus links the two streams together, just as Umāpati himself does with the TP and the TMT.

A̱riyum Neri (the method of knowing): Umāpati acknowledges the role of life experience in his presentation of the methodology that leads to knowledge. He speaks of the "twofold karma," which, when it is balanced, will render the soul fit to receive Śiva's śakti. One sense of this karma is action within the world; the other is the influence of karma on the soul. Karma can have a positive influence on the soul, at least in an early stage of progression toward salvation. The influence of karma on the soul allows humankind to learn from worldly experience. For example, humankind begins to make distinctions (knowing that there is a person who performs actions, the actions that are performed, the results of those actions, and the person who experiences the results of those actions), yet humankind is able to understand that these distinctions are fundamentally related, which leads to knowledge of the soul (which is the continuity underlying all discrete things, or the foundation).

Most of the poems chosen to illustrate the "method of knowing" provide lists of modes of worship that keep one's mind focused on the Lord and will thus ultimately lead to the realization of God. There are methods of discipline to control the mind, including meditation, yoga, the discipline of leaving attachments, and the channeling of four mental processes (*antarakāraṇa*s) into a single path of pure knowledge (*citti*). The poems also indicate appropriate emotional dimensions of the methodology, including love that is sincere, sowing the seeds of bhakti, and desiring ñāṉa (*jñāna*). In contrast to the tone in the section on the soul, the emotions here are free of despair: Appar offers a prayer, after which he weeps, his heart melting; in another poem, he splits his sides in embarrassed laughter, realizing that he can hide nothing from God. Ultimately, these activities and attitudes will lead to a recognition that the Lord is knowledge itself. The last few poems in this section suggest that humankind eventually realizes this identity between the Lord and the soul.

The polemic toward the Buddhists and Jains that is frequently found in Campantar's and Appar's hymns is represented by only two examples in Umāpati's anthology. They are the antithesis of the soul's progression toward pati in their nature as "beings of the flesh." In contrast, one can save oneself by becoming a servant to the Lord as a path of discipline.

Uyir Viḷakkam (the enlightenment of the soul): In this chapter, the soul is at the threshold of salvation. The mature soul recognizes its own limitations and is thus prepared for the full experience of the encompassing, protective power of grace. These limitations and knowledge of them may be individually defined to make individualized experiences of grace, appropriate to each soul.

The poems Umāpati has selected for this category reveal distinctive themes in each mūvar's experience. Appar speaks of the experience of complete identification between soul and Lord that is possible when one loses one's attachment to self. Campantar speaks of the salvation of those who reach the Lord through their identification with him. Cuntarar berates himself for thinking there is separation between himself and the Lord and vows to keep the Lord in his mind always, with true understanding of his nature as the grace that pervades the world.

I<u>n</u>pu<u>r</u>u Nilai (the nature of experiencing bliss): This chapter of the TP explores the Tamil Śaiva Siddhanta understanding of the advaita relationship between Lord and humanity. The sense of advaita here is not "monism" but an acknowledgment of duality within unity. A well-known demonstration of this sense of advaita concerns the Tamil word *tāṭalai*, which is composed of *tāḷ* (foot) and *talai* (head). When these two terms are joined, the Tamil letters change to create a matching sound (sandhi) to facilitate pronunciation. The retroflex *ḷ* and the alveolar *t* join to become a retroflex *ṭ*: The result is neither two letters nor one letter. So, too, when a soul joins with the Lord: They are neither two essences nor one. The experience of this advaita relationship is bliss.

The five poems in this category indicate that when one sees Śiva through praise or meditation one experiences the bliss of identification with him. The bhaktas participate in his perfection. This participation, according to one of the poems by Appar, is freedom from the pendulum of desire, which is replaced by the equilibrium of detachment. In Śaiva Siddhānta, this state is imagined as *tā<u>l</u>maṇi*, the pendulum of a temple bell. The correct state is for the pendulum to be at rest in the center of the bell, not swinging from side to side. The sides represent desire; the pendulum at rest is thus symbolic of the soul's detachment. The state of bliss is this detachment.

Ante<u>l</u>uttu Aruḷ Nilai (the nature of the grace of the five syllables): According to Umāpati, the five-syllabled mantra (*pañcākṣara mantra*), or Nama(ḥ)śivāya, encompasses all religious knowledge and ultimate reality. This is illustrated by the following values given to each syllable: *Na* (Tirobhāva, the concealing power of the Lord), *ma* (āṇava mala), *śi* (Lord), *vā* (grace), and *ya* (soul). For Umāpati, the traditional recitation of the mantra in this order is an impediment to salvation because it does not represent the reality of the human condition. Instead, he insists that the soul must be between darkness (āṇava) and the Lord (pati); thus, the mantra must be recited in the order of Śi (Lord), vā (grace), ya (soul), na (Tirobhāva), and ma (āṇava). This revised order prioritizes both salvation through the Lord and humankind's ultimate struggle. If the reciter begins with *na* and *ma*, the individual affirms the control of elements of darkness and concealment over him. In contrast, if the reciter begins with *Śi* and *vā*, he is beginning with those realities that will set him free.

From the many poems the mūvar composed that mention the recitation of this mantra, Umāpati has carefully chosen the ones that are in keeping with his version of its correct recitation. Both Campantar and Appar have composed entire poems devoted to the sacred syllables,[50] which repeat the mantra as a refrain in each verse. But neither of these poems is included in Umāpati's selection because they give the mantra as "Namaccivāya" instead of "Civāyanama." The mūvar appear to have considered both mantras to be equally efficacious. But Umāpati has discovered two verses of one patikam that give the mantra as "Civāyanama." In the selected poems, the mantra is recited with Śiva's names, which is instrumental to receiving the Lord's grace. In the TP, Umāpati describes the mantra as the essence of all knowledge; in the final poem of this section, Appar says that it is all we really need to understand to attain the Lord.

Aṇaintōr Taṉmai (the state of those who have attained): For Umāpati, this state represents pure knowledge (Skt. *śuddha-jñāna*, Tam. *cutta-ñāṉam*) of the Lord as ultimate reality. Those who are in this state are enjoyers of the world through the bliss of Śiva. They are free from causation: They do not experience birth and death, they no longer cause the Lord to perform the five cosmic actions for their benefit, and all of their actions are selfless. They do not seek worldly ends, for the reward of their selfless action is truth itself, yet they remain in the world and have compassion for those who are still bound by ignorance.

The first several poems in this section (10.1, 3, 4, 5) describe various ways of worship. According to the Sanskrit Śaiva Siddhānta, these modes of worship (as well as portions of the āgamas) should be classified distinctively, in a hierarchical order of knowledge and efficacy: lowest is caryā (proper conduct), then kriyā (ritual), and yoga (discipline), with the highest jñāna (knowledge). The ways of worship represented in the mūvar's poems could be characterized as caryā (Appar: sweeping the floor of the temple), kriyā (Campantar: singing, ritually offering sandalwood paste, flowers, and incense), yoga (Campantar: controlling the breath and the mind), and jñāna (Campantar: knowing the arts, beginning with the Vedas). Indeed, some understand the mūvar, plus Māṇikkavācakar, as embodying these stages: Appar is caryā, Campantar is kriyā, Cuntarar is yoga, and Māṇikkavācakar is jñāna. However, Umāpati rejects this hierarchical view; for him, the composers of the hymns are gurus to others by their attainment of the Lord. Their hymns present several ways of participating in the ultimate state of bliss.

Other verses in the category affirm the salvific power of Śiva's grace and the unity of the soul with pati. There is a confidence, even a defiance, to the hymns, which suggests the certainty of salvation. "Those who have attained" live simply, having truly given up attachments. When one bhakta sees another, recognizable by ashes on the forehead and other insignia of Śaivism, he feels love for him and serves him as he would Śiva. In the language of Śaiva Siddhānta, the bhaktas are gurus.

The mūvar and their hymns held a special interest for the Tamil Śaiva Siddhāntins as examples of the direct experience of God's grace and, as such, predecessors in a Tamil lineage of gurus. Direct experience had been a feature of the hymns themselves, but it had become increasingly marginalized in the context of ritual performance in the temple, which had contributed to Cēkkiḻār's consistent representation of direct access to Śiva in the stories of the nāyaṉmār. Through connecting the hymns to his philosophical methodology of grace, Umāpati also recentralized the hymns' quality of direct experience.

Further, Umāpati connected traditions even within Tamil Śiva-bhakti tradition that had seemingly become increasingly disparate: He bound hymn and story together in a canon. The *Tirumuṟai* begins with the hymns of the mūvar and ends with the stories of the nāyaṉmār. In between, a variety of distinctive texts were brought together, including the mystical verses of Tirumūlar, the bhakti poems of Māṇiccavācakar, the hymns of Kāraikkāl Ammaiyār, and court-inspired songs in praise of Śiva. The *Tirumuṟai* was a written canon that encompassed all known compositions and framed them with nāyaṉmār Śiva-bhakti. Yet this written canon contained an oral canon, for the hymns of the mūvar (the first seven books of the canon) were organized first by author and then by melody (*paṇ*). The order of the hymns in the beginning of the written canon is thus quite distinctive from their order in Cēkkiḻār's narrative, for he arranges them by place, in the context of the mūvar's pilgrimages.

The pilgrimage Umāpati envisioned was toward salvation, echoing the emphasis in Nampi Āṇṭār Nampi's verses on the saints. A fifth of the poems he chose for the anthology do not explicitly localize Śiva in a Tamil town. Poems that include the local stories of the bhaktas and the local deeds of Śiva are not included in the collection. The TP's category of Patimutu (the original, cosmic Lord), as opposed to Pati (the Lord who acts in the world), in effect excluded the relevance of these sorts of poems to the philosophical agenda. In Śaiva Siddhānta philosophy, Śiva is not a local god, although this was an important aspect of him in the *Tēvāram* and *Periya Purāṇam*. As a corollary, the mūvar's love of seeing Śiva, which was intimately related to their sense of him as a locally concerned God with a presence to which they could pilgrimage, also became relativized by the philosophical premise that the Lord and the Lord's grace are intangible, save for the embodiment of grace in the guru.

Tamil Śaiva Siddhānta defined the sacredness of place by the presence of a guru, who as the embodiment of grace represented the apotheosis of understanding the spiritual significance of human life. The nāyaṉmār, as direct experiencers of Śiva, and the temple priests, as the leaders who ritually honor Śiva, remained important, but they were not, according to Tamil Śaiva Siddhānta, the interpreters who could help people understand the ultimate meanings and obligations of human life. This is the role of the Tamil Śaiva Siddhānta philosophers as gurus. Building on historical circumstance, the Tamil Śaiva Siddhānta philosophers developed Chidambaram, which was already famous as the home of the dancing Śiva, as the center for their ideas and institutions. According to Umāpati, prior to his time it was the setting for all the important events in the postnāyaṉmār life of Śiva-bhakti, including the "discovery" of the *Tēvāram* manuscripts in the temple and the writing and presentation of the *Periya Purāṇam* in the temple courtyard. During his era, all of the cantāṉācāryas hailed from Chidambaram. Tradition links Umāpati directly to the development of maṭhs (religious communities) headed by gurus that exist today in the region of Chidambaram. But beyond any geographical place, the guru stood at the center of Tamil Śaiva Siddhānta.

Concluding Remarks

If scholars of the nineteenth and early twentieth centuries tended to focus more on the definition of bhakti than its context, which resulted in a consensus on bhakti as "devotion to a personal deity" and an appeal to Christian influence, the trend seems to have been reversed in contemporary scholarship on bhakti, with much more attention to the variety of examples of bhakti, especially from diverse regional contexts, and much less on the definition of bhakti.

In calling this book *The Embodiment of Bhakti*, I emphasize two aspects of the study of Tamil Śiva-bhakti that have implications for the study of bhakti more generally. First, bhakti is a theology of embodiment. Its thesis is that the range of human experiences is religiously significant if grounded in the experience of God. Bhakti's emphasis is on participation, variously envisioned in texts as doing one's dharma, reviving a wilted woman who personifies bhakti, singing the Lord's praises in one's mother tongue, and performing acts of service. Second, bhakti's thesis on embodiment guided agents who developed bhakti as a religious path. In particular, story, sculpure, and sainthood, all of which illuminated the character and activities of bhaktas, became primary ways of understanding the nature and significance of bhakti. In these portraits of bhaktas, interpreters of bhakti related its thesis on embodiment to their own circumstances. Often, their work responded to challenges to bhakti from members of other religious worldviews. For example, Cēkkiḻār responded to the marginalization of Tamil Śiva-bhakti in āgamic temple worship by representing Appar as providing the foundation of such worship. The Tamil Śaiva Siddhānta also responded to the āgamic perspective on bhakti in a distinctive yet related way by asserting that the mūvar were primary examples of the direct experience of the Lord and by rejecting the centrality of temple worship.

Academic discussions of bhakti that focus on the image of God, including monotheism and nirguṇa and saguṇa, and those that focus on social movements, including reform, revolution, and revival, tend to obstruct scholarly recognition of the pattern of concern with embodiment common to bhakti's proponents and interpreters. Such discussions tend to overlook these agents' attempts to create continuity while insisting that the developing tradition respond to their own historical circumstance. If the categories of monotheism, revival, and so on are invoked in academic discussion, then the source of that representation of bhakti should be made clear, as well as the issues at stake.

Relating to the Lord through bhakti hymns was a cornerstone of the mūvar's and medieval interpreters' perspectives in Tamil Śiva-bhakti tradition. A single hymn by Appar can illustrate their distinctive yet overlapping perspectives on the meaning of bhakti:

> Inside this house called the body
> the heart is the lamp;
> Pour knowledge that dispels ignorance as the ghee,
> fashion the soul as the wick,
> take the supreme fire of ñāṉa as the flame,
> and the vision of the One
>   whose feet are decorated with anklets
>   and whose son enjoys the kaṭampu tree
> will be yours.

Appar uses a metaphor of the body to convey the experience of Śiva by mapping the body with ways of worship. Love and knowledge of the self and Śiva culminate in a vision of the Lord, and hearers are invited to experience this way of worship as well as the vision for themselves. In the context of the temple, this hymn provides a homology between the body-as-temple and the enactment of the pūjā ceremony. Through this homology, the ritual lighting of a lamp before Śiva (*āratī*) is both an act of honor and a symbol of the spiritual participation in the event by each person there, whether ritual specialist or member of the audience that observes. For Tamil Śaiva Siddhāntins, the hymn describes humankind's defeat of ignorance, as the soul becomes filled with the highest knowledge of Śiva (civañāṉa) and a mystical union with the Lord is attained. These perspectives were tied to distinctive images of the place of bhakti, from the "wide world" of the mūvar, to the network system of imperial temples, to the guru of Tamil Śaiva Siddhānta. Through these changes, the significance of the experiencer became understood through the increasingly important role of the interpreter.

The three streams of tradition may also be viewed as developing related meanings of the term *bhakti* through the questions they asked and the perspectives they promoted. For example, the hymnists sought to create a method of approaching God; in their poetic expressions of the method, they highlighted active engagement with the Lord through love. In the temple context, interpreters of the bhakti hymns sought to demonstrate how their approach to God was accessible to others; thus, they imagined the appearance and the lives of the hymnists in detail. Official singers of the hymns evoked the mūvar's own performances; images of the hymnists became part of the temple dāna system; and stories asserted the salvific quality of the nāyaṉmār's Śiva-bhakti and its application to people in many walks of life who chose to participate in the worship of Śiva. Philosophers writing texts in Tamil focused on the shared essence of humankind and the divine as they sought to define the nature of a religious leader. To them, a guru was absolutely necessary to lead humankind to a recognition of the truth of this shared essence; however, there were two distinctive categories of guru. One category, the leaders of "religion," represented the nāyaṉmār, and was a closed category. The other category, the leaders of "the lineage," represented the living tradition of the Śaiva Siddhānta philosophers. The former could lead one to the truth by example; the latter could teach one philosophical understanding of the truth.

Such compatibilities are characteristic of tradition, but they do not outweigh the distinctions each group made in their respective representations of bhakti. Indeed, there are considerable contrasts in their worldviews that developed in contexts of conflict, competition, and accommodation. The bhakti of the hymnists was brought into alternative, dominant systems that sought to encompass the poets' formulations. In the temples, Śiva-bhakti was represented as a regionally based support for āgamic worship. In Tamil Śaiva Siddhānta, Śiva-bhakti was represented as an early predecessor that led to a mature system of philosophy. Both of these contexts encompassed bhakti; yet the reverse is also true. Insofar as the Tamil poets located bhakti in the human heart, they created a paradigm of aspirations that compel people to participate in spite of real and imagined limitations.

APPENDIX A

Umāpati Civācāryār's *Tēvāra Aruḷmuṟaittiraṭṭu*

TRANSLATION

Index to the poems follows the translation.

Midway through translating this text, I came across a translation of it and the philosophical text by Umāpati, which I translate in appendix B, in V. A. Devasenapathi, *Tiruaruṭpayaṉ and Aruṇmuṟaittiraṭṭu, with an English Rendering* (Thanjavur: Tamil University, 1987). It was helpful as I reviewed my translations of both texts. However, the translator provides no notes, nor does he offer any explanatory essay, which he leaves to others: "A study of these companion works is not merely of academic interest but is also of value for spiritual practice. The grammar of philosophy must be understood with reference to the literature of religion at the focal point of one's own experience. . . . The present work is an invitation to the academically and spiritually adventurous to follow the train in this treasure hunt" (Preface). I am also much indebted to Norman J. Cutler, Indira V. Peterson, and A. K. Ramanujan, for their work in creating conventions for translating Tamil poetry into English. Peterson's *Poems* was especially helpful, although I discovered with mild surprise that with very few exceptions the *Tēvāram* poems she has translated there do not overlap with Umāpati's collection that I translate here. In the translation, each poem has a title: for example, 1.1 Campantar 1.1.1/1 *Tiruppiramapuram*. The first number refers to its place in the *Tēvāra Aruḷmuṟaittiraṭṭu*, followed by the name of the author, its number in the *Tirumuṟai* canon, and its traditional title (which is often a place name).

1. Patimutu Nilai / The Nature before Pati

1.1 Campantar 1.1.1/1 *Tiruppiramapuram*[1]

His ear adorned with an earring,
riding on a bull,
crowned by the pure white moon,
smeared with ashes from the cremation ground,
He stole my heart.
This one is Pemmā<u>n</u> who resides at great Piramāpuram,
where He bestowed Grace upon the One of the lotus
who worshiped Him in days of yore.

1.2 Appar 4.63.3/4780 *Tiru Aṇṇāmalai*

Oh, our Perumā<u>n</u>,
    who stands as the great deeds of birth and death
    for all the universe that is classified as body and soul,
stay at Aṇṇāmalai where water flows and makes fertile the land.
Since I approached the king of the gods
I need no other wealth besides his beneficial feet.

1.3 Appar 5.97.2/6196

A light appears in the heavens
that has passed through the darkness that pervades the worlds.
Upon perceiving that light, whoever here is knowledgeable
will call it Vētiya<u>n</u>, who traps the pure moon in his locks.

1.4 Campantar 3.54.5/3376 *Tiruppācuram*

Oh people of great virtue!
You need not search hard for the Lord
by means of the logic of causes and argumentation;
Our Lord of Light is all-brilliant.
Great Sādhus,
live with your minds fixed on the Light
and you will experience release from great sorrows.
Come before the Lord!

1.1 Line 5, heart, *uḷḷam*. Line 6, Piramāpuram, Brahmāpuram (Skt.). Line 7, the One of the lotus, Brahmā.

1.2 Line 4, water flows . . . mikku aruvi po<u>n</u> coriyum—in Tamil poetry it is typical to use the term *gold* to convey the wealth of fertility that water brings; line 6, ma<u>rr</u>oru māṭu il ē<u>n</u> ē.

1.3 Line 1, light, cuṭar. Line 2, darkness, iruḷ. Line 4, Vētiya<u>n</u>, he who is the source, meaning, knowledge, or Vedic knowledge.

1.4 Line 3, logic of causes and argumentation, ētukkaḷālum eṭutta mo<u>l</u>iyālum. Line 4, Lord of Light, enkaḷ cōti. Line 5, Great Sādhus, cātukkaḷ mikkīr.

1.5 Campantar 3.54.3/3374 *Tiruppācuram*
He gracefully cures the karma
of those who wake up thinking upon
the One who has no mother and father and
who smears Himself with ashes, thinking them sandalwood paste.
Though He is my Father,
how can I tell you of His ways?

1.6 Campantar 3.54.4/3375 *Tiruppācuram*
If one should ask about the excellence of the Lord,
beginning with the ways He grants Grace to those He rules,
we would not be able to say;
for it is without limit.
Those who stand here worshiping the Lord's feet
so that karma and attachments remain at bay
truly deserve to hear these things I'm saying.

1.7 Appar 6.35.2/6605 *Tiruveṇkāṭu*
The Lord of the feet that remain upon the earth as its only support;
the Lord of the feet that pass through the seven netherworlds;
the Lord of the feet that stand as the way of no sorrows;
the Lord of the feet that are one with the seven worlds.
After the roar of the sea rose up and spread forcefully
then calmed, submerging the whole world,
the Lord heard the sound of the Vedas on the vina
and resided with love at Veṇkāṭu.

1.8 Campantar 1.21.3/219 *Tiruccivapuram*
The Lord is the first Being
who gracefully intends to destroy all the ensouled beings
that abound in races such as celestials, demons, and humans,
in all the worlds, first among them the earth
that lies at the side of the faultless sea.
This Lord resides at Civapuram,
ornamented with fertility and jewels;
the fame of the one who worships Him in this temple
will spread throughout the world.

1.5 Line 6, entaiyār avar evvakaiyār kolō?

1.6 Line 5, alternate translation: those here bowing their heads and standing worshiping.

1.7 This poem uses the theme of the deluge to describe the greatness of Śiva. The entire world as the body of God is known as Viṣvarupa. After the destruction, the Lord hears the sweet music of the vina that is the Vedas themselves, the lone sound in a newly becalmed world, and the sound that initiates the re-creation of the world.

1.8 The modern name for Civapuram is Cīrkāḻi. Line 1, or the first form—that is, the form that produces and destroys. Line 2, intends to destroy, aḻi vakai niṉaivoṭu. Line 8, temple, nakar.

1.9 Campantar 3.119.4/4082 *Tiruvīḻimiḻalai*

The Lord of the third eye
who made all things in antiquity
was fit to wear the bones of the two
when the time came that they could no longer bear them.
Thinking upon this Lord of Vīḻimiḻalai,
where the flowers from the betel, coconut,
young creeper, champak, jackfruit, olive, kino,
and makiṟa trees block the sunshine,
karma will be destroyed.

1.10 Campantar 1.21.1/217 *Tiruccivapuram*

He who meditates upon Śiva at Civapuram
who sits on His lotus throne,
full of graceful thoughts toward
heaven, wind, fire, water, earth,
the sixty-four arts, the famous Vedas, the three guṇas,
the ways of the wise, the devas above, all other beings,
and the actions that result from their births,
will have a prosperous life on this earth.

1.11 Appar 6.94.1/7174

The Lord of the feet and the long, unkempt matted hair
can assume many forms:
the eight forms,
the wide earth, fire, water, the souls of humanity,
the wind that blows, the changing moon, the sun, the firmament;
the forms of good and evil,
woman and man,
any of the forms of those who are born,
His own form,
yesterday, today, and tomorrow.

1.12 Appar 6.54.5/6799 *Tiruppuḷḷirukkuvēḷūr*

The Lord at Puḷḷirukkuvēḷūr
has the form of lightning;
He is one in the heavens,
two in the wind that blows forcefully,
three in the form of the red fire,

1.9 Line 1, Lord of the third eye, kaṇṇutal paramar. Line 3, bones, aṅkam, one limb, possibly the skull. Line 3, the two, Brahmā and Hari (Viṣṇu), who return to Śiva at the end of time and die, at which time Śiva bears their bones.

1.10 This poem can be seen as the creative corollary to the the destruction in poem 1.8. Line 5, famous Vedas, urai maṟai. Line 6, the devas reside at Tivam, which is the Sanskrit Svarga.

four in the water that flows,
five in the earth,
a refuge that does not diminish.
His form is a great coral flame,
a pearl,
bright light,
a diamond,
gold without blemish.
I dismiss as in vain all days not spent worshiping Him!

1.13 Campantar 1.21.2/218 *Tiruccivapuram*

The one who meditates upon Paraṉ at Civapuram of the stone walls,
the Lord who resides in Hari's heart,
who is consciously sleeping in the midst of the great ocean,
deep in contemplation to keep all things permanent:
heaven where the celestials stay
and the world where human beings follow the ways of the Vedas
on the earth that is made fertile by mountains,
will be blessed with prosperity in this world.

1.14 Appar 4.8.2/4242 *Tirucivaṉeṉumōcai*

Our Lord is not
the sun of reaching rays
the moon
the customs according to the Vedas
the heavens, the earth, and the three winds
the fire that destroys
the water that cleanses;
He comes with graceful compassion
as half Umā of the eyes with red lines,
on His chest a shining garland of snakes.
This Lord is of neither the celestials nor mortals.

1.12 This poem uses numbers to suggest the relation between the five elements and the human senses; the heavens are one, the sense of sound; the wind is two, the senses of sound and touch; fire is sound, touch, and sight; water is sound, touch, sight, and taste; earth is sound, touch, sight, taste, and smell. The refuge of Śiva is both the cosmos and the microcosm of the human body.

1.13 This poem emphasizes the preservation theme; compare 1.8 and 1.10. Line 8, blessed with wealth, wealth is personified in the poem as Lakṣmī, Tirumakaḷ.

1.14 Line 9, eyes with red lines indicates youth and beauty. Line 11, neither the celestials nor mortals, lit. "those who do not blink" (imaiyārum) and "those who do blink" (imaippārum).

1.15 Cuntarar 7.56.8/7812 *Tirunīṭūr*

The Lord who destroys the māyā of the mind
the Lord who is knowledge inside the mind
the Lord who makes the māyā that is the body
the Lord who takes the form of wind and fire
the Lord who creates the disease that makes the body die
the Lord who quickly destroys the powerful karmas
the Lord who is half Umā with the bamboolike shoulders
the King who lives at Nīṭūr—
    can we ignore His worship?

2. Uyiravai Nilai / The Nature of Categories of the Soul

2.1 Appar 6.25.6/6511 *Tiruvārūr*

At first, human life is an embryo, like a stew.
Then it thickens,
    forming the brain, black veins, and white bones
    that join together as one to form a body.
In the world
    the body is born and brought up in the care of a woman;
    in the end, it dies along with the soul.
I will not forget your fragrant feet, Lord!
Even if birth occurs again I shall not go the way of forgetfulness,
Oh husband of Umā at Tiruvārūr!
May I not forget you,
Oh Lord of Tiruttenkūr, Oh Ēkampaṉ!

2.2 Appar 4.33.4/4496 *Tirumaṟaikkāṭu*

The body is a house
    with legs as the foundation
    two arms as the height
    bones as the bricks
    flesh as the plaster
    skin as the paint
    blood as support for the walls
    the two that are appropriate as entryways
    the seven as windows that receive delusions—
  and the Lord who lives at great Maṟaikkāṭu keeps the soul.

2.1 Line 6, although the body is brought up in the care of a woman, she cannot provide for the soul; Appar pleads with the Lord to take care of his soul. Line 12, Ēkampaṉ, he who is one with the mango, perhaps a reference to the sacred mango tree at Śiva temples.

2.2 Each phrase of the original poem includes a verb, for example, having given the legs; this can be interpreted either as the Lord making the body or the sexual act of creation. Line 8, the two entryways are the mouth and anus. Line 9, the seven windows are eyes, ears, nose, and birth canal. Line 9, delusions, māl.

2.3 Appar 4.67.5/4822 *Tirukkoṇṭīccuram*

Oh Lord of Tirukkoṇṭīccuram with the radiant red body!
I am tortured by the effects of the ever-increasing twosome:
the pain of the ninety-six tattvas
and the five senses
    that stay in the body
    which has bad smells
    is crowded with nasty maggots
    and is impermanent.

2.4 Cuntarar 7.60.8/7856 *Tiruviṭaimarutūr*

The five senses became king
and ruled without letting up,
never leaving me;
because of their desires
I followed them all
and did not know how to leave them.
Oh Civalōkam! Oh fire-hued Lord! Oh Civaṉ! Oh Dancer on ashes!
How will you deliver me?
Be Graceful enough to tell me, Oh Lord of Iṭaimarutūr!

2.5 Appar 4.67.1/4818 *Tirukkoṇṭīccuram*

I am unable to control the five senses,
sinking into this illusive hut that is the body
    whose births are without limit,
and I do not see any way out of it.
Oh Lord who wears the shiny snake about your waist!
Tell me, "Do not fear,"
Oh Lord of Tirukkoṇṭīccuram
    where watered fields are fences.

2.6 Appar 4.26.7/4434 *Tiruvatikai Vīraṭṭāṉam*

I could not dispel the disease of desire that is kāma
nor could I break the bond called passion;
looking out with the eyes of flesh
I was unable to see with the open eyes of wisdom.
I have got many things called karma that are due to ignorance;
I did not stop these things
and I have become tired,
Oh Lord at Atikaivīraṭṭaṉam!

2.5 Line 2, into the illusive hut, māyap puraiyulē, that is, temporary shell.

2.7 Appar 4.78.3/4925
I have earned many sins,
especially that of desire.
First, I engaged my mind in it;
then, I was unable to think about the future.
In previous days I should have worshiped the One who is First,
but I could not as desire intensified.
I am like a neglected dog,
unable to dispel desire.
Why have I been born?

2.8 Appar 4.31.6/4478 *Tirukkaṭavūr* (*Vīraṭṭam*)
Squandering nourishing water
for the sake of this body of faults,
this wasteland,
I am unable to live a good life;
nor am I able to pierce māyā.
Battered by the five senses
my life is all but destroyed,
a boat at the end of a narrow waterway,
Oh, Lord of līlā at Kaṭavūr!

2.9 Appar 6.95.9/7192
I am lacking in family
I am lacking in character
I am lacking in aims;
my faults increase,
and I am lacking in the goodness of beauty.
Inside, I am no good either;
I am not a wise man
I do not join with good people
I am in between being an animal and not being an animal
I am very good at saying things that people hate
I lack riches
if anyone begs I do not give.
Why have I been born? I am impoverished in every way!

2.7 In Śaiva Siddhānta philosophy, desire is twofold: love of self and the craving of worldly sense pleasures. In this poem, the moment the poet thinks he cannot escape from desire, he has, in fact, moved beyond it. Line 7, like a neglected dog: chasing after unclean things? Unloved?

2.8 The commentator for the edition I used interprets kaḻi as uppankaḻi, backwaters. Manavalan suggested the interpretation that the boat is at the end of the backwaters, symbolizing the poet looking back on a lifetime that has been wasted.

2.9 Line 1, I am lacking in family, kulam pollēṉ; *kulam* can mean family, group, caste. Line 2, character, kuṇam.

2.10 Appar 4.99.6/5130 *Tiruvēkampam*

Since the day of my conception
my mind melted,
longing for the sight of your feet alone
and I was distressed at not seeing them.
Oh, Lord of Tiruvoṟṟiyūr!
Oh, Lord of Ālavāy!
Oh, Lord of Ārūr!
Seeing that I have not reached you,
don't You pity me?
Oh, Ēkampaṉ at Kacci!

2.11 Cuntarar 7.67.7/7918 *Tiruvalivalam*

I came to Valivalam and saw the Lord:
Destroyer of the powerful karma that binds
Remover of the wide sea of births
Opener of the gates of Civalōkam
whose feet are easily reached by the meditation
of His servants, who gain tapas by intensive yoga
the One who lives in the hearts of those who worship Him.

2.12 Cuntarar 7.7.7/7303 *Tiruvetirkoḷpāṭi*

Forsake shyness
forsake fault
forsake anger of the mind
forsake passions of the household
that arise from the intrigue of women
with fragrant plaited hair—
join with love for the Lord
adorned with bones riding on a bull
let us reach Him at the temple of Etirkoḷpāṭi.

3. Iruḷmala Nilai / The Nature of the Bond That Is Dark

3.1 Appar 4.76.2/4906

Using the plow of truth
sowing the seeds of love
plucking the weeds of falsehood
pouring the water of patience;

2.10 Lines 2 and 3, melting for the sight of your feet, uṉ pātamē kāṇpataṟku urukiṟṟu. This is a characteristic formulation in nāyaṉmār Śiva-bhakti.

2.12 Line 1, shyness, kūcam, in this context possibly the hypocritical shyness one may have in worshiping publicly. The poem is about clearing one's mind and filling it with love for worship, in this instance, in a temple.

they look directly into themselves
and build fences of virtue.
If they remain rooted in their good ways,
the Bliss of Śiva will grow.

3.2 Appar 4.75.4/4898
Inside this house called the body
the heart is the lamp;
pour knowledge that dispels ignorance as the ghee,
fashion the soul as the wick,
take the supreme fire of ñāṉa as the flame
and the vision of the One
    whose feet have anklets
    and whose son enjoys the kaṭampu tree
will be yours.

3.3 Appar 6.19.4/6447 *Tiruvālavāy*
The Master of all the worlds, from heaven to earth
the Wearer of the speckled snake around his waist
the Dancer in the forest surrounded by powerful pēy
the Destroyer of all the faults upon me,
    following the favorable gaze of Umā
the Nectar of honey that has taken over the mind
    of me, His servant—
indeed, I have been blessed to meditate upon the feet
of Śiva of Tiru Ālavāy, known as Teṉkūṭal.

3.4 Appar 6.62.2/6875 *Tiruvāṉaikkā*
You became my flesh
my soul
my consciousness
and all other things;
You came inside me without my knowing
and enabled me to distinguish good from evil.

3.1 A beautiful poem using agricultural motifs to describe the cultivation of bhakti. Line 5, look directly into themselves, tammaiyum nōkkik kaṇṭu, suggesting that they self-consciously tend to their inner goodness, then protect that goodness with external "fences of virtue," virtuous acts. Line 8, the bliss of Śiva, Civakati.

3.2 Line 3, ignorance, maṭam. Line 5, ñāṉa is the Tamil transliteration of the Sanskrit jñāna. Line 8, whose son enjoys the kaṭampu tree, Murugan/Skanda is the son of Śiva.

3.3 Line 3, pēy, demonlike creatures who witness Śiva's dance on the cremation ground. Line 5, following the favorable gaze of Umā, kaṭaikkaṇṇāl maṅkaiyaiyum nōkkā, a look of kindly disposition from the goddess to the worshiper of Śiva: because the worshiper has her favor, he must also have the Lord's. Line 9, Teṉkūtal, south Madurai, to distinguish it from Mathurā in north India, Kṛṣṇa's birthplace.

Oh, Lord who wears the ko<u>nr</u>ai flowers full of honey
Oh, Lord of Ni<u>nr</u>iyūr
Oh, Śiva who lives at Tiru Ā<u>n</u>aikkā
You became my knowledge.
If I can reach your golden feet
what need your servant worry about afflictions?

3.5 Appar 4.76.7/4911
I cannot express myself at all
due to that passion called desire;
even though You remain inside me
I am not able to ingest You
as I would honey from a bowl;
even though you are my life
You remain hidden.
Oh, Mother
How can I see You?

3.6 Campantar 1.103.6/1117 *Tirukka<u>l</u>ukku<u>nr</u>am*
He can bear the bursting ko<u>nr</u>ai flowers
in His wide matted locks
along with the entire Flood,
He can steathily remain in the minds of all His little servants
who worship His tinkling ankleted feet
and dance there,
this Lord who loves to live at Ka<u>l</u>ukku<u>nr</u>am.

4. Aruḷatu Nilai / The Nature of Grace

4.1 Campantar 1.17.6/179 *Iṭumpāva<u>n</u>am*
This is Iṭumpāva<u>n</u>am
on a hill full of fragrant flowers
surrounded by fields overflowing with water.
It is the place of the Lord of perfect guṇas
who gracefully grants knowledge
to those who approach Him as the aim
through meditative knowledge,
be they the celestials in the heaven of light
or mortals on the path.

3.6 Line 3, flood, allusion to the myth of Śiva catching the full Gaṅgā River in his matted hair, to save the world from its destructive force.

4.1 Line 2, hill, taru ku<u>nr</u>il, suggesting a man-made mound, perhaps for a palace; the locus is near Chidambaram, where there are no natural hills. Line 4, perfect guṇas; whereas human beings have various levels of the six guṇas (essences), which determine our characters, bodily states, and so on, the Lord is complete in all the guṇas.

4.2 Appar 6.13.6/6386 *Tiruppuṟampayam*
The Lord whose neck swallowed poison,
smeared with white ashes,
bearing the snake tied above the beautiful tiger skin,
this one of coral hue came to me in my sleep
with half His form as the lady of the soft fingers hennaed red
announcing, "I have a mixed body,"
and beat His drum
such that I woke up frightened;
I am unable to say more.
Crowned with the Gaṅgā in His unkempt matted locks,
He called, "Puṟampayam is Our town" as He left.

4.3 Appar 6.35.5/6608 *Tiruveṇkāṭu*
He came as one whose heart was seized with interest
to the place where the stout bhūtas with heavy gold earrings
dance the koṭukoṭṭi dance and sing;
but I was unable to see Him,
so I turned back.
His sight is that of a thief's;
with the eyes one will not see Him,
because even though He is in the eye
He remains hidden.
The Lord of the matted locks that bear the Flood,
the Lord who chants the Vedas
the Lord Vikirtaṉār who loves to live at Veṇkāṭu.

4.4 Appar 6.13.2/6382 *Tiruppuṟampayam*
Covered with ashes
crowned with the crescent moon
wearing the sacred thread,
He counts my shining glass bangles one by one
while I sleep.

4.2 Line 6, "I have a mixed body," parāyttuṟaiyēṉ; it is an obscure phrase, perhaps comprised of a form of parvi (mixed) and uṟai (cover, body), as suggested by Manavalan. V. A. Devasenapathi takes it as a place-name. Either interpretation is relevant to the content of the poem: The Lord appears as half female, and he calls the name of Puṟampayam to his servant, implying that he should follow him there. The poem implies that the Lord himself is on a pilgrimage.

4.3 Line 2, bhūtas (Tam. pūta) are the helpers of Śiva. Line 12, Vikirtaṉār, can suggest the one who is spoken of in the Vedas (cognate of "speech"), or the one full of light.

4.4 This poem is of the genre nāyaka-nāyaki bhāva, in which the poet is the female lover to God, who is the beloved. Here, the Lord playfully counts the persona's glass bangles while she sleeps, which awakens and confuses her.

I have no one to help me;
while I lie confused, as though I have lost consciousness,
the Lord who makes a girdle of the snake from the anthill
    and is surrounded by bhūtas
calls, "Puṟampayam is Our town," as He leaves.

4.5 Appar 4.75.9/4903
The Lord of the matted locks that bear the Flood
came to me as if to ask something;
dreamy from sleep I approached this One who entered my heart
and asked, "Are you a thief who has entered?"
He made love to me
looked directly at me
smiled at me:
"We are innocent," He said.
Oh Lord of the shining new moon!

4.6 Appar 5.97.17/6211
Who else can be our refuge?
When the senses stop functioning and life weakens
as death approaches
He will remove our sins;
is He not the Destroyer of the triple citadels?

4.7 Campantar 2.86.9/2407 *Tirunāraiyūr*
Let us worship the Lord of fertile Tirunāraiyūr,
the red-hued Śiva who, as the fiery liṅgam,
defeated the competing Tirumāḷ and
Perumāṉ who lives in the lotus that rises from the mud.
He improves the nature of our lives:
He destroys karma, sorrows, and great enmity in our bodies
and makes our minds clear with a truth that overpowers concealment.

4.5 This poem participates in the genre described in the note to 4.4. Line 8, "We are innocent," veḷḷarōm, lit., we are white, we are pure.

4.6 Line 1, refuge, caraṇam. Line 5, alludes to the myth of Śiva's destroying the triple cities of the demons.

4.7 Line 2, fiery liṅgam, eriyāy; liṅgam is implied since the poem alludes to the myth in which Śiva demonstrated his superiority over both Viṣṇu (Tirumāḷ) and Brahmā (Perumāṉ of the lotus) by becoming a liṅgam so encompassing that the former could not find the bottom of it, nor the latter the top.

4.8 Appar 6.54.4/6798 *Tiruppuḷḷirukkuvēḷūr*

The Lord who destroys the darkness of a darkened mind
the Lord who clears my dull mind, impoverished though I am,
  gracefully bestowing knowledge of the path to His Civalōkam
the Lord who is the first great tapas
the Lord whose meaning is beyond the four Vedas and six limbs
the Lord of Puḷḷirukkuvēḷūr
I have wasted many days not going there and worshiping.

5. Aruḷuru Nilai / The Nature of the Form of Grace

5.1 Appar 6.75.10/7007 *Tirukkuṭantaikkīḻkkōṭṭam*

He destroyed the troubles of this birth
for me, grown weary in the midst of a sea of afflictions
calling me there—
it seems He gave me the six nameless guṇas
in order to penetrate all the worlds of the devas.
Oh, Our Dancer of Kuṭantaikkīḻkkōṭṭam
  surrounded by tīrthas with leaping waters:
  the Kāvēri, good Yamunā, Gaṅgā, Sarasvati,
  Golden lotus tank of Madurai, other tanks,
  the clear water of the Godāvarī, and Kumari.

5.2 Appar 6.43.4/6685 *Tiruppūnturutti*

The Lord who is crowned with the intoxicating koṉṟai flowers
who stays at Veṇkāṭu
  where the white elephant came and worshiped
who rescued me
  His ignorant servant ensnared by a sea of afflictions
  by showing me, saying, "This indeed is the path"
who terminates all types of daily torments
who is a symbol of purity, wearing the speckled snake
who is always there—
I myself saw Him at Pūnturutti.

5.1 The locus of this poem is a temple in Kumbakonam. Line 4, the six nameless guṇas, kuṟiyil aṟukuṇattu, suggesting that they are perfected, and not of this world, in contrast to the sea of afflictions that result from the karma of the speaker. Line 5, possessing the powers of the perfected six guṇas, one can even penetrate the higher worlds of the devas; according to Śaiva Siddhānta, if one obtains the six guṇas, one can penetrate āvidya, "not seeing," or ignorance. Line 7, tīrtha (Tam. tīrttam), the poem suggests that some of the most famous tīrthas of both north and south India are located around (or maybe their waters are within) the temple tank at Kumbakonam.

5.2 Line 3, white elephant, refers to a myth that Śiva saved a white elephant (Indra's vehicle Airāvata) from a sage's curse when the elephant worshiped him at Venkāṭu. Line 9, who is always there, taṉṉai poyiliyai, lit., one who is without falsehood, in the sense of the illusion of impermanence.

5.3 Appar 6.20.6/6460 *Tirunaḷḷāṟu*

The Lord who is able to destroy alternative tenets
and thus gives us a family of bhaktas,
the Lord whose left side is the simple lady of the mountains,
the Lord of the Vedas who drenches us in His tīrtha of Grace
which destroys the malas,
the Lord of the red matted locks in which the young moon crawls,
the Lord who destroys deception and gives goodness
to all who submit to the path of philosophy
that says Grace is the source of all virtues,
the Lord who lives at Naḷḷāṟu—
I, His servant, meditated upon Him and was saved.

5.4 Appar 6.43.1/6682 *Tiruppūnturutti*

The Lord who holds the gushing Gaṅgā in His matted locks
the Lord who made my mind remember though it forgets
the Lord who taught me all I did not know
the Lord who showed me all I did not see
told me all I had not been told
followed me
enslaved me, His servant;
the pure One who destroyed my evil diseases
the source of all virtues—
I myself saw Him at Pūnturutti.

5.5 Appar 6.95.3/7186

If made to dance is there anyone who will not dance?
If made to obey is there anyone who will not obey?
If made to run is there anyone who will not run?
If made to melt is there anyone who will not melt?
If made to sing is there anyone who will not sing?
If made to serve is there anyone who will not serve?
If shown is there anyone who will not see?
Oh, Lord with the eye in His forehead!
Who will see if you do not show us?

5.6 Appar 4.25.8/4425 *Tiruvatikai Vīraṭṭāṉam*

Someone came and entered me while I slept night and day,
joining me by entering the temple of my mind;

5.3 Lines 1 and 2, lit., having given a family, usually taken as the community of bhaktas; the other part of the line may also be taken as "the Lord who removes the influence of the planets," which would not be connected to the idea of family as I understood it in my translation. Line 4, grace is implied. Line 8, philosophy, tattuvattiṉvaḻi. Line 9, grace as the source of all virtues, tayāmūlataṉmam.

5.5 Line 4, melt, uruku, in *Tēvāram* and other bhakti poems (such as the works of Māṇikkavācakar), the verb means that the bhakta's heart melts.

His gaze burned the archer of the five arrows named Kāma;
He lives at Atikaivīraṭṭāṉam
where fences surround
agricultural lands filled with lilied waters.

5.7 Appar 5.93.8/6160
Can I who am prone to deception henceforth forget
the light that shone even while I slept,
the virtue that remains in my mind, causing me to remember
the Lord who subdued the poison in His throat?

6. Aṟiyu Neṟi / The Method of Knowing

6.1 Appar 6.25.1/6506 *Tiruvārūr*
Controlling the breath
gazing fixedly
drawing Your image on the canvas of the mind;
if the soul is made a sale deed
and handed over to You,
You will live together with those who are understood by You.
Oh, Lord of things subtle
who rides on a bull instead of Indra's ivory elephant
and rules Ārūr instead of heaven!
Oh Mother!
Those who are not seen by Your graceful eyes
might as well not exist.

6.2 Appar 6.1.5/6259 *Kōyil*
The Lord is an invaluable companion
a rare nectar that dispels the sorrows of His servants
a great helper always
for those born on this wide earth
who have left the attachments of family and friends
subdued the strong senses within
turned away from the pleasures of going to bed with women
and, separating Him from other gods,
are able to think of Him alone—

6.1 This poem participates in the genre, maṭakku, in which one term is used in many senses; four of the eight lines begin with the phrase *uyirā vaṇam* (bondage of breath, sale deed of soul, Indra's elephant, Lord of things subtle). Line 6, those who are understood by You, this poem suggests that the ways of yoga are not only a method for knowing God but are also ways for him to know, and to see, you. Lines 8 and 9, the Lord is contrasted with Indra, Lord of heaven: the servants to Śiva are found on earth—here, in Ārūr—not in heaven.

6.2 Line 8, separating him from other gods, potu nīkki, lit., removing commonness or removing equivalents; an idiomatic expression for distinguishing one god above others.

this Lord of great Tiger Town—
all days not spent speaking of Him
might as well not arise.

6.3 Appar 4.32.9/4491 *Tiruppayaṟṟūr*
If we can control the senses
place the mind in deep concentration
leave different kinds of activity
and remove the two,
the Lord of Tiruppayaṟṟūr
will be able to make the malas as one
and replace anger and other passions of the mind with enjoyment.

6.4 Appar 5.48.4/5720 *Tirukkacci Ēkampam*
By our own motivation
let us go to Ēkampam together to pray
to the One who is nectar known in the minds
of those who control the outflow of the senses,
focus their minds,
and think upon Him.

6.5 Appar 4.97.4/5115 *Tirunallūr*
The Lord whose throat bears poison
His body a fiery red jyōti
  a collection of coral
  shining like a pearl
lives at Nallūr.
I once saw Him in my dreams and bowed, worshiping;
He remains in my mind without departing
He remains always.

6.3 Line 1, controlling the senses, pulaṉkalaip pōka nīkki; the senses are twofold, made up of both the organs of sense (e.g., nose) and the sensation of sense (e.g., smell). "Controlling the senses" means checking the outward flow of the senses, so that, for example, the nose should not indulge in smelling. Line 3, different kinds of activity, iṉankaḷai; the Tamil word means simply "class, kind, species, race." I translate it as "different kinds of activity" in the context of the verse, to highlight the yoga of the first two lines; it could also be in the more specific sense of "other kinds of worship"; Devasenapathi translates it as the six yogic centers. Line 4, removing the two, could be the internal and external desires, or it could be the separation of ego. In a Śaiva Siddhānta reading, it would be understood as karma and māyā. Line 6, malas, malaṅkaḷai, probably refers to the transformation of the three guṇas (tamas-darkness, rajas-passion, sattva-truth) into the highest guṇa, sattva; it could also be taken in the technical sense of Śaiva Siddhānta as the āṇava mala. Line 7, enjoyment, pōkam.

6.4 Line 1, by our own motivation, kuṟippiṉāl.

6.5 Line 2, jyōti, a blazing bright light.

6.6 Appar 4.113.6/5234
Śankara is crowned with the young crescent moon
and uṉmattaka flowers;
worshiped by the world
He carries many skulls from the cremation ground
and wanders from house to house seeking alms;
day and night He is inseparable from my mind.

6.7 Appar 4.77.5/4919
Five wicked thieves have entered the field of the mind;
wreaking havoc,
they take plunder;
they are thorns that prevent cultivation of the pure path.
If we stand hiding in the shadow
of the feet of the Lord with the third eye
we can pierce them with our arrows of knowledge.

6.8 Campantar 1.126.7/1365 *Tirukkaḻumalam*
The Lord will make as Himself
those who will reach the highest shining truth
    by sowing the seeds of bhakti
    guarding against the engagement of the five senses
    thinking of ways to cut off these enemies
    closing the openings of the three guṇas
        that stop progress to mukti
    and channeling the four discordant antarakaraṇas
        into the single path of citti.
This Lord lives at the fertile town of Kaḻumalam
    where people are well versed in the six aṅgas
    and unceasingly join with His shining feet of goodness.

6.9 Campantar 1.132.6/1421 *Tiruvīḻimiḻalai*
In the temple at Miḻalai
the Lord of the purāṇas
is in the lotus hearts
of those whose love is sincere
    who have subdued the six enemies
    controlled the five senses
    and desire ñāṉa.

6.7 Line 1, the five thieves, representing the five senses.

6.8 Line 1, make as Himself, tāṉ ākac ceyumavaṉ. Line 3, bhakti, patti; similarly, line 7, mukti, mutti. Line 8, the antarakaraṇas are the "internal instruments," citta, manas, buddhi, and ahankāra. They are often described as "managers" between the soul and the senses. Line 9, citti, the correct goal or aim, here salvation.

Outside,
shining groups of conches
    lie in water as clear and bright as gems
    with lotuses as red as fire,
and flowers from numerous pu<u>n</u>ku trees
    thick like popped rice
    emit their fragrance.

6.10 Appar 6.40.7/6661 *Tirumaḻapāṭi*
I prayed:
    Oh my Perumā<u>n</u> of the curly matted hair
        who destroys the sorrows of births
        that are like a whirlwind;
    Oh my Guide of the purest clear water
        who destroys the births
        arising from pacu and pācam
        that are difficult to go beyond;
    Oh my great Lord
    Mother!
    Light that blameless Tirumāḷ and Aya<u>n</u> could not see,
    Strong pillar of Maḻapāṭi
        who wears the Vedas on His crest
        who guides us on the path—
then I melted, weeping.

6.11 Campantar 1.131.10/1414 *Tirumutuku<u>nr</u>am*
Those who wear ocher robes
and those who wear mats spread as robes
are not worthy of association;
understand yourself
without taking heed of these fleshly beings' words;
save yourself at Mutuku<u>nr</u>am, be a servant to the Lord!
There, silent sages rich in ñā<u>n</u>a,
    complete in knowledge of the four Vedas
    and destruction of the five senses
    live alone, performing tapas.

6.12 Appar 4.75.3/4897
I wasted much time
as a thief engaged in a pretense of service.

6.11 The modern-day name for this town is Viruttācalam; it lies on the road from Madras to Trichinopoly. Lines 1 and 2, ocher robes and mats as robes refer to the Buddhists and Jains, respectively. This is one of only two verses in the collection (the other is 8.5) that alludes to the polemic frequently found in the poems of Campantar and Appar. Line 5, fleshly beings, ū<u>n</u>ikaḷāy uḷḷār, suggesting their mortality, their concern with the flesh; a polemical insult.

6.12 Line 4, found, kaṇṭē<u>n</u>, lit., I saw.

Then, becoming clear in my mind,
I sought You, desired You, and found You,
at last ashamedly realizing
that You know everything because
You are with all of our thoughts.
Embarrassed, I split my sides laughing.

6.13 Cuntarar 7.21.9/7452 *Tirukkaccimēṟṟaḷi*
I was constantly thinking of Your feet,
thinking of You, my Lord!
But really it was You who made me think of You;
I got rid of my hypocrisy.
Oh Lord of the mountain who lives
  at Tirumēṟṟaḷi, surrounded by great walls of thick stone,
I happily worship none besides You.

6.14 Campantar 1.45.1/481 *Tiruvālaṅkāṭu*
He comes while I sleep
and makes me worship Him.
Dispelling my lies,
He enters my mind
and makes me think of Him.
Oh Lord of the sacred feet
who lives at the ancient town of Ālankāṭu
  which is feared by those who have heard
  that a woman who deceived her husband previously
  has had her life spoiled.

6.13 Tirumēṟṟali is a temple in Kāñcipuram.

6.14 The second part of this poem can refer to one or both of two stories, one local and the other a story of one of the nāyaṉmār. Line 7, the ancient town of Ālaṅkāṭu, can also read as the proper name, Paḻayaṉūr Ālaṅkāṭu. The former term is the name of a small village near Ālaṅkāṭu. The story centering around this village tells of a woman named Nili who was killed by her merchant husband. Subsequently, he came to Paḻayaṉūr to do business. Just outside the village, he was approached several times by a female ghost. He ran into town, telling of what he had seen. A crowd of seventy villagers assembled; they explained to him that she was no ghost but a lady and that he should respond to her pleas by marrying her. A village council confirmed the idea, and he married her. Then she killed him. The villagers were distressed, feeling that the blame was on them for convincing him to marry her. They prayed to Śiva, who delivered them from their fear by saying that the two were truly husband and wife. The other story is of Kāraikkāl Ammaiyār, who deceived her husband with a mango that Śiva had given her. The husband could taste the divine sweetness in the mango and became frightened by his wife's intimate relationship with the Lord. Subsequently, the lady asked to be released from her womanly body-beauty, to witness Śiva's dance at the cremation ground at Ālaṅkāṭu. For a telling of the story and translations of her poetry, see Cutler, *Songs of Experience*.

7. Uyir Viḷakkam / The Enlightenment of the Soul

7.1 Appar 6.25.7/6512 *Tiruvārūr*

First, she heard His name
then she heard about His color and form
and His Ārūr.
Though dissuaded, she became mad for Him
and left her mother and father that very day,
abandoning the customs of the world.
Losing herself,
forgetting her own name,
this girl placed her head at the Lord's feet.

7.2 Cuntarar 7.51.6/7758 *Tiruvārūr*

The Lord who burned the cities
drawing against His body
the mountain as the bow, the strong cobra as the bowstring,
and Agni and Hari as the arrows—
I am a fool not to think of Him first.
Bearing this body,
How long can I remain separate
from my Lord of Ārūr?

7.3 Appar 4.5.5/4215 *Tiruvārūr*

I, the impoverished one,
the one of the evil body
listening to the words of evil people
chewing areca nut
wandering aimlessly
eating food placed in my hands here and there,
should have taken refuge in His golden body.
Without taking the Lord of Ārūr into myself
I am ensnared and made ignorant by those who deny causes.

7.1 This poem draws upon the Caṅkam tradition of *akam* (interior) poetry, especially those poems of the kuriñuji landscape in which the impassioned lovers meet secretly.

7.2 Line 4, Agni and Hari as arrows, Devasenapathi interprets that Agni (Lord of fire) is the tip of the arrow, while Hari (Viṣṇu, Lord of water) is the shaft. This can be interpreted in other ways as well: Agni and Hari are agents of the all-powerful Śiva, or the arrows can be viewed as the elements, fire and water, of destruction—water can be considered more powerful than fire because it can extinguish fire.

7.3 Lines 7 and 8, should have taken shelter in His golden body / without taking the Lord of Ārūr into myself, poṉ ākattu aṭiyēṉaip pukap peytu poruṭpaṭutta Ārūrarai yeṉ ākattu iruttātē, lit., (I) ignored placing I, the servant, in the golden body; without making the one of Ārūr stay in my body.

7.4 Cuntarar 7.91.4/8161 *Tiruvoṟṟiyūr*
He steals my beauty and my honor
this Lord of Oṟṟiyūr
which shines in a forest of flowering puṉṉai trees.
Previously, He would make me think of Him;
now, He is constantly in my mind.

7.5 Campantar 2.40.1/1895 *Tiruppiramapuram*
My Lord who is nectar to me
the Lord of those who reach Him
the One who holds fire in His hands
the beggar Kāpāli
the One who skinned the great fearsome elephant
the poison-throated One
He of the heavens lives in Piramapuram
surrounded by fragrant gardens.

7.6 Appar 5.93.3/6155
He weeps aloud, crying and crying "Lord, Lord!"
The Lord is not separate from my mind.
Since I have taken Him into my mind
how could I possibly forget Him?

7.7 Appar 4.29.1/4453 *Tiruccempoṉpaḷḷi*
He is easy to know
for those who have purified the soul in the body.
He is full of guile and unknown to the gods in heaven.
The Lord of Tiruccempoṉpaḷḷi
is sweet nectar and honey
in the minds of the bhaktas
and if the knowers of ñāṉa say "I" it means "He."

7.8 Appar 5.50.6/5743 *Tiruvāymūr*
If they say
"In any of our actions we are not ourselves but You,"
it suits the Lord whose greatness has no limits.
He lives in Vāymūr as the Great God.
Is His entering my mind, saying "Go!"
a delusion?

7.7 Line 6, bhaktas, pattar. Line 7, knowers of ñāṉa, ñāṉattār.

7.8 This poem suggests that the Lord provides the motivation for pilgrimage by his telling Appar to go to Vāymūr.

7.9 Campantar 1.42.4/451 *Tiruppēnu Peruntuṟai*
The Lord lives at Peruntuṟai
where many virtuous people live
who have subdued earth, heaven, water, fire, and wind,
which are the five senses,
and removed all falsehoods.
Smeared with white ash,
they have no good or evil apart from Him
their minds are elevated
they are free of the malas and faults.

7.10 Appar 6.62.3/6876 *Tiruvāṉaikkā*
I wandered forgetting Your good nature
living such that I clung to the ways of the world
staying with those who perform tapas in the wrong way
eating leftover rice obtained by begging.
You came, making me realize You everywhere,
becoming Master over me.
Oh, Lord of beautiful Āṉaikkā
Oh, Father of the celestials!
If I of this body of sorrows
can reach Your golden feet
what need Your servant worry?

7.11 Cuntarar 7.59.3/7840 *Tiruvārūr*
The Lord whose Grace showers down
like rain on the black hills,
the Lord who gives support
to the souls who look to Him
and to all the arts and philosophies as their Meaning.
The Lord who remains as day and night,
the Lord of the ears that listen
the tongue that knows sweetness
the eyes that see,
the Lord of the roaring sea and the mountains—
is it possible to forget You?

7.12 Cuntarar 7.4.7/7273 *Tiruvañcaikkaḷam*
"You are the Creator, Destroyer, and Maintainer," say I.
"You are the Speaker of words and their Meaning," say I.
"You are the tongue, the eye, and the ear," say I.
Oh Lord of goodness,
only today have I understood You well.
Oh, Father of Añcaikkaḷam in Makōtai
surrounded by groves
on the shore of the sea that roars
bringing up boats laden with treasure.

8. Inpuru Nilai / The Nature of Experiencing Bliss

8.1 Appar 6.67.3/6927 *Tirukkīlvēlūr*

Those who seek
the beautiful One who wears the snake
from the mouth of the anthill,
the One who makes love grow for His servants
who desire Him,
the One who is the Meaning of true knowledge,
the One who is wisdom,
the One who will undergo any suffering
for the sake of the bhakti of the bhaktas,
and who will not suffer for others,
the One who is without limit,
the One who cleanses the fault from my mind
and enters into it,
the King who rules Kīlvēlūr,
the One who is indestructible,
will never perish.

8.2 Appar 6.84.3/7089 *Tiruccenkāṭṭankuṭi*

I myself have seen at Ceṅkāṭṭaṅkuṭi
the Lord who is the honey that saturates the servants
whose minds melt,
whose locks bear the crest-jewel,
who is Knowledge for those whose aim
is the ultimate state of Truth,
who is the Meaning of the Vedas
to the brahmans who preserve them,
who is Absolute over Ayan on the fragrant flower
and Māḷ,
who is Help for those of true tapas,
whose body is half Umā of the thick plaited hair.

8.3 Appar 4.26.6/4433 *Tiruvatikaivīraṭṭāṉam*

My mind leaves one thing and grabs hold of another,
like a swing on two ropes;
it goes here and there.

8.1 Line 6, Meaning of true knowledge, meyññāṉapporuḷ āṉāṉai. Line 7, another Sanskrit term suggesting perfected knowledge.

8.2 Line 8, brahmans, antaṇars. Cuntarar begins his list of the nāyaṉ the antaṇars of Tillai.

Oh Lord of the matted locks that bear the crescent moon
and look like great ropes for a swing,
I became as a swing whose ropes have broken at Your feet.
Oh You of Atikaivīraṭṭāṉam!

8.4 Cuntarar 7.84.7/8093 *Tirukkāṉappēr*
The One who skinned the great elephant and wore its hide
the One who does not approach deceitful people of tainted minds
the Primordial form from which the three forms arise
the Rider on the great bull that stays close to Him
the Nectar for those who hold the truth without illusion
in their minds
the Supreme Lord who bathes in the five substances,
including milk, fragrant ghee, and curds
the virile Lord who lives at Kāṉappēr
surrounded by the muddy fields;
To think of the Lord as my protector—
when will I reach this state of mind?

8.5 Campantar 2.106.10/2625 *Tiruvalañcuḻi*
The violent Jains and Buddhists are devoid of knowledge;
they perform tapas in vain,
they say things contrary to the path:
Do not trust in them!
If one enumerates the achievements
of those who are not separate from Perumāṉ
who loves to live at Valañcuḻi
where the Kāvēri's waves always swell across the land
there will be no limit.

9. Aintеḻuttu Aruḷ Nilai / The Nature of the Grace of the Five Syllables

9.1 Appar 5.46.5/5700 *Tiruppukalūr*
Thinking of the King crowned by the moon in the open sky,
reciting His names and the five syllables;
if you ask where His feet can be seen,
my heart will say the Lord of Virtue at Pukalūr.

8.3 Lines 2 and 5, the ropes of the swing are a simile for the senses; when they are broken, one will reach the feet of Śiva.

8.4 Line 3, the primordial form, lit., the root embryo; the three forms could be Śiva, Viṣṇu, and Brahmā, or Pati, Paśu, and Pāśa. Lines 7 and 8, the five substances are those from a cow, āṉaintu (āṉ + aintu), the list of which is completed by butter (veṇṇey) and buttermilk (mōr).

9.2 Appar 4.94.6/5087 *Tiruppātirippuliyūr*
When I was an embryo
I thought only of Your feet.
After birth I recited Your names and,
wearing sacred ash,
said "Civāyanama," which sanctified my mouth by Your Grace.
Oh, Lord of Pātirippuliyūr, grant me the Bliss of Śiva!

9.3 Appar 4.94.5/5086 *Tiruppātirippuliyūr*
Unless we recite "Civāyanama,"
considering it as our treasure to be kept,
enclosing it in our minds,
uniting it with our minds,
how will we obtain the Grace
of the Lord of Pātirippuliyūr
  who is like the moon surrounded by its beams?
Oh, my simple mind that lacks knowledge!

9.4 Appar 5.60.1/5841 *Tirumāṟpēṟu*
For those who recite even though they lack knowledge of anything
and for those who understand the five syllables,
the Lord of Māṟpēṟu and His Lady
will happily enter their minds
without distinguishing between them.

10. Aṇaintōr Taṉmai / The State of Those Who Have Attained

10.1 Appar 6.31.3/6566 *Tiruvārūr*
Oh my mind
if you think to achieve the ultimate state, then come!
Enter the temple of our Lord daily
sweep it before dawn
smear the floor with cow dung
decorate Him with flower garlands and worship
sing songs of praise
bow in worship with your hands above your head
and dance,
crying "Victory to Śankara, Hail! Hail!"
"My Highest Lord, whose red locks bear the waves of water!"
"Lord of Ārūr!"
over and over and louder and louder.

9.2 Line 6, Bliss of Śiva, Civakati.

10.2 Campantar 3.37.4/3193 *Tiruppiramapuram*
The Destroyer of the city of enemies
who, along with His great Lady, is praised by brahmans
lives in the temple at Piramapuram
where female birds sport with their mates.
If people praise the deeds of the Lord
who wears garlands of fragrant koṉṟai flowers,
this will be the reason
for their attainment of Civalōkam without impediment.

10.3 Campantar 1.21.4/220 *Tiruccivapuram*
The servants who always tread on the path
worship Him thoughtfully,
with sandalwood paste, flower buds and blossoms, incense,
bright lights, and copious water.
They think of Him at Civapuram
where water is contained in tanks;
the powerful place where the Lord who has the guṇa of Grace
grants them the proper state without deficiency.
Those who think of Him here
will become the husband of the goddess of Victory.

10.4 Campantar 1.21.5/221 *Tiruccivapuram*
The beautiful form of the Lord
is worth seeking
for those who always realize His Meaning
that arises on the flower
with all their minds,
subduing the six agitated enemies
and the increasing senses,
and controlling the breath.
Those who think upon the Lord of Civapuram
which is encircled by thick walls
will prosper with things given by the goddess of the Arts.

10.5 Campantar 1.21.6/222 *Tiruccivapuram*
Those who customarily perform rare tapas
and subdue the senses in the body,

10.3 Line 10, the husband of the goddess of victory, ceyamakaḷ taliavarē. Ceya, victory, is here personified as a goddess, suggesting Jayalakṣmī. The one who marries her will himself be victorious; to achieve this marriage, one needs to do the things mentioned in the passage.

10.4 Lines 3 and 4, meaning that arises on the flower, malarmicai eḻutaru poruḷ, the flower may be that used in worship, or that the God is seated on flowers, usually 1,000 flowers. Line 11, goddess of the arts, kaḷaimakaḷ, suggesting Sarasvatī.

following the path in such a way
that the many beings of the world will praise them,
and knowing without fault the good and many arts
beginning with the Vedas,
think upon the Lord in order to obtain His feet.
Those who think upon this Lord of Civapuram
    which is filled with holiness
will have their famous progeny prosper on this earth.

10.6 Appar 5.91.9/6141
The luminous nectar
that is pure and clear and sweet
perfects the mind.
How did it arise in me?
I am a hypocrite, full of anger, engulfed in a sea of troubles.

10.7 Appar 6.26.4/6526 *Tiruvārūr*
Oh you five
    who are signified by the properties of your form,
    taste, sight, touch, sound, and smell—
Aiyo! The whole world is not enough
for you to enjoy by your instincts.
I instead will unite with
the golden form of the celestials
the hill of southern Ārūr
the aspect of Śiva which is the beauty of the world
the One who gives His form to enter my mind
my Father.
You vainly try to put Him at a distance!

10.8 Appar 6.98.1/7216
We are bound to no one
we do not fear Yama
we will not experience pain in hell
we are not deceitful
we will rejoice
we do not know disease
we do not submit.
All days we feel bliss, not sorrow,
for we are humbly joined
with the flower-laden red feet of
Śankara
    whose nature is bound to no one
    who is a king with the good white conch earring in one ear
    and whose rule redeems us.

10.9 Appar 6.95.2/7185

The severe punishments of Yama will not come to us
the fierce enemy karma will gradually be reduced
we are cured of our distress
we have no afflictions
we are not lowly;
where will the sun arise for us?
The Lord is in my mind
crowned by the river through His beautiful red matted locks
dancing with fire
pleased by bathing with the five substances of the cow
bearing a red complexion like coral, the hills, the heavens.

10.10 Appar 5.12.5/5357 *Tiruvīḻimiḻalai*

Our people gather round
the One who has the bull on His flag of victory;
we are mendicants, eating what we obtain by begging;
what we destroy is the severe karma that keeps us down.
Causing this to go, we depart for Vīḻimiḻalai.

10.11 Appar 4.94.3/5084 *Tiruppātirippuliyūr*

The Lord who has the bull
desires me and is in my mind;
from this day troubles will not approach us here,
difficult karma will not connect with us,
we are not afraid of Yama.
Is there anything that is difficult
for the servants who serve the servants
of the Lord of Pātirippuliyūr
where beings like Ayaṉ of the gracious lotus live?

10.12 Appar 6.61.3/6867 *Tirukkaṉṟāppūr*

The Lord of Kaṉṟāppūr
is seen in a post
and in the hearts of His servants,
who worship not only Him
but also whomever they should see
who bears the sacred ash on the forehead
and other Śaiva marks.
When the servants see such persons
they are glad, thinking them also servants,
and joyfully look upon them.
They say, "This one is a deva, that one is a deva,"
without separating the two.
They honor them as having the nature of the Lord,
without distinguishing the two.

10.13 Appar 5.13.5/5368 *Tiruvīḻimiḻalai*
Oh Lord who is the Source,
Oh Lord who is unique as the Foundation
for everything and everyone of clear mind,
Oh Lord who is Holy
remaining as the soul and knowledge,
Oh Lord who is the Source in Tiruvīḻimiḻalai,
take me, Your servant, as Your signified.

10.14 Cuntarar 7.51.4/7756 *Tiruvārūr*
I came here
subject to the afflictions of birth
and I am becoming tired.
My Lord of Ārūr came there
as a rare medicine that rules me
so I will not lose strength.
How can I be separated from Him anywhere,
my nectar,
the Lord whose great form is the blazing fire,
the Lord whose hand holds the deer?

10.15 Cuntarar 7.26.4/7497 *Tirukkāḷatti*
Oh Lord who holds the deer in His hand,
Oh Lord who is cloaked with the skin of the great elephant,
Oh my Aim,
Oh my Foundation,
I shall do Your least bidding.
Oh Knowledge that stays at Tirukkāḷatti,
whom the servants on the path contemplate,
I shall neither think of nor praise
anyone besides You.

10.16 Campantar 1.3.8/30 *Tiruvalitāyam*
The Lord who swallowed the poison
in the primordial sea
as though it were water,
who danced while the celestials worshiped
and praised Him,
who gracefully subdued the power
of the king of mighty Ilaṅkai,
lives in the temple at Valitāyam
which abounds with the sweet sap
of the jack tree and the betel nut tree with shining leaves.
If one worships Him
for as long as the soul shines in the body
the troubles of the mind will be gone.

INDEX TO *TĒVĀRAM* HYMNS TRANSLATED FROM THE *TĒVĀRA ARUḶMUṞAITTIRAṬṬU*

Although the numbering of hymns in different editions of *Tēvāram* can vary, they all usually provide the first words of each hymn in an index; here I provide the first word or words of each hymn, so that the reader can locate them easily in Tamil sources. As is the custom, I have given the words in the metered form of the verse, in Tamil alphabetical order. Numbers in parentheses key the poem to my translation in Appendix A, followed by an identification of the author and volume of *Tirumuṟai*.

puvamvaḷikaṉalpuṉal (1.10; Campantar 1)
puḷḷuvar aivarkaḷvar (6.7; Appar 4)
pokkamāy niṉṟapollāp (2.3; Appar 4)
poṟippu laṉkaḷaip (6.4; Appar 5)

malaipalavaḷar (1.13; Campantar 1)
maṟicērkaiyiṉaṉē (10.15; Cuntarar 7)
māṭṭiṉēṉ maṉattai (2.7; Appar 4)
māya māya (1.15; Cuntarar 7)
māvai yurittataḷ (8.4; Cuntarar 7)
miṉṉuruvai (1.12; Appar 6)
muṟṟoruvar pōla (4.4; Appar 6)
muṉṉa mavaṉuṭaiya (7.1; Appar 6)
meymmaiyām uḻavaic (3.1; Appar 4)
mēṉiyiṟcī varattārum (6.11; Campantar 1)

yātē ceytu (7.8; Appar 5)

varaikilēṉ pulaṉkaḷaintum (2.5; Appar 6)
vaṉṉāka nāṇvaraivil (7.2; Cuntarar 7)
vāṉa mituvellā (3.3; Appar 6)
viṭaiyāṉ virumpiyeṉ (10.11; Appar 4)
viṇṇi ṉārmati (9.1; Appar 5)
virikatirñāyiṟallar (1.14; Appar 4)
viḷḷattān oṉṟu (3.5; Appar 4)
venta cāmpal (1.5; Campantar 3)
vempavaru kiṟpataṉṟu (10.9; Appar 6)
veḷḷanīrc caṭaiyaṉār (4.5; Appar 4)
veḷḷamellām viri (3.6; Campantar 1)
veṟiyār malark (5.2; Appar 6)
vēṟuyar vāḻvutaṉmai (4.7; Campantar 2)
vaitta poruṇamak (9.3; Appar 4)

APPENDIX B

Umāpati Civācāryār's *Tiruvaruṭpayaṉ*

TRANSLATION

Analysis of the text follows the translation.

In preparing this translation, I have benefited from consulting previous translations: J. M. Nallaswami Pillai, *Thiruvarutpayan of Umapathi Sivacharya* (Dharmapuram: Gnanasambandam Press, 1945 [1896]); Rama Ghose, *Grace in Śaiva Siddhānta* (Varanasi: Ashutosh Prakashan Sansthan, 1984); and, less helpful but still a good read, G. U. Pope, *The Tiruvāçagam or "Sacred Utterances" of the Tamil Poet, Saint, and Sage Māṇikka-vācagar* (Oxford: Clarendon Press, 1900). The discussion in Dhavamony, *Love of God*, 275–288 was also helpful.

1. Patimutu Nilai / The Nature before Pati

1.1 The Lord is like the vowel *a*, permanently pervading everywhere as knowledge; yet he is incomparable.
1.2 Our Lord is not separate from śakti, which gives its essence to eternal souls as their nature.
1.3 The Lord is unequaled in his unique benefit, his wide grace, his subtlety, and his greatness.
1.4 After making all things become and maintaining them, the Lord destroys them along with the fault and becomes the refuge from which they will not depart.
1.5 The Lord has no form and form; to the learned his form is knowledge.

1.1 In Tamil, as in other Asian languages, *a* is a default vowel, meaning that it is always added to the consonant unless otherwise modified (by a stop or by another vowel). I have used a small *a* rather than a capital because the Tamil does not use capital letters. Compare *Tirukkuṟaḷ*, 1.1.

1.4 Fault, ācu, is the āṇava mala. "Destruction" in this couplet does not mean annihilation but a returning to Śiva.

1.6 Our Lord has no one above him that compares to his nature, by which the numerous souls possess knowledge.

1.7 The celestials do not understand his greatness, but for his servants he remains as inseparable knowledge.

1.8 He remains as one with everything everywhere like heat in hot water; yet he is himself alone.

1.9 To those who do not approach him he is not good; to those who do approach him he is good. Caṅkaraṉ is the name of the impartial one.

1.10 Set your mind upon him without doubt, for he is the medicine that will cure your everlasting births.

2. Uyiravai Nilai / The Nature of Categories of the Soul

2.1 The number of those who have been and will be released is the same as the number of days that have passed and those yet to arise.

2.2 The souls are divided into those that have three malas [bonds], those that have gone beyond one of them, and those that possess only one.

2.3 All three categories possess the root mala [āṇava mala]; those who are most bound do not know of [the Lord's] succor.

2.4 The agency of āṇava mala is of such great power it makes things seen everyday confused in dreams.

2.5 *A<u>r</u>ivu* is [hardly] the best name for understanding perceived only through the sense organs.

2.6 What can light, darkness, and the world affect if there is no clarity in the open eye?

2.7 *Sat* [reality] does not join *asat*; *asat* does not know the place of *sat*; therefore, the soul experiences these two as *satasat*.

1.7 Servants, aṭiyavār.

Title, Section 2 "Avai" can be the pronoun "those," or it can mean an assembly (Skt. *sabhā*). I have taken it as descriptive of the categories of souls. Cf. title to section 7.

2.2 The three malas are āṇava, māyā, and karma; those who are bound by all three are called Sakalas; those who have gone beyond māyā only are called Pralayakalas; and those who have gone beyond māyā and karma and are bound by only the root mala (the āṇava mala; also called the mūla mala or root mala) are called Vijñānakalas.

2.4 Āṇava mala is implied in the text.

2.5 "A<u>r</u>ivu" is intelligence or knowledge; this passage should be taken as ironic. It is literally "understanding that perceives nothing without the sense organs."

2.7 According to Vai. Irattiṉacapāpati, *satasat* is a combination specific to the Śaiva Siddhānta and is not found outside its philosophy. *Sat* means something that exists unchanging; *asat* does not mean nonexistence because this idea does not have a place in Śaiva Siddhānta, which admits three eternal realities and thus is often called *realism* or *realistic pluralism*. *Asat* connotes unreality. In explaining the meaning of the term *satasat*, an image of a sky-lotus (a lotus flower suspended in the sky) is often used. Śaiva Siddhānta views the sky as real, and the lotus as real, but the relationship between them is unreal, or *asat*. The soul experiences realities but is confused as to their relationships.

2.8 Are there not things in the world that become completely dark in darkness and illuminated in light?
2.9 Like the eye of the owl for which even light is great darkness we cannot see certain things but for the eye of God.
2.10 Alas! The souls will continue to bear up until that day when, knowing the Lord's grace, their afflictions will be no more.

3. Iruḷmala Nilai / The Nature of the Bond That Is Dark

3.1 It is not possible by any means to say that the sorrows of many births, bliss, and their auxiliaries do not exist.
3.2 The reality that persists as one with everything is nothing but that which is dark.
3.3 Darkness does not reveal anything but it does show its form; this [āṇava mala] does not reveal either.
3.4 Since the beginning, darkness has been contained in the midst of the soul with its inner light, and remains there up until today.
3.5 The base lady of darkness embraces many persons, though her "chastity" is unknown to her husband.
3.6 Why use many words? Darkness makes truth unknown to the intelligent soul.
3.7 If darkness does not exist then why is there suffering? If it is of the soul's essence then when it is made to go they will depart as one.
3.8 If the fault has a beginning, what is the reason that it binds? If we cannot say, then the bonds will attach even in the state of mukti.
3.9 If the soul does not grasp the increasing light of grace, then darkness will never leave it.
3.10 Like a lamp that lasts up until dawn, māyā comes to karma through the body and other instruments.

2.8 An implicit comparison with the soul.

2.9 The eye of God (man̲ kaṇ) is the eye of ñān̲a.

3.1 In this couplet, Umāpati sets down the possible polarities of human existence: the sorrows of births or the joy of (divine) bliss. It is up to human beings to decide which course they will pursue.

3.2 and 3.3 Although the bond (āṇava mala) is dark, it is unlike darkness in that it does not show itself.

3.6 "Why use many words?" in the sense that the soul under āṇava mala is ignorant. Intelligent soul, uṇarum pān̲mai.

3.8 Fault, ācu. The āṇava mala is real and eternal (without beginning). Before enlightenment, it has power over the soul, but it is not part of the soul.

3.9 Soul, uḷḷam. This term, unlike uyir, implies an advaita relation between God and soul. Unlike Śankara's use of the Upaniṣadic term, which reduced all things to one essence, the Śaiva Siddhānta understanding of advaita acknowledges two things that remain as one. This relationship is envisioned in several ways by Śaiva Siddhānta, including camavāya (a relation of essentiality, such as the relation between heat and hot water) and tātān̲miyam (the relation of one thing that remains as two, such as two tumblers of water, or Śiva and his śakti).

4. Aruḷatu Nilai / The Nature of Grace

4.1 There is nothing in this world that is greater than grace, just as there is nothing above the things that the soul needs.

4.2 Grace pervades everywhere like the great light of the sun and touches the karma that is ripe.

4.3 The body does not know anything; nor does the soul know these things. How can one who does not know become one who knows?

4.4 Though the souls have grace as their nature, they flounder about in a sea of confusion like fish in an ocean of milk.

4.5 The soul will not realize knowledge with the five senses, like a wanderer who does not realize that help approaches.

4.6 Even those who move about the earth do not know the earth; how much less do those of the world understand higher things.

4.7 Those who would bring the mountain to ruin, those who would bring the earth to ruin, those who would bring the heavens to ruin, and those who would bring the highest knowledge to ruin have only brought themselves to ruin.

4.8 The person who is most deceived feels thirst even though up to his neck in a flood, and takes complete darkness for dawn.

4.9 Listen to this teaching after subduing your desires; else you will be like a cat on top of a full jug of milk who yet desires to eat a cockroach.

4.10 "Release" is too much to expect for the empty souls who are not at all familiar with Grace though they have been joined to it up to today.

3.10 Māyā is not "illusion" as in the Advaita philosophy of Śankara; rather, in Śaiva Siddhānta, māyā is able to give a small light for the soul to understand reality, particularly through practical experiences. There are four products by which māyā comes: ta\underline{n}u (body), karaṇa (instruments), puva\underline{n}am (world; also thought of as an embodiment of śakti), and pōkam (Skt. bhoga, enjoyment). Karma also assists the soul through action and knowledge. Thus both māyā and karma help the soul toward realizing Śiva, although they are imperfect aids and eventually the soul must transcend them. They are the small lamp in the darkness before grace dawns.

4.3 The implied answer is that one needs the Lord's agency of grace.

4.4 "In an ocean of milk," milk is useless for fish; similarly, confusion is useless for humankind. Further, fish do not realize that milk is a sacred and nourishing food; similarly, the soul does not recognize the sacrality and benefit of grace.

4.5 I take this couplet to suggest that the wanderer cannot realize who will help him from sense data alone; that is, the people or village he approaches may be friend or foe, but he cannot necessarily tell from sight. The wanderer is an illustration of the principle that people in the world cannot gain knowledge through the five senses. Other interpreters have taken help, tuṇai, as a synonym for the Lord; just as the wanderer has the Lord as assistance but does not know it, people have his assistance but cannot know this through the senses.

4.7 In Umāpati's time, this would have been a rhetorical statement; no one could "ruin" a mountain, or the earth, or the heavens. The idea is that those who would bring these to ruin repudiate their own foundation, by denying the realities that order one's life, both mundane (earth, mountain) and sacred (heaven, knowledge [ñā\underline{n}am]). The "highest knowledge" is a manifestation of grace: To deny grace is to deny one's foundation and bring oneself to ruin.

4.9 "Desires," parappu.

4.10 "Release," vīṭu.

5. Aruḷuru Nilai / The Nature of the Form of Grace

5.1 The Lord's grace, which will never depart, protected you during the state of ignorance and will appear again as a sign.

5.2 Aside from the one who has a disease inside himself, will the people of the world know anything about it?

5.3 Who of the earth would recognize the sign that came to bestow grace in ways not previously granted?

5.4 The one who lacks intellect because perception and mind are darkened by falsehood can barely see the two truths.

5.5 The world does not know that the Lord comes in the cloak of human form to catch and hold people, like a decoy for animals.

5.6 Think not, "What is to me and which things are to others;" for authority [in spiritual matters] you require him [the guru].

5.7 The vision of the guru will make darkness go, just as a vision [of a mongoose] in true meditation cures snake poison better than a mongoose itself.

5.8 The Lord Himself graciously comes to the Sakalas, removes the karma of the Pralayakalas, and bestows the grace that gives release to the Vijñānakalas.

5.9 Who will know anything if the Great Knower who gracefully manifests the path of release for all does not come?

5.10 Wisdom will arise without the guru if crystal can glow without light.

5.1 The sign, kuṟiyaka; here it is a term for grace; in a later couplet, 5.3, it is more specifically the guru.

5.2 The state of ignorance, due to the influence of the three malas, is understood to be like a "disease." Just as the one who has overcome a disease is the one who knows most about it, so the guru is the one who knows about the soul's condition and the way to remedy it.

5.3 The guru is understood to be the "sign."

5.4 Intellect, pōtam; perception, poṟi; mind, cintai. The two truths are grace and the guru as the form of the Lord's grace.

5.6 Do not compare your knowledge to that of a guru. Just as a gold merchant knows about gold and a textile worker about cloth, the guru ("him") is a specialist concerning spiritual knowledge.

5.7 Meditation, pāvakaṉ, which means "making oneself as one." It is a method of meditation in which you envision the form of an object, then you develop a mantra, and by constant chanting you "become" the form (in your vision). In this case, the object is a mongoose, the enemy of snakes. The mongoose itself cannot remove the poison but the meditative vision of the mongoose, which invokes the animal's powers and acquires them for oneself, can. Such is the mental power of the guru (ivaṉ) in curing your spiritual diseases, chief among them darkness, āṇava mala.

5.8 Here Umāpati summarizes the statuses and spiritual needs of souls. The Sakalas, whom he mentions by this term in the couplet, suffer from all three malas and need his presence in the form of a guru. The Pralayakalas (implied in the couplet) need to have their karma removed, and the Vijñānakalas (implied in the couplet) will receive the Lord's grace to overcome the influence of the āṇava mala.

6. Aṟiyum Neṟi / The Method of Knowing

6.1 When the endless twofold karma becomes balanced it is possible to receive the Lord's śakti.

6.2 One, many, darkness, karma, and the twofold māyā; these six are beginningless.

6.3 Know that the one who is saved exists as the one who performs actions, the actions that are performed, the fruit of these actions, and as the one who attains the fruit of these actions.

6.4 The body lives because of the soul, and the soul is one with the body; similarly, the soul is one with the Supreme Intellect.

6.5 Like the golden sun that gives the crystal its own color and many other colors, grace gives the world its own and many colors.

6.6 As with the way of conventional seeing, if the light of grace is not in its midst the eye of the soul cannot see.

6.7 Consider that the Lord's actions are related to yours in the manner that actions of the senses are related to mundane activities.

6.8 Do not undertake research or scrutinize anything; do not project from yourself; see the Lord who has seen you.

6.9 After you recognize that worldly pleasures are only excesses of the senses, take refuge as a ray in the light of knowledge.

6.10 Take things in this way of taking them: see things in the way they have been shown to you, and do not see things that have not been shown to you.

6.1 Śakti is catti in the text. The twofold karma: (1) the karma by which the soul gets experience, for example, good actions and bad actions; this karma has a beginning and an end; and (2) karma as a possession of the soul, as a potentiality, like icca (will, desire), kriyā, and jñāna; this karma is beginningless. The couplet can be understood to suggest that śakti (the technical term is *śakti nipāta*) descends on a ripened soul, that is, one that has matured, which is symbolized by the balance of the two karmas (iruviṉaiyum). It can also be understood to suggest that the equality or balance of the two karmas is achieved with the help of grace.

6.2 One is God, many is souls, darkness is āṇava mala, karma is karumam, twofold māyā is aśuddha māyā, mixed with karma and not acted upon by Śiva directly; and śuddha māyā, acted on by Śiva directly and having as its evolutes forms of jñāna and kriyā, separately and combined. It is also possible that the couplet suggests that there are two ways to understand each element (iraṇṭu āka modifying the set, rather than māyai alone). Each element can be understood on its own and as implying its complement; for example, darkness implies the existence of light.

6.3 Ceyvāṉum, ceyviṉaiyum, cērpayaṉum, cērppavaṉum. We gain knowledge of the soul by observing it as the continuity among these observable realities; similarly, we know that karma exists because of the inequalities we see in the world.

6.4 Supreme Intellect, tāṉ uṇarvu.

6.7 The Lord motivates our actions, just as the senses motivate worldly actions. The pulaṉ ceyal, actions of the senses, are the indrīyas.

6.8 Compare 6.10.

7. Uyir Viḷakkam / The Enlightenment of the Soul

7.1 Just as no one need be told to seek refuge under cool shade, the soul will join with grace in the same way.

7.2 At the time of bilious affliction, even milk that is sweet will be bitter; after the tongue recovers, the bitterness will subside.

7.3 He will see only when the light shows itself in darkness; on what day will the vain sin of seeing by his own agency depart?

7.4 Light and darkness are of one nature, but the action of the former is enlightenment and the latter, unenlightenment.

7.5 Except for those of worthy and good friendship, who will bear your burdens now?

7.6 When the thief stole the valuables that were kept, was the owner asleep or had he gone out? Say.

7.7 As a crystal prism catches light without shadow to itself, grace renders darkness powerless to take hold.

7.8 One who has attained the state of grace should stand behind truth just as one who holds a torch stands behind the emitted light.

7.9 If what you see is dependent upon the five senses, then besides grace what is the competence of the senses and the soul to know?

7.10 Is it possible to consider that his giving to you is due to your own will? What is the competence of the soul to know?

8. In̲pu̲ru Nilai / The Nature of Experiencing Bliss

8.1 Those who experience bliss go behind the light that arises in darkness; those who experience sorrow go before it; therefore, go behind.

8.2 There will not be any fruit of bliss between two women; it is experienced between a man and a woman.

7.1 This couplet suggests not only that the soul will naturally be drawn to grace but also that it will be within grace, just as the body is covered by the shade.

7.2 The influence of the āṇava mala early in the soul's path toward enlightenment does not irreparably damage the soul; when the affliction of āṇava is dispelled, the soul will fully realize its good potential and grace. Also, the bitterness of life with subside when one is in the state of grace.

7.3 Vain sin of seeing by his own agency, tān̲ kaṇṭa vīṇ pāvam.

7.4 Both light and darkness are of one nature because they show their own powers; however, only the power of the former is helpful to enlightenment.

7.5 Likens grace to friends (kēṇmaiyārkku) who carry one's burdens. The couplet can also be interpreted as suggesting that God takes on the burdens of only those souls who have a special relationship to him, one that is defined by grace.

7.9 In this and the next couplet, an idiomatic expression is used, tām ār ata̲rku/ ivan̲ ār ata̲rku, lit., what is this with respect to that; here I translate the phrase to mean asking on what grounds the soul can know, which implies its own limitations. Grace here is implied, atu o̲liya.

8.1 Bliss, in̲pu, happiness.

8.3 The Lord of bliss bestows it upon those who reach him; therefore, the weight of bliss does not remain with his own form.

8.4 As the words join to make *tāṭalai* [*tāḷ* + *talai*], losing their otherness, take your joining with bliss as one.

8.5 If there is only one then it cannot unite; if there are two then sound will not arise [from the two hands that are held apart]; if this be the case, there is neither one nor two.

8.6 The ones who are freed from the cycle of birth and death are those who join with bliss, those who receive bliss, and those who adhere silently without cease.

8.7 Remain without performing any actions up until the nature of a pēy arises.

8.8 Only the fruit of grace and nothing else is experienced by those who join the highest truth; they view all else as things that drop from the hand of those who sleep.

8.9 Bliss does not appear separately from the three natures that are completely joined together; what else is there to say?

8.10 This is the state of love: If he finds sweetness in bliss today, he will attain it today.

9. Ainteḻuttu Aruḷ Nilai / The Nature of the Grace of the Five Syllables

9.1 The books of grace, the Vedas, and others besides elucidate the threads of truth in the five syllables.

9.2 Lord, śakti, pāśa, the power of māyā, and the soul all remain within the syllable Ōṃ.

8.4 The couplet uses Tamil sandhi (the joining together of letters to make a "matching" sound easier to pronounce) as a metaphor for the union of the soul with God. Here, the retroflex *ḷ* of tāḷ combines with the alveolar *t* of talai, producing a retroflex *ṭ*. The next couplet also tries to provide an image of the Tamil Śaiva Siddhānta view of this union.

8.7 A pēy is a possessed being, often associated with the wildness of Śiva's dance of destruction, as in the story of Kāraikkāl Ammaiyār, in which she pleads to Śiva for the removal of her flesh (her femininity) and then sits as an ematiated, cross-legged figure, enraptured with the vision of the Lord's dance. The pēy is a socially constituted antisocial being, and its common translation into English as *demon* reflects this. The couplet advocates sitting in meditation until the time of complete mental absorption in Śiva.

8.8 The highest truth, oṇ poruḷ.

8.9 The three natures are Śiva (the source), the soul (the experiencer), and bliss (the experienced). In worldly experience, knowledge, knower, and known are assumed to be separate entities; in the experience of bliss, the underlying connection among them is seen.

8.10 The state of love, aṉpu nilaiyē.

9.1 The books of grace, the āgamas; the Vedas, āraṇam. The five syllables are the mantra to Śiva: Na-ma-ci-vā-ya! Homage to Śiva! This set of couplets is devoted to explaining the correct way to pronounce this mantra.

9.2 The five realities listed here are reduced to the three realities in the three sounds that make up Ōṃ (Aum), a is God, u is soul, m is pāśa. An alternate reading of the couplet would be to take the first item as the Lord's śakti (instead of two items, Lord, śakti).

9.3 Seek the soul between the actions of the flesh on one side and the dance of knowledge on the other.

9.4 The expanding "na" and "ma" will not release the soul that combines with them until the soul is able to end the great karma [of birth and death].

9.5 If concealment [na] and fault [ma], fraught with illusion, come first, will things ever change? The things that are highest are what set the soul free.

9.6 Who is your basic foundation? The Mūlātāram? Alas, do not continue to think this way! Recite the highest things first.

9.7 If you adopt the method of recitation with Śiva first, your births will end; recite it in this way.

9.8 "Vā" gracefully endows the soul and causes it to prosper in "Śi," Śiva-bliss. That same grace becomes the unblemished form of the soul.

9.9 Because of the grace this flawless form will not stand between "na" and "vā"; it will stand between "Śi" and "vā."

9.10 All of these methods are mentioned knowing that the soul cannot remain separated from the Lord.

10. Aṇaintōr Taṉmai / The State of Those Who Have Attained

10.1 Those in the state of samādhi are submerged in the highest knowledge and overcome by bliss in their minds; what else is there to say?

10.2 They do not desire to perform the five cosmic actions, or to be the agents of actions, or to seek the enjoyment of passionate actions.

9.3 The values assigned to the mantra, which will be elaborated in later couplets but are alluded to here, are na, Tirobhāva-śakti, concealment; ma, āṇava mala; ci, Śiva; vā, grace; ya, soul. The couplet gives us a clue that Umāpati wants to put the order of the mantra in the reverse, for the signifier of the soul, ya, is supposed to be between the signifiers of "the actions of the flesh" (na, ma) and those of "the dance of knowledge" (ci, vā); therefore, the correct order of the mantra is Ci-vā-ya-na-ma.

9.5 Concealment, tirōtam (Tirobhāva); fault, malam (mala)

9.6 The couplet begins with "ār āti ātāram," which means "who is [your] first foundation?"; however, the mention of ātāram immediately brings to mind the āṟu ātāraṅkaḷ or the six power centers of the body in the discipline of yoga. These six cakras—the lowest at the base of the spine culminating in the highest at the eyebrow—are Mūlātāram, Cuvātiṭṭāṉam, Maṇipūrakam, Anākatam, Vicutti, Āññai. Thus, the mention of āti ātāram would immediately suggest the Mūlātāram, and I have translated the couplet as such. The couplet makes the point that the way of beginning in yoga—going from the bottom to the top—is not suited to the recitation of the mantra, which should begin with the highest realities. The foundation of the soul is grace, not the seat of the spinal cord.

9.7 The mantra is to be recited: Ci-vā-ya-na-ma.

9.9 Refining what he has said earlier, Umāpati says that the soul that has attained grace will stand between Śiva and grace, instead of between knowledge and flesh.

10.1 The couplet says tūṅkuvār, those who sleep, which I have glossed as a meditative state.

10.2 The ones who have attained do not desire to perform the actions of Śiva (creation, preservation, destruction, concealment, and bestowal of grace), or ordinary actions, or passionate actions.

10.3 Even though they are in a position to know everything, they do not want to know anything except the One.

10.4 After subduing the senses they enter into their own essences without reemerging, like a tortoise that withdraws its limbs into its shell.

10.5 Where is a place that is separate from the Lord? Even if a place does not exist, he is everywhere. His existence is not separate from the liberated soul.

10.6 For those who view things internal and external as of one nature, there is nothing whose nature is reproachful.

10.7 The world is the fruit of gainful work, while truth is the fruit of selfless action.

10.8 The accumulated karma will end with the death of the body; if more karma appears in the midst of this birth, then grace alone will burn it.

10.9 For those of mature understanding, actions that give the threefold result will not be kindled; even the actions of future births will come to fruition in this birth.

10.10 When those committed to the truth reflect upon the sorrows of those committed to deceit, they are filled with compassion.

ANALYSIS OF THE *TIRUVARUṬPAYAN̲*

The *Tiruvaruṭpayan̲* (hereafter TP) is not an expository text in the sense of providing explanations and thus is not traditionally regarded as a place to begin an inquiry into Tamil Śaiva Siddānta; rather, Man̲avācakam Kaṭantār's *Uṇmai Viḷakkam* has this status.[1] Unlike the *Uṇmai Viḷakkam*, which is in the question-and-answer format conducive to teaching, the TP is a series of one hundred couplets, each of which invites philosophical meditation and discussion. The TP conveys philosophical concepts by images, using few words. That the concepts the text conveys are part of the system of Śaiva Siddhānta provides a point of entry into its understanding.[2]

The TP is celebrated by Tamil Śaiva Siddhāntins today as an "original" Tamil work, which has never been viewed or claimed as a translation or interpretation of a Sanskrit text. Indeed, many scholars have convincingly argued that the closest "ancestor" of the TP is Tiruvaḷḷuvar's *Tirukkur̲aḷ* (sacred collection), a Tamil work of 1,330 couplet-aphorisms that scholars have dated anywhere from two centuries before the first millennium to the sixth or seventh century A.D.; if the latter, then the author would be a contemporary of Appar. There are parallels between the texts. The TP is, for example, written in the same meter as the *Kur̲aḷ*, the *kur̲aḷ veṇpā*.

10.5 "Even if a place does not exist," that is, a place conceived of in the mind.

10.7 "Selfless" action, var̲untoḻir̲ku, lit., empty action.

10.8 Alludes to the different classes of karma: *Sañcita* karma is the karma from an earlier time (a former birth) that gets carried forward through subsequent lives, *prārabdha* karma is the karma that will come to fruition in the present life, and *āgamin* karma will come to fruition in a future birth.

10.9 The threefold result probably refers to the classes of karma alluded to in the previous couplet.

And like the *Kuṟaḷ*, the TP begins with a couplet on the letter *a* and its nature as a symbol of God. The *Kuṟaḷ* is traditionally divided into three sections, the *muppāl*: virtue (*aṟam*), wealth (*poruḷ*), and love (*iṉpam*). As many have noted, these appear to correspond to the *puruṣārtha*s of dharma, ārtha, and kāma found in classical Sanskrit sources such as the *Manusmṛti* and the *Mahābhārata* (Śantiparva). The connection between the *Kuṟaḷ* and the TP on structural grounds has led many to suggest a relationship in terms of content, as well. In this light, the TP is viewed as describing the goal of life, *vīṭu* (Skt. *mokṣa*), which is pursued after one has lived life according to dharma, ārtha, and kāma; Umāpati's text is thus as an appendix to Tiruvaḷḷuvar's. One author, Veḷḷiyampala Muṉivar, included the TP in his work, *Mutumoḻi mēlvaippu*, as the fourth division of the *Kuṟaḷ*.[3]

However, if the TP does in some way "complete" the *Kuṟaḷ*, it does so on its own terms by connecting salvation directly to Śaiva Siddhānta philosophy, in contrast to the commonsense wisdom of the *Kuṟaḷ*. In the TP, salvation is explicitly linked to Divine Grace, which is prominent as the title of the work indicates; according to scholars, the text's central concern with grace is historically important.[4] Philosophically understood, grace is the primary way for humankind to attain Śiva; it permits humankind to disentangle itself from bonds or fetters and to realize God. In Śaiva Siddhānta, the human condition is believed to be a mediating position between God and the fetters; this is represented by the concepts *pati* (Lord), *uyir* (soul, Skt. *paśu*), and *iruḷmala* (the bond that is dark, Skt. *pāśa*). Umāpati begins by exploring the nature of each before turning to grace in the fourth set of couplets. The entire text illustrates the path of humankind from ignorance to salvation. In the following analysis, I explore Umāpati's vision of this path through a consideration of each section title and the meanings with which the section couplets invest it.[5]

The first collection of ten couplets is entitled "Patimutu Nilai." Pati is Lord, one of the three irreducible realities according to Śaiva Siddhānta thought, along with uyir/paśu (soul) and iruḷmala/pāśa (bond). Nilai is state or nature. Previous translators have rendered the title of this section as "The Nature of God." In so doing, they leave out the term *mutu*, which is a modifier suggesting temporal distance—that is, old, ancient, in some cases connoting originality.[6] In the examples given in dictionaries, one usually finds *mutu* as a prefix to the word it is modifying. However, in this first section title, it follows *pati*. Therefore, it appears to be modifying *nilai*, which could then be translated as "The Nature before Pati."

What would be before Pati? Śaiva Siddhānta imagines that the Lord has many modifications: two foundational images are the Lord as *svarūpa lakṣaṇa* and as *tatastha lakṣaṇa*. The former is the "self-form-quality" of Śiva. Explained by way of folk etymology, which is a common technique in traditional exegesis, Śiva is made up of two syllables: Śi, meaning pervasiveness, and va, meaning that he is an embodiment of grace; grace is his śakti (power). This is viewed as his original existence. The tatastha lakṣaṇa is the "that-standing-quality" of the Lord. It is an image of Śiva as One who benefits humankind as the doer of five actions, the *pañca-kṛtya*: *paṭaittal*, creation; *kāttal*, maintenance; *aḻittal*, destruction; *maṟaittal*, concealment; and *aruḷal*, bestowing grace. Both images are appropriate for meditation; the one implies the other, and neither is reducible to the other. It is characteristic of Tamil

Śaiva Siddhānta not to collapse pluralities, but it does tend to hierarchize them. In calling the section "The Nature before Pati," it is assumed that pati is the tatastha lakṣaṇa that humankind knows before realizing the svarūpa lakṣaṇa, because it is a condition of humankind that we first become aware of God through his actions. Later, through meditation and knowledge, humankind may know the original nature of Śiva, the svarūpa lakṣaṇa.

The first section of the TP, then, is about the svarūpa lakṣaṇa. The text begins with a metaphor based upon lingistic structure. From the first couplet, we learn that he is like the vowel *a*, which is a default vowel that always follows a consonant unless modified, in Tamil script as in many South Asian scripts. The simile suggests God's foundational status in the world and his omnipresence. Moreover, the letter *a* is a vowel, which is wind to a consonant's hard sound, suggesting life; *a* also begins the Tamil alphabet; and the comparison also links God to a sound invested with the potentiality of language. Similar associations of pervasiveness, life, importance, and a link to philosophical knowledge can also be attributed to the couplet's statement that his presence is "as knowledge" (*a̲rivāki*). Knowledge provides a link between the subtlety of God and the capacity of humankind, and it is the primary methodology of Śaiva Siddhānta. Yet this methodology points to its own limits, for "He is incomparable." The svarūpa lakṣaṇa is somewhere between likeness and uniqueness, pervasive yet alone; the closest description of him is knowledge. This trope is used in several other couplets as well: He is unequaled in qualities that are nevertheless enumerated (1.3), he has no form, though the learned know his form as knowledge (*a̲rivām*, 1.5; 1.6); he is like heat in hot water (1.8); he is impartial, between the extremes of like and dislike (1.9). Through language, the TP points to its own limitations as language in its attempt to describe the nature before pati.

Though God is hard to describe, the TP asserts that he has a relationship with humankind. Most commonly, the text points to knowledge as the way to the self-formed Lord. But this is not the only way of human awareness or the only form of God. The Śaiva Siddhānta does not reduce pluralities, so the svarūpa lakṣaṇa implies the tatastha lakṣaṇa. Therefore, we also learn of the agency of the Lord, which is actualized by his śakti, a power that is inseparable (*pin̲n̲amilān̲*) from both him and the nature (*tan̲ nilaimai*) of souls (1.2). We hear of his benefit, which is unequaled (1.3); his creation, maintenance, and destruction of all beings (= *tatastha*), at which time they are reabsorbed into him as a refuge (= *svarūpa*; 1.4); his inseparability from his human servants (*aṭiyavarkku*) as knowledge, to the exclusion of celestials; and, last, his role as medicine for the disease of rebirth.

The language of the first set of couplets is of metaphor and simile, to point the reader toward an awareness that God is beyond pati but is nevertheless also pati who acts for the benefit of humankind; this is summarized by the first and last couplets in the section. In between these framing couplets, the philosopher suggests several paths for constituting the relationship between God and humankind, for both God's śakti and his knowledge are inseparably with the souls of humankind. This relationship becomes the focus of the second set of couplets.

The "Nature of Categories of the Soul" section begins with the positive assertion that "those who have been and will be released are equal to the number of days that have been and are yet to be." In this couplet, the possibility of release is described in terms of the limitlessness of time itself. But by the end of the section, the reader or hearer knows that the path is difficult. The last couplet laments that the souls will bear their burdens up until the day they know the Lord's grace; then their afflictions will be no more. Within these parameters, the section describes the categories of souls at various stages on the path to liberation.

The Lord is inseparable from the souls, but his existence does not derive from them; they come to know of him through his actions full of grace (*aruḷ-śakti*) in the world. They are predisposed to gain this knowledge of the Lord, for the souls stand upon (*nil*) the Lord for their existence; however, the ability of the unenlightened soul to gain this knowledge is compromised by the āṇava mala. The soul is the middle term of the three fundamental realities in Śaiva Siddhānta; just as it stands on the reality of God, the third term, *bond*, called *āṇava mala*, stands upon the soul for its existence. The eighth couplet brilliantly describes the relations of the three: "Reality (*sat*) is not bound by unreality (*asat*); unreality does not know the place of reality; therefore the soul experiences *satasat*."[7] Sat, as the Lord, has no contact with asat, the āṇava mala, and the converse is true. The soul, as the intermediary term, has contact with both of them, so it experiences satasat.

The experience of the souls reflects their position between pati and pāca. The souls will experience liberation, but until that day they will bear the burdens of bodily existence—chief among them, the experience of both reality and unreality in a struggle toward ultimate truth. Three broad categories of experience characterize the souls' journey from the unreality of āṇava to the reality of God (2.2). The Sakalas experience all three malas; āṇava, māyā, and karma. The Pralayakalas have gone beyond māyā, and the Vijñānakalas have gone beyond māyā and karma and wrestle only with āṇava mala. Although all of the classes of souls are influenced by āṇava mala, which hangs on until the last because it is a fundamental element in the universe according to Śaiva Siddhānta, they have different experiences corresponding to their respective stages. The Sakalas experience the ordinary perception of ordinary things; this is pāśa-jñāna, or knowledge of worldly things. The Pralayakalas recognize a difference between the soul and the body (thus they are beyond māyā), as well as a difference between the experiencer and the experience; this is paśu-jñāna. Finally, the Vijñānakalas experience God; this is pati-jñāna. This hierarchy describes a trajectory of knowledge from the crude to the subtle.

On this path, the souls move from the realm of the perceptible to the imperceptible. In the main, the first section of couplets emphasized the realm of the imperceptible; the connection between the Lord and the souls was envisioned as knowledge of God and awareness of his śakti. In the second section, the author is concerned to describe the realm of perception. Although the souls who are most bound may know of the world, they do not know of the imperceptible assistance of the Lord (2.3). Moreover, the power of āṇava is such that it "confuses in dreams things seen everyday" (2.4), thereby disputing even ordinary perception. The Sakalas' reliance on the sense organs for knowledge is much to blame (2.5).

Sight, chief among the sense organs, in Umāpati's text becomes a metaphor both for problems inherent in knowledge through perception and for the realm of higher knowledge through God's grace. Just as one needs to have clarity in the eye to get around in the world, one needs clarity in the eye of the soul to progress on the path toward liberation (2.6). For the soul, the world is divided into dark and light (2.8); the former, signifying the āṇava mala, conceals all objects within it and blocks the experience and knowledge of those things, whereas the latter illuminates those same objects and allows the eye and the soul to distinguish them clearly.[8] In a scathing simile, Umāpati compares the bound soul to an owl, which cannot see in the light. This simile points to the reality that one needs assistance from the "eye of God" in order to see (2.9). The nature of the path is that God will assist humankind (2.3, 2.9), yet when the soul is under the influence of the malas, it is unable to see this clearly. Only when the soul recognizes the grace of the Lord will it achieve freedom from fetters (2.10).

Before that nature of grace can be recognized, one must first clearly understand the nature of the āṇava mala. The reality of the āṇava mala cannot be denied, just as the grace of God cannot; the first couplet of the third section of "The Nature of the Bond That Is Dark" describes the two poles of human existence as the sorrows of (re)birth and the bliss of Śiva. The polarity challenges readers to determine which path they are on.

The locus of āṇava mala is the soul, in whose midst it remains, along with the inner light (3.4), yet it is not of the essence of the soul. It exists distinctively from the soul and fundamentally, generating suffering from which the soul can ultimately gain release (3.7). Like the two other fundamental realities, the āṇava mala does not have a beginning (3.4, 3.8), and it is therefore without an end, but its influence on the soul can be almost completely eclipsed. It is never destroyed, but as knowledge of pati increases, the influence of the āṇava mala becomes correspondingly less.

Why is it difficult to gain release from the influence of āṇava? In part, this difficulty is due to its permeation of all things as their dark side (3.2). To the last, it competes with the inner light of the soul; its method of competing is concealment. Like darkness, the āṇava conceals the true nature of things from view; it is the reason that truth is unknown to the intelligent soul (3.6). But it is more treacherous than darkness because, unlike darkness, which reveals itself (that is, it is seen as darkness), the āṇava conceals itself as well (3.3). Thus, it does not represent a bond that can be seen, identified, and renounced, like the household to an ascetic. The āṇava mala is a bond of ignorance that touches all and ensnares one's sense of reality with deception, like a wayward wife to her unsuspecting husband, according to Umāpati (3.5).

The auxiliaries of āṇava are māyā and karma, which also serve to engage the soul in experiences or actions that are counterproductive to the soul on its path toward release. Yet, they also play a role in leading the soul to enlightenment, for as agents of pati they facilitate the soul's knowledge of āṇava. The Lord does not come into direct contact with a soul burdened by the āṇava mala; instead, māyā as his agent gives a small light of understanding to the soul through practical experiences, which help to determine the circumstances for the enlightenment that karma will eventually bring through good action. In a significant departure from the philosophical theories of other schools, Śaiva Siddhānta admits that māyā and karma provide a flicker of light in the darkness of āṇava (3.10).

Māyā and karma are auxiliaries of both āṇava and pati, but just as the ignorance of āṇava is greater than the negative powers of māyā and karma, so is the grace of the Lord greater than their enlightening powers. Beyond these two auxiliaries, it is the grace of God that permits the soul to break the bond of āṇava. The small light of māyā and karma takes the soul through the night of āṇava until the dawn of grace (3.10); when grace dawns, the soul must seize it, or else the darkness will never depart (3.9). In Śaiva Siddhānta, the soul must act in its own progress toward liberation.

The fourth section of couplets, "The Nature of Grace," answers questions on grace that are provoked by both the problems and the solutions described in the chapter about darkness. This section begins by stating that grace is above everything (4.1) and that it is the śakti of the Lord that comes to fulfill the things the soul needs, including knowledge and salvation, to be liberated (4.10). Grace is itself one of the soul's needs, for the soul that relies only on the powers of the senses is like a wanderer ignorant of assistance (4.5). Thus the soul can travel only so far along the path with conventional knowledge or, indeed, even with some knowledge of the Lord. Grace itself must take the soul the rest of the way to salvation. This occurs when the soul has already worked toward its own knowledge through māyā and karma, resulting in karma that is "ripe" (4.2; perukka nukar viṉai). The karma has been brought to maturity and is ready to fall off when "touched" by the salvific light of grace.

If the soul does not work at its knowledge of higher realities, it will not come to know grace, even though grace is part of its essential nature (4.4, 4.10). The soul under the control of the āṇava, before it has commenced on the path of liberation, is like the body (4.3). It will remain that way, confused and unable to recognize its own nature and sustenance (4.4), until the soul can subdue its desires, or else the soul will be like a cat hungry for prey even though it sits upon on a full jug of milk (4.9).

Finally, there are those who remain under the influence of the āṇava mala, which blocks their knowledge of grace. Umāpati describes them as the most deceived (4.8; kaḷḷat talaivar). These souls know not of grace and live a torturous existence, likened to those who feel thirsty though up to their necks in water and those who take darkness for dawn (4.8). These unfortunate souls unwittingly deny their very existence by seeking to ruin the stable elements of their world, including earth, mountains, the heavens, and even grace itself (4.7).

The nature of the Lord's assistance to humankind on the path to enlightenment is explored in section 5, "Nature of the Form of Grace." Grace assists the three classes of souls in distinctive ways, appropriate to their condition. None is irredeemable because all have grace as their essence, which protects the souls in the state of ignorance and will appear as a sign (5.1) to the souls as they gain greater knowledge of things as they truly are. Grace comes to the Sakalas, for they do not know to come to the Lord. Grace removes the karma of the Pralayakalas, who have extricated themselves from māyā through their own activites. And grace grants release to the Vijñānakalas (5.8). The form of Grace by which this assistance is rendered is the guru.

A guru's teachings are relevant for the progression of all categories of soul but perhaps most importantly for the Sakalas because the guru is a visible sign of God.

The Sakalas, afflicted by all three malas, are the ones who have not yet begun their journey on the path of knowledge to enlightenment and liberation, and they need grace to take on a form within their midst. Umāpati describes the guru as like a decoy (*pārvai*) for animals; similarly, the Lord puts on a cloak (*pōrvai*) of human form to attract human beings (5.5). The problem is that the Sakalas in the world do not know this (5.5, 5.3) because the faculties of their intellect, including perception and mind (note that perception is relevant for gaining knowledge in the realm of the Sakalas), are darkened by falsehood (*poy*), so they can neither recognize the guru nor discern grace (5.4).

Umāpati insists that the guru is necessary for initiating the unenlightened on the path of liberation. He appeals to two commonsense examples to prove the authority of the guru. First, the guru has the necessary experience: Just as someone who has survived a disease has knowledge of its affliction and its cure, the guru has knowledge of the bonds of the human condition and freedom from them (5.2). Second, Umāpati asks us to recognize the authority of the guru in spiritual matters (5.6). Even in ordinary life there are various specialists, for example, the merchant who knows about cloth and the goldsmith who knows about gold; therefore, there is an authority for spiritual matters, and this is the guru. Instead of comparing our knowledge to the guru's, we should listen to him. Since the guru is none other than the Lord's śakti, he has the power to cure the disease of the malas and rebirth. The vision of the guru will cure the soul just as a powerful mantra will remove the poison from a snakebite (5.7). Umāpati emphasizes the power of the guru as a teacher: "Will anyone know anything if [the guru] does not come?" and "Ñāṉam [knowledge] will arise without the Guru if crystal can glow without the sun." As a dispeller of all hardships and doubts that may afflict the soul, the guru leads the disciple to correct knowledge and salvation.

Section 6 is on the methodology of knowing. The chapter begins with two premises. The first is that the soul is fit to receive the Lord's śakti when it has balanced the twofold karma (6.1). Śaiva Siddhānta understands the twofold karma as the karma of worldly experience gained through performing actions and the karma that the soul possesses as a component of its essential nature (for example, knowledge is karma). As I noted before, according to the Śaiva Siddhāntins, karma and māyā can empower as well as disable the soul; their role depends on the progress of the soul and the decisions made by the human agent, whether to go the way of ignorance or the way of enlightenment. It is not necessarily the case that only when the karmas are balanced is the soul fit for receiving grace; earlier chapters suggested that grace seeks to aid the soul even in its ignorance. But because this couplet specifically mentions the balance of karmas, I interpret it as suggesting that the type of knowledge revealed within this chapter is best fit for the souls that have resolved the influences of karma, namely, the Vijñānakalas. In addition, it is this category of soul, as I discussed earlier, that is at the limit of human agency toward salvation. This is the point in the progression of the soul where it can be taken no further by one's own powers but needs to have grace assist it to reach the highest reality of God.

The second premise is that there are six beginningless realities: God, souls, darkness (āṇava), karma, and the twofold māyā (6.2). This may appear to contradict the Śaiva Siddhānta premise that there are three essential realities, but it does not, because karma and māyā are the auxiliaries of God and āṇava, and they are included in the experience of all souls. The methodology of knowledge expounded in this chapter deals primarily with what the soul can know from its experiences; the Vijñānakalas are the one class of soul that has experienced it all in the embodied state, from the lowest possible realities (āṇava and its powers) to the highest (God and grace).

Indeed, half of the couplets in this section (6.3–6.7) are based on an analogy between what can be known by perception and what can be known, though imperceptible. The relationship between the two is philosophically argued, with the former as signifier and the latter as signified. One couplet points to the experiencer of karma as a signifier for the existence of the soul (6.3). Our perception tells us that there are many observable aspects of karma: We know that there is a person who performs actions, actions that are performed, the results of those actions, and the person who experiences the results of the actions. Yet reflection reveals that these are all related entities. There is a continuity of the experiencer through the performance of actions and their results over time. What is this continuity? It is the soul, "he who is saved" (uyvāṉ). The existence of the soul is signified by the observable fact that we experience actions and their results. This is the method of knowing the soul.

Other couplets offer analogies that support the method of knowing God. We can see that the soul vivifies the body; therefore, the soul is closely joined to the body (6.4). The same relationship exists between the soul and God, the latter identified as an imperceptible power, the intellect (tāṉ uṇaṟvu). We can also come to know about God through our actions (6.7). Just as sense perceptions animate or even motivate mundane activities, so the Lord is related to our (nonmundane) activities. Grace is also signified by human experience in the world. Grace is to the world as the sun is to a crystal (6.5). The sun will show its own color through a crystal, and it will illuminate the colors of objects around it; similarly, grace will show itself though the world and the many objects in the world. Like the sun, the light of grace is pervasive, and it allows us to see things as they truly are. In a related analogy, grace also makes it possible for the soul to see (6.6). In ordinary sight, the eye needs light to apprehend not only the objects around it but also its own position in relation to those objects. Similarly, the eye of the soul cannot see higher realities or understand its position in relation to them without the light of grace.

The final couplets of the section deconstruct this method of analogy to clarify differences in the ways of knowing. An analogy is a comparison, and a comparison presupposes difference, even if its effect is to emphasize similarity. One couplet insists that the way of knowing higher realities is not like the method of gaining ordinary knowledge (6.8). It advises that research, close scrutiny, and the projection of yourself, all of which mean one's own agency, are ultimately futile methods for the knowledge of soul, grace, and God, even though appropriate for worldly knowledge. The method here becomes not only seeing but also being seen by the Lord (pārtta taṉai pār). The implication is that because the Lord has seen you, therefore, you can see him. This passive sense of things beyond one's own agency, which was suggested by the first couplet, is echoed in the final couplet (6.10), in which the hearer is urged to see things that have been shown. The double reference here is to the text itself and to the agency of God. The couplet creates a limit; there are many things that can be seen but only a few that are shown. This is the difference between ordinary knowledge and the way of knowing described in this section. To those who grasp this difference, the world will be seen as an excess of the senses (6.9), and the knowers can take refuge (oḷi, lit. hide) in the light of jñāna.

The next decade of couplets, "Enlightenment of the Soul," intensifies the teaching that the soul is limited in its knowledge. This section serves as a counterpoint to section 2, "Nature of the Categories of the Soul." The progression of the soul that occurs between chapter 2 and chapter 7 is immense. The former outlined the categories of the souls (uyiravai) and their capacities or lack thereof, whereas the latter imagines the soul as an individual at the threshold of salvation. In the Śaiva Siddhānta philosophy of this text, salvation happens to an individual in a way especially appropriate to him.

The distinction between the two chapters on the soul may be further understood with reference to the hierarchy of knowledge envisioned by the Śaiva Siddhānta. Each of the four stages of knowledge is progressively subtle in comparison to the crudeness of its predecessor, yet all four are required for an understanding of the world. The highest knowledge is Śiva-cit-śakti, knowledge of God. Prior to it is jīva-cit-śakti (ātma-cit-śakti), which is knowledge of the soul that is directly catalyzed by God.[9] Next are the four internal instruments, the *antaḥkaraṇa*: manas (mind), buddhi (power of discrimination, description; in the realm of karma), citta (a storehouse of decisions and aims), and ahamkāra (a stage of mental activity of the mind that is ready to act or eager to know; this, unlike āṇava, works for the benefit of the soul). Finally, there is sensual knowledge, the jñānendrīyas. Section 2 concerned ways for the soul to know itself; section 7 focuses on the soul's knowledge of grace. To know grace, the soul must become aware of its own limitations (7.2, 7.3, 7.6, 7.9, 7.10). When this is done, the soul will be receptive to grace, which several couplets describe as an encompassing, protective source (7.1, 7.4, 7.5, 7.7, 7.8).

Section 8 of the text describes the experience of grace, which is characterized as Bliss (iṉpu; 8.1). One is possessed by bliss (8.7); alternatively, bliss is like the love between a man and a woman (8.2, 8.10). The images are complete engagement in bliss, yet there remains a distinction between the soul and bliss. How is this distinction to be understood? The Tamil Śaiva Siddhānta recognizes different relationships that describe the stages of the soul's knowledge and experience of God. One is camavāya, in which two realities share an essential nature and cannot be divided without losing their essence. Examples include fire and heat, water and wetness, and heat in hot water. This imperfectly describes the relationship between God and soul because, ultimately, God is greater than the soul (see 1.8). The second relationship is called tātāṉmiyam, which admits the pluralism that one thing can remain as two. Examples include water that is in a pot and water that is in a tumbler and one woman who is both a mother and a teacher. This relationship describes the nature of Śiva and śakti. Finally, there is the relation of advaita, which is two things remaining as one. It also admits a plurality but does so in the service of a unity. The two things are understood to be distinctive, yet they remain as one. This is a very different understanding of advaita than that of Śankara, who used the term to describe everything as one, actively discarding a sense of plurality in the relationship by designating the plurality as māyā in the sense of illusion. It is also distinct from the Sanskrit Śaiva Siddhānta ideology of "becoming a Śiva" discussed in part 4. There is no indication in the TP that the soul "becomes a Śiva" or is equal to Śiva (*Śivasamavāda*), both of which are premises of the Sanskrit-language Śaiva Siddhānta.[10] Some of the reasons for this difference, as I suggested previously, are the influence of advaita philosophy in late medieval times and the idea that the Tamil Śaiva Siddhāntins did not localize their philosophy in a specific temple tradition. The TP suggests that the way of salvation is in the teaching of the knowledge contained in texts, not temple praxis.

In this advaitic relationship, the soul does not "become" God; God shares his nature by granting bliss to the soul (8.3). It is an acknowledgment of the shared essence yet distinction among God as the source, bliss as the experience, and the soul as the experiencer (8.9). Like the letters *ḷ* and *t* that become one to make the letter *t* in tāṭalai (foot, *tāḷ*; head, *talai*), each sharing its own distinctive nature (the retroflex *ḷ* contributes its retroflex pronunciation, whereas the alveolar *t* contributes its form; the result is a retroflex *ṭ*), God and the soul remain distinct, but they are joined as one in bliss (8.4). Indeed, the tendency of humankind to view the soul as either the same as the Lord or completely different is criticized in the next couplet. If there is only one, then what good is talk of unity? If there are two opposed in nature, then what good is talk of unity? There must be neither two nor one (8.5, 8.9). The experience of bliss, achieved by those who join the bliss (ur̲r̲ār), those who receive the bliss (per̲r̲ār), and those who silently adhere to the bliss (urai oḷiyap par̲r̲ār), results in liberation from the cycle of births and deaths (8.6). At this stage, bliss is the only experience, which renders all others irrelevant (8.8).

Umāpati turns next to interpret philosophically the pañcākṣara-mantra (five-syllable mantra), namaccivāya (Skt. namaḥ śivāya; homage to Śiva!), an ancient mantra that scholars believe appeared for the first time in the Sanskrit *Śatarudrīya*.[11] Umāpati introduces the mantra in the section of couplets that stands between the categories of "Experiencing Bliss" and "Those Who Have Attained," which can be interpreted in three overlapping ways: (1) the mantra is most efficacious if used by people who have reached this point in the path of salvation; (2) it is only at this juncture in the text that Umāpati believes he has explained enough of the Tamil Śaiva Siddhānta philosophy for the reader to understand his interpretation of the mantra, for he offers nothing less than a complete reconstitution of the mantra, from the way it is pronounced to the meanings embedded therein[12]; and (3) Umāpati uses the discussion of the mantra to provide the hearer with images to further describe the soul's movement toward God. All three of these ideas are possible reasons as to why Umāpati chose to focus on the five-syllable mantra at this point in the text.

To begin with, Umāpati tells us that the āgamas (the books of grace) and the Vedas, plus other books (probably the texts viewed as limbs or supplements to the Vedas, though the couplet does not specify), elucidate the threads of truth in the five syllables (9.1). Rather than stating that the mantra encapsulates the books, Umāpati appears to suggest that mantra is the prior whole and that the role of the books is to follow and explore its threads of truth (poruḷ nūl). The five-syllable mantra is thus the basis for the knowledge that fills volumes.

The mantra encapsulates the realities according to Śaiva Siddhānta. Umāpati lists five realities: God, śakti, pāśa, the power of māyā, and the soul, as contained within the universal sound, Ōṃ, which precedes the mantra and is considered its sixth syllable. When the mantra is pronounced as five syllables, excluding the Ōṃ, the syllables correspond to each of the five realities. Ōṃ, made up of the three letters, *a* + *u* + *m*(a), represents a further reduction of the realities to the three essential realities of Śaiva Siddhānta, pati, paśu, and pāśa, in that śakti and māyā can both be considered modalities of the Lord. In this way, *a* is Lord, *u* is soul, and *m*(a) is pāśa. The couplet asserts that whenever we say Ōṃ, we are articulating the world according to Śaiva Siddhānta.

The remaining couplets in this section further identify the values of the five syllables, give a philosophical interpretation that makes changing the order of the syllables not only meaningful but also necessary, and teach reciters of the mantra how to locate themselves in the mantra and thus in the larger meanings of Śaiva Siddhānta. For example, one couplet (9.3) tells the reader to locate the soul between the actions of the flesh and the dance of knowledge. In terms of the philosophy learned from earlier sections, we know this means that the soul stands between pāśa and pati, respectively. What it also means, however, is that the order of the mantra is changed. If the Śaiva Siddhānta values were assigned to the mantra in the traditional sequence, the soul would be located at the end of the mantra, that is, Na (Tirobhāva-śakti, the concealing power of the Lord), ma (āṇava mala), śi (Lord), vā (grace), ya (soul). But in this couplet, Umāpati says that the soul is *between* the highest and the lowest realities. Therefore, the proper order is Śi-vā-ya-na-ma.

The struggle for the soul's release is played out with respect to the correct pronunciation of the mantra. Umāpati explains that the ma (āṇava) and na (Tirobhāva) expand and will never release the soul until it is liberated from birth and death, for the āṇava in conjunction with concealment is the cause for birth and death (9.4). Therefore, in terms of reciting the mantra, the soul will not progress toward release if the reciter begins with na and ma (9.5) because by saying these syllables first, the individual affirms their control over him; things will not change. Instead, those realities that will set the soul free should be recited first, that is, Śi and va. The text urges the hearer to recite the mantra in this way so that his births will end, and thus the āṇava will no longer have a hold on the soul (9.7).

Umāpati further suggests that it is a common strategy in Indian thought to begin at the bottom and work one's way up (9.6). This is the case, for example, in yoga, where one begins concentration on the lowest cakra (power center) at the base of the spine, the Mūlātāram, and brings the power (kundalini) up to the cakra at the level of mideyebrow, the Āññai.[13] But Umāpati asserts that thinking of anything other than Śiva or his grace as the soul's foundation is incorrect, and thus one must recite the syllables of the highest realities first.

If one does recite the mantra in this way, then grace, which comes directly before the soul and thus has influence over it prior to mention of the harmful realities, will act as a facilitator between the soul and God by endowing the soul with its own flawless form and causing it to prosper in the bliss of the Lord (9.8).[14] Indeed, because of the influence of grace, the soul will really stand no longer between grace (vā) and Tirobhāva (na); in effect, the soul will stand between the Lord (Śi), and grace (vā) (9.9). The mantra itself demonstrates that the soul cannot be separate from the Lord (9.10).

In the final section, the reader encounters a series of couplets on the nature of "Those Who Have Attained" the Lord, which is understood in Tamil Śaiva Siddhānta as the advaita relationship in which the two are as one (10.5). The souls are meditative enjoyers: They enjoy the highest knowledge and bliss (10.1), and though they can know anything they want only to know the Lord (10.3). They are no longer agents of causality in the world: Because they are free, they no longer cause the Lord to perform the five cosmic actions for their benefit, nor are they agents or experiencers of actions (10.2). Therefore, whatever actions they do are selfless, and their reward is truth, not the world that is suited to gainful work (10.7). They have withdrawn from sensual perception to realize their own essences of grace (10.4), so they are not affected by the worldly polarities of like and dislike (10.6). They are freed from the cycles of birth; their understanding (leading to selfless action) will not give rise to karmic result, and should karma appear, grace will take care of them by burning it (10.9). Last, though they are no longer subject to the cycles of birth and death, part of their selfless action is to be filled with compassion for those still bound (10.10).

As this last section of couplets demonstrates, the TP is written from the perspective of śuddha-jñāna (Tam. cutta-ñāṉam), or "pure knowledge." The text has led the hearer or reader through the three initial essential categories that define the human condition as a polarity between darkness and salvation, with the soul as an intermediary term, then continues with a series of categories that suggest stages on a path that culminates in pure knowledge. However, at no point is the cumulative knowledge divorced from experience: The soul goes from being an experiencer of a mixture of knowledge and ignorance, of grace and the material pull of desires and consequences, and of joy and sorrow, to being an experiencer of pure grace, pure bliss, and pure knowledge of the Lord. At this point, the soul is no longer between grace and Tirobhāva-śakti but between the Lord and grace. As with the relationship between the Lord and grace, it is impossible to say that the soul and God are one and impossible to say that they are two. The Tamil Śaiva Siddhānta envisions an advaitic relationship that is between monism and dualism. Similarly, the "attained" are in the world, but they are not subject to the conditions of the world; their link to the everyday is not through the experiences of the senses but through the experience of compassion. They live in the world as compassionate examples to others. To illustrate the nature of these exemplars, Umāpati turned to the nāyaṉmār.

Notes

Introduction

1. The term appeared as such in English-language dictionaries; for example, the *Oxford English Dictionary Supplement*, 1st ed. (1933), defined *bhakti* as "religious devotion, piety, or devoted faith as a means of salvation," citing M. Monier-Williams (1887, *Hinduism*), art historian E. B. Havell (1911, *Ideals of Indian Art*), and historian of Christianity T. R. Glover (1921, abbr. *Jesus Exper. Men*). The second edition of the *OED Supplement* (1976) adds H. H. Wilson (1832, *Journal of the Asiatic Society* (*Bengal*); his 1828 *Asiatic Researches* article is cited under *bhakta*) as the earliest and cites Indologist N. MacNicol (1915, *Indian Theism from the Vedic to the Muhammadan Period*) and writer-novelist E. M. Forster (1953, *Hill of Devi*). Of related interest is *Webster International*, 2d ed. (1948), which gives "religious devotion, love directed toward a personal deity."

2. See J. Samuel Preus, *Explaining Religion: Criticism and Theory from Bodin to Freud* (New Haven and London: Yale University Press, 1987).

3. Weber's theories on this appear in several of his writings, including *Indische Studien* 1:400ff. and 2:398ff., *Über die Kṛishṇajanamāsṭami* (Berlin: Akademie der Wissenschaften, 1867), and a paper on the Kṛishṇajanamāsṭami he delivered before the Akademie on June 17, 1867, of which extracts appear in English translation as "An Investigation into the Origin of the Festival of Kṛishṇajanmāshṭami," *Indian Antiquary* 3 (1874):21–25 (on the history of Western scholarship on whether Kṛṣṇa worship is derived from Christianity), 47–52 (on the date he believes Kṛṣṇa worshipers borrowed from Christianity), and 6 (1877):161–180 (reviews Hindu literary sources for the festival, thirteenth to eighteenth centuries, including some transliteration and translation), 281–301 (comparative discussion of pictorial images, including Egyptian and Byzantine), and 349–354 (conclusion).

The discussion in *IA* 3:21–23 gives a remarkable history of the confusion of the terms Kṛṣṇa and Christ, tracing it to the missionary arguments recorded in P. Georgi, *Alphabetum Tibetanum* (Rome, 1762), 253–263. See also the discussion of this confusion in contemporaneous and subsequent works in John Stratton Hawley, *At Play with Krishna*: *Pilgrimage Dramas from Brindavan* (Princeton: Princeton University Press, 1981), 56–61. Note also Max Müller's assimilation of the names of Vedic gods to those of Roman and Greek mythology.

4. The comparisons were made in an explanatory appendix to his translation of the *Bhagavad Gītā* (M. F. Lorinser, *Die Bhagavad Gita uebersetzt und erläutert* [Breslau, 1869]); an English translation of this appendix is in *Indian Antiquary* 2 (1873): 283–296.

5. On Weber: "Garbe's Introduction to the *Bhagavad Gītā*," *Indian Antiquary*, 47 (Supplement, 1918): 15–17; A. Barth, *The Religions of India*, 4th ed., trans. J. Wood (London: Kegan Paul, Trench, Trübner & Co., 1914, 219–224. (Much of Barth's book was originally published as an article in the *Encyclopédie des Sciences Religieuses*, ed. Lichtenberger, Paris, 1879; subsequently it was published as a book, *Religions de l'Inde*.) Weber was frequently critiqued by Bombay scholar R. G. Bhandarkar: see *IA* 2 (1873): 59–64, esp. 59–60; 94–96, 238–240 (on the date of Patañjali); 123–124 (on Rāmāyaṇa). Weber responded to many of these criticisms in *IA* 4 (1875): 244–251. Subsequent to the translation of Lorinser's thesis in *IA*, Edinburgh scholar J. Muir responded in a three-part *IA* article (4 [1875]: 77–81), which was subsequently reprinted and expanded as the Introduction to his *Metrical Translations from Sanskrit Writers* (London: Trübner, 1879). First, he translated part of an article by Professor Windisch of Heidelberg that criticized Lorinser for not knowing other Indian literatures and commentaries; then he reported his communication with A. Weber:

> Although [Weber] regards this attempt of Dr. Lorinser's to be overdone, he is not in principle opposed to the idea which that writer maintains, but regards it as fully entitled to a fair consideration, as the date of the *Bhagavad Gītā* is not at all settled, and therefore presents no obstacle to the assumption of Christian influences, if these can be otherwise proved. He adds that he regards Wilson's theory that the *bhakti* of the later Hindu sects is essentially a Christian doctrine, as according well with all that we know already about the Śvetadvīpa, the Kṛishṇajanmāshṭamī, &c.

The third part is Muir's criticism of Lorinser's translations and "renderings." Barth's later survey cuts the discourse to the quick: "[Lorinser] arrives at the singular conclusion that the author of the Hindu poem was well read in the Gospels and the Christian fathers" (221, n. 2). See also Monier-Williams's partial approval and partial critique in his *Indian Wisdom, or Examples of the Religious, Philosophical, and Ethical Doctrines of the Hindus*, 4th ed. (London: Luzac, (1895), 122–143, esp. 131–132.

6. R. G. Bhandarkar, "Allusions to Kṛishṇa in Patanjali's *Mahābhāshya*," *Indian Antiquary* 3 (1874): 14–16.

7. Bhandarkar, "Basis of Theism, and Its Relation to the So-Called Revealed Religions," *Collected Works of Sir R. G. Bhandarkar* (Poona: Bhandarkar Oriental Research Institute, 1927–1933) 2:603–616; originally published in 1883 by the Cheap Literature Committee of the Theistic Association of Bombay. This paper is also interesting because Bhandarkar offers reasons for giving his lecture in English rather than the usual Marathi. The quotation and surrounding discussion are on pages 611–616 of this article.

8. See my discussion of George A. Grierson's early-twentieth-century encyclopedia article on bhakti in part I and my discussion of bhakti as revival in contemporary scholarship in chapters 2 and 4.

9. On the *prasthānatrayā* status of the *Gītā*, see Krishna Sharma, *Bhakti and the Bhakti Movement: A New Perspective* (New Delhi: Munshiram Manoharlal, 1987), 82–83. Eric Sharpe reminds us that although we tend to think of the *Gītā* as a popular text, its popularity is a recent phenomenon; see Eric J. Sharpe, "Some Western Interpretations of the Bhagavad Gītā, 1785–1885," in Peter Slater and Donald Wiebe, eds., *Traditions in Contact and Change* (Waterloo, Ontario: Wilfrid Laurier University, 1983), 65–85, esp. 84–85.

10. Dnyāneśwar (or Jñāneśwar, Dnyānadev, Jñānadeo) wrote a colloquial commentary on the Gītā in A.D. 1290, known as *Dnyāneśwarī*; see Dnyaneshwar, *Jnāneshvari: A Song-*

Sermon on the Bhagavad-gītā, trans. V. G. Pradhan, ed. H. M. Lambert (London: George Allen and Unwin, 1967–1969).

11. A recent example would be *Devotion Divine: Bhakti Traditions from the Regions of India. Studies in Honour of Charlotte Vaudeville*, ed. Diana L. Eck and Françoise Mallison (Groningen: Egbert Forsten; Paris: École Française d'Extrême-Orient, 1991), which contains essays on regions of India from Indo-Pakistan to Tamilnadu, yet lacks any collective discussion of what constitutes bhakti.

12. John B. Carman, "Bhakti," in *The Encyclopedia of Religion*, ed. Mircea Eliade (New York: Macmillan, 1987), 2:130.

13. Two recent anthologies on bhakti in north India have sought to revise the definition of *bhakti* as "devotion to a personal deity" by including both saguṇa and nirguṇa images in the category. See Karine Schomer and W. H. McLeod, eds., *The Sants: Studies in a Devotional Tradition of India* (Berkeley: Berkeley Religious Studies Series; Delhi: Motilal Banarsidass, 1987) and David N. Lorenzen, ed., *Bhakti Religion in North India: Community Identity and Political Action* (Albany: State University of New York Press, 1995). See also the theoretical discussion in Sharma, *Bhakti and the Bhakti Movement*.

14. The distinction was primarily observed by commentators on the Hindi bhakti poetry, not by the poets themselves. See John Stratton Hawley, "The Nirguṇ/Saguṇ Distinction in Early Manuscript Anthologies of Hindi Devotion," in *Bhakti Religion in North India*, ed. David N. Lorenzen (Albany: State University of New York Press, 1995).

15. A famous example would be Mīrābaī's portrait of a Bhil woman; see the translation of this poem in John Stratton Hawley and Mark Juergensmeyer, *Songs of the Saints of India* (New York: Oxford University Press, 1988), 137. This is not to say that awareness of caste is not expressed in some bhakti poetry, notably that of untouchable poets.

16. Rajeswari Sunder Rajan, *Real and Imagined Women: Gender, Culture, and Postcolonialism* (London: Routledge, 1993).

17. Ibid., 10.

18. On the dimensions of the Tamil Nationalism movement, see the discussions in K. Nambi Arooran, *Tamil Renaissance and Dravidian Nationalism, 1905–1944* (Madurai: Koodal, 1980), esp. 1–34, 252–267. There was controversy in some quarters in viewing the hymns as representative of Tamil culture because they draw upon Sanskrit religious terminology and ideals.

19. I prefer not to engage in this discourse, which invokes the political agenda of Tamil nationalism, although other contemporary authors have. See the interesting comments on this theme in the review article of literature on Tamil bhakti by Vasudha Narayanan, "Hindu Devotional Literature: The Tamil Connection," *Religious Studies Review* 11, no. 1 (January 1985): 12–20.

Part I

1. Grierson, "Bhakti-Mārga," 539.

2. Ibid., 540. He may have had in mind Manu's description of the traditional sacred Vedic region, *Manava Dharma Śāstra* 8.92.

3. Ibid., 543.

4. Ibid., 547. He suggests answers to the question by appealing to the familiar discussion of Christian influence and adds the possibility of Islamic influence as well, which earlier scholars had noted in their discussions of Kabīr and the Sikhs.

5. Grierson, "Modern Hinduism and Its Debt to the Nestorians," *Journal of the Royal Asiatic Society* (January–June, 1907): 317. For a brief discussion of this article in the con-

text of the Christ-Kṛṣṇa debate in contemporaneous and subsequent works, see Hawley, *At Play with Krishna*, 56–61.

6. Grierson, "Modern Hinduism," 319.

7. Ibid., 314. He reproduces selections from A. B. Cowell's translation in an appendix, under the title "The Official Hindū Account of *Bhakti*."

Chapter 1

1. Examples of the assertion that bhakti is present in the Vedas include A. B. Keith in *JRAS* (1915), V. Raghavan, *The Indian Heritage* (Bangalore, 1956), and Solomon in *History of Religions* 10, no. 1 (1970), all cited in Miller, "*Bhakti* and the Ṛg Veda: Does It Appear There or Not," in *Love Divine*, ed. Karel Werner (Richmond, Surrey: Curzon, 1993), where *bhakti* is defined as "devotion to a personal god."

2. Biardeau, *Hinduism: The Anthropology of a Civilization*, trans. Richard Nice (Delhi: Oxford University Press, 1989), 89–90. The term *englobe* is from Hiltebeitel, "Toward a Coherent Study of Hinduism," *RSR* 9, no. 3 (July 1983): 206–212.

3. Biardeau and Malamoud, *Le sacrifice dans l'Inde ancienne* (Presses Universitaires de France, 1976), 106, 132. Emphasis added.

4. Biardeau, *Hinduism*, 90.

5. Biardeau notes that this school was "mainly responsible for the re-reading of the Revelation which bhakti constitutes," and adds that she cannot explain why at present (ibid., 15). Note that orientalists A. Weber and A. B. Keith translated texts from the Taittirīya school. The *Śatarudrīya-stōtra* is a chain of chants in praise of Rudra in the *Yajurveda*.

6. Ibid., 28. Elsewhere, she indicates that *Śvetāśvatara* is virtually a bhakti text (Biardeau and Malamoud, *Le sacrifice*, 79–80).

7. Biardeau, *Hinduism*, 28.

8. Ibid., 102.

9. Ibid., 84.

10. Ibid., 86–87.

11. Ibid., 87.

12. Ibid., 88.

13. A survey of the use of the term *bhakti* in epics was done many years ago by E. Washburn Hopkins, "The Epic Use of Bhagavat and Bhakti," *Journal of the Royal Asiatic Society of Great Britain and Ireland* (1911): 727–738. He concluded that the term *Bhāgavat* is always sacred (the sense of Adored), whereas *bhakti* can have ordinary meanings of affection.

14. Minoru Hara ("Note on Two Sanskrit Religious Terms: Bhakti and Śraddhā," *IIJ* 17, no. 2/3 [1964]: 124–145) provides an interesting discussion of *bhakti* as a technical term, in a comparison of śraddhā and bhakti. Although Hara tends to dichotomize the terms ("impersonal and personal, intellectual and emotional, and Vedic-Brahmanic and Hinduistic"), the conclusion that śraddhā is a "fundamental principle" with bhakti as "a developed mode of it" is a significant image for the development of *bhakti* as a technical term.

15. Wilson, *The Religious Sects of the Hindus* (London: Christian Literature Society for India, 1904), 82. Wilson and Henry Thomas Colebrooke are credited with the first discussions of bhakti in Western scholarship. Colebrooke's discussion of the *Bhāgavatas* was first read in 1827 and published the same year in the first volume of *Transactions* of the Royal Asiatic Society (549–579).

16. Monier-Williams, *Religious Thought and Life in India: An Account of the Religions of the Indian Peoples* (London: John Murray, 1883), 135. This work was subsequently republished many times with different descriptive phrases following "Religious Thought and Life in India."

17. Sharma, *Bhakti and the Bhakti Movement*, 109–114.

18. Edward C. Dimock Jr., *The Place of the Hidden Moon: Erotic Mysticism in the Vaisnava-sahajiyā Cult of Bengal* (Chicago: University of Chicago Press, 1989), 16.

19. David Haberman, *Acting as a Way of Salvation: A Study of Rāgānugā Bhakti Sādhana* (New York: Oxford University Press, 1988), 145.

20. Norman J. Cutler, *Songs of Experience: The Poetics of Tamil Devotion* (Bloomington: Indiana University Press, 1987), esp. 12–13, 19–37.

21. Helpful bibliographies of the literature on bhakti in English include: Norvin J. Hein, "Hinduism," in *A Reader's Guide to the Great Religions*, ed. Charles J. Adams (New York: Free Press, 1968); Eleanor Zelliot, "The Medieval Bhakti Movement in History: An Essay on the Literature in English," in *Hinduism: New Essays in the History of Religions*, ed. Bardwell L. Smith (Leiden: E. J. Brill, 1976), and Mariasusai Dhavamony, "A Bibliography on Bhakti in Hinduism," *Studia Missionalia* 30 (1981): 279–306.

22. Examples include Thomas J. Hopkins, *The Hindu Religious Tradition* (Belmont, Calif.: Wadsworth, 1971), 91; Glenn E. Yocum, "Personal Transformation through Bhakti (A Hindu Path to Release)," *Studia Missionalia* 30 (1981): 351; Fuller, *Servants of the Goddess: The Priests of a South Indian Temple* (Cambridge: Cambridge University Press, 1984), 16; Thomas B. Coburn, *Encountering the Goddess: A Translation of the Devī-Māhātmya and a Study of Its Interpretation* (Albany: State University of New York Press, 1991), 16; and Miller, "*Bhakti* and the Ṛg Veda."

23. This position is epitomized in Monier-Williams's separation of his treatment of these three in brief chapters on "reforming theistic sects" that formed appendages to his main chapter on Vaiṣṇavism. For Monier-Williams, Kabīr exemplified the true radical other of reformist tendencies because his religious perspective, in contrast to mainstream Vaiṣṇavism, definitively repudiated "idol worship": "But he did more than all other Vaishṇava reformers. He denounced all idol-worship and taught Vaishṇavism as a form of strict monotheism. True religion, according to Kabīr, meant really nothing but devotion to one God, who is called by the name Vishṇu, or by synonyms of Vishṇu such as Rāma and Hari, or even by names current among Muhammadans" (*Religious Life and Thought in India*, 159).

24. For example, Śankara, following Upaniṣadic traditions, distinguishes between Brahmā (nirguṇa) and Īśvara (saguṇa; the conditioned or sopādhika aspect of Brahmā); in his commentary on the *Brahmasūtra* he also relates this to bhakti. See, for example, Dasgupta, *A History of Indian Philosophy* (Delhi: Motilal Banarsidass, 1988), esp. vol. 4, and Susmita Pande, *Birth of Bhakti in Indian Religions and Art* (New Delhi: Books and Books on behalf of Indian History and Cultural Society, 1982), 170ff. On the division of regional-language bhaktis into nirguṇa and saguṇa, see Hawley and Juergensmeyer, *Songs of the Saints of India*, 3–7; and A. K. Ramanujan, *Speaking of Śiva* (Baltimore: Penguin, 1973), 35 n. 9. On nirguṇa bhakti, see Schomer and McLeod, eds., *The Sants*, in which a minority of two scholars remain unconvinced that nirguṇa is bhakti: Frits Staal, "The Ineffable *Nirguṇa* Brahman" (41–46), and Wendy Doniger O'Flaherty, "The Interaction of *Saguṇa* and *Nirguṇa* Images of Deity" (47–52).

25. R. Garbe, for example, resolved the problem by asserting that "in the older poem is preached Kṛishṇaism based philosophically on Sāmkhya-yoga [theism]; the Vedānta philosophy is taught in the additions (made at the time) of the revision" (in N. B. Utgikar, trans., "Garbe's Introduction to the *Bhagavadgītā*," *Indian Antiquary* 47 supplement [1918]): 5–6; this statement is italicized in the article. The orientalists had primarily relied upon the *Bhagavad Gītā* and other Sanskrit literature for their conception of bhakti, although they were aware that poetry associated with Caitanya was in Bengali and that the poetry of Kabīr was in Hindi. In fact, some Bengali bhakti poetry, plus excerpts from the Hindi "Caitanya-caritāmṛta," had been translated early on by John Beams, "Chaitanya and the Vaishnava Poets of Bengal," *IA* 2 (1873):1–7.

26. Rāmachandra Shukla, *Hindi Śabda Sāgara* (Nāgari Prachārani Sabhā, 1929, 1939); cited in Sharma, *Bhakti and the Bhakti Movement*, 69–70. Other pioneering studies include Pitambar D. Barthwal, *The Nirguna School of Hindi Poetry: An Exposition of Medieval Indian Santa Mysticism* (Benares: Indian Book Shop, 1936; reprinted as *Traditions of Indian Mysticism Based upon the Nirguna School of Hindi Poetry* [New Delhi: Heritage Publishers, 1978]); and Parashuram Caturvedi, *Uttari Bhārat ki sant-paramparā* (Allahabad: Bharati Bhandar, 1972 [1952]). The term *nirguṇa* was itself used in bhakti poetry: "For the Sants already, as for earlier Shaiva and for later Vaishnava bhaktas, *nirguṇa* is a somewhat magic word. They would talk of the ultimate object of their own bhakti as *nirguṇa*, but for them, *nirguṇa* should not be interpreted as 'that which is deprived of qualities but rather as 'that which is beyond the three *guṇas*' (inherent to material nature, *prakṛti* and even beyond the traditional distinction between the *nirguṇa* and *saguṇa* aspects of the Godhead)" (Charlotte Vaudeville, "*Sant Mat*: Santism as the Universal Path to Sanctity," in Schomer and McLeod, eds., *The Sants*, 21–40, esp. 27–28.

27. Hawley, "The Nirguṇ/Saguṇ Distinction in Early Manuscript Anthologies of Hindi Devotion."

28. Ramanujan, "The Myths of Bhakti: Images of Śiva in Śaiva Poetry," *in Discourses of Śiva: Proceedings of a Symposium on the Nature of Religious Imagery*, ed. Michael W. Meister (Philadelphia: University of Pennsylvania Press, 1984), 212.

29. Krishna Sharma, *Bhakti and the Bhakti Movement*, 109–129. See also Arvind Sharma, *The Hindu Gītā: Ancient and Classical Interpretations of the Bhagavād Gītā* (LaSalle, Ill.: Open Court), 1986.

30. For example, Zelliot, "The Medieval Bhakti Movement in History," 146; see also Cutler, *Songs of Experience*, 1–2.

31. Kinsley, "Devotion," in *Encyclopedia of Religion*, ed. Mircea Eliade (New York: Macmillan, 1987), 4:321–326.

32. See Scott, "Devotion and Devotional Literature," in *The Encyclopædia of Religion and Ethics*, James Hastings, ed. (Edinburgh: T. & T. Clark, 1911), 693–967.

33. Hallisey, "Devotion in the Buddhist Literature of Medieval Sri Lanka" (Ph.D. dissertation, University of Chicago, 1988), esp. 1:1–6, 18–68.

34. Ibid., 1:5–6, 56–57, 68. Hallisey's complicated argument would be difficult to reproduce here. He uses a theory of signs from Charles Morris to explicate Wach's typology of devotion (1:2–5).

35. Auguste Barth, *The Religions of India*, see also H. H. Wilson, *The Religious Sects of the Hindus* (London: Christian Literature Society for India, 1904), 82.

36. For example, Ronald Inden's translation of bhakti as "conscious participation," *Imagining India* (London: Basil Blackwell, 1990), 114; also Peterson, *Poems to Śiva: The Hymns of the Tamil Saints* (Princeton: Princeton University Press, 1989), 49; and Cutler's analysis of Tamil hymns as communion between devotee and god, and author and audience, *Songs of Experience*, 11, 51–52. There are other examples of the use of participation in scholarship, notably, the association of participation with primitive societies in the work of anthropologist Levy-Bruhl and religious historian Betty Heiman's analysis of bhakti as "reciprocal participation" according to the formula of *do ut des* (for a critique of the latter, see Dhavamony, *Love of God* according to Śaiva Siddhānta [Oxford: Clarendon, 1971], 21).

Chapter 2

1. This identification of bhakti as a "popular religion" included the idea that Vāsudeva was a patronym indicating a real person, who, like the other great classical Indian reformer, the Buddha, was from the kṣatriya caste.

2. M. G. Ranade, *Rise of the Maratha Power and Other Essays* (Bombay: University of Bombay, 1960 [1900]), 4–5; cited in Eleanor Zelliot, "Chokhamela and Eknath: Two *Bhakti* Modes of Legitimacy for Modern Change," in *Tradition and Modernity in Bhakti Movements*, ed. Jayant Lele (Leiden: E. J. Brill, 1981), 140.

3. For example, Monier-Williams, *Religious Thought and Life in India*, 116, 139.

4. Sharma reviews and critiques the Indian scholars R. S. Sharma, Irfan Habib, K. A. Nizami, D. D. Kosambi, and Romila Thapar in *Bhakti and the Bhakti Movement*, 26–35; Zvelebil reviews and critiques the Soviet scholars Smirnova and Pyatigorsky and the Tamil scholars S. Vaiyapuri Pillai, Cāmi Citamparaṉār, and C. Rakunātaṉ in *The Smile of Murugan: On Tamil Literature of South India* (Leiden: E. J. Brill, 1981), 191–199.

5. Peterson, *Poems to Śiva*, 270. See Zvelebil, *The Smile of Murugan*, 192–193.

6. Ramanujan, *Hymns for the Drowning:* Poems for Viṣṇu by Nammāḻvār (Princeton: Princeton University Press, 1981), 136.

7. Ibid., 137. In many of his writings on bhakti and on folklore, Ramanujan has characterized Sanskrit as a "father tongue" and regional languages as a "mother tongue."

8. K. Sharma, *Bhakti and the Bhakti Movement*, 24–25. Cf. David N. Lorenzen, "Introduction: The Historical Vicissitudes of Bhakti Religion," in *Bhakti Religion in North India*, ed. D. N. Lorenzen, 1–32, esp. 13–21.

9. Ramanujan calls the language of Mahādēviyakka "spontaneous rhetoric," in *Speaking of Śiva*, 37–42.

10. Jayant Lele, "The *Bhakti* Movement in India: A Critical Introduction," in *Tradition and Modernity in Bhakti Movements*, ed. J. Lele (Leiden: E. J. Brill, 1981), 15.

11. Lele, "Community, Discourse, and Critique in Jnanesvar," in ibid., 111.

12. Guha, "Dominance without Hegemony and Its Historiography," in *Subaltern Studies VI: Writings on South Asian History and Society*, ed. R. Guha (Delhi: Oxford University Press, 1992), 259, 262.

13. Ibid., 263–264.

14. Burton Stein, "Social Mobility and Medieval South Indian Hindu Sects," in *Social Mobility in the Caste System in India*, ed. James Silverberg (The Hague: Mouton, 1968); Lynn Vincentnathan, "Nandanar: Untouchable Saint and Caste Hindu Anomaly," *Ethos* 21, no. 2 (1993): 154–179; and Eleanor Zelliot, "Chokhamela and Eknath," 153, whose arguments are summarized in her more recent article, "Chokhāmeḷā: Piety and Protest," in David N. Lorenzen, ed., *Bhakti Religion in North India*, 212–220.

15. Philip Lutgendorf, "Interpreting Rāmrāj: Reflections on the *Rāmāyaṇa*, Bhakti, and Hindu Nationalism," in *Bhakti Religion in North India*, ed. D. N. Lorenzen, 267, 280. Ayodhya is understood to be the birthplace of Rāma.

16. Ibid., 280.

17. Hawley and Juergensmeyer, *Songs of the Saints*, 5–6.

18. See, for example, Dehejia, *Slaves of the Lord: The Path of the Tamil Saints* (New Delhi: Munshiram Manoharlal, 1988), frontispiece; Zvelebil, *The Smile of Murugan*, 190; and Dhavamony, *Love of God*, 101–102.

19. In translation, the *Bhāgavata Māhātmya* is often appended to the *Bhāgavata Purāṇa*; for example, *The Bhāgavata-Purāṇa*, part I, translated and annotated by Ganesh Vasudeo Tagare, vol. 7 in the Ancient Indian Tradition and Mythology Series, ed. J. L. Shastri (Delhi: Motilal Banarsidass, 1976), lxxi-cv, esp. lxxvi. It is from the *Padma Purāṇa* (Uttarakhanda chap. 6, 193.51); see *The Padma-Purāṇa*, part IX, translated and annotated by N. A. Deshpande, vol. 9 in the Ancient Indian Tradition and Mythology Series, ed. G. P. Bhatt (Delhi: Motilal Banarsidass, 1991), 2974. Sharma says that the passage is in the *Skanda Purāṇa* as well, but gives no exact citation; see *Bhakti and the Bhakti Movement*, 298. The encyclopedic *History of Dharmaśāstra* by P. V. Kane (Poona: Bhandarkar Oriental Research Insti-

tute, 1953) mentions just the *Bhāgavata Māhātmya* and the *Padma Purāṇa* as sources, vol. 5, part II, p. 979.

20. My telling is based on the editions of the *Bhāgavata Māhātmya* and the *Padma Purāṇa*, cited in the previous note, and on Sharma, *Bhakti and the Bhakti Movement*, 298–301, 303–308.

21. In the *Padma Purāṇa*, Pārvatī says that she has heard the greatness of the *Gītā* and now wishes to hear the *Bhāgavata*, which is "best among the purāṇas." Śiva tells the story of Śaunaka and Sūta.

22. *Yavana* is the Sanskrit term for Greeks, Muslims, or foreigners in general.

23. *Vairāgya* is also translated as "detachment," "passionlessness," and sometimes even "asceticism"; the term is associated with Jñāna Yoga.

24. On the sons, the *Padma Purāṇa* says, in Deshpande's rather obscure translation: "These two, for want of receivers, have not become young. It appears that they are asleep here due to a little joy to them." Tagare's translation of the *Bhāgavata Māhātmya* says: "These two (sons of yours) do not shed off their decrepitude due to absence of people accepting them. Their deep sleep is regarded as a result of the partial satisfaction of their self."

25. Similarly, the sweet mango fruit is distinguished from the tree, and the ghee is separated from the milk.

26. See the section on this text in Hardy, *Virāha-Bhakti: The Early History of Kṛṣṇa Devotion in South India* (Delhi: Oxford University Press, 1983); that the text was composed in the south is generally accepted by scholars. However, van Buitenen offers the caveat that neither Rāmānuja nor Yāmuna, both medieval philosophers who were concerned with bhakti, quoted the *Bhāgavata Purāṇa*; see "On the Archaism of the Bhāgavata Purāṇa," in *Krishna: Myths, Rites, and Attitudes*, ed. Milton Singer (Honolulu: East-West Center Press, 1966), 26.

27. Jean Filliozat "proves" that the *Māhātmya* gives the history of bhakti, through his appeal to dates from other sources that indicate the appearance of bhakti in specific regions. The earliest regional-language bhakti appears in Tamil around the seventh century, then in other languages elsewhere at different times, the latest being in Hindi, around the sixteenth century. However, the chronology of bhakti in regional languages does not prove that bhakti was a unified movement. See his "Les dates du *Bhāgavatapurāṇa* et du *Bhāgavatamāhātmya*," in *Indological Studies* (New Haven: American Oriental Society, 1962).

28. The āgamas are sectarian works that expound on mythological, philosophical, and ritual themes and often have the status of "fifth Veda" in their communities. Those associated with Śaivism are Śaiva Āgamas; with Vaiṣṇavism they are often called Saṃhitās, and with Śāktism they are often called Tantras. Davis, "Ritual in an Oscillating Universe" (Ph.D. dissertation, University of Chicago, 1988), 10–25, discusses the transmission of Śaiva Siddhānta knowledge through networks created by traveling members of lineages in medieval times; the detail of this discussion was not included in his book of the same title. There were regional purāṇas that were localized in caste groups; see the discussion in chapter 4.

29. On the polemic against Gujarat in the text, Sharma notes that there may have been many Jains in Gujarat and that there is no record of a Gujarati Viṣṇu-bhakta before Narsimha Mehtā (1415–1481); *Bhakti and the Bhakti Movement*, 309. This bhakta thus slightly predates Vallabha.

30. The Caṅkam poetry of the Tamils dates to around 2,000 years ago. The history of these poems, however, is complicated, because it appears that, unlike many of the Sanskrit texts, they were largely forgotten until their "rediscovery" by U. Vē Cāminātaiyar in the latter part of the nineteenth century.

31. See, for example, "Dravidians (South India)," in *Encyclopædia of Religion and Ethics*, edited by James Hastings (Edinburgh: T & T Clark, 1912), 5:21–22, citing Thurston, *Castes and Tribes of Southern India*.

32. Ibid., 22.

33. Grierson, "Bhakti-Mārga," 551.

34. G. U. Pope, *The Tiruvāçagam or "Sacred Utterances" of the Tamil Poet, Saint, and Sage Māṇikka-Vācagar* (Oxford: Clarendon Press, 1900).

35. Ibid., ix; see also x. In his brief note on bhakti, he claimed that bhakti is equal to *pietas* (loving piety), compared it to a psalm, argued with H. H. Wilson, dated Māṇikkavācakar, and maintained that the *Gītā* was the source for bhakti (lxvii n. 8).

36. Bhandarkar, *Vaiṣṇavism, Śaivism and Minor Religious Systems* (Varanasi: Indological Book House, 1965 [1913]), 142. Note that the āgamas were not widely known or studied at that time. Richard Davis has tried to correct this omission, *Ritual in an Oscillating Universe* (Princeton: Princeton University Press, 1991).

37. Others had translated canonical works in Tamil from the Śaiva Siddhānta school, too. For example, the *Civañāṉa Pōtam* of Meykaṇṭār and the *Civappirakācam* of Umāpati Civācāryār had been translated by Henry R. Hoisington (*Journal of the American Oriental Society* 4 [1853–1854], 31–102, 127–244), and the *Tiruvaruṭpayaṉ* had first been translated into English in 1896, under the supervision of the Dharmapuram maṭh: Nallaswami Pillai, *Thiruvaruṭpayaṉ of Umapathi Sivacharya* (a year earlier, the maṭh had published his translation of *Civañāṉa Pōtam*). From this point on, very brief mentions of Ṣaiva Siddhānta were made in the main academic journals.

38. Whitehead, *The Village Gods of South India* (New Delhi: Asian Educational Services, 1983); Elmore, *Dravidian Gods in Modern Hinduism* (Madras: CLS for India), 159.

39. This could be expanded into the broader orientalist classification of "cold-climate" and "hot-climate" countries, in which the former represent more advanced societies; this classification is sometimes applied within a country, such as India, as well.

40. Shulman, *Tamil Temple Myths: Sacrifice and Divine Marriage in the South Indian Śaiva Tradition* (Princeton: Princeton University Press, 1980); Hart, *The Poems of Ancient Tamil: Their Milieu and Their Sanskrit Counterparts* (Berkeley: University of California Press, 1975); Hardy, *Virāha-Bhakti*.

41. For example, Beck, "The Goddess and the Demon: A Local South Indian Festival and Its Wider Context." *Puruṣārtha* 5 (1981):83–136.

42. Sharma, *Bhakti and the Bhakti Movement*, 6, n. 1.

43. Krishna Sharma makes the point about the *Gītā* as prashāntrayā, ibid., 109–114. The philosophical comparison I present is based on my readings of *Sri Sankara's Gita Bhashya*, trans. C. V. Ramachandra Aiyar (Bombay: Bharatiya Vidya Bhavan, 1988); and J. A. B. Van Buitenen, *Rāmānuja on the Bhagavadgītā* (Delhi: Motilal Banarsidass, 1968). See also Patricia Y. Mumme, "Haunted by Śankara's Ghost: The Śrivaṣṇava Interpretation of Bhagavad Gītā 18:66," in *Texts in Context: Traditional Hermeneutics in South Asia*, ed. Jeffrey R. Timm (Albany: State University of New York Press, 1992), 69–84.

Part II

1. Their formal spiritual names are, respectively, Tiruñāṉacampantar ("He who is related [to the Lord] through Divine Knowledge"), Tirunāvukkaracar ("The King of Sacred Speech"), and Cuntaramūrtti ("The Handsome One"); Cuntarar is also called Nampi Ārūrar, indicating that he is from Ārūr. The poetry of Māṇikkavācakar is in the Tamil Śiva-bhakti canon (the complete canon is known as the *Tirumuṟai*, in twelve volumes), and it is very well known, especially his *Tiruvācakam*, but Māṇikkavācakar himself was not included on the authoritative list of sixty-three Śiva-bhakti "leaders" (nāyaṉmār).

2. Recently, an additional hymn attributed to Campantar was discovered as an inscription on the wall of the temple Tiruviṭaivāy in Tanjavur district. See Peterson, *Poems to Śiva*, 22, text and n. 7.

3. A text purporting to describe the canonization of the hymns, the *Tirumuṟaikaṇṭapurāṇam*, which is dated to the fourteenth century, tells us that originally the number of verses was much greater, with 16,000 composed by Campantar, 49,000 by Appar, and 38,000 by Cuntarar. The text relates that many of the hymns were destroyed by white ants and then specifies that Śiva himself claimed to have preserved all the hymns that were necessary for humankind (vv. 14–16, 17, 22). Judging from the canon we possess today, the text suggests that only 25 percent of Campantar's hymns survived, only 6 percent of Appar's, and a meager 2.5 percent of Cuntarar's. I discuss this text and the agenda of its author, as well as its role in forming the *Tirumuṟai* canon, in chapter 8.

4. Indira Peterson provides a telling of each of the mūvar's stories from later sources with correlation to the hymns in *Poems to Śiva*, 270–322.

5. Ibid., 333. A translation of Appar's verse by David Shulman offers an alternative meaning: "I am the servant of the servants of the King of the Holy Tongue (Tirunāvukk'-araiyaṉ), who took for himself that excellence that is imbued with splendor." As Shulman notes, in this brief description, Cuntarar is quoting a line from Appar's poetry (4.8.1). See his *Songs of the Harsh Devotee: The Tēvāram of Cuntaramūrttināyaṉār* (Philadelphia: Department of South Asia Regional Studies, University of Pennsylvania, 1990), 240 and 244 n. 23.

Chapter 3

1. Stella Kramrisch, *The Hindu Temple* (Delhi: Motilal Banarsidass, 1976 [1946]), 1 n. 3.

2. Modern ethnographically based monographs of Hindu pilgrimage also support this image of regionalism and make us aware of local practices and motives. Examples include, on Maharashtra, I. Karve, "On the Road: A Maharashtrian Pilgrimage," trans. Dinkar Dhondo Karve, *Journal of Asian Studies* 22 (1962): 13–29, and D. B. Mokashi, *Palkhi: An Indian Pilgrimage*, trans. Philip Engblom (Albany: State University of New York Press, 1987); on Rajasthan, Ann Grodzins Gold, *Fruitful Journeys: The Ways of Rajasthani Pilgrims* (Berkeley: University of California Press, 1988); and on Tamilnadu, chapter 7 ("Equilibrium Regained") of E. Valentine Daniel, *Fluid Signs: On Being a Person the Tamil Way* (Berkeley: University of California Press, 1984).

3. Diana Eck, "India's Tīrthas: 'Crossings' in Sacred Geography," *History of Religions* 20, no. 4 (1981): 324–329.

4. *The Mahābhārata*, vol. 2, books 2 and 3, ed. and trans. J. A. B. van Buitenen (Chicago: University of Chicago Press, 1973), 374.

5. Ibid., 375.

6. Ibid., 374. The idea of getting out of actually journeying to perform pilgrimage is important but one that goes beyond the scope of this paper. We could point to the pilgrimage-like activities at large Hindu temple compounds, where worshipers circumambulate a number of satellite shrines before entering the main temple, for example, activities at the Ekāmbareśvara Temple as described in Agehananda Bharati, "Pilgrimage in the Indian Tradition," *History of Religions* 3, no. 1 (Summer 1963), 135–167, esp. 165. See also Allan G. Grapard, "Flying Mountains and Walkers of Emptiness" *History of Religions* 20, no. 2 (February 1982), 195–227, esp. 207, for a description of performing a symbolic pilgrimage to Shikoku at the temple precincts of Sennyū-ji. Also outside the scope of this essay is the notion of an "inner pilgrimage," such as that advocated by the reformers Guru Nānak (the founder of Sikhism) and Dayānanda Saraswatī (the founder of the Ārya Samāj). It is worth

pointing out that in Indian culture the notion of inner pilgrimage is literal as well as metaphorical; it depends on a schema of yoga, in which areas of the body are mapped as power regions.

7. See the map in Bhardwaj, *Hindu Places of Pilgrimage in India* (Berkeley: University of California Press, 1973), 44.

8. Ibid., 67.

9. Ibid., 58–79.

10. P. V. Kane systematically reviews the vast purāṇic references to tīrthayātrā, noting that the major purāṇas *Matsya*, *Kūrma*, *Vāyu*, *Padma*, and *Narasiṃha* refer to the Kāvēri, whereas the *Matsya*, *Kūrma*, and *Garuḍa* refer to Rāmeśvara; see his *History of Dharmaśāstra* vol. 4, sec. 4, "Tīrthayātrā," 552–827; listings on 795, 767.

11. Bhardwaj, *Hindu Places*, 34–35; see also Eck, "India's Tīrthas," 336.

12. Bhardwaj, *Hindu Places*, 61. There is a large literature on regionalism and its meanings in the corpus of scholarship on India. Two pieces to which I am indebted in what follows are Burton Stein, "Circulation and the Historical Geography of Tamil Country," in his *All the King's Mana: Papers on Medieval South Indian History* (Madras: New Era, 1984), 249–301, and Bernard S. Cohn and McKim Marriott, "Networks and Centres in the Integration of Indian Civilisation," *Journal of Social Research* 1, no. 1 (September 1958): 1–9.

13. Unless otherwise specified, poems found in the body of this book are my translations from the *Tēvāra Aruḷmuṟaittiraṭṭu*; numbers following the author's name indicate the poem's position in this text, and in the corpus of *Tēvāram*. See also appendix A.

14. See George W. Spencer, "The Sacred Geography of the Tamil Shaivite Hymns," *Numen* 17 (1970): 237–238. Tradition views the composition and singing of a hymn as simultaneously occurring in a single spontaneous event before God. However, a poem of Campantar alludes to his poems as manuscripts (Cam. 3.345.1–2; the written hymns were cast into a fire when Campantar sang in a king's court); see Peterson, *Poems to Śiva*, 273, 280.

15. For example, Appar 6.4/5.48.4, Cuntarar 10.14/7.51.4; see appendix A.

16. Das, *Structure and Cognition: Aspects of Hindu Caste and Ritual* (Delhi: Oxford University Press, 1982), 32: "Thus the creation of the Brahmans transforms a mere physical space into a tīrtha, which is a category of social space."

17. Pechilis, "To Pilgrimage It," *Journal of Ritual Studies* 6, no. 2 (Summer 1992): 59–91; see also my article, "Pilgrimage" in *The HarperCollins Dictionary of Religion*, ed. Jonathan Z. Smith (San Francisco: HarperSanFrancisco, 1995), 841–843.

18. Expressions used in the poem include "sacred Tamil" (*tiru tamiḻ*), "a garland of Tamil verse" (*tamiḻ-mālai*), "the Tamil Veda" (*tamiḻ maṟai*), and "Tamil song" (*icait tamiḻ*), as discussed by Peterson, "Singing of a Place: Pilgrimage as Metaphor and Motif in the *Tēvāram* Hymns of the Tamil Śaivite Saints," *Journal of the American Oriental Society* 102, no. 1 (January–March 1982): 77.

19. Ibid., p. 71.

20. M. A. Dorai Rangaswamy, *The Religion and Philosophy of Tēvāram: With Special Reference to Nampi Ārūr (Sundarar)* (Madras: University of Madras, 1991), 3; see also 5–18.

21. See, for example, Campantar 6.9/1.132.6.

22. *Ūrāṉ ōr tēvakulam*, as discussed in the ancient grammar, *Tolkāppiyam*, in the second book.

23. Indira Peterson explores this sentiment: The poems "concentrate on the goal, the experience of 'when you are there'; they contain detailed descriptions of the sacred places but not of the journey or the route. . . . The flavor and symbolism of 'being there' pervades them," in "Lives of the Wandering Singers: Pilgrimage and Poetry in Tamil Śaivite

Hagiography," *History of Religions* 22, no. 4 (1983): 345. In contrast to the "being there" nature of the hymns, the later *Periya Purāṇam* biographies detail aspects of the pilgrimage journey—which the text places squarely within the context of imperial stone temples.

24. Campantar composed a song, *Tirukcēttirakkōvai* (Garland of Sacred Places, 2.39), listing places he visited; he also composed the *Tiruvūrkkōvai* (Anthology of Sacred Places, 2.175); see the translation in Peterson, *Poems to Śiva*, 159–60. Cuntarar composed three hymns on this theme: the *Tirunāṭṭut tokai* (List of the Nāṭus, 7.12; see the translation in Shulman, *Songs of the Harsh Devotee*, 74–79); the *Tiru Iṭaiyāṟu* (the title is the name of a town which serves as a refrain in the hymn; 7.31; see the translation in Shulman, *Songs of the Harsh Devotee*, 188–192); and the *Ūrttokai* (List of Sacred Towns, 7.47; see the translation in Shulman, *Songs of the Harsh Devotee*, 295–300, and in Peterson, *Poems to Śiva*, 160–161). Appar's song, *Aṭaivu Tiruttāṇṭakam* (6.71), attempts to classify places of worship to Śiva in several categories: Paḷḷi, Vīraṭṭāṇam, Kuṭi, Ūr, Kōyil, Kāṭu, Vāyil, Iccuram, Malai, Āṟu, and Tuṟai. Many of these terms suggest both natural and constructed places (respectively: temple, site of Śiva's deeds, house, town, temple, uncultivated land, doorway, trees?, hill, river or path, port or refuge). Compare Peterson: "'Temple' is probably a misnomer for the dwellings of Śiva which the *nāyaṉmār* visited. . . . There are references to many kinds of *kōil* (the word for 'temple' in modern Tamil) in the Tēvāram, with descriptive prefixes which indicate that some of these *kōils* were no more than small open-air shrines in woods, on the banks of rivers and on beaches" ("Singing of a Place," 72 n. 18).

25. Or, socially constituted antisocial space. For example, the poetry of the woman nāyaṉār Kāraikkāl Ammaiyār portrays her at the feet of Śiva in Ālankāṭu, with kāṭu suggesting wild lands (or forest) as opposed to nāṭu, cultivated lands. She describes herself as watching the wild dance of Śiva at the cremation ground, which is uncontested land in social terms because of the pollution rules in Hindu society; yet, the Lord inhabits that land.

26. Ramanujan and Cutler, "From Classicism to Bhakti," in *Essays on Gupta Culture*, ed. Bardwell L. Smith (Columbia, Mo.: South Asia Books, 1983); also Ramanujan, *Hymns for the Drowning*, Appendix. In his many translations of Tamil poems A. K. Ramanujan has introduced the topics of akam and puṟam; I will not rehearse the details here.

27. Most often Śiva's role as a benefactor in the bhakti hymns is presented as a religious role; for example, he saves the mūvar from bad karma. However, three of Cuntarar's hundred hymns focus on gaining material wealth; see Peterson, "In Praise of the Lord: The Image and Tradition of the Royal Patron in the Songs of Saint Cuntaramūrtti and the Composer Tyāgarāja," in *The Powers of Art: Patronage in Indian Culture*, ed. Barbara Stoler Miller (Delhi: Oxford University Press, 1992), 123–130.

28. The gods are Māyōṉ (the dark one), Cēyōṉ (the red one), Vēntaṉ, and Varuṇa. Some scholars suggest that Māyōṉ was later homologized to Viṣṇu, and Cēyōṉ to Murukaṉ.

29. On Kāraikkāl Ammaiyār and the three early Vaiṣṇava poets, see Cutler, *Songs of Experience*, 117–130.

30. The *Tirumantiram* of Tirumūlar is the tenth volume of the canon. The poems of Kāraikkāl Ammaiyār and the *Tirumurukāṟṟuppaṭai*, attributed to Nakkīratēvar, are found in the eleventh volume.

31. *Paripāṭal* 15, translated by Norman Cutler in Ramanujan and Cutler, "From Classicism to Bhakti," 188–189.

32. Translated by Ramanujan, *Poems of Love and War* (New York: Columbia University Press, 1984), 215–217, 226–228.

33. *Cēvaṭi paṭarum cemmal uḷḷamoṭu* (lit., "the red feet thinking the king/Lord with the mind"). See discussion and transliteration in Dhavamony, *Love of God*, 125–127.

34. For discussion and translation, see Cutler, *Songs of Experience*. For a transliteration, see Dhavamony, *Love of God*, 132–138.

35. Dhavamony, *Love of God*, 127.

36. Peterson, *Poems to Śiva*, 100; citing *Tirumantiram*, Tantiram 2. This section of the *Tirumantiram* also contains stanzas on the eight heroic deeds of Śiva, which are also celebrated by the three poets.

37. Cutler, *Songs of Experience*, 51. Cutler primarily locates this "communion" in the ritual context of the temple: "It is useful to think of Tamil bhakti poetry as a poetic corollary of a theology of embodiment. . . . The poetics of bhakti . . . mirrors the religious ideology implicit in temple worship, for just as the presence of divinity is thought to be literally embodied in a properly consecrated stone or metal image of god, similarly the saint's communion with divinity is literally embodied in the recitation of his or her poetry in a consecrated ritual environment" (112–113).

38. In Biardeau's view (discussed in chapter 1), bhakti contributed to the creation of Hinduism. Here, I use the term *Hinduism* to stress the connections the nāyaṉmār were trying to forge between their religious vision and established religious ideals.

39. Jan Gonda identifies these recensions and versions in "The Śatarudrīya,"in *Sanskrit and Indian Studies*, ed. Masatoshi Nagatomi, et al. (Dordrecht: D. Reidel, 1980), 75–76. Indira Peterson, *Poems to Śiva*, 26, notes that of these recensions the *Black Yajurveda Taittirīya Saṃhitā* is used in south India. For the translated text, she points to C. Sivaramamurti, *Śatarudrīya: Vibhūti of Śiva's Iconography* (Delhi: Abhinav, 1976). Note that A. Weber was among the first to translate the Taittirīya rescension into a Western language (with various readings of the Kaṭha and the Vājasaneya); see A. Weber, *Indische Studien* 2, 13–47. See also A. B. Keith, *The Veda of the Black Yajus School Entitled the Taittiriya Samhita*, Harvard Oriental Series 19 (Cambridge: Harvard University Press, 1914), 353–362. J. Bruce Long gives a new translation of chapter 16 of the *Vājasaneya-Saṃhitā*, in "Rudra as an Embodiment of Divine Ambivalence in the *Śatarudrīya Stotram*," in *Experiencing Śiva*, ed. Fred W. Clothey and J. Bruce Long (New Delhi: Manohar, 1983), 123–128.

40. In K. A. Nilakanta Sastri, "An Historical Sketch of Śaivism," in *The Cultural Heritage of India* (Calcutta, 1956), 4:70; cited in Long, "Rudra," 106–107, 120 n. 20.

41. He cites Appar II.5 and on the following page calls attention to the formula in the *Cilappatikāram*, XI.128–130. Indira Peterson, *Poems to Śiva*, also calls attention to the pañcākṣara mantra (in Tamil, the mantra is namaccivāya) in several of the nāyaṉmār's poems, including: Campantar III.307 *Namaccivāyat Tiruppatikam* (217–218), which uses the mantra as a refrain; Appar IV.11 *Namaccivāyat Tiruppatikam* (218); Cuntarar VII.48 *Pāṇṭikkoṭumuṭi* (220–221); Appar IV.95.6 *Pātirippuliyūr* (228); and Appar VI.312.4 *Marumārrat Tirut Tāṇṭakam* (294). I have translated four hymns in which the mantra, or an allusion to it, appear, in appendix A, section 9.

42. Long, 'Rudra," 112; emphasis added.

43. *Śatapatha Brāhmaṇa* 9.1.1.1., cited in Gonda, "The Śatarudrīya," 75.

44. *Aitareya Brāhmaṇa* 3.33–34, in O'Flaherty, *Asceticism and Eroticism in the Mythology of Śiva* (Oxford: Oxford University Press, 1973), 29–31.

45. See Long, "Rudra," 108–111.

46. Ibid., 103–105.

47. Gonda, "The Śatarudrīya," 87–88. His discussion of this transition represents the classic scholarly perspective: "Thus the Vedic litany was interpreted in the light of a *bhakti* religion of later, post-Vedic times and transformed into a eulogy that was fully acceptable to the adherents of Śivaite *bhakti* movements. This was not very difficult. Every cult of a divine personality may involve some form of *bhakti* and the Śatarudrīya contains many passages that may strike those who feel inclined to adore, in a spirit of contemplative personal devotion, a mighty god who may have pity even upon the man whom he is to punish."

48. For details, see ibid., 83–87.

49. Ibid., 83.
50. This is according to Davis, *Ritual in an Oscillating Universe*, 12–15.
51. Peterson, *Poems to Śiva*, 132 n. 51; cf. 200 n. 118.

Chapter 4

1. Peterson, "Singing of a Place," 79–80, 85–87; citing Appar 4.73, translated appendix II.1; and Appar 4.49, translated in Peterson, *Poems to Śiva*, 201–220, 327–329.
2. There are two recent translations of this hymn; Peterson, *Poems to Śiva*, 331–336, and Shulman, *Songs of the Harsh Devotee*, 239–248.
3. Peterson, *Poems to Śiva*, 323–330, provides translations and discussion.
4. The other form of first person plural in Tamil, *nāṅkaḷ*, excludes the hearer.
5. This poem is one of the few extensive descriptions of supposedly ordinary bhaktas in a community. I use Indira Peterson's beautiful translation; Appar 6.312 (*Maṟumāṟṟat tirut tāṇṭakam*), in Peterson, *Poems to Śiva*, 293–296. Peterson notes the political understanding of the hymn in modern times: "The opening lines of this hymn: 'nāmārkkuṅ kuṭiy allōm namaṉaiy añcōm' ('We are slaves to no man, nor do we fear death') not only have become the Tamil Śaiva credo but are seen as the manifesto of the Tamil spirit in general. Though many of the references are specific to Appar's life, the use of the first person plural gives the ideas in this hymn a more general application to the Śaiva community" (293 n. 240).
6. The first line of the fourth verse, *uṟavu āvār uruttirapalkaṇattiṉōrkaḷ*, extends the kinship to all who worship Śiva: "They are kin, those of the many groups [who worship] Śiva the destroyer."
7. Veena Das, *Structure and Cognition*, 55. Although there are many studies of the renouncer-householder paradigm, Das's ideas are most relevant to my study because she emphasizes the role of a regional community in creating a distinctive order of Hindu categories, thereby creating their own identity: "The categories of caste in addition to those of kingship and renunciation provide the conceptual tools for describing the structural order of Hinduism in the Dharmaranya Purana" (9).
8. Ibid., 32. In an epilogue written for the 1982 edition, Das discusses the applicability of her study to understanding Hindu categories more generally.
9. Ibid., 45.
10. Discussed in ibid., 38–51. This list I present here combines selections from Das's list that are specifically relevant to my own comments.
11. However, on occasion, tapas is described as a method for attaining Śiva's feet (e.g., 2.11 in appendix A).
12. *Cākkiya* is Tamil for Śākya, the clan name of the Buddha (Śākyamuni): Appar IV.49, *Karukkai Vīraṭṭāṇam*, v. 6; Cuntarar VII.39, *Tiruttoṇṭattokai*, v. 6. See the translations in Peterson, *Poems to Śiva*, 328, 333. In Śiva-bhakti, Cākkiyaṉ's stone throwing is understood to be a unique form of worship of which the Lord approves: Cuntarar's poem says that Cākkiyaṉ "devoutly threw stones at the feet of the Lord."
13. Appar specifically mentions in his poetry that he was a monk in the Jain order; see Appar IV.39, *Tiruvaiyāṟu*, in ibid., 286.
14. Aside from Zvelebil, whom I quote later, and Dhavamony, *Love of God*, most of the academic sources on Buddhism in medieval south India (which has been much more widely studied than Jainism during that period) reproduce the as-yet unproved thesis that the Kaḷabhra kings, allegedly ruling in central south India just prior to the Pallavas, were Buddhists, as the historical context of the bhakti revival. See P. V. Kane, *History of Dharmaśāstra*, vol. 5, part 2, sec. 5, "Causes of the Disappearance of Buddhism from India," 1003–1030; Trevor Ling, *Buddhist Revival in India* (New York: St. Martins Press, 1980); T. N. Vasudeva

Rao, *Buddhism in the Tamil Country* (Annamalainagar: Annamalai University Press, 1979); Mylai S. Venkatasami, *Pauttamum Tamiḻum* (Tinnevelly: Saiva Siddhanta Works, 1965 [repr.]); Glenn Yocum, "Buddhism through Hindu Eyes: Śaivas and Buddhists in Medieval Tamilnadu," in *Traditions in Contact and Change*, ed. by Peter Slater and Donald Wiebe (Waterloo, Ont.: Wilfrid Laurier University Press, 1980); K. A. Nilakanta Sastri, "An Episode in the History of Buddhism in South India," in *B.C. Law Volume, Part I*, ed. D. R. Bhandarkar, et al. (Calcutta: Indian Research Institute, 1945); Amaradasa Liyanagamage, "A Forgotten Aspect of the Relations between the Sinhalese and the Tamils," *Ceylon Historical Journal* 25, nos. 1–4 (October 1978): 95–142; and Shu Hikosaka, *Buddhism in Tamilnadu: A New Perspective* (Madras: Institute of Asian Studies, 1989).

15. Kamil Zvelebil, *The Smile of Murugaṉ*, 199. This kind of analysis continues in sourcebooks on Hinduism that are widely used in the present day; for example, R. C. Zaehner portrays bhakti as a passionate protest against the passionless religions of Brāhmanism, Jainism, and Buddhism in *Hinduism* (Oxford: Oxford University Press, 1962), 171. Compare Dhavamony, *Love of God*, 96–102.

16. Most scholars consider these works to predate the mūvar; however, this view could change because it is based on the tenuous identification of a Sri Lankan king. It may be that the epics should be dated contemporaneous to, or even later than, the hymnists. For lists of Jain texts and discussion, see Asim Kumar Chatterjee, *A Comprehensive History of Jainism* (Calcutta: Firma KLM, 1978), vol. 1, chapter 7; and Srimati Aparna Banerji, *Traces of Buddhism in South India (c. 700–1600 A.D.)* (Delhi: Motilal Banarsidass, 1975), 28. See also Paula Richman's discussion of how the *Maṇimēkalai* came to be "a text without a community" in *Women, Branch Stories, and Religious Rhetoric in a Tamil Buddhist Text* (Syracuse: Syracuse University Maxwell School of Citizenship and Public Affairs, 1988), esp. chapter 1.

17. See Chatterjee, *A Comprehensive History*, 40–41. The two groups hold widely divergent views on the life of Mahāvīra and subsequent Jain history. The Śvetambara group preserved some ancient texts in a Prākrit (close to Mahārāṣṭrī Prākrit), whereas the Digambaras preserved some ancient texts in Śauraseni Prākrit and developed other canonical texts in Sanskrit; see Jaini, *The Jaina Path of Purification* (Delhi: Motilal Banarsidass, 1979), 47–87. My description here is based on scholarly accounts either of practices and ideas that both groups had in common or of practices and ideas specific to the Digambaras.

18. The following discussion is based on R. Champakalaksmi, "South India," in *Jaina Art and Architecture*, ed. A. Ghosh (New Delhi: Bharatiya Jnanpith, 1974), 1:93–102.

19. Ibid., 96.

20. Some scholars believe that Jain images were of great antiquity in north India; see Jaini, *The Jaina Path*, 191–192; also Prasad Jain, "The Genesis and Spirit of Jaina Art," in *Jaina Art and Architecture*, ed. A. Ghosh (New Delhi: Bharatiya Jnanpith, 1975), 1:35–40. But we do not have support for this kind of assertion in south India; see later.

21. R. Champakalaksmi explains that Vaṭṭeluttu "is a cursive script, which evolved out of Brāhmi in the southern region" ("South India," 94 n. 1).

22. K. R. Srinivasan, "South India," in *Jaina Art and Architecture*, ed. A. Ghosh (New Delhi: Bharatiya Jnanpith, 1975), 2:209–212. These cave temples were later appropriated and converted into Śaiva temples, a phenomenon the article briefly discusses. The author connects these events with the bhakti conversion of a king (in this case Campantar's conversion of Kūṉ Pāṇḍya [= Arikeśari-Mūravarmaṉ, 670–700]), as do many other scholars. This "history" relies on the *Periya Purāṇam* as a source, as I discuss in part III.

23. See the list of the fourteen guṇasthānas in Jaini, *The Jaina Path*, 272–273.

24. My brief discussion cannot do justice to the complicated nature of *samyak-darśana*, which describes the transformation of consciousness and behavior as well as the cultivation of perfection according to the *aṣṭānga* "eight limbs" system.

25. Jaini, *The Jaina Path*, 141.

26. Ibid., 190. He points out that this is Somadeva's list, which became the standard one. Jinasena's list has vārtā (profession) rather than guru-upāsti. According to Jaini, the former list had been: "1. *sāmāyika*, the practice of equanimity (meditation); 2. *caturviṃśatistava*, praise of the twenty-four Tīrthaṅkaras; 3. *vandana*, veneration (of the mendicant teachers); 4. *pratikramaṇa*, expiation (for transgressions); 5. *kāyotsarga*, abandonment of the body (standing or sitting motionless for various lengths of time); 6. *pratyākhyāna*, renunciation (of certain foods, indulgences, or activities, for a specified period)," 190.

27. Ibid., 289–291.

28. Ibid., 292.

29. These inscriptions are from Śāttamaṅgalam, in the Wandiwash Tāluk of North Arcot district. All of them were found on a natural rock formation; the Jain temple they describe is no longer extant; see Chatterjee, *A Comprehensive History*, 211–213, and also 177–226 for a general discussion with inscriptional references from many areas. At the time of the Pallava period, the Digambaras were being patronized by both the Chalukyas in the southern Deccan and the Gangas in Karnataka; the former were rivals of the Pallavas and the latter sometime allies. It was within this cultural nexus that the Pallavas patronized Jainism.

30. Martin E. Marty and R. Scott Appleby, eds., *Fundamentalisms Observed* (Chicago: The University of Chicago Press, 1991), vii–xiii, in which also see articles by Daniel Gold (vol. 1), and Robert Eric Frykenberg, Ainslie T. Embree, and Peter van der Veer (vol. 2); see also the articles by Philip Lutgendorf, Peter van der Veer, and Susana B. C. Devalle in Lorenzen, ed., *Bhakti Religion in North India*. There are several book-length studies, including Peter van der Veer, *Religious Nationalism: Hindus and Muslims in India* (Berkeley: University of California Press, 1994); and feature-length documentary films, including *In the Name of God*, directed by Anand Patwardan.

31. Daniel Gold, "Organized Hinduisms: From Vedic Truth to Hindu Nation," in Marty and Appleby, eds., *Fundamentalisms Observed*, 580–581.

Part III

1. For a survey discussion of early Pallava and Pandya temples, see Susan L. Huntington, *The Art of Ancient India: Buddhist, Hindu, Jain* (New York: Weatherhill, 1985), 291–321. For more technical discussions, see the articles by K. R. Srinivasan and K. V. Soundara Rajan in *Indian Temple Architecture* (Delhi: Academy of Arts, 1979).

2. See the discussions on dating Māṇikkavācakar in Younger, *The Home of the Dancing Śivan̲* (New York: Oxford University Press, 1995), 128, 134–135.

Chapter 5

1. This conversion scene takes place in "Appar Purāṇam," verses 1410–1411. Tradition interprets the poem of Appar that I discussed in chapter 3 (VI.312, translated by Peterson) to be Appar's defiant response to the king, but in his poetry Appar mentions only one trial, that of the rock, for which he blames the Jains, not the king. See Peterson, *Poems to Śiva*, 293, 296.

2. Mahēndravarman I represents himself through inscriptions to be an innovator in the creation of stone temples (for example, his Maṇḍagapaṭṭu inscription records the king's fascination with the stone building as "the brickless, timberless, metalless, and mortarless temple which is a mansion for the [gods] Brahmā, Iśvara, and Viṣṇu") (*Annual Report of Epigraphy* [hereafter *ARE*] 1905, no. 56; *Epigraphia Indica* [hereafter *EI*] xvii, no. 5 and plate; *South Indian Inscriptions* [hereafter *SII*] xii, no. 12), as well as in music (for example,

the Kuḍumiyāmalai inscription [*ARE* 1904, no. 354; *EI*, xii, 227; *SII*, xii, no. 7], and the Māmaṇḍūr inscription [*ARE* 1888, no. 38; *SII* iv, no. 136]); a play, the *Mattavilāsa*, is also attributed to him. Scholars vary on their dates of the Pallava rulers, though with much overlap; see the chart of influential scholars' dating schemes for the Pallavas in C. R. Srinivasan, *Kāñchīpuram through the Ages* (Delhi: Agam Kala Prakashan, 1979), 25.

3. Tradition represents Appar to be the oldest of "the three" nāyaṉmār because of his long association with Jainism prior to his conversion (he allegedly attained the title of Dharmasēna, indicating a leadership role in Jainism) and because the child-saint Campantar is said to have called him "Appar," Father.

4. See the text and translations of the Sanskrit inscription in *SII* 1: 29–30.

5. Emphasizing the importance of the Kāvēri, the temple contains an image of Śiva Gaṅgādhara (Śiva bearing the Gaṅgā River in his matted locks), homologizing the Kāvēri to the Gaṅgā.

6. The extensive wordplay in the inscription is discussed by Michael Lockwood and A. Vishnu Bhat, "The Philosophy of Mahendravarman's Tiruchirapalli Epigraph," *Studies in South Indian Epigraphy* 3 (1977): 100–103. See also R. Nagaswamy's criticism in *Śiva Bhakti* (New Delhi: Navrang, 1989), and Michael D. Rabe's discussion in "Royal Temple Dedications" in Donald S. Lopez, ed., *Religions of India in Practice* (Princeton: Princeton University Press, 1995): 235–243.

7. Kingship has been a major topic of study in Indology; for a review of orientalist and postcolonial studies of it, see Inden, *Imagining India*, 162–212. I do not focus on the nature of the king or the state, but on the ways in which Tamil Śiva-bhakti became part of imperial temple culture.

8. Ronald Inden, "The Ceremony of the Great Gift (Mahādāna): Structure and Historical Context in Indian Ritual and Society," *Asie du Sud, Traditions et Changements* (1979): 131–136.

9. Inden mentions five imperial groups: the Pratihāra dynasty in north India, the Pāla in east India (as Inden notes, the Pālas are associated with Buddhism, not Hinduism), the Rāṣṭrakūṭa in the Deccan, and the Pāṇḍya and Pallava in south India.

10. Inden, "The Ceremony of the Great Gift," 135.

11. Ibid., 133.

12. Ibid.

13. Ibid., 135.

14. Ibid.

15. Nicholas B. Dirks, "Political Authority and Structural Change in Early South Indian History," *Indian Economic and Social History Review* 13, no. 2 (1976): 125–157.

16. Both *pallava* and *toṇḍai* may mean "creeper" or "shoot," suggesting new growth on an established plant; this was not an uncommon image for indicating a new generation or lineage.

17. Dirks ("Political Authority," 130) notes that "the ritual performances of the Pallavas are better explained by looking north, not south. . . . Nonetheless, though the Pallavas apparently looked north, they were firmly implanted in the south."

18. Ibid., 133.

19. For example, see the Hirahaḍagali plates of the Pallava Śivaskandavarman I (ca A.D. 300–325), in Mahalingam, *Inscriptions of the Pallavas* (New Delhi: Indian Council of Historical Research; Delhi: Agam Prakashan, 1988), 35–39, no. 3.

20. Dirks, "Political Authority," 144.

21. Ibid., 142.

22. It may be that some of the grants from this early period were issued from victory camps, although they invoke the capital city of Kāñcīpuram. Of particular interest are the

Maidavōlu Plates of Yuvamahārāja Śivaskandavarman, the Hirahaḍagali Plates of Śivaskandavarman (I), the Vesanta (Jalālpuram) Plates of Simhavarman (II), the Udayēndiram Plates of Nandivarman (I), and the Chendalūr Plates of Kumārarviṣṇu (III); other grants from this early period were issued from victory camps. See C. R. Srinivasan, *Kāñchīpuram through the Ages*, 15.

23. For a detailed analysis of the horse sacrifice see Dirks, "Political Authority," 137–139. See also Inden, "The Ceremony of the Great Gift," 135: "Formulated before the rise of the Buddhist imperial state, the horse sacrifice, the combative rite par excellence of the ancient Kṣatriya, could do no more than evoke the very world of dispersed power and agonistic rivalries it was meant to overcome."

24. Dirks, "Political Authority," 145.

25. What the king gave was expanded as well. Along with land grants and temples, the king gave structures of public works, including irrigation and other administrative necessities. As Dirks points out, these gifts were parallel to the earlier sacrificial rituals, ibid., 145–146, 149.

26. Ibid., 150, 151.

27. On dating, see K. R. Srinivasan, *Cave Temples of the Pallavas* (New Delhi: Archaeological Survey of India, 1964), 6, and Robert Sewell, ed., *The Historical Inscriptions of Southern India* (Madras, 1932), 23, cited in C. R. Srinivasan, *Kāñchīpuram*, 57–58.

28. Dirks, "Political Authority," p. 144.

29. Inden, *Imagining India*, 249.

30. For example, Campantar 3.276, 3.277; Appar 4.49.4, 4.65.3; and Cuntarar 7.55.4, 7.65.1, 7.66.2, 7.98.11. This king is also mentioned by the Vaiṣṇava saint Tirumaṅkai A̲lvār (*Periya Tirumo̲li* 6.6.8), who claims that this king has built seventy temples, three of which are Vaiṣṇava. K. A. Nilakanta Sastri notes that this saint "makes the achievements of Kōcceṅgaṇān and his worship at Tiruva̲raiyūr the refrain of his song," *The Cō̲las* (Madras: University of Madras, 1975), 52.

31. For a translation of Campantar's poem, Ā*lavāy* (Madurai), in which he praises this queen in every other verse, see Peterson, *Poems to Śiva*, 273–276.

32. "[Śiva] afflicts those kings who refuse tribute to the Pallavas, the rightful guardians of this world," Cuntarar (7.90.4/916); translated by Shulman, *Songs of the Harsh Devotee*, 569. The refrain of the hymn localizes Śiva at Puliyūr, an ancient name for Chidambaram.

33. Dirks, "Political Authority," 146–148. The reign of Nandivarman Pallavamalla represents a "dynastic revolution" in terms of genealogy as well as choice of main deity: Earlier Pallava kings were from the Siṃhaviṣṇu family line, whereas Nandivarman Pallavamalla was from a collateral branch of the Pallavas, the line of Bhīmāvarman through Hiraṇyavarman. See C. R. Srinivasan, *Kāñchīpuram*, 38.

34. Dorai Rangaswamy cites *Madras Epigraphical Reports* [hereafter *MER*] 433/1903, 423/1908, 624/1909, 129/1914, 349/1918, 139/1925, 99/1928–29 and 149/1937, in *Religion and Philosophy*, 17.

35. This discrepancy applies to *MER* 423/1908, 624/1909, 129/1914. The other records he cites have not been available to me at the time of this writing; however, D. R. Nagaswamy has dated 99/1928–29 to the reign of the Chola king Parāntaka I (ca A.D. 917–925), in *Śiva Bhakti*, 216.

36. *SII* 3.1 (no. 43): 92–94.

37. *SII* 3.1, nos. 44, 45, 47, 49; no. 46 is from a stone slab built into the floor of the temple and is thus considered to be original. See the discussion in S. R. Balasubrahmanyam, *Early Chola Art: Part One*, 215–220.

38. The identification of the king mentioned in the inscription (named as Vijaya-Nandivikramavarman) with Nandivarman Pallavamalla is difficult and somewhat controversial,

although scholars seem to agree that the inscription is late Pallava. The inscription is located on the north wall of the maṇḍapam in the Bilvanatheśvara temple in Tiruvallam (see *SII* 31: 92–94; also see E. Hultzsch's explanation of the identification in *EI* 4: 180–82). Balasubrahmanyam, *Early Chola Art: Part One*, 217.

39. However, this inscription does not include the Sanskrit genealogy found in some other inscriptions described by Dirks. This grant is in Tamil, and it details the logistics of a land transfer.

40. Introductory text accompanying the inscription, *SII* 3.1: 92–93. T. V. Mahalingam identifies this chieftain as Bāṇavidyādhara (A.D. 850–896), in *Inscriptions of the Pallavas*, cv, 397–399.

41. On the meaning of *cavaiyār*, I am following Fabricius's dictionary, in which he refers the reader to *capai* (hall of assembly; an assembly) for the more obscure *cavai*. He notes that both words are from the Sanskrit.

42. *SII* 3.1 (no. 43): 95.

43. See Peterson, "Singing of a Place," 71, where she notes that today all such places are known by this designation.

Chapter 6

1. See Burton Stein's discussion of the segmentary state, which he acknowledges is derived from Aidan Southall's work, in *Peasant State and Society in Medieval South India* (Delhi: Oxford University Press, 1980), 264–285. Two responses to Stein's image of the segmentary state that have been helpful to me from a wide literature are Ronald Inden's criticism of Stein on his concept of the *nāṭu*, in *Imagining India*, 206–211; and Noboru Karashima, *South Indian History and Society: Studies from Inscriptions A.D. 850–1800* (Delhi: Oxford University Press, 1984), who discusses discontinuities between villages and brahmadēyas in contrast to Stein's alliance of these two entities. Other scholars who explore aspects of polity and land tenure include James Heitzman, David Ludden, George Spencer, and Y. Subbarayalu.

2. Stein, *Peasant State*, 76–89. We possess no evidence on the Kaḷabhras save polemics against them in inscriptions from other dynasties who claim to have vanquished them. These polemical inscriptions refer to them as both Kaḷabhra and as kali aracar (either "kings of the kali era" or "kings of darkness") and criticize them for supporting Buddhism and Jainism. See "The Vēḷvikkuḍi Copper Plates of Pāṇḍya Neḍunjaḍaiyan" in T. N. Subrahmaniam, ed., *Ten Pandya Copper Plates* (Madras, 1967), 1–18.

3. Stein, *Peasant State*, 87.

4. Ibid., 81.

5. Ibid., 324.

6. Local goddesses probably did receive representation in temples, as part of the general ethos to incorporate regional elements. However, this is not a phenomenon to be derived from the mūvar's hymns: "As for the Goddess, we see that compared to her prominence in the later literary sources of Tamil Śaivism and later versions of Tamil temple myths (*talapurāṇam*), her role in the *Tēvāram* is a relatively subdued one. Here she is most often invoked as the inseparable 'consort' and companion of the Lord, the lovely and gentle feminine figure who tempers the harshness of his personality, the sensitive witness of his heroic deeds" (Peterson, *Poems to Śiva*, p. 101).

7. My discussion in this paragraph draws upon Stein, *Peasant State*, 81–84.

8. The period I discuss in this section corresponds to "sub-period one" as identified by B. Sitaraman, Noboru Karashima, and Y. Subbarayalu in their analysis of Chola inscrip-

tions, "A List of the Tamil Inscriptions of the Chola Dynasty," *Journal of Asian and African Studies* (Tokyo) 11 (1976): 89. See also Y. Subbarayalu, *Political Geography of the Chola Country* (Madras: State Department of Archaeology, Government of Tamilnadu, 1973).

9. Nilakanta Sastri, *The Cōḻas*, 111.

10. Ibid., 110.

11. Ibid., 113, 115.

12. Balasubrahmanyam, *Early Chola Art: Part One*, 146–170. Balasubrahmanyam indicates that all of these places were sung by the mūvar, but neither Tiruchchatturai nor Tiruvilakkudi—in his spelling—is represented on lists of places sung by the nāyaṉmār that I have consulted; if these towns are known by other names, he does not specify. In his discussion of Tiruvaiyāṟu, Balasubrahmanyam notes: "Appar, Sambandar and Sundarar have glorified this Lord by their immortal *devaram* hymns; so this temple should have been a living institution even before the seventh century A.D. But the present central shrine of stone is to be ascribed to the days of Aditya I"; ibid., 149–150. I questioned this assumption in part II. It is widely acknowledged among scholars that Balasubrahmanyam's comprehensive work, while important, could use a thorough critical review.

13. These formulae occur numerous times in the inscriptions; I provide one example in the following discussion of Sembiyan Mahādevī.

14. On Sembiyan Mahādevī and other queenly patrons, see Venkataraman, *Temple Art under the Chola Queens* (Faridabad: Thomson Press, 1976): 11–64; Dehejia, *Art of the Imperial Cholas* (New York: Columbia University Press, 1990), 1–47; and George W. Spencer, "When Queens Bore Gifts: Women as Temple Donors in the Chola Period," in *Śrīnidhiḥ: Perspectives on Indian Archaeology, Art and Culture*, ed. K. V. Raman (Madras: New Era Publications 1983), 361–373. The queen is also mentioned in surveys of Chola art and architecture, for example, S. R. Balasubrahmanyam, *Early Chola Temples: Parantaka I to Rajaraja I* (Bombay: Orient Longman, 1971), 158, 168–69, and 181–183.

15. Leslie C. Orr, "Women's Patronage and Power: Chola Royal Women and the Politics of Religious Endowments," paper presented at the Association of Asian Studies annual meeting, April 2–5, 1992, Washington, D.C. See also her "Women of Medieval South India in Hindu Temple Ritual: Text and Practice," *Annual Review of Women in World Religions* 3 (1994): 107–141.

16. Cynthia Mary Talbot made this argument with respect to Rudramadevī, a sixteenth-century Andhra queen, in her paper, "Rudramadevī, the Queen Who Ruled: A Study of Female Power and Identity in South India," on the same AAS panel. Venkataraman discusses many other Chola royal women, such as Kundavai and Lōkamahādevī, in *Temple Art*.

17. Her first known inscription is in the thirty-fourth year of Parāntaka I, recording her gift of sheep for maintaining a lamp to Śiva at Uyyakoṇṭaṉ-Tirumalai (*SII* 2, no. 75). The last known inscription mentioning the queen is on the southern base of the Śivalōkamuṭaiya Paramaśvāmin temple at Tiruvakkarai, dated to the sixteenth regnal year of Rājarāja I, recording that the queen built the temple (*ARE* 200 of 1904). This latter inscription is cited by Balasubrahmanyam, *Middle Chola Temples: Rajaraja I to Kulottunga I* (Faridabad: Thomson Press, 1975), 164–65; he also mentions an inscription relating to the queen from A.D. 1006 but does not cite its source.

18. An epithet of her husband, Gandarāditya, specifies that he "rose and went west," the direction of death. See Balasubrahmanyam, *Early Chola Temples*, 157.

19. Venkataraman, *Temple Art*, 21–22.

20. However, Venkataraman suggests that she "rebuilt" it, based on the knowledge that both Appar and Cuntarar sang of this place (ibid., 25–26); I criticized this perspective earlier.

21. Appar 5.43; Campantar 1.85.

22. For a discussion of inscriptional records at this temple, see Balasubrahmanyam, *Early Chola Temples*, 165–174.

23. *SII* 3.3 nos. 146, 147: 295–297. I discuss here inscription no. 146. Number 147 describes Sembiyan as the mother of Uttama Chola and declares that her temple was built by one Śattan Gunabattan, who is pictured below the inscription.

24. See plate no. 167 in Balasubrahmanyam, *Early Chola Temples*.

25. *SII* 3.3, nos. 151, 151A: 300–322. The content of the inscription is continuous, basically refining and extending an original grant by Sembiyan Mahādevī; however, it is actually a series of different inscriptions over time.

26. During this period of Chola inscriptions, there are many mentions of lamp donations; in some cases, they were a way for various people (chiefs, dancers, and so on) to participate in the royal pattern of dāna; in other cases, they were symbols of expiation for those who had performed criminal acts.

27. The period of Sembiyan Mahādevī is well known for its masterful bronzes, and many of them can be found in the Kōnērīrāja temple; see Dehejia, *Art of the Imperial Cholas*, 4–10. I have found no art historian who will date bronze images of the nāyaṉmār to this period; however, N. Nagaswamy claims that an inscription dated to Parāntaka I's thirty-eighth year (A.D. 945) at the Tiruvidaimarudur temple describes festival (that is, bronze) images of the mūvar (*Śiva Bhakti*, 216). He does not cite a source, and I find no mention of this inscription in Balasubrahmanyam's discussion of inscriptions from that site (*Early Chola Art: Part One*, 173–176).

28. Andanallur, whose ancient name is Andavanallur, is in the Kāvēri delta, lying some seven miles from Tiruchirapalli on the road to Karūr. On the identity of Sembiyan Irukkuvel, see the remarks by Balasubrahmanyam, *Early Chola Temples*, 118–131. The relevant inscriptions he lists are 337, 348, 357, 358, 359, and 360, all from 1903.

29. 358/1903 (= *SII* 3: 139). See also Nagaswamy, *Śiva Bhakti*, 215–216.

30. Nagaswamy, *Śiva Bhakti*, 216. He cites, respectively, 99/1928–29, 129/1914, *SII* 19: 69.

31. *SII* 2 contains Rājarāja I's inscriptions at the temple.

32. Noted by K. A. Nilakanta Sastri, who says, "The temple was altogether a creation of Rājarāja's policy" (*The Cōḻas*, 185).

33. Women did perform service in temples during Rājarāja I's reign: An inscription mentions the appointment of four hundred women as "temple women" (*taḷippeṇṭir*); see the chart of their names and where they served in Venkataraman, *Rājarājēśvaram: The Pinnacle of Chola Art* (Madras: Mudgala Trust, 1985), 338–48. However, Leslie Orr has argued that women's roles in the temple were marginalized: "In neither [the āgamas or Chola period inscriptions] is there any insistence on the ritual participation of women; women are marginal and optional to temple ritual, and the tasks they are assigned may also be performed by men" ("Women in Hindu Temple Ritual," 127). Orr suggested in "Women's Patronage and Power" that royal women's roles in the patronage of temples were greatly reduced in the reign of Rājarāja I. In this vein, B. Suresh states that Rājarāja's temple represents an "aryanization" of Tamil religion, in that it displaces indigenous Tamil goddess cults with male, Aryan, Brahmanic Hinduism. His conclusions are based on his study of inscriptional and iconographic evidence at the Bṛhadīśvara temple. He characterizes the period of Rājarāja I as the "propagation of canonized religion in Tamilnad" (unfortunately, later in the article he conflates "canonization" with "aryanization"). B. Suresh, "Raajaraajeesvaram at Tancaavuur," in *Proceedings of the First International Conference Seminar of Tamil Studies, Kuala Lumpur, 1964* (Kuala Lumpur: International Association of Tamil Research, 1968), 449; cited in B. Stein, *Peasant State*, 324ff.

34. *S.I.I.* 2, no. 69, 312 ff., and no. 70, 328 ff. Compare Burton Stein, *Peasant State*, 332–333.

35. Venkataraman, *Rājarājēśvaram*, 88–89. Gary J. Schwindler, "Speculations on the Theme of Śiva as Tripurāntaka as It Appears during the Reign of Rājarāja I in the Tañjāvūr Area, c. A.D. 1000," *Ars Orientalis* 17 (1987): 163–178.

36. Younger, *The Home of Dancing Śivaṉ*, 98. Younger discusses in detail the building and donative activities of the Chola kings in several sections of his book.

37. Venkataraman, *Rājarājeśvaram*, 254, citing *SII* 2, no. 65.

38. For a list of these musicians' names, see ibid., 363–364, and note 2, 371–372. Dorai Rangaswamy states that sectarian religious centers (*maṭam*, pl. *maṭankaḷ*) were named after the mūvar during the reigns of Rājarāja I and his son, Rājēndra. These structures were perhaps houses for the temple singers, as in the grant of Sembiyan Mahādevī; see *Religion and Philosophy*, 23–24.

39. *Madras Epigraphical Records*, 333/1906, cited in Dorai Rangaswamy, *Religion and Philosophy*, 18.

40. Singers of the mūvar's hymns in temples today are Vēḷāḷas or Śaiva Piḷḷais. Christopher Fuller offers this observation about the modern-day participants in the Madurai Mīnākṣi temple: "The devotional singers (Tam. *otuvār*) are non-Brahmans, usually belonging to the vegetarian Vellalar or Saiva Pillai caste, which traditionally ranks above most other non-Brahman castes. Brahmans never work as singers in Saiva temples"; see *Servants of the Goddess*, 38. My discussions in 1992 and 1993 with young men training to become ōtuvārs at a school in Chidambaram revealed this caste association as well.

41. Some scholars suggest that temple priests in this region were not originally brahman, but took on a brahman identity as ādiśaivas; see my discussion in chapter 7.

42. Venkataraman, *Rājarājeśvaram*, 88, 91. See also the line drawing of the vestibule on 115.

43. The vestibule was in disuse when Professor S. K. Govindaswamy discovered the art there in the 1930s. Subsequently, the Department of Archaeology has restored some of the surfaces, discovering that in many cases the Nāyaks painted over Chola works; some of the Chola paintings are exposed, and the panels depicting Cuntarar are dated to the Chola era. Today, the vestibule is generally off-limits to the casual spectator; entrance is granted only to those with permission from the Archaeological Survey of India.

44. For a description of this and other Tanjavur paintings, see Venkataraman, *Rājarājēśvaram*, 118–147, esp. 120–124. For a telling of Cuntarar's story, see Peterson, *Poems to Śiva*, 302–321.

45. Cuntarar *Tēvāram* VII.1.1, VII.17, VII.62.5, translated in Peterson, *Poems to Śiva*, 303–304. David Shulman discusses the traditional understanding of the hymn at Veṇṇeynallūr (VII 1.1) as first among Cuntarar's compositions and provides a translation of it in *Songs of the Harsh Devotee*, xxviii, xxxix, 1–6.

46. B. Venkataraman, *Rājarājeśvaram*, 123.

47. Noted by Peterson, *Poems to Śiva*, 320, note to poem 258.

48. There is a discrepancy in the descriptions of these figures by Dorai Rangaswamy, *Religion and Philosophy of Tēvāram*, 1022; and Venkataraman, *Rājarājēśvaram*, 123.

49. Venkataraman suggests that a text attributed to "Cēramāṉ Perumāḷ," the *Tirukkailāya ñāṉavulā*, which is one of the texts in the eleventh volume of the Śiva-bhakti canon, the *Tirumuṟai*, is a source for the mural's depiction of Śiva's heavenly scene in the final panel (*Rājarājēśvara*, 124). This text is described in the *Encyclopedia of Tamil Literature*, vol. 1 (Madras: Institute of Asian Studies, 1990), as follows:

> In [the literary genre of] *ulā*, the god or the patron goes in procession around and women of different age groups from five to forty are depicted as falling in love with him. *Ātiyulā*, meaning the first *ulā*, also known as *Tirukkailāya Ñāṉaulā* was com-

posed by Cēramān Perumāḷ of the eighth century A.D. The literary significance of this genre consists in its being able to create the appropriate dramatic situations in which women of varying age groups express their love for the hero. The three great *ulās* by Oṭṭakkūttar are on the three Cōḻa rulers. The later ages witnessed an endless chain of *ulās* (87).

50. Peterson assumes these are waves (*Poems to Śiva*, 320, note to poem 258), as does Dorai Rangaswamy, who notes, "Beneath them are found the waves with fish" (*Religion and Philosophy*, 1022). In contrast, Venkataraman considers them to be "involuted cloud designs," *Rājarājēśvaram*, 123.

51. Shulman provides translation and paraphrase of some verses from this scene in Cēkkiḻār's *Periya Purāṇam* in *The King and the Clown in South Indian Myth and Poetry* (Princeton: Princeton University Press, 1985), 253–256. According to this story, when the king is asked by Śiva to explain how he ascended, he replies by likening the ocean waves to the Lord's mercy.

52. B. Venkataraman, *Rājarājēśvaram*, 124.

53. David Shulman interprets this mural as an example of the king and alter-ego clown motif he says is widespread in Tamil literature. See *The King and the Clown*, 246–256, 401–408. Note that Rājarāja I was not the only Tamil king to use the stories of the nāyaṉmār as a frame for interpreting one's own kingly power, although he was the most powerful king who did so. Nicholas B. Dirks notes that the late medieval Uttumalai Maravars of the Pudukkottai region used the *Periya Purāṇam* story of Kaṇṇappar the hunter in their vaṃcāvaḷis (family histories) to illustrate their own transformation from hunters to little kings. See *The Hollow Crown: Ethnohistory of an Indian Kingdom* (Cambridge: Cambridge University Press, 1987), 75–107, esp. 82.

54. *SII* 2, 29. We know from inscriptions that some sixty-six metal images were donated to this temple; only two are extant, an image of Naṭarāja and his consort Umā Paramēśvarī, both now housed in the Naṭarāja maṇḍapam.

55. Venkataraman, *Rājarājēśvaram*, 153.

56. The task of this man, as described in an inscription (*SII* 2: 38), was to weigh and measure the "bronzes" (a mixture of metals) and then record the results on the stone wall of the temple. The king had given other bronzes of Śiva and his consort to the temple (for example *SII* 2: 1).

57. See the summary of the royal agents and their gifts in Venkataraman, *Rājarājēśvaram*, 154–158. None of the queens appears to have had the power or reputation of Sembiyan Mahādevī.

58. *SII* 2: 38. This inscription dates to the twenty-ninth year of the king's reign, A.D. 1013, four years after the completion of the temple. It is the earliest reference we have of images of the nāyaṉmār cast in bronze (excluding the unidentified source Nagaswamy cites in *Śiva Bhakti*).

59. Vidya Dehejia has given the English equivalent of the Tamil measurements in *Slaves of the Lord*, 144.

60. For a discussion of these grants, made over a period of two years (1013–1015), see ibid., 144–145.

61. *SII* 2: 40. The inscription says *periya perumāḷukku tēvāratēvarāka eḻuntaruḷiviṭṭa tirumēṉi*.

62. See Gangoly, *South Indian Bronzes* (Calcutta: Nababharat, 1978), plates 15–19, and explanation with some brief translations from āgamic texts on 119–121.

63. Venkataraman, *Rājarājēśvaram*, 156; Dorai Rangaswamy, *Religion and Philosophy*, 27–35, esp. 28.

64. Dorai Rangaswamy is convinced that, prior to the fifteenth century, *tēvāram* meant private worship. In support of his interpretation, he cites many inscriptions from this medieval period that detail the special cult of a particular saint at various temples, the naming of maṭhs (*maṭam*) after certain saints, and the naming of people after the saints. See *Religion and Philosophy*, 24–27.

65. See Dehejia, *Slaves of the Lord*, 170; also Venkataraman, *Rājarājēśvaram*, 286.

66. *SII* 2: 43. For a translation of the *Periya Purāṇam* story of Ciṟuttoṇṭar and its continued importance in Tamilnadu and other south Indian regions, see Hart, "The Little Devotee: Cēkkiḻār's Story of Ciṟuttoṇṭar," in *Sanskrit and Indian Studies*, ed. Masatoshi Nagatomi, et al. (Dordrecht: D. Reidel, 1980).

67. Discussion in Dehejia, *Slaves of the Lord*, 146–147.

68. Dehejia cites the creativity of fifteenth-century bronzes from Kalahasti, ibid., 147.

69. This image is also interpreted by contemporary observers to be the crowning of the king by Śiva. A photo of this panel, taken by Richard H. Davis, appears as the frontispiece to Norman Cutler's *Songs of Experience*.

70. In addition to evidence from within Tamilnadu, note that Vidya Dehejia reports the find of a complete set of bronze images of the sixty-three nāyaṉmār from the eleventh century in Polonnaruwa, Sri Lanka, which was part of the Chola empire for some seventy-five years; *Slaves of the Lord*, 142–143.

71. *MER* 137/1912, cited in Dehejia, *Slaves of the Lord*, 140. This inscription is in a temple at Tiruvoṟṟiyūr and is attributed to Rājēndra, aka Rājādhirāja (1018–1054) in the year 1046. There are many inscriptions at this temple complex over the period of the middle Cholas, up to Vijayanagar. See the discussion in Balasubrahmanyam, *Middle Chola Temples*, 299–309. In the *MER* I have consulted, the "General Remarks" of the epigraphist indicate that 137/1912 mentions the *Tiruttoṇṭattokai* and images of the bhaktas (part II, p. 99), but the summary in the record of the inscription makes no mention of these (appendix B, p. 21).

72. For example, Richard Kieckhefer and George D. Bond, eds., *Sainthood: Its Manifestations in World Religions* (Berkeley: University of California Press, 1988), and John Stratton Hawley, *Saints and Virtues* (Berkeley: University of California Press, 1987).

73. Vidya Dehejia has a brief comparative discussion of the nāyaṉmār and Christian saints in *Slaves to the Lord*, 1–5.

74. See Reynolds and Capps, eds., *The Biographical Process: Studies in the History and Psychology of Religion* (The Hague: Mouton, 1976).

75. The history of making Christian saints illuminates these processes, and they have comparative value in understanding the making of Tamil Śiva-bhakti saints. I have found helpful the discussion of these historical processes in Woodward, *Making Saints: How the Catholic Church Determines Who Becomes a Saint, Who Doesn't, and Why* (New York: Simon and Schuster, 1990).

76. The *Periya Purāṇam* speaks, however, of a special connection between Cuntarar and Tiruvoṟṟiyūr, namely, that his second marriage to Caṅkili took place there (3155–3563; see Shulman, *Songs of the Harsh Devotee*, xxvii).

77. *Aṭi* also means "foot"; thus, the refrain can be translated as "I serve the feet of . . ."; see the discussion in Shulman, *Songs of the Harsh Devotee*, 242. Tamil Śiva-bhakti plays upon the dual meanings of *aṭi* as servant and foot. There are two recent translations of the *Tiruttoṇṭattokai*; see Shulman, ibid., 239–248; and Peterson, *Poems to Śiva*, 331–336.

78. Cuntarar uses the term *pattarāy* (patikam 10, line 1), which Shulman and Peterson agree is "as a bhakta" or "as a devotee" (*patti* is the Tamil transliteration of *bhakti*). For a breakdown of which names come from which poet's hymns, see Dorai Rangaswamy, *Religion and Philosophy* 1.1: 114–118.

79. Shulman, *Songs of the Harsh Devotee*, 240.

80. There are several interesting scholarly meditations on lists. For example, see Jack Goody, *The Domestication of the Savage Mind* (Cambridge: Cambridge University Press, 1977), 74–111, who stresses the list as a bridge between orality and writing. Also see Michel Foucault's delight in the taxonomy of a Chinese encyclopedia, *The Order of Things* (New York: Vintage, 1970), 1ff.; and Stanley Fish's experiment with a list in *Is There a Text in This Class?* In this section, I primarily draw on Jonathan Smith's reflections in *Imagining Religion* (Chicago: University of Chicago Press, 1982), 36–52, esp. 44–52, because he explicitly links list with canon, the latter as a "subtype of the genre *list*" (44).

81. Contemporary editions of *Tēvāram* note that the *Tiruttoṇṭattokai* was assigned the *kollikauvāṇam paṇ*, an ancient Tamil musical tune. On meter, poetry, and song, see Peterson, *Poems to Śiva*, chapters 4 and 5, esp. 60–64, 76–82. On a related theme, Jack Goody suggests that a list is related to both oral and written communication in *Domestication*, 81–82.

82. Smith, *Imagining Religion*, 48.

83. Scholars have arrived at this date for Nampi Āṇṭār Nampi by equating the reference to Rājarāja Abhaya in a fourteenth-century work attributed to Umāpati Civācāryar, the *Tirumuṟaikaṇṭa Purāṇam*, with Kulōttunga I. There is some debate on this point; some scholars would view this king as Rājarāja I. See the discussion in Dorai Rangaswamy, *Religion and Philosophy*, 22–23. I discuss this text in part IV.

84. See the list in Cutler, *Songs of Experience*, 5.

85. Zvelebil, *Tamil Literature*, vol. 10 in the series *A History of Indian Literature*, ed. Jan Gonda (Weisbaden: Otto Harrassowitz, 1974), 109. Zvelebil also credits other authors contemporaneous with Nampi with this revolution in writing, including the Śaiva Pattiṉattār and the Vaiṣṇavas Tirumaḻicai Aḻvār and Tirumaṅkai, before the style culminated in the fifteenth-century work of Aruṇakiri.

86. Ibid., 109–110.

87. For example, Nampi's *Kōyil tiruppaṇṇiyar viruttam* and *Āḷuṭaiyapiḷḷaiyār tiruccaṇpai viruttam*. On this meter, see ibid., 97, 105. Indira Peterson notes that "the *viruttam* style . . . is considered to have ancient connections with the hymns of the saints, and it is known today as the style that is truly characteristic of *Tēvāram* singing," *Poems to Śiva*, 61.

88. Cuntarar and Nampi Āṇṭār Nampi both listed sixty-three nāyaṉmār, including Cuntarar and his parents, along with the other bhaktas. Cēkkiḻār added nine others for an ultimate total of seventy-two nāyaṉmār, expanding upon categories of people Cuntarar grouped in his list. Since the later texts follow the order of the Cuntarar's list, I have considered it closure.

89. Elaborating on the "many other places" that Nampi's text leaves unexplored, the *Periya Purāṇam* locates Appar's visit to Nallūr in the midst of his pilgrimage, not as the conclusion of it, which he places at Pukalūr. For Cēkkiḻār, the incident at Nallūr represents the Lord's branding of Appar with his lotus feet, in response to a request Appar made at Tiruvāvaṭuturai. See Peterson, *Poems to Śiva*, 222, 297, 301.

90. Note that the term *pēy* in Cuntarar's text does not specify gender; Nampi's text does. In her own poetry, Kāraikkāl Ammaiyār refers to herself as a *pēy*; Norman Cutler has translated the first two verses of her *Tiruvālaṅkāṭṭu-mūtta-tiruppatikam* in *Songs of Experience*, 121.

91. I discuss the controversial assertion that Nāḷaippōvāṉ left his lowly pulai status in chapter 7, where I translate Cēkkiḻār's version of this story.

Part IV

1. Burton Stein, *All the King's Mana*, 45–46. Stein views brahmanical ritual kingship as only one of three models fused in the Chola praxis of kingship; the other two are Tamil heroic kingship of the puṟam poems and Jain moral kingship.

2. Davis, *Ritual in an Oscillating Universe*, 14.

3. Richard Davis discusses the pan-Indian nature of the school: "the peripatetic monastics documented in medieval inscriptions and the authors of Sanskrit Śaiva Siddhānta *paddhati* texts saw themselves as member of a single pan-Indian Śaiva order composed of several interrelated lineages or monastic orders;" "Aghoraśiva's Background," *Journal of Oriental Research* 56–62 (1986–1992): 369.

4. Davis discusses Śaiva Siddhānta as "system" in *Ritual in an Oscillating Universe*, 19–21.

5. Peterson, *Poems to Śiva*, 42–43.

6. Davis, *Ritual in an Oscillating Universe*, 38.

7. Ibid., 39.

8. The *Cīvakacintāmaṇi* is the hagiography of the Jain hero, Jīvaka (Tamil Cīvakaṉ), which details his gradual progression through the stages of perfection (*guṇasthānas*) to ultimate salvation. The story is the theme of many works in Sanskrit, Prākrit, and Kannada; the Tamil version was composed by Tiruttakkatēvar and is dated to the late eighth–early ninth centuries. Tamil stories suggest that Cēkkiḻār's *Periya Purāṇam* was a polemic against the Jaina story:

> The influence which *Cīvakacintāmaṇi*, and Jainism in general wielded over the masses as also the intelligentsia may be seen from the well-known account relating to the composition of the *Periyapurāṇam* by Cēkkiḻār. We are told that *Cīvakacintāmaṇi* was adored by Anapāya Kulōttunkaṉ II (A.D. 1113–1150). His minister, Cēkkiḻār, advised him not to be misled by the Jaina work which was full of false beliefs, and implored him to listen to the exploits of Lord Civaṉ instead (*Tiruttoṇṭar Mākkatai* vv. 21, 22). It may also be pointed out at this juncture that the concept of sixty-three divine Caivaite saints probably originated as a countermeasure to the well-established tradition of the sixty-three *śalākha puruṣas* of Jaina mythology. (*Encyclopaedia of Tamil Literature*, 210)

9. In recognizing the historical separation between the Sanskrit canon and the Tamil canon, I refer to the Sanskrit Śaiva Siddhānta and the Tamil Śaiva Siddhānta schools in this chapter, although some contemporary Śaiva Siddhānta philosophers I have spoken with in Madras resist such a classification and prefer simply "Śaiva Siddhānta."

Chapter 7

1. Venkataraman, *Rājarājēśvaram*, 231.

2. The mural is in chamber 10, on the inner jamb facing north; ibid., 119. The king and his guru appear as the two devotees carved beside the image of Lakṣmī; ibid., 45. On the *Tiruvicaippā*, see ibid., 231.

3. *SII* 20: 90, 96; and 2: 96. See Nagaswamy's discussion of Guru Iśāna Paṇḍita as a "Rājaguru" to Rājarāja I in "Iconography and Significance of the Bṛhadīśvara Temple, Tañjāvūr," in *Discourses on Śiva: Proceedings of a Symposium on the Nature of Religious Imagery*, ed. Michael W. Meister (Philadelphia: University of Pennsylvania Press, 1984), 174–175.

4. On the priests at this temple, see Davis, *Ritual in an Oscillating Universe*, 6. His book is devoted to describing and analyzing āgamic temple rituals in this medieval period, and I draw on his work in this section.

5. Ibid., 69–72.

6. Venkataraman, *Rājarājēśvaram*, 288.

7. Davis, *Ritual in an Oscillating Universe*, 10.

8. The architectural portions of the the influential *Kāmikāgama* may have been developed in dialectic relationship to Chola architecture of the eleventh century, possibly via the *Mayamata*; see ibid., 13. Davis discusses historical problems in dating the āgamas on pp. 12–14.

9. The ground of the temple is made sacred by a vāstumaṇḍala. On this topic see Stella Kramrisch, *The Hindu Temple*, 2 vols. (Delhi: Motilal Banarsidass, [1946] 1976), 1: 19–97.

10. Inden, "The Ceremony of the Great Gift," 134.

11. Gregory D. Alles, "Surface, Space, and Intention: The Parthenon and the Kandāriya Mahādeva," *History of Religions* 28, no. 1 (August 1988): 1–36.

12. For an architectural description of this temple, see Venkataraman, *Rājarājēśvaram*, 72–101; and the essay by K. R. Srinivasan in *Encyclopaedia of Indian Temple Architecture: South India, Lower Drāviḍadēśa*, ed. Michael W. Meister (New Delhi: American Institute of Indian Studies; Philadelphia: University of Pennsylvania Press, 1983), 234–241.

13. For a list and diagram of these images, see Venkataraman, *Rājarājēśvaram*, 88–89.

14. Davis, *Ritual in an Oscillating Universe*, 62.

15. Ibid., 64.

16. At Darasuram; for the relationship between the Darasuram friezes and the *Periya Purāṇam* see J. R. Marr, "The *Periya Purāṇam* Frieze at Tārācuram: Episodes in the Lives of the Tamil Śaiva Saints," *Bulletin of the School of Oriental and African Studies*, 42, part 2 (1979), 268–289.

17. This discussion is based on Davis, *Ritual in an Oscillating Universe*, 42–47. See also R. Nagaswamy's comments on the role of the *Makuṭāgama* in worship at the Tanjavur temple, "Iconography and Significance," 176–177.

18. These categories can also represent paths appropriate to a priest who is a renouncer and a priest who is a householder. Ibid., 46–47.

19. Richard Davis calls the latter "becoming a Śiva," in *Ritual in an Oscillating Universe*; I draw on his second and fourth chapters for my discussion of embodiment.

20. Ibid., 51.

21. See ibid., 47ff.

22. Ibid., 132.

23. See Brunner, "Les catégories sociales védiques dans le sivaïsme du sud," *Journal Asiatique* 252, no. 4 (1964): 454–455.

24. Ibid., 463.

25. Gotras are traced back to a founding figure, often a ṛṣi (seer or sage); the five most often mentioned are Kāśyapa, Kauśika, Bharadvāja, Gautama and Atreya (Agastya); see ibid., 457. Here I am following the texts' descriptions of the respective privileges of the five categories. Brunner suggests that the ādiśaivas may have been nonbrahman in origin (464–465), and modern sociological studies support the view that the status of the ādiśaivas is not as elevated as the texts suggest; for example, Fuller, *Servants of the Goddess*, 50–71, 186 n. 7.

26. See ibid., 456–457. Compare Davis, *Ritual in an Oscillating Universe*, 69–70.

27. *Kāmikāgama* (4.6–7), cited in Davis, *Ritual in an Oscillating Universe*, 69.

28. Brunner discusses several historical hypotheses on this point, including the possibility that Śaivism spread in areas where śūdras were powerful (such as the Kāvēri delta, where many Vēḷāḷa agricuturalists lived, who were technically of śūdra status but had a more positive social standing than this would suggest) or that originally Śaivas were śūdras. In either case, she views the attention in the texts to the correct origins of the ādiśaivas as part of an attempt to legitimize this religious group in the wider world of Vedic varṇas, "Les catégories," 464–465.

29. Brunner notes, "But to receive the title of *ācārya* is one thing, to exercise all the powers of *ācārya* is another"; ibid., 462.

30. Davis, *Ritual in an Oscillating Universe*, 70–71.

31. The text is translated and discussed by Pierre-Sylvain Filliozat, "Le droit d'entrer dans les temples de Śiva au XIe siècle," *Journal Asiatique* 263, facs. 1 and 2 (1975): 103–117. Quotations from the text in the following discussion are taken from page 115.

32. Filliozat states: "The text has, however, no particular connection with this province [Kashmir]. One sees there, on the contrary, mention of hymns in the *drāviḍa* language that one must identify as being the Tamil *Tēvāram*. And it is certain that the author considers the rules that he pronounces as applicable to all temples and all *śaiva*s in every region of India"; ibid., 103.

33. Śiva appears in this form in the *Mahābhārata* and in the *Śiva Purāṇa*, among other texts. See O'Flaherty, *Hindu Myths: A Sourcebook* (Harmondsworth; Baltimore: Penguin, 1975), 38, 160–168, et passim for examples. The mūvar and other proponents of Śiva-bhakti praised Śiva's capacity both to cause happiness to and to bestow ultimate bliss on his bhaktas.

34. Davis, *Ritual in an Oscillating Universe*, 136.

35. On the location of sections on Cuntarar in the *Periya Purāṇam* see Shulman, *Songs of the Harsh Devotee*, xxvii.

36 Cēkkiḻār claims that the composition of the *Tiruttoṇṭattokai* was the main reason for Cuntarar's birth on earth; *Periya Purāṇam* v. 35, cited by Shulman, *Songs of the Harsh Devotee*, xvi.

37. For example, the traditional Śaivite distinction between *vaṉroṇṭar* ("hard devotee") and *meṉroṇṭar* ("soft devotee"); many attribute the genesis of this classification to a hymn of Cuntarar's, which speaks of both *nal aṭiyār* (good servants) and *val aṭiyār* (harsh servants); *Tirvalivalam*, 7.67.2. A late-nineteenth-century Tamil scholar, Aṟumuka Nāvalar, provided a threefold classification:

> 1. *Guru bhakti*: Intense devotion to the preceptor, human or divine: 12 saints including Appar, Campantar, and Tirumūlar, besides Appūti, Kaṇanātar, Nilakaṇṭayālppāṇar, etc. 2. *Liṅka bhakti*: Worship of the *Civa-liṅkam* in which the devotee makes undreamt of sacrifices: 32 devotees of whom Kaṇṇappar and Nāḻaippōvār (Nantaṉār) may be mentioned as well known examples. 3. *Caṅkama bhakti*: Worship and service to Civaṉ's *caṅkam*, community of *aṭiyār*. This is also called *makēcuvarapūcai*, the worship of the Lord: 19 devotees of whom Ciruttoṇṭar, Kāraikkālammaiyār, Amarniti and Viṟalmiṇṭar may be mentioned at random. (Aṟumuka Nāvalar, *Tiruttoṇṭar Periyapurāṇam* [in prose] [Madras, 1889], 39; cited in *Encyclopedia of Tamil Literature* 1: 295).

38. Peterson, "Lives of the Wandering Singers." In the article, she points to some differences between the *Periya Purāṇam* and Nampi's text, noting that in the stories of the mūvar, Nampi emphasizes "miracles" (*aṟputam*), whereas Cēkkiḻār focuses on a sequential depiction of the saints' journeys, emphasizing their "virtues or attainments" (343–344).

39. For example, Hart, "The Little Devotee"; and Dennis D. Hudson, "Violent and Fanatical Devotion among the Nāyanārs: A Study in the *Periya Purāṇam* of Cēkkiḻār, in *Sanskrit and Indian Studies*, ed. Masatoshi Nagatomi, et al. (Dordrecht: D. Reidel, 1980).

40. G. Vanmikanathan, *Periya Puranam: A Tamil Classic on the Great Saiva Saints of South India by Sekkizhaar. Condensed English Version* (Mylapore: Sri Ramakrishna Math, 1985). A fourteenth-century Śaiva Siddhānta philosopher understood the *Periya Purāṇam* to be the culmination of nāyaṉmār Śiva-bhakti, which I discuss in the next chapter.

41. Dennis Hudson has described the *Periya Purāṇam* as an "establishment" text that "provides Śaiva kings with religious justification for their rule"; "Violent and Fanatical Devotion," 374.

42. Burton Stein discusses these developments in "Social Mobility," 78–94.

43. His work, entitled *Nantaṉār Charitram*, uses the term *varukalāmo?*, meaning "May I come?" as the first word of his story and as a refrain throughout. Nantaṉār had to yell this phrase when he came to the entrance of each street as a warning to higher caste people that they should take cover from his polluting presence. At the other end of the street, he would make another announcement to signify that the coast was clear. It is the degradation of his social condition that makes Nantaṉār long to visit Tillai. If Cēkkiḻār's telling of the story is about temples, Bharati's is about streets. For a discussion of Bharati's story, see Vanmikanathan, *Periya Puranam*, 564–567; and B. Natarajan, *The City of the Cosmic Dance: Chidambaram* (New Delhi: Orient Longman, 1974), 101–103. Natarajan's condensed telling includes an episode specific to Bharati's work. When Nantaṉār finally decides to go to Tillai, he needs to get permission from his "master" (the owner of the land). His master tells him that he must plow all the lands and transplant the rice seedlings before the next morning, an impossible task; however, overnight Naṭarāja intervenes and does all the work, freeing Nantaṉār to go to Chidambaram. On other differences between the two tellings and a discussion of Bharati and the development of the *kālakṣēpam* genre, see Zvelebil, *Tamil Literature*, 227–230. Selections from Gopalakrishna Bharati's composition were performed by faculty and students from Madras University's Department of Indian Classical Music at the Music Academy, December 25, 1996.

44. Three films called *Nandanar* were made during this period: by the New Theatres in 1933, by Asandas Classical Talkies in 1935, and by Gemini Studios in 1942. In the Gemini Studios version, a female singer, K. B. Sundarambal played the lead, and received the noteworthy remuneration of Rs. 1,00,000 (a lakh of rupees) for her work. According to a Tamil friend who saw this version of the film when it came out, it was "the talk of the town" over the perceived controversy of a "brahman" (character in the movie) bowing down to a "harijan"; additionally, the "brahman" was played by a man, while the "harijan" (Nandanar) was played by a woman. Later, Annadurai wrote the screenplay for a film that was a take-off on the Nandanar legend, *Nallathambi* (1949). See S. Theodore Baskaran, *The Eye of the Serpent: An Introduction to Tamil Cinema* (Madras: EastWest Books, 1996).

45. Lynn Vincentnathan, "Nandanar," 174.

Chapter 8

1. See my discussion in Prentiss, "A Tamil Lineage for Śaiva Siddhānta Philosophy," *History of Religions* 35, no. 3 (February 1996): 231–237. I draw on this article here.

2. According to tradition, Meykaṇṭār was born in Tiruvenkāṭu, near Cīṟkāḻi, some 20 km from Chidambaram; Aruṇanti was born in Tiruttuṟaiyūr, near Paṉṟutti, approximately 25 km west of Cuddalore and 50 km north of Chidambaram; and Maṟaiñāṉa Campantar was born in Tiruppeṇṇākāṭam, near Viruttāccalam, also near Chidambaram (Tiruppeṇṇākāṭam is connected with the story of Meykaṇṭār as well; his father was born here and the ācārya's samādhi took place here). Umāpati was from Chidambaram itself.

3. There was a scholarly debate on whether Meykaṇṭār's *Civañāṉa Pōtam* was a translation of the "pāśamocana paṭhala" of the *Rauravāgama*, but no editions of the latter, including the most recent, have these sūtras in them. See Siddalingaiah, *Origin and Development of Saiva Siddhanta up to 14th Century* (Madurai: Madurai Kamaraj University, 1979), 94–95. For a translation of the *Civañāṉa Pōtam* and the relevant verses from the *Rauravāgama*, see Dhavamony, *Love of God*, 327–334.

4. The lineage of Tamil philosopher-seers begins with Meykaṇṭār, who tradition says had forty-nine disciples. Except for the first two authors of the canon, who came before Meykaṇṭār, the other authors are claimed to be among these forty-nine. That the first two authors wrote their treatises before Meykaṇṭār wrote his appears to have bothered later in-

terpreters of Tamil Śaiva Siddhānta. The *Cantāṉavaralāru* (eighteenth century?), a prose work on the history of the cantāṉācāryārs ("leaders of the lineage," the canonical authors), explains that the two prior authors, both named Uyyavanta Tēvanāyanār, belonged to the Viññāṉatēvar Cantāṉam, which was "like" the Meykaṇṭatēvar Cantāṉam. One day they placed their works before Meykaṇṭār and prostrated themselves. He approved of their work, thus legitimating them for inclusion in the canon (*śāstras*). See Siddalingaiah, *Origin and Development*, 86, n. 65. Otherwise, Meykaṇṭār was the guru, Aruṇanti was his preceptor-cum-disciple, Maṉavācakam was a disciple of Meykaṇṭār, and Umāpati was the disciple of Maṟaiñāṉacampantar, who had received instruction from Aruṇanti. A special status is given to two pairs of guru-disciples: Meykaṇṭār, Aruṇanti, Maṟaiñāṉacampantar, and Umāpati are known as the four cantāṉācāryārs. See ibid., 97–98, 108, 110.

5. This has been briefly noted by Davis, *Ritual in an Oscillating Universe*, 18.

6. The influence of advaita was noted many years ago in a scholarly article by the famous turn-of-the-century interpreter of Tamil Śaiva Siddhānta, J. M. Nallaswami Pillai; see the chapter on "Advaita According to the Śaiva Siddhānta" in his *Studies in Saiva-Siddhanta* (Madras: Meykaṇdān Press, 1911), 244–272. See also Dhavamony's remarks on advaita in his discussion of the *Śivañāṉapōtam* in *Love of God*, 200–223.

7. The Tamil text of the simile (*uvamam*) is: *vētam pacuvataṉpāl meyyā kammanālvar ōtun tamiḻ ataṉiṉ uḷḷuṟuney pōtamiku neyyiṉ uṟucuvaiyām nīḷveṇṇey meykaṇṭāṉ ceyttamiḻ nūliṉ tiṟam*; see Siddalingaiah, *Origin and Development*, 93–94. According to tradition, Tiruveṇṇeynallūr ("veṇṇey" in the simile; located in South Arcot district) is the place where Meykaṇṭār achieved samādhi; it is also the place where Cuntarar was "enslaved" by the Lord.

8. Ibid., 73.

9. Meykaṇṭār, whose name forms the title of the canon, wrote one text, the *Civañāṉa Pōtam*, that is considered to be foundational, though not chronologically first. The traditional order of the fourteen canonical śāstras (Tam. *cāttiraṅkaḷ*), which scholars take as chronological, is: *Tiru Untiyār* by Tiruviyalūr Uyyavanta Tēva Nāyaṉār (ca. A.D. 1147), *Tirukkaḷiṟṟuppaṭiyār* by Tirukkatalūr Uyyavanta Tēva Nāyaṉār (ca. A.D. 1177); *Civañāṉa Pōtam* by Tiruveṇṇeynallūr Meykaṇṭa Tēvar (1221); *Civañāṉa Cittiyār* by Tirutturaiyūr Aruṇanti Civācāriyār (1253), who also wrote *Irupā Irupatu* (1254); *Uṇmai Viḷakkam* by Tiruvatikai Maṉavācakamkaṭantār (1255); and eight by Umāpati Civācāriyār (of Koṟṟavaṉkuṭi): *Civappirakācam* (1306), *Tiruvaruṭ Payaṉ* (1307), *Viṉā Veṇpā* (1308), *Pōṟṟip Paṟoṭai* (1309), *Koṭikkavi* (1309), *Neñcuviṭu Tūtu* (1311), *Uṇmaineri Viḷakkam* (1312; a minority opinion among scholars attributes the authorship of this text to Cīṟkaḻi Tattuva Natar), and *Caṅkaṟpa Nirākaraṇam* (1313; the Śāka equivalent of this date is given in the text itself). These widely accepted dates are taken from Dhavamony, *Love of God*, part 2. We do not know when this corpus was constituted as a canon, or by whom. An anonymous verse enumerates the fourteen śāstras: "*Undikaḷiṟu uyar bōdam siddiyār, pindirupā uṇmai pirakāsamvaṇda arutpaṇbu viṉā pōṟṟi koḍi pāśamilā neñcuviḍu, uṇmaineṟi sankaṟpa muṟṟu*," quoted in Siddalingaiah, *Origin and Development*, 72 n. 7. S. S. Janaki states that the earliest place this verse is found is in the Madurai Nāyakan's 1866 edition of these fourteen works in a single collection; Janaki, "Umāpathi Śivācarya: His Life, Works, and Contribution to Śaivism," in *Śaiva Siddhanta* 24, no. 2 (April–June 1989): 56. The issue of closure may not have been settled early on; for example, some scholars argue that the *Tukaḷaṟu Pōtam* by Cīṟkāḻi Ciṟṟampalanāṭikaḷ replaces *Uṇmai Viḷakkam* as one of the fourteen śāstras. However, there is a great deal of internal coherence in the canon if taken as the fourteen texts already described, and Umāpati Civācāryār may have played a role in establishing the Tamil Śaiva Siddhānta canon. I discuss later the likelihood of his role in creating the Tamil Śivabhakti canon.

10. *Civappirakācam*, stanza 5, in Vai. Irattiṉacapāpati, *Meykaṇṭa Cāttiraṅkaḷ* (Ceṉṉai [Madras]: Ceṉṉaip Palkalaik Kaḻakam, Caiva Cittāntat Tuṟai [Madras University, Tamil Department], n.d. [Author's Preface, 1988]), 190. Unless otherwise specified, the Tamil canonical texts I consider in this article are from Irattiṉacapāpati's volume.

11. Dīṭcitar, a title for the group of priests at Chidambaram, is from the Sanskrit term for initiation, *dīkṣā*. S. S. Janaki has compiled a list of the sources for Umāpati's biography, which are in Tamil and Sanskrit: *Pārthavana māhātmyam* (*Koṟṟavaṉguḍi Purāṇam*), in 240 Sanskrit verses, also found in the *Chidambarasara* as a dialogue between Brahmānanda Yati and Śankarācārya; *Rajendrapura* (*Tillai*) *māhātmya* or *Umāpati-vijaya*, 108 Sanskrit verses by Tillai Civānanda Dīṭcitar (both of these Sanskrit sources are found in the Introduction to the *Pauṣkara bhāṣya*, one of Umāpati's Sanskrit works); a 15-verse biography by Chidambara Brahma Yati, found in Umāpati's *Kuñcitāṅghristava*; and the *Cantāṉācārya Purāṇa* by Svāminatha Dīṭcitar. This last work, in Tamil, is from the eighteenth century. See S. S. Janaki, "Umāpathi Śivācarya," 54. T. B. Siddalingaiah adds a few Tamil sources, including the *Pulavarpurāṇam* and the invocatory poems by various later poets, for example, the *Enāṭkaṇṇi* of Tāyumāṉavar; see *Origin and Development*, 124.

12. Younger, *The Home of the Dancing Śivaṉ*.

13. See translations in ibid., 201–210; and Peterson, *Poems to Śiva*, 190–192. Gandarāditya's *Tiruvicaippā* also follows this trend.

14. Translations of Tirumūlar and Māṇikkavācakar on Tillai are in Younger, *The Home of the Dancing Śivaṉ*, 192–201.

15. Translation, ibid., 217.

16. Ibid., 231, n. 24, remarks on these instances of hesitation.

17. Shulman, *Songs of the Harsh Devotee*, xxix.

18. As Shulman notes (242, n. 1), there are several ways this first line can be translated, including "I am a slave to the feet of the brahmans who live in Tillai." Tradition, beginning with Nampi Āṇṭār Nampi, understands the brahmans themselves to be the servants of Śiva; thus, the meaning of the phrase is in effect, "I am the servant of the servants who are the brahmans who live at Tillai."

19. It is fairly certain that Umāpati authored the *Kōyil Purāṇam*, the *Tirumuṟaikaṇṭa Purāṇam*, and the *Cēkkiḻār Purāṇam*, all of which I discuss in this chapter.

20. A comparison of the two texts by section theme is as follows: Introduction/ *Citamparamāhātmya* sections 1–4, *Kōyil Purāṇa* verses 1–29; On Viyākirapāta/ *C* 6–10, *KP* 30–59; On Patañjali/ *C* 11–18, *KP* 60–158; On Naṭarājaṉ/ *KP* 159–229; On Hiraṇyavaramaṉ/ *C* 19–26, *KP* 229–362; On festivals/ *KP* 363–415. This detailed comparison is from Younger, "The Home of the Dancing Śivaṉ" (manuscript), Story 3. In the following, I draw primarily upon Younger's discussion in the manuscript; some, but not all, of this discussion appeared in the published book.

21. Younger suggests that the claims in this story were made in the thirteenth-century context of many north Indian pilgrims traveling to Chidambaram and questioning the legitimacy and authority of the priests; *The Home of the Dancing Śivaṉ*, 175–176.

22. For example, *Kōyil Purāṇam* 138ff.; discussed ibid., 179–180.

23. The distinction between priestly activity and Śaiva Siddhānta knowledge is also found in the tradition surrounding Umāpati's canonical text, the *Koṭikkavi* (The Flag Song). Tradition says that, on one occasion, the temple flag, which is raised to commence important festivals, would not ascend. It was only when Umāpati was brought to the temple to deliver a mini-discourse on Śaiva Siddhānta that the flag went up. The discourse was the *Koṭikkavi*, in four verses: the first verse describes the darkness of ignorance and the light of knowledge; the second describes the realities of God and the soul; the third "explains the 'advaita'

relationship of God with soul"; and the fourth is on the recitation of the pañcākṣara mantra, which can be recited as five syllables, six syllables, or eight syllables. See Siddhalingaiah, *Origin and Development*, 125, 146–148; and Dhavamony, *Love of God*, 318–320.

24. Some scholars believe he is the author of *Śatamaṇikkōvai*, but T. B. Siddhalingaiah disagrees; see *Origin and Development*, 120–124.

25. *Paṭṭa kaṭṭaiyiṟ pakaṟkuruṭu ēkutu pārir*, see ibid., 124.

26. A maṭh (some people refer to it as a temple) is there today, a small building housing an image of Umāpati that is washed and decorated each day by a Vīraśaiva caretaker. According to the caretaker, the Vīraśaivas have been in control of the maṭh for many years.

27. Meykaṇṭār's text, the *Civañāṉa Pōtam*, is the source; Aruṇanti's text, *Civañāṉa Cittiyār*, says that it is related to Meykaṇṭār's text (verse 3), and tradition considers it a vaḻinūl ("derived text;" *vaḻ* in general meaning "way," in this context, "son"); Umāpati's *Civappirakācam* is possibly organized using the twelve sutras of Meykaṇṭār's text (see Siddhalingaiah, *Origin and Development*, 135 n. 2), and tradition considers it cārpunūl, "a supplementary treatise" (*cārpu* meaning "reliance" or "connection"). Aruṇanti's *Irupā Irupatu* is in question-and-answer form, for example, as is Tiruvatikai Maṉavācakamkaṭantār's *Uṇmai Viḷakkam*. Another notable genre in the Tamil śāstras is *pūrva-pakṣa siddhānta*, in which rival schools are refuted; for example, Aruṇanti's *Civañāṉa Cittiyār*, of which the first half, the parapakkam (Skt. *parapakṣam*), refutes the tenets of other schools, whereas the second half, the cupakkam (Skt. *svapakṣam*), expounds the Śaiva siddhānta perspective; also Umāpati's *Caṅkaṟpa Nirākaraṇam*.

28. Umāpati is credited with several "miracles" at Chidamabaram beside the raising of the festival flag, including the presence of Śiva Naṭarāja at Koṟṟavaṉkuṭi instead of the temple at Chidambaram; the initiation of a low-caste man, Pettāṉ Cāmpāṉ, into the highest initiation, the Nirvāṇa Dīkṣa; granting Liberation to a plant; and controlling a serpent at the Kalpaka Viṇāyaka temple at the Chidambaram temple complex's west gopuram. On the possibility that Umāpati made a donation to the temple, see Smith, "The Dance of Śiva."

29. Umāpati praises Śiva Naṭarāja as a teacher in his śāstra *Pōṟṟip Paṟoṭai* (Song of Praises).

30. For information on three Tamil Śaiva Siddhānta maṭankaḷ (pl.), Tiruvāvaṭuturai maṭam, which traces its lineage to Umāpati, the Tarumapuram maṭam, and Tiruppaṉantāḷ maṭam, see K. Nambi Arooran, "The Changing Role of Three Saiva Maths in Tanjore District from the Beginning of the 20th Century," in *Changing South Asia: Religion and Society*, ed. Kenneth Ballhatchet and David Taylor (London: Asian Research Service for the Centre of South Asian Studies at SOAS, 1984), 51–58. The Dharmapuram Āṭiṉam is linked to Umāpati's guru; see Siddhalingaiah, *Origin and Development*, 119. See also *Mutt and Temples* (Dharmapuram: Dharmapuram Adhinam, 1981).

31. A few scholars may dispute Umāpati's authorship for these five texts, but it remains significant that tradition closely associates Umāpati with these representations of nāyaṉmār Śiva-bhakti.

32. Subsequent anthologies of *Tēvāram* are numerous, including contemporary pamphlets from which pilgrims can sing the appropriate hymns at the sites of which the mūvar sang; many of these pamphlets are published by the Tirumai Āṭiṉam. There is also an anthology, claimed to be traditional, of twenty-five hymns of the mūvar (ten from Campantar, eight from Appar, and seven from Cuntarar), which is said to bestow the benefits of reciting the entire *Tēvāram* if one recites merely the twenty-five hymns therein; see Yāḻppāṇattunallūr Aṟumukakarāvalaravarkaḷ, *Akattiyamakāmuṉivar Tiraṭṭiyaruṉiya Tēvārattiraṭṭu* (Ceṉṉai: Jīvakāruṇya Vilāca Accukūṭttiṟa, 1909).

33. But note T. B. Siddhalingaiah's comment: "[Umāpati] collected a few padikams of the Tirumuṟais and classified them under ten headings, on the basis of the chapters given in

his Tiruvaruṭpayaṉ. The Tēvāram hymns obviously were the basis for the composition of the Tiruvaruṭpayaṉ"; *Origin and Development*, 133. Evidence suggests that Umāpati applied these categories to other texts; for example, he may have used them as a method for organizing the Sanskrit ślokas of āgamic philosophy that he collected in his *Śataratnasaṅgraha* (Compendium of One Hundred Gems). N. R. Bhatt suggests that there is some overlap in the content matter of the *Tiruvaruṭpayaṉ* and the *Śataratnasaṅgraha*: TP vv. 1–10=*Ś* 7–17; TP vv. 11–20=*Ś* 18; TP vv. 21–30=*Ś* 19–33; TP vv. 31–70=*Ś* 34–70; TP vv. 71–90=*Ś* 71–78; TP vv. 91–100=*Ś* 79–91, but the categories from the *Tiruvaruṭpayaṉ* are not provided as titles in the *Śataratnasaṅgraha*, nor is the similarity convincing in all sections. See N. R. Bhatt, "Paśu and Pāśa in Śataratna-Saṅgraha," in *Umāpati Śivācārya: His Life, Works, and Contribution to Śaivism*, ed. S. S. Janaki. See also P. Thirugnanasambandhan, *Śataratnasaṅgraha of Śri Umāpati Śivācārya* (Madras: University of Madras, 1973).

34. K. Sivaraman considers these each to be a type of revelation; he calls the third type "personal revelation through direct experience;" see *Śaivism in Philosophical Perspective: A Study of the Formative Concepts, Problems, and Methods of Śaiva Siddhānta* (Delhi: Motilal Banarsidass, 1973), 24–30.

35. The *Tirukkaḻiṟṟuppaṭiyār* by Uyyavanta Tēva Nāyaṉār of Tirukkaṭavūr, v. 9; the words I place in brackets are pronouns in the Tamil. Compare Dhavamony, *Love of God*, 184, who translates "those who" as "Śiva-bhaktas," with which I agree.

36. K. Sivaraman explores the link between Tamil Śaiva Siddhānta philosophy and the *Periya Purāṇam*: "Personal revelation defies all categories. . . . Authentic accounts of lives of saints and their awakening to the reality of Divine Revelation alone can be our evidence. Tense moments of crises in such lives are also moments of self-revelation of Grace. *Periyapurāṇam* the book on saints and saintly life by a saint is therefore, intrinsically the most valuable document for Śaiva Siddhānta"; *Śaivism in Philosophical Perspective*, 30.

37. Verse 54. See also verses 53, on the nāyaṉār Cēntaṉār, and 52, on Kaṇṇappar—in which he quotes Māṇikkavācakar's phrase *kaṇṇappaṉ oppatōr aṉpiṉmai* (Kaṇṇappar's incomparable love); see Dhavamony *Love of God*, 190–191. Verses 70–71 praise the poetry of each of the four camayācāryas (the mūvar plus Māṇikkavācakar).

38. Dhavamony has identified a few examples from the text: "The bhaktas' union with Śivaṉ is so intimate that he makes them partake of his own divine way of acting (*tāṉ ceyyumtaṉmaikaḷum avaṉ aṉparkku ākkiyiṭum*, 69.3–4). He takes possession of them (*aṉparai vantāṇṭatu*, 90.3) in such a manner that he becomes the doer of all their actions, the agent of their knowledge and love" (followed by a translation of verse 64); *Love of God*, 197–198.

39. The text of the *Tirumuṟaikaṇṭa Purāṇam* can be found printed in some editions of the *Periya Purāṇam*. I have used *Cēkkiḻārcuvāmikaḷaruḷicceyta Tiruttoṇṭarpurāṇameṉṉum Periyapurāṇam*, vol. 1, ed. Āṟumukat Tampirāṉ Cuvāmikal, with commentary (Ceṉṉai [Madras]: Pā. Cōmaiyaravarkaḷatu, 1888); and Tiruvāvaṭuturai Ātiṉam: *Cēkkiḻār Perumaṉ Aruḷiya Periya Purāṇam eṉa valaṅkum Tiruttoṇṭar Purāṇam* (Tiruvāvaṭutuṟai: Tirukkayilaya Paramparait Tiruvāvaṭutuṟai Ātiṉam, 1988). I provide a translation of the *Tirumuṟaikaṇṭapurāṇam* in an unpublished manuscript, "On the Making of a Canon"; for a summary of the text in English, see Dorai Rangaswamy, *Religion and Philosophy*, xix–xx.

40. *Rājarāja* is "king of kings," *maṉṉaṉ* is "king," and *apayakulacēkaraṉ* is "fearless leader of the clan." Scholars agree that this was a Chola king, but they differ on their identification of which one. Kamil Zvelebil discusses Tamil scholars' identifications of this king before settling upon Kulōttunga I (A.D. 1070–1122) as the most likely candidate, with the period of Āditya I and Parāntaka I (907–955) a secondary possibility (Brill, *Tamil Literature*, 133–134). Compare Dorai Rangaswamy's agreement, *Religion and Philosophy*, 22–23. On the king's reaction, note that Tiruvārūr is especially sacred to the bhakti poet-saint,

Cuntarar: "This town becomes Cuntarar's home and a fixed point in all the stories about him; his restless wanderings always, eventually, bring him back to Tiruvārūr (note that he also bears the name of the god of this town, as Nampi Ārūraṉ)"; Shulman, *Songs of the Harsh Devotee*, xxviii. It was at Tiruvārūr that Cuntarar composed his list of saints, the *Tiruttoṇṭattokai*. At that time, Cuntarar had just returned from a pilgrimage to Chidambaram. The first line of the poem, which was provided by Śiva for the tongue-tied Cuntarar, is in praise of the priests of Chidambaram, as I discussed before. See ibid., xxix.

41. The text says that originally, there were 16,000 verses by Campantar, 49,000 by Appar, and 38,000 by Cuntarar. Some view the text as a classical authority on the number of patikams composed by the three hymnists, although I do not take up this issue here; see Dorai Rangaswamy, *Religion and Philosophy*, 36–41.

42. Contra M. A. Dorai Rangaswamy's suggestion that the text originally ended with the twenty-fourth verse: "The twenty-sixth verse, at once abruptly starting to mention in the most summary way the other hymns and poems of other Śaivite Saints and poets without any explanation about them, comes as a surprise . . . one may not be wrong in believing that this part was a later addition and that the original Tirumuṟaikaṇṭa Purāṇam must have closed with the first twenty-four verses"; *Religion and Philosophy*, 20.

43. Ibid., 27–29.

44. Umāpati's *Kōyil Purāṇam*, v. 381. For this parallel and the following discussion of this text I rely on Younger, *The Home*, 176–182. Younger notes that festivals are more conservative than priestly worship; the festival section of the text describes many that are performed today, in contrast to the section on daily worship, which is quite different from that practiced today. However, the festival involving the procession of Patañcali is described in the text but not performed today. The procession is not mentioned in the Sanskrit *sthālapurāṇa* of Chidambaram, the *Citambaramāhātmya*.

45. *Cēkkiḻār Purāṇam*, 96, cited in Dorai Rangaswamy, *Religion and Philosophy*, 20.

46. My discussion of Umāpati's role is at variance with two very influential studies of the history of *Tēvāram* (and *Tirumuṟai*), Dorai Rangaswamy, *Religion and Philosophy*, esp. 19–35, and Vellaivāranaṉ, *Pannirutirumuṟai Varalāṟu* (Aṇṇāmalai: Aṇṇāmalaip Palkalaikkaḻakam, n.d.), 1: 1–48. The basic difference in our positions is that they view Umāpati Civācāryār's *Tirumuṟaikaṇṭa Purāṇam* as a description of earlier times, especially the time of Nampi Āṇṭār Nampi, whereas I view the text as a history of its own period, the early fourteenth century.

47. The language of grace and other terms and images associated with the Tamil Śaiva Siddhānta worldview recur throughout the text; compare vv. 2, 13, 20–22, 24, 26–27.

48. For example, Campantar 2.183.11, Cuntarar 7.65.2; see Peterson, *Poems to Śiva*, 40, 189, 329.

49. Even this hymn's iconographic description of Śiva can be understood philosophically, as I discuss in the notes to this poem in appendix A.

50. Campantar 3.37, Appar 4.11. See Peterson's partial translations of these patikams, *Poems to Śiva*, 217–218.

Appendix A: The Translation of Tēvāra Aruḷmuṟaittiraṭṭu

1. A Śaiva Siddhānta Interpretation for Campantar 1.1.1. The first two lines are the most significant:

tōṭu uṭaiya ceviyaṉ viṭai ēṟiyōr tūvu eṉa mati cūti
kāṭu uṭaiya cuṭalai poṭi pūciyeṉ uḷḷam kavarkaḷvaṉ

Tōṭu, "earring," is a symbol of "Ōm." It is made up of the letters *t* and *ō*. T is the seventh letter of the consonants, denoting the seven kinds of births and deaths. The long *o* is the tenth letter of the alphabet, which in Tamil begins with the vowels. The number ten signifies the soul. Thus, *tōṭu* is a symbol of the body and the soul, both in terms of the numerical content of the letters and also in the sense that the consonant is the body and the vowel is the soul (compare the beginning of the *Tiruvaruṭpayaṉ*, which begins with the letter *a* as a symbol of the Lord). The meaning of *ceviyaṉ* can be taken in the sense that the Lord has ears to hear the grieving of the souls, and he responds to them by giving them different and appropriate mantras (which the souls speak and he hears) to overcome the five senses. *Viṭai* means bull, which signifies *aṟam* or "ethics," "virtue." Ōr *(ēṟiyōr)* signifies "one" in the sense of "only"; in combination with purity and virtue (*tūvu*) and whiteness (*eṉa*), it suggests that the soul has achieved the uppermost levels of ñāṉa (Skt. jñāna). Mati, moon, is also a symbol of the soul. These associations yield an interpretive understanding of line one of the poem:

> The Lord who hears the grieving of the embodied souls,
> who bears virtue,
> who is crowned with the pure virtuous souls of cutta ñāṉa

Line 2: Kāṭu is a burial ground, as distinct from cuṭalai, which is a cremation ground. In Śaiva Siddhānta understanding, these are two different ways for souls to be purified. The burial ground is a symbol for the soul's maturity through ñāṉa; in the next birth, the soul can easily obtain ñāṉa. The cremation ground is a symbol for the ñāṉa-agni, the fire of knowledge that destroys and removes the impurities of the soul. Śiva smears ashes on the souls in the burial ground and the cremation ground for their purification and protection—it is the way the Lord bears the souls of the dead. By implication, the ashes are from the elemental fire, one of the five bhūtas (earth, water, fire, air, ether) that compose the body and the world. Two of the bhūtas, earth and water, are considered to be formed, while two others, air and ether, are considered formless. Fire, which stands between formed and formless, is therefore appropriate in this context because of the in-between status of the souls. The last part of the line can be interpreted as the Lord's stealing one's mind; the mind goes off to him without permission, suggesting that effort to go to the Lord is useless. An interpretive understanding of line 2 of the poem:

> The Lord who smears ashes from the bhūta of fire
> on the souls from the burial ground and the cremation ground,
> protecting them in their helplessness;
> The Lord who takes my mind without my effort.

Lines 3 and 4 describe the Lord's giving grace to Brahmā. I am grateful to Dr. Vai. Irattiṉacapāpati for sharing his philosophical ideas on this verse with me.

Appendix B: The Analysis of Tiruvaruṭpayaṉ

1. For example, C. N. Singaravelu considers *Uṇmai Viḷakkam*, which is in the format of a disciple asking his guru philosophical questions and requesting his answers, as a primer for Śaiva Siddhānta; see his *Uṇmai Viḷakkam* (*The Exposition of Truth*)*: A Primer of Saiva Siddhanta* (Tellipazhai, Sri Lanka: Siddhanta Maha Samajam, 1981). The writer of the foreword indicates that one usually studies *Uṇmai Viḷakkam* before proceeding to the *Civañāṉa Pōtam*, the *Civañāṉa Cittiyār*, and the *Civappirakācam*. I studied the TP for the academic year 1992–1993 with Dr. Vai. Irattiṉacapāpati, professor of Śaiva Siddhānta Philosophy emeritus of the University of Madras. I am grateful to him for sharing his deep understanding of philosophy and for his patience.

2. In general, Umāpati creates instructive images in the TP with nontechnical Tamil terms, and I have translated the text accordingly. However, because the philosophical ideas illustrated by the images are expressed elsewhere in Sanskrit (and, indeed, many of the Sanskrit terms are transliterated into Tamil), I have felt free to use this vocabulary in my expository discussion here. An excellent resource for the general study of Śaiva Siddhānta is Sivaraman, *Śaivism in Philosophical Perspective*. The author uses both Sanskrit and Tamil sources in his study.

3. Veḻḻiyampala Muṉivar lived in the middle of the seventeenth century and held the position of a junior head of Dharmapuram Ātiṉam. He was a scholar in both Tamil and Sanskrit.

4. For example, K. D. Thirunavukkarasu notes that the early-twentieth-century orientalist, John Mackenzie (*Hindu Ethics* [London: Oxford University Press, 1922], 128–130) believed there to be no Hindu text on grace; in contrast, Dhavamony (*Love of God*) lauds the TP as being "the only work in the religious literature of India exclusively devoted to the theology of divine grace, as far as we know" (275). See K. D. Thirunavukkarasu, "Tiruvaruṭpayaṉ," in *Umāpati Śivācārya: His Life, Works, and Contribution to Śaivism*, S. S. Janaki, ed. (Madras: Kuppuswami Sastri Research Institute, 1996). For a study of the TP that explores the nature of grace in classical and later Hindu sources, see Ghose, *Grace in Śaiva Siddhānta.*

5. For a couplet-by-couplet interpretation, see Ghose, *Grace in Śaiva Siddhānta*, part II.

6. Fabricius's *Tamil and English Dictionary* (Tiruchirapalli: Tranquebar, 1972 [1897]) identifies *mutu* as an adjective, "old, ancient, original," and gives nouns, such as *mutumoḻi*, *mutuvar*, below the adjective. The *Tamil Lexicon* identifies *mutu* as a noun, "vast knowledge," and lists all the nouns beginning with *mutu* separately.

7. According to Irattiṉacapāpati, the term *satasat* is not found outside of Śaiva Siddhānta philosophy. *Sat* and *asat* denote any number of oppositions: truth, falsehood; intelligence, ignorance; good, bad, and so on. Here, the contrast is between that which is real and that which is unreal. Unreal does not connote "nonbeing"; the āṇava mala is one of the fundamental realities of the world according to Śaiva Siddhānta. Unreal means that it is a distortion, the antithesis of the truth embodied by pati.

8. Irattiṉacapāpati has made an interesting point with respect to Umāpati's emphasis on the metaphors of darkness and light. In terms of physical properties, light can penetrate darkness, but light will not admit any darkness; thus, in philosophical terms, āṇava (darkness) admits grace (light), but grace (light) will not admit āṇava (darkness).

9. Śaiva Siddhānta traditionally recognizes the four stages of knowledge that I discuss here, but the nineteenth-century saint Ramalingaswamy made an important contribution to this schema by introducing a stage of jīva after jīva-cit-śakti. He stated that jīva is the knowledge gathered by the soul from the experience of each and every birth, the total of which helps the soul understand the world.

10. But see N. R. Bhatt, "Paśu and Pāśa in Śataratna-Sangraha" in (S. S. Janaki, ed., *Umāpati Śivācārya*), in which he states that Umāpati agrees with gurus Sadyojyoti, Rāmakaṇṭha, Nārāyanakaṇṭha, and Aghoraśiva in his understanding of *Śivasamavāda* in his Sanskrit text the *Śataratna-Saṅgraha* but disagrees with them, positing a relationship of oneness (*Śivatādātmya*), in his Sanskrit text the *Pauskarabhāṣya*. It could be that Umāpati had at least two different opinions, or it could be that there were two differet Umāpatis. This is one reason why I strictly localize my interpretations in the TP.

11. It appears in the eighth *Anuvāka* of the Taittirīya version. See my discussion of this text in chapter 3.

12. Umāpati was not the first to change the order of the syllables in the recitation of the mantra. Tirumūlar's *Tirumantiram* mentions it (vv. 2797–2798), and Māṇikkavācakar knew of it (for example, *Tiruvācakam* section 38, no. 553; Pope's translation), and the *Tēvāram*

poets knew of it (see my translations in appendix B, section 9). Ultimately, there were three ways to pronounce the pañcākṣara-mantra: (1) Tūlapañcākkaram (Namacivāya), signifying respect to Śiva; (2) Cūkkampañcākkaram (Civāyanama), signifying contemplation exclusively on Śiva; and (3) Āticūkkampañcākkaram (Civāyaciva), signifying union with God for eternal happiness. The terms (Sanskrit, transliterated into Tamil) *tūlam* and *cūkkam* are antonyms; the former means "material matter" and the latter, "subtlety."

Other texts extend the meaning of the mantra to different realms, such as the śāstraic *Uṇmai Viḷakkam* by Maṉavācakam Kaṭantār of Tiruvaṭikai (verse 33), which describes the dance of Śiva in terms of the mantra: na = feet, ma = navel, śi = shoulder, vā = face, and ya = crown; or, following Tirumūlar, śi = hand that holds the drum, vā = extended hand, ya = hand in abhāya mudra, na = hand that holds fire, and ma = foot placed on the demon. For a summary, see Siddhalingaiah, *Origin and Development*, 109–110.

13. There are, of course, many philosophies of yoga, but this is the method that Umāpati alludes to in this couplet.

14. Note that, when saying the mantra, the sound from the prior syllable extends over the syllable yet to be pronounced.

Bibliography

Abbreviations

ARE	*Annual Report of Epigraphy*
EI	*Epigraphia Indica*
IA	*Indian Antiquary*
MER	*Madras Epigraphical Records*
SII	*South Indian Inscriptions*

Tamil Texts and Translations

Cēkkiḻār Cuvāmikaḷ Eṉṉum Aruṇmoḻittēvar Aruḷiya Tiruttoṇṭar Purāṇam. Edited and commentary by C. K. Cuppiramaniya Mutaliyār. 6 vols. Coimbatore: Kōvait Tamiḻc Caṅkam, 1964–1968.

Civappirakācam. By Umāpati Civācāryar. Translated by K. Subramanya Pillai. Dharmapuram: Gnanasambandam Press, 1945.

Meykaṇṭa Cāttiraṅkaḷ. Edited by Vai. Irattiṉacapāpati. Madras: University of Madras, 1990.

Śataratnasaṅgraha of Śri Umāpati Śivācārya. Sanskrit text. Introduced, translated, and explained in English by P. Thirugnanasambandhan. Madras: University of Madras, 1973.

Tēvāra Aruḷmuṟait Tiraṭṭu. By Umāpati Civācāryar. Commentary by P. Irāmanāta Pillai. Madras: South Indian Saiva Siddhanta Works Publishing Society, 1961.

Tēvāram: Hymnes Śivaïtes du Pays Tamoul. Vol. 1, *Ñāṉacampantar.* Edited by T. V. Gopal Iyer. Publications de l'Institut Français d'Indologie no. 68.1, General Editor, François Gros. Pondichéry: Institut Français d'Indologie, 1984.

———. Vol. 2, *Appar et Cuntarar.* Edited by T. V. Gopal Iyer. Publications de l'Institut Français d'Indologie no. 68.2, General Editor, François Gros. Pondichéry: Institut Français d'Indologie, 1985.

———. Vol. 3, *Tēvāram Āyvuttuṇai: Tēvāram études et glossaire Tamouls.* Edited by T. V. Gopal Iyer. Publications de l'Institut Français d'Indologie no. 68.3, edited by François Gros. Pondichéry: Institut Français d'Indologie, 1991.

Tēvāram and *Tiruvācakam.* Translation of selected verses in F. Kingsbury and G. P. Phillips, *Hymns of the Tamil Saivite Saints.* Delhi: Sri Satguru Publications, 1988 [1921].

Thiruvarutpayan of Umapathi Sivacharya. Translated with notes and introduction by J. M. Nallaswami Pillai. Dharmapuram: Gnanasambandam Press, 1945 [1896].

Tirumantiram. By Tirumūlar. With commentary by P. Irāmanāta and notes by A. Citamparaṉār, 2 vols. Madras: South Indian Saiva Siddhanta Works Publishing Society, 1992.

Tirumantiram: A Tamil Scriptural Classic. By Tirumūlar. Translated and annotated by B. Natarajan and edited by N. Mahalingam. Madras: Sri Ramakrishna Math, 1991.

Tirumuṟaikaṇṭapurāṇam. In *Cēkkiḻārcuvāmikaḷaruḷicceyta Tiruttoṇṭarpurāṇameṉṉum Periyapurāṇam*. Edited with commentary by Āṟumukat Tampirāṉ Cuvāmikal. Ceṉṉai: Pā. Cōmaiyaravarkaḷatu, 1888.

Tiruttoṇṭar Mākkaṭai (Periya Purāṇam). With historical notes by P. Irāmanāta Pillai and textual notes by Cu. A. Irāmacāmip Pulavar. Madras: South India Saiva Siddhanta Works Publishing Society, 1970.

Tiruttoṇṭar Tiruvantāti. By Nampi Āṇṭār Nampi. With notes by Guruñāṉcampanta Tēcika Paramācāriya Cuvāmikaḷ. Tarumapuram: Tarumai Ātiṉam, 1986 [1963].

The Tiruvāçagam or "Sacred Utterances" of the Tamil Poet, Saint, and Sage Māṇikka-Vāçagar. With an English translation, introduction and notes, and a translation of the *Tiruvaruṭpayaṉ* by G. U. Pope. Oxford: Clarendon Press, 1900.

Tiruvaruṭpayaṉ & Aruṉmuṟaittiraṭṭu. By Umāpati Civācāryar. With an English rendering by V. A. Devasenapathi. Thanjavur: Tamil University, 1987.

Uṇmai Viḷakkam (The Exposition of Truth) of Manavasagam Kadanthar. Tamil text, translation in English with notes, and index by C. N. Singaravelu. Madras: Saiva Siddhanta Maha Samajam, 1981.

Books and Articles

Balasubrahmanyam, S. R. *Four Chola Temples*. Bombay: N. M. Tirupathi, 1963.

———. *Early Chola Art: Part One*. Bombay: Asia Publishing House, 1966.

———. *Early Chola Temples: Parantaka I to Rajaraja I*. Bombay: Orient Longman, 1971.

———. *Middle Chola Temples: Rajaraja I to Kulottunga I*. Faridabad, Haryana: Thomson Press, 1975.

———. *Later Chola Temples: Kulottunga I to Rajendra III*. Madras: Mudgala Trust, 1979.

Barrett, Douglas. *Early Cōḻa Bronzes*. Bombay: Bhulabhai Memorial Institute, 1965.

———. *Early Cōḻa Architecture and Sculpture, 866–1014*. London: Faber, 1974.

Beams, John. "Chaitanya and the Vaishnava Poets of Bengal: Studies in Bengali Poetry of the Fifteenth and Sixteenth Centuries." *Indian Antiquary* 2 (1873): 1–7.

Beck, Brenda E. F. "The Goddess and the Demon: A Local South Indian Festival and Its Wider Context." In Madeleine Biardeau, ed., *Autour de la Déesse Hindoue*, 83–136. Paris: Éditions de l'École des Hautes Études en Sciences Sociales, 1981.

Bhandarkar, R. G. *Vaiṣṇavism, Śaivism, and Minor Religious Systems*. Varanasi: Indological Book House, 1965 [1913].

Bharati, Agehananda. "Pilgrimage in the Indian Tradition." *History of Religions*, 3, no. 1 (Summer 1963): 135–167.

Bhardwaj, Surinder Mohan. *Hindu Places of Pilgrimage in India: A Study in Cultural Geography*. Berkeley: University of California Press, 1973.

Bhatt, N. R. "Development of Temple Rituals in India." In S. S. Janaki, ed., *Śiva Temple and Temple Rituals*, 24–45. Madras: Kuppuswami Sastri Research Institute, 1988.

Bhattacharyya, N. N., ed. *Medieval Bhakti Movements in India*. New Delhi: Munshiram Manoharlal, 1989.

Biardeau, Madeleine. *Études de mythologie hindoue*. Vol. 1, *Cosmogonies Purāṇiques*. Paris: École Française d'Extrême Orient, 1981.

———. *Hinduism: The Anthropology of a Civilization*. Translated by Richard Nice. Delhi: Oxford University Press, 1989.

Biardeau, Madeleine, and Charles Malamoud. *Le sacrifice dans l'Inde ancienne*. Paris: Presses Universitaires de France, 1976.

Brunner, Hélène. "Les catégories sociales védiques dans le sivaïsme du sud." *Journal Asiatique* 252, no. 4 (1964): 451–472.

———. "Importance de la littérature āgamique pour l'étude des religions vivants de l'Inde." *Indologica Taurinensia* 3–4 (1975–1976): 107–124.

———. "The Four Pādas of Śaivāgamas." *Journal of Oriental Research* 56–62 (1986–1992): 260–278.

Carman, John B. "Bhakti." In *Encyclopedia of Religion*. vol. 2. Edited by Mircea Eliade. New York: Macmillan, 1987.

Catāciva Paṇṭārattār, Ti. Vai. *Piṟkālaccōḻar Varalāṟu*. 3 vols. Aṇṇāmalai: Aṇṇāmalaippal-kalaikkaḻakam, 1971.

Champakalakshmi, R. "South India." In A. Ghosh, ed., *Jaina Art and Architecture*. Vol. 1, 92–103. New Delhi: Bharatiya Jnanpith, 1974.

———. "Religion and Social Change in Tamil Nadu (c. A.D. 600–1300)." In N. N. Bhattacharyya, ed., *Medieval Bhakti Movements*, 162–173. New Delhi: Munshiram Manoharlal, 1989.

Chatterjee, Asim Kumar. *A Comprehensive History of Jainism*. Vols. 1 and 2. Calcutta: Firma KLM Private, 1978, 1984.

Civakurunātap Piḷḷai, Mā. *Tēvāra Mūvar Talayāttirai*. Tañcāvūr: Yu. Cupramaṇiyaṉ Aṟak-kaṭṭaḷai, 1990.

Clothey, Fred W., and J. Bruce Long, eds. *Experiencing Śiva: Encounters with a Hindu Deity*. New Delhi: Manohar, 1983.

Cohn, Bernard S., and McKim Marriott. "Networks and Centres in the Integration of Indian Civilisation." *Journal of Social Research* 1, no. 1 (September 1958): 1–9.

Colebrooke, H. T. *Essays on History, Literature, and Religions of Ancient India: Miscellaneous Essays*. Vol. 1. New Delhi: Cosmo Publications, 1977 [1837].

Cutler, Norman J. *Songs of Experience: The Poetics of Tamil Devotion*. Bloomington: Indiana University Press, 1987.

Daniel, E. Valentine. *Fluid Signs: On Being a Person the Tamil Way*. Berkeley: University of California Press, 1984.

Das, Veena. *Structure and Cognition: Aspects of Hindu Caste and Ritual*. Delhi: Oxford University Press, 1982 [1977].

Das Gupta, Shashibhusan. *Obscure Religious Cults*. Calcutta: Firma K. L. Mukhopadhyay, 1969 [1946].

Dasgupta, Surendranath. *A History of Indian Philosophy*. Vol. 5, *Southern Schools of Śaivism*. Delhi: Motilal Banarsidass, 1988 [1922].

Davis, Richard H. "Ritual in an Oscillating Universe." Ph.D. diss., University of Chicago, 1988.

———. *Ritual in an Oscillating Universe*. Princeton: Princeton University Press, 1991.

———. "Aghoraśiva's Background." *Journal of Oriental Research* 56–62 (1986–1992): 367–378.

Dehejia, Vidya. *Slaves of the Lord: The Path of the Tamil Saints*. New Delhi: Munshiram Manoharlal, 1988.

———. *Art of the Imperial Cholas*. New York: Columbia University Press, 1990.

Devasenapathi, V. A. *Śaiva Siddhānta As Expounded in the Śivajñāna-Siddhiyār and Its Six Commentaries*. Madras: University of Madras, 1960.

Dhavamony, Maraisusai. *Love of God according to Śaiva Siddhānta*. Oxford: Clarendon Press, 1971.

———. "A Bibliography on Bhakti in Hinduism." *Studia Missionalia* 30 (1981): 279–306.

Dimock, Edward C., Jr. *The Place of the Hidden Moon: Erotic Mysticism in the Vaiṣṇava-sahajiyā Cult of Bengal*. Chicago: University of Chicago Press, 1989 [1966].

Dimock, Edward C., Jr., Edwin Gerow, C. M. Naim, A. K. Ramanujan, Gordon Roadarmel, and J. A. B. van Buitenen, eds. *The Literatures of India: An Introduction*. Chicago: University of Chicago Press, 1978 [1974].

Dirks, Nicholas B. "Political Authority and Structural Change in Early South Indian History." *Indian Economic and Social History Review* 13, no. 2 (1976): 125–157.

———. *The Hollow Crown: Ethnohistory of an Indian Kingdom*. Cambridge: Cambridge University Press, 1987.

Dnyaneshwar. *Jñāneshvari: A Song-Sermon on the Bhagavad-gītā*. 2 vols. Translated by V. G. Pradhan and edited by H. M. Lambert. London: George Allen and Unwin, 1967–1969.

Dorai Rangaswamy, M. A. *The Religion and Philosophy of Tēvāram: With Special Reference to Nampi Ārūr (Sundarar)*. 4 vols. Madras: University of Madras, 1991 [1958–1959].

Eck, Diana L. "India's Tīrthas: 'Crossings' in Sacred Geography." *History of Religions* 20, no. 4 (1981): 323–344.

Eck, Diana L., and Françoise Mallison, eds. *Devotion Divine: Bhakti Traditions from the Regions of India. Studies in Honour of Charlotte Vaudeville*. Groningen: Egbert Forsten; Paris: École Française d'Extrême-Orient, 1991.

Elmore, Wilber Theodore. *Dravidian Gods in Modern Hinduism*. Madras: CLS for India, 1929; Lincoln: University Studies of the University of Nebraska, 1915.

Encyclopedia of Tamil Literature. Vol. 1. Edited by G. John Samuel. Madras: Institute of Asian Studies, 1990.

Epigraphia Indica. Multiple volumes. Edited and translated by E. Hultzsch. Calcutta: Government of India, 1895–.

Fabricius, Johann Philip. *A Tamil and English Dictionary*. Tiruchirapalli: Tranquebar Publishing House, 1972 [1897].

Filliozat, Jean. "Les dates du *Bhāgavatapurāṇa* et du *Bhāgavatamāhātmya*." *Indological Studies* 70–77. New Haven: American Oriental Society, 1962.

———. "The Role of the Śaivāgamas in the Śaiva Ritual System." In *Experiencing Śiva*, ed. Fred W. Clothey and J. Bruce Long. New Delhi: Manohar, 1983.

Filliozat, Pierre-Sylvain. "Le droit d'entrer dans les Temples de Śiva au XIe Siécle." *Journal Asiatique* 263 (1975): 103–117.

Fuller, C. J. *Servants of the Goddess: The Priests of a South Indian Temple*. Cambridge: Cambridge University Press, 1984.

Gangoly, O. C. *South Indian Bronzes*. Calcutta: Nababharat, 1978 [1915].

Ghose, Rama. *Grace in Śaiva Siddhānta (A Study of Tiruvaruṭpayaṉ)*. Varanasi: Ashutosh Prakashan Sansthan, 1984.

Gold, Daniel. "Organized Hinduisms: From Vedic Truth to Hindu Nation." In *Fundamentalisms Observed*, ed. Martin E. Marty and R. Scott Appleby. Chicago: The University of Chicago Press, 1991.

Gonda, Jan. *Medieval Religious Literature in Sanskrit*. Vol. 2, *A History of Indian Literature*. Wiesbaden: Otto Harrassowitz, 1977.

———. "The Śatarudrīya." In *Sanskrit and Indian Studies*, ed. Masatoshi Nagatomi et al. Dordrecht: D. Reidel, 1980.

Grierson, George A. "Modern Hinduism and Its Debt to the Nestorians." *Journal of the Royal Asiatic Society* (January–June 1907): 316–332.

———. "Bhakti-Mārga." In *Encyclopædia of Religion and Ethics*, edited by James Hastings. New York: Charles Scribner's Sons, 1910.

Guha, Ranajit. "Dominance without Hegemony and Its Historiography." In *Subaltern Studies VI: Writings on South Asian History and Society*, ed. Ranajit Guha. Delhi: Oxford University Press, 1992.

Haberman, David L. *Acting as a Way of Salvation: A Study of Rāgānugā Bhakti Sādhana*. New York: Oxford University Press, 1988.

Hallisey, Charles. "Devotion in the Buddhist Literature of Medieval Sri Lanka." 2 vols. Ph.D. diss., University of Chicago, 1988.

Hara, Minoru. "Note on Two Sanskrit Religious Terms: Bhakti and Śraddhā." *Indo-Iranian Journal* 17, no. 2/3 (1964): 124–145.

Hardy, Friedhelm. *Virāha-Bhakti: The Early History of Kṛṣṇa Devotion in South India*. Delhi: Oxford University Press, 1983.

Harman, William P. "Two Versions of a Tamil Text and the Contexts in Which They Were Written." *Journal of the Institute of Asian Studies* 5, no. 1 (September 1987): 1–18.

Hart, George L., III. *The Poems of Ancient Tamil: Their Milieu and Their Sanskrit Counterparts*. Berkeley: University of California Press, 1975.

———. "The Little Devotee: Cēkkiḻār's Story of Ciṟuttoṇṭar." In *Sanskrit and Indian Studies*, ed. Masatoshi Nagatomi et al. Dordrecht: D. Reidel, 1980.

Hastings, James, ed. *Encyclopædia of Religion and Ethics*. Edinburgh: T & T Clark, 1912.

Hawley, John Stratton. *At Play with Krishna: Pilgrimage Dramas from Brindavan*. Princeton: Princeton University Press, 1981.

———. *Saints and Virtues*. Berkeley: University of California Press, 1987.

———. "The Nirgun/Sagun Distinction in Early Manuscript Anthologies of Hindi Devotion." In *Bhakti Religion in North India*, ed. David N. Lorenzen. Albany: State University of New York Press, 1995.

Hawley, John Stratton, and Mark Juergensmeyer. *Songs of the Saints of India*. New York: Oxford University Press, 1988.

Hein, Norvin J. "Hinduism." In *A Reader's Guide to the Great Religions*, ed. Charles J. Adams. New York: Free Press, 1968.

Hiltebeitel, Alf. "Toward a Coherent Study of Hinduism." *Religious Studies Review* 9, no. 3 (July 1983): 206–212.

Hopkins, E. Washburn. "The Epic Use of Bhagavat and Bhakti." *Journal of the Royal Asiatic Society of Great Britain and Ireland* (1911): 727–738.

Hudson, Dennis D. "Violent and Fanatical Devotion among the Nāyanārs: A Study in the *Periya Purānam* of Cēkkiḻār." In *Sanskrit and Indian Studies*, ed. Masatoshi Nagatomi et al. Dordrecht: D. Reidel, 1980.

Inden, Ronald. "The Ceremony of the Great Gift (Mahādāna): Structure and Historical Context in Indian Ritual and Society." *Asie du Sud, Traditions et Changements* (1979): 131–136.

———. *Imagining India*. London: Basil Blackwell, 1990.

Jaini, Padmanabh S. *The Jaina Path of Purification*. Delhi: Motilal Banarsidass, 1979.

Janaki, S. S., ed. *Śiva Temple and Śiva Ritual*. Madras: Kuppuswami Sastri Research Institute, 1988.

———. "Umāpathi Śivācārya, His Life, Works, and Contribution to Śaivism." *Śaiva Siddhānta* 24, no. 2 (April–June 1989): 53–62.

Jash, Pranabananda. *History of Śaivism*. Calcutta: Roy and Chaudhury, 1974.

Kane, P. V. *History of Dharmaśāstra*. Poona: Bhandarkar Oriental Research Institute, 1953.

Karashima, Noboru. *South Indian History and Society: Studies from Inscriptions A.D. 850–1800*. Delhi: Oxford University Press, 1984.

Kieckhefer, Richard, and George D. Bond, eds. *Sainthood: Its Manifestations in World Religions*. Berkeley: University of California Press, 1988.

Kinsley, David. "Devotion." *Encyclopedia of Religion*, vol. 4. Edited by Mircea Eliade. New York: Macmillan, 1987.

Kramrisch, Stella. *The Presence of Śiva*. Princeton: Princeton University Press, 1981.

Lele, Jayant, ed. *Tradition and Modernity in Bhakti Movements*. Leiden: E. J. Brill, 1981.

Ling, Trevor. *Buddhist Revival in India*. New York: St. Martins Press, 1980.

Long, J. Bruce. "Rudra as an Embodiment of Divine Ambivalence in the *Śatarudrīya Stotram*." In *Experiencing Śiva*, ed. Fred W. Clothey and J. Bruce Long. New Delhi: Manohar, 1983.

Lorenzen, David N., ed. *Bhakti Religion in North India: Community Identity and Political Action*. Albany: State University of New York Press, 1995.

Lorinser, M. F. "Traces in the Bhagavad-Gita of Christian Writings and Ideas." *Indian Antiquary* 2 (1873): 283–296.

Lutgendorf, Philip. "Interpreting Rāmarāj: Reflections on the *Rāmāyaṇa*, Bhakti, and Hindu Nationalism." In *Bhakti Religion in North India*, ed. David N. Lorenzen. Albany: State University of New York Press, 1995.

Mahābhārata, trans. J. A. B. van Buitenen, vol. 2, bks. 2 and 3. Chicago: University of Chicago Press, 1973.

Mahalingam, T. V. *Inscriptions of the Pallavas*. New Delhi: Indian Council of Historical Research: Delhi: Agam Prakashan, 1988.

Marr, J. R. "The *Periya Purāṇam* Frieze at Tārācuram: Episodes in the Lives of the Tamil Śaiva Saints." *Bulletin of the School of Oriental and African Studies* 42, no. 2 (1979): 268–289.

Meister, Michael W., ed. *Discourses on Śiva: Proceedings of a Symposium on the Nature of Religious Imagery*. Philadelphia: University of Pennsylvania Press, 1984.

Meister, Michael W., M. A. Dhaky, and Krishna Deva, eds. *Encyclopædia of Indian Temple Architecture*. 2 vols. Princeton: Princeton University Press, 1988.

Miller, Jeanine. "*Bhakti* and the Ṛg Veda: Does It Appear There or Not." In *Love Divine*, ed. Karel Werner. Richmond, Surrey: Curzon Press, 1993.

Monier-Williams, Monier. "The Vaishnava Religion, with Special Reference to the Śikshā-patri of the Modern Sect Called Svāmi-Nārāyana." *Journal of the Royal Asiatic Society of Great Britain and Ireland* n.s. 14 (1882): 289–316.

———. *Religious Thought and Life in India: An Account of the Religions of the Indian Peoples, Based on a Life's Study of Their Literature and on Personal Investigations in Their Own Country. Part I: Vedism, Brāhmanism, and Hindūism*. London: John Murray, 1883.

———. *Hinduism*. London: SPCK, 1894.

Nagaswamy, R. "Chidambaram Bronzes." *Lalit Kalā* 19 (1979): 9–17.

———. "Iconography and Significance of the Bṛhadīśvara Temple, Tañjāvūr." In *Discourses on Śiva: Proceedings of a Symposium on the Nature of Religious Imagery*, ed. Michael W. Meister. Philadelphia: University of Pennsylvania Press, 1984.

———. *Śiva Bhakti*. New Delhi: Navrang, 1989.

Nagatomi, Masatoshi, B. K. Matilal, J. M. Masson, and E. C. Dimock, Jr., eds. *Sanskrit and Indian Studies: Essays in Honour of Daniel H. H. Ingalls*. Dordrecht, Holland: D. Reidel, 1980.

Nallaswami Pillai, J. M. *Studies in Saiva-Siddhanta*. Madras: Meykaṇdān Press, 1911.

Nambi Arooran, K. *Tamil Renaissance and Dravidian Nationalism, 1905–1944*. Madurai: Koodal, 1980.

Narayana Ayyar, C. V. *Origin and Early History of Śaivism in South India*. Madras: University of Madras, 1974.

Narayanan, Vasudha. "Hindu Devotional Literature: The Tamil Connection." *Religious Studies Review* 11, no. 1 (January 1985): 12–20.

Nilakanta Sastri, K. A. "An Episode in the History of Buddhism in South India." In *B.C. Law Volume, Part I*, ed. D. R. Bhandarkar, et al. Calcutta: Indian Research Institute, 1945.

———. *The Cōḻas*. Madras: University of Madras, 1975 [1955].

———. *Development of Religion in South India*. New Delhi: Munshiram Manoharlal, 1992 [1963].

O'Flaherty, Wendy Doniger. *Asceticism and Eroticism in the Mythology of Śiva*. Oxford: Oxford University Press, 1973.

Orr, Leslie. "Women of Medieval South India in Hindu Temple Ritual: Text and Practice." In *The Annual Review of Women in World Religions*, vol. 3, ed. Arvind Sharma and Katherine K. Young. Albany: State University of New York Press, 1994.

Pechilis, Karen P. "To Pilgrimage It." *Journal of Ritual Studies* 6, no. 2 (Summer 1992): 59–91.

Peterson, Indira V. "Singing of a Place: Pilgrimage as Metaphor and Motif in the *Tēvāram* Hymns of the Tamil Śaivite Saints." *Journal of the American Oriental Society* 102, no. 1 (January–March 1982): 69–90.

———. "Lives of the Wandering Singers: Pilgrimage and Poetry in Tamil Śaivite Hagiography." *History of Religions* 22, no. 4 (1983): 338–360.

———. *Poems to Śiva: The Hymns of the Tamil Saints*. Princeton: Princeton University Press, 1989.

———. "In Praise of the Lord: The Image and Tradition of the Royal Patron in the Songs of Saint Cuntaramūrtti and the Composer Tyāgarāja." In *The Powers of Art: Patronage in Indian Culture*, ed. Barbara Stoler Miller. Delhi: Oxford University Press, 1992.

Prentiss, Karen Pechilis. "A Tamil Lineage for Śaiva Siddhānta Philosophy," *History of Religions* 35, no. 3 (February 1996): 231–257.

Raghavan, V. "Tamil Versions of the Purāṇas." *Purāṇa* 2, nos. 1–2 (July 1960): 225–242.

———. *The Great Integrators: The Saint-Singers of India*. New Delhi: Government of India Ministry of Information and Broadcasting, 1965.

Rajan, Rajeswari Sunder. *Real and Imagined Women: Gender, Culture, and Postcolonialism*. London: Routledge, 1993.

Ramachandran, T. N. *Pati-Pasu-Paasam*. Dharmapuram: International Institute of Saiva Siddhanta Research, 1988.

———. *Saiva Siddhantam*. Vol. 2. Dharmapuram: International Insitute of Saiva Siddhanta Research, 1988.

Ramanujan, A. K. *Speaking of Śiva*. Baltimore: Penguin, 1973.

———. *Hymns for the Drowning: Poems for Viṣṇu by Nammāḻvār*. Princeton: Princeton University Press, 1981.

———. "On Women Saints." In *The Divine Consort: Radha and the Goddesses of India*, ed. John S. Hawley and Donna Marie Wulff. Berkeley: Berkeley Religious Series and Graduate Theological Union, 1982.

———. "The Myths of Bhakti: Images of Śiva in Śaiva Poetry." In *Discourses on Śiva: Proceedings of a Symposium on the Nature of Religious Imagery*, ed. Michael W. Meister. Philadelphia: University of Pennsylvania Press, 1984.

———. *Poems of Love and War*. New York: Columbia University Press, 1984.

Ramanujan, A. K., and Norman Cutler. "From Classicism to Bhakti." In *Essays on Gupta Culture*, ed. Bardwell L. Smith. Columbia, Mo.: South Asia Books, 1983.

Ramaswami Ayyangar, M. S. *Studies in South Indian Jainism*. Part 1, *South Indian Jainism*. Delhi: Sri Satguru Publications, 1982 [1922].

Reynolds, Frank E., and Donald Capps. *The Biographical Process: Studies in the History and Psychology of Religion*. Religion and Reason 2, ed. Jacques Waardenburg. The Hague: Mouton, 1976.

Satyamurti, T. *The Nataraja Temple: History, Art, and Architecture*. New Delhi: Classical Publications, 1978.

Schomer, Karine, and W. H. McLeod, eds. *The Sants: Studies in a Devotional Tradition of India*. Berkeley: Berkeley Religious Studies Series; Delhi: Motilal Banarsidass, 1987.

Scott, W. Major. "Devotion and Devotional Literature." In *The Encyclopædia of Religion and Ethics*, vol. 4, ed. James Hastings. Edinburgh: T. & T. Clark, 1911.

Sharma, Krishna. "Bhakti." In *Problems of Indian Historiography*, ed. D. Devahuti. Delhi: D. K. Publications, 1979.

———. *Bhakti and the Bhakti Movement: A New Perspective*. New Delhi: Munshiram Manoharlal, 1987.

Shulman, David Dean. *Tamil Temple Myths: Sacrifice and Divine Marriage in the South Indian Śaiva Tradition*. Princeton: Princeton University Press, 1980.

———. *The King and the Clown in South Indian Myth and Poetry*. Princeton: Princeton University Press, 1985.

———. *Songs of the Harsh Devotee: The Tēvāram of Cuntaramūrttināyaṉār*. Philadelphia: Department of South Asia Regional Studies, University of Pennsylvania, 1990.

Siddalingaiah, T. B. *Origin and Development of Saiva Siddhanta up to 14th Century*. Madurai: Madurai Kamaraj University, 1979.

Sivaramamurti, C. *South Indian Bronzes*. Bombay: Lalit Kalā Akademi, 1963.

Sivaraman, K. *Śaivism in Philosophical Perspective: A Study of the Formative Concepts, Problems, and Methods of Śaiva Siddhānta*. Delhi: Motilal Banarsidass, 1973.

Smith, David. "The Dance of Śiva as Portrayed in the Kuñcitāṅghristava of Umāpati." *Journal of Oriental Research* 56–62 (1986–1992): 154–161.

Smith, Jonathan Z. *Imagining Religion*. Chicago: University of Chicago Press, 1982.

———. *To Take Place: Towards Theory in Ritual*. Chicago: University of Chicago Press, 1987.

Somasundaram, J. M. *The University's Environs: Cultural and Historical*. Annamalai: Annamalai University, 1963.

South Indian Inscriptions. Multiple volumes. Edited and translated by E. Hultzsch. Madras: Government Press, 1890–1933.

Spencer, George W. "The Sacred Geography of the Tamil Shaivite Hymns." *Numen* 17 (1970): 232–244.

Srinivasan, C. R. *Kāñchīpuram through the Ages*. Delhi: Agam Kala Prakashan, 1979.

Srinivasan, K. R. "South India." In *Jaina Art and Architecture*, ed. A. Ghosh. New Delhi: Bharatiya Jnanpith, 1975.

Stein, Burton. "Social Mobility and Medieval South Indian Hindu Sects." In *Social Mobility in the Caste System in India*, ed. James Silverberg. The Hague: Mouton, 1968.

———. *Peasant State and Society in Medieval South India*. Delhi: Oxford University Press, 1980.

———. *All the King's Mana: Papers on Medieval South Indian History*. Madras: New Era Publications, 1984.

Surdam, Wayne. "The Vedicization of Śaiva Ritual." In *Śiva Temple and Śiva Ritual*, ed. S. S. Janaki. Madras: Kuppuswami Sastri Research Institute, 1988.

Tamil Lexicon. 6 vols. and supplement. Madras: University of Madras, 1982 [1936].

Turner, Victor W. "The Center Out There: Pilgrim's Goal." *History of Religions* 12, no. 3 (1973): 191–230.

Van Buitenen, J. A. B. "On the Archaism of the Bhāgavata Purāṇa." In *Krishna: Myths, Rites, and Attitudes*, ed. Milton Singer. Honolulu: East-West Center Press, 1966.

Vasudeva Rao, T. N. *Buddhism in the Tamil Country*. Annamalainagar: Annamalai University Press, 1979.

Vellaivāranaṉ, Ka. *Paṉṉirutirumuṟai Varalāṟu*. 2 vols. Aṇṇāmalai: Aṇṇāmalaip Palkalaikkaḻakam, n.d.
Venkataraman, B. *Temple Art under the Chola Queens*. Faridabad, Haryana: Thomson Press, 1976.
———. *Rājarājēśvaram: The Pinnacle of Chola Art*. Madras: Mudgala Trust, 1985.
Vincentnathan, Lynn. "Nandanar: Untouchable Saint and Caste Hindu Anomaly." *Ethos* 21, no. 2 (1993): 154–179.
Weber, Albrecht. "An Investigation into the Origin of the Festival of Kṛishṇajanmāshṭami." *Indian Antiquary* 3 (1874): 21–25, 47–52; 6 (1877): 161–180, 281–301, 349–54.
Werner, Karel, ed. *Love Divine: Studies in Bhakti and Devotional Mysticism*. Durham Indological Series 3. Richmond, Surrey: Curzon Press, 1993.
Whitehead, Henry. *The Village Gods of South India*. New Delhi: Asian Educational Services, 1983 [1921].
Wilson, H. H. *The Religious Sects of the Hindus*. London: Christian Literature Society for India, 1904. First published in *Asiatic Researches* 16 and 17 (1828–1832).
Woodward, Kenneth L. *Making Saints: How the Catholic Church Determines Who Becomes a Saint, Who Doesn't, and Why*. New York: Simon and Schuster, 1990.
Yocum, Glenn E. "Buddhism through Hindu Eyes: Śaivas and Buddhists in Medieval Tamilnadu." In *Traditions in Contact and Change*, ed. Peter Slater and Donald Wiebe. Waterloo, Ont.: Wilfrid Laurier, 1980.
———. "Personal Transformation through Bhakti (A Hindu Path to Release)." *Studia Missionalia* 30 (1981): 351–375.
Younger, Paul. *The Home of the Dancing Śivaṉ*. New York: Oxford University Press, 1995.
Zelliot, Eleanor. "The Medieval Bhakti Movement in History: An Essay on the Literature in English." In *Hinduism: New Essays in the History of Religions*, ed. Bardwell L. Smith. Leiden: E. J. Brill, 1976.
———. "Chokhamela and Eknath: Two *Bhakti* Modes of Legitimacy for Modern Change." In *Tradition and Modernity in Bhakti Movements*, ed. Jayant Lele. Leiden: E. J. Brill, 1981.
Zvelebil, Kamil V. *The Smile of Murugaṉ: On Tamil Literature of South India*. Leiden: E. J. Brill, 1973.
———. *Tamil Literature*. In *A History of Indian Literature*, vol. 10, ed. Jan Gonda. Weisbaden: Otto Harrassowitz, 1974.
———. *Tamil Literature*. In *Handbuch der Orientalistik*. Second Section: *Indien*, ed. Jan Gonda. Vol. 2: *Literatur und Bühne*, part 1. Leiden: E. J. Brill, 1975.

Index